Diversity and Its Discontents

Diversity and Its Discontents

CULTURAL CONFLICT

AND COMMON GROUND

IN CONTEMPORARY AMERICAN

SOCIETY

EDITED BY NEIL J. SMELSER
AND
JEFFREY C. ALEXANDER

PRINCETON UNIVERSITY PRESS

PRINCETON, NEW JERSEY

Library of Congress Cataloging-in-Publication Data

Diversity and its discontents : cultural conflict and common ground in
contemporary American society / edited by Neil J. Smelser and
Jeffrey C. Alexander.
p.   cm.
Includes bibliographical references and index.
ISBN 0-691-00436-6 (cloth : alk. paper). — ISBN 0-691-00437-4
(pbk. : alk. paper)
1. Pluralism (Social sciences)—United States.   2. Culture
conflict—United States.   3. Social values—United States.
4. Postmodernism—Social aspects—United States.   5. United States—
Social conditions—1980–   I. Smelser, Neil J.   II. Alexander,
Jeffrey C.
E184.A1D57   1999
303.48′2′0973—dc21   98-31391
CIP

This book has been composed in Times Roman

The paper used in this publication meets the minimum requirements of
ANSI/NISO Z39.48-1992 (R1997) (*Permanence of Paper*)

http://pup.princeton.edu

Printed in the United States of America

1   2   3   4   5   6   7   8   9   10

1   2   3   4   5   6   7   8   9   10
(pbk)

CONTENTS

Seyla Benhabib is Professor of Government at Harvard University and Chair of the Committee for the Degree on Social Studies. She is also Senior Research fellow at the Center for European Studies. She is the author of *Situating the Self: Gender, Community and Postmodernism in Contemporary Ethics* (1992), and *The Reluctant Modernism of Hannah Arendt* (1996).

Jean L. Cohen is Professor of Political Science at Columbia University. She is the author of C*lass and Civil Society: The Limits of Marxian Critical Theory* and co-author of *Civil Society and Political Theory*.

Reynolds Farley is Vice President at the Russell Sage Foundation.

Claude S. Fischer is Professor of Sociology at the University of California, Berkeley. His recent books include *America Calling: A Social History of the Telephone to 1940* (1992) and, as senior author, *Inequality by Design: Cracking the Bell Curve Myth* (1996). He is currently writing a book on American social history.

Frank F. Furstenberg, Jr. is Zellerbach Family Chair of Sociology at the University of Pennsylvania where he is also an Associate in the Population Studies Center. His most recent book, *Managing to Make It: Urban Families and Adolescent Success*, will be published this year by the University of Chicago Press.

John Higham is Professor of History Emeritus at The Johns Hopkins University and a former President of the Organization of American Historians. Most recently he edited and co-authored *Civil Rights and Social Wrongs: Black–White Relations Since World War II* (1997).

David A. Hollinger is Chancellor's Professor of History at the University of California, Berkeley. His two most recent books are *Science, Jews, and Secular Culture* (Princeton University Press, 1996) and *Postethnic America: Beyond Multiculturalism* (Basic Books, 1995).

Steven Seidman is Professor of Sociology at the State University of New York at Albany. He is the author of, among other books, *Embattled Eros: Sexual Politics and Ethics in Contemporary America, Contested Knowledge,* and *Difference Troubles: Queering Social Theory and Sexual Politics*.

Marta Tienda is Director, Office of Population Research and Professor of Sociology and Public Affairs at Princeton University. She is co-author of *The Hispanic Population of the United States* (Russell Sage Foundation, 1987).

David Tyack is Vida Jacks Professor of Education and Professor of History at Stanford University.

R. Stephen Warner is Professor of Sociology at the University of Illinois at Chicago.

Robert Wuthnow is Gerhard R. Andlinger Professor of Sociology and Director of the Center for the Study of American Religion at Princeton University. He is the author of *Poor Richard's Principle: Recovering the American Dream Through the Moral Dimension of Work, Business, and Money.*

Viviana A. Zelizer is Professor of Sociology at Princeton University. She is the author of *Morals and Markets: The Development of Life Insurance in the United States, Pricing the Priceless Child: The Changing Social Value of Children,* and *The Social Meaning of Money.*

PART ONE

Introduction: Sources of Cultural Conflict

CHAPTER ONE

Introduction: The Ideological Discourse of Cultural Discontent

PARADOXES, REALITIES, AND ALTERNATIVE WAYS OF THINKING

JEFFREY C. ALEXANDER AND NEIL J. SMELSER

POLITICAL and academic arguments about social justice over the last decade—and the controversies they ignited—have shown a notably cultural face. The language is revealing: moral majority, family values, cultural pluralism, cultural diversity, multiculturalism, and culture wars. Wuthnow (ch. 2 in this vol.) refers to this development as a "discourse of discontent." It reaches deeply into American social structure, identifying crises in family, marriage, religion, education, and race relations. This discourse also draws attention to shifts in social behavior and social process, pointing to public displays of homosexuality and cultural difference, massive new waves of legal and illegal immigration, and economic and cultural globalization. Moreover, this growing chorus of complaint has struck a chord in American public life because it meshes with *cultural* themes that carry great symbolic weight.

The core of the complaint concerns common values in American society. Critics at both ends of the political spectrum claim that such values are disappearing or have disappeared. Conservatives complain that the solidarity of American society has become fragmented, that the very fabric of society has been ruptured. They claim that unprecedented developments are undermining the cultural homogeneity on which a democratic society depends. In response, conservatives assert, traditional values must be revitalized. For their part, radical critics celebrate the end of common cultural values. Arguing that *diversity* and *difference* constitute the high moral goods of society, they view any attempt to connect this diversity to shared values oppressive. In the academy, this leftist position has contributed to the appearance and vitality of "cultural studies," a new field challenging traditional disciplinary authority. Originating in British neo-Marxism and highly influenced by Foucault, cultural studies stress hegemony rather than common culture, and domination rather than civil solidarity. It has been in centers of cultural studies that the more radical programs in race, gender, and ethnic studies have been launched.

A glance at earlier twentieth-century periods of intense, polarized cultural conflict highlights not only the uniqueness of the contemporary cultural emphasis but also the unique polarizing nature of this rhetoric.

- In the 1930s, American society experienced intense and divisive social conflict. Because this crisis was triggered by the collapse of the American economy and its consequent large-scale unemployment and poverty, the dominant frames of discourse in that era were those of economic and political stability, the viability of capitalism as compared with socialist alternatives, and the possibilities of achieving social justice through structural reforms. Although cultural themes certainly were not absent, the integrity of American cultural values did not enter significantly into the conflicting social and political dialogues of the time. Indeed, as many have since pointed out, the "popular front" ideology espoused by the left in the 1930s was as "American as apple pie."
- In the 1960s, dramatic and polarizing turmoil was triggered by demands—first by African Americans, later by feminists and by other racial minorities—for deepening the nation's long-established constitutional and cultural commitments to civil rights. Countercultural issues of the youth movement sometimes obscured this traditional framing, as did the often violent conflicts generated by the moral and political debacle of the Vietnam War. The discursive framework of that decade of protest, however, was clearly established by the model of citizenship. Social justice and inclusion were to be achieved by making citizenship more real for outgroups and more binding for ingroups. Radicals and conservatives both agreed on the necessity for achieving greater "equality of opportunity," the cultural theme that Tocqueville had already discerned in American society almost a century and a half earlier.
- During the last period of massive immigration, from the 1880s to the early 1920s, conflict over economic and political issues was indeed permeated by rhetoric about the salience and stability of traditional cultural values. Conservative WASP intellectuals raised cries of alarm that the new, largely Catholic and Jewish immigration would undermine homogeneity. In mounting a defense of the new immigrant groups, progressive intellectuals proclaimed not only that they could easily be assimilated—that immigrant values were complementary to traditional American ones—but that the new immigrants fervently sought such cultural incorporation. From the current perspective, what is remarkable about this debate is that the existence and legitimacy of a dominant, "hegemonic" national culture was assumed on all sides. American culture was not itself the object of debate. The issue that divided Americans was whether or not immigrant groups could be brought to come to terms with it.

The uniquely cultural orientation of contemporary social complaints and conflicts, however, should not imply that we ourselves should adopt a purely "culturalist" approach in studying them. Of course, we must do our best to understand radical and conservative complaints interpretatively, from within their own framework of ideas and symbols. At the same time, as social scientists we must remain skeptical of the reality claims that emanate from the contenders on both sides. Our goal is not simply to provide a "thick description" of these discourses, to employ the term by which Clifford Geertz (1973a) illuminated hermeneutical interpretation, but to explain them as well. In order to achieve this goal, we must examine these critical complaints not simply from the inside (as coherent cultural discourses) but from the outside (as ideological constructions).[1]

Moreover, rather than simply understanding the symbolic structure of ideology (Geertz 1973b), we are interested in finding out whether these discourses are realistic descriptions of contemporary American society or whether they distort it in potentially damaging ways. Does the widely shared discourse of complaint fairly represent the actual practices of Americans today? Does it accurately and responsibly describe contemporary institutions and interactions? The discourse of discontent has been created by intellectuals of the left and the right and has become part of the rhetoric of political leaders and aspirants, ideologically sophisticated media figures, and highly visible "movement intellectuals" (Eyerman and Jameson 1990) who articulate and oppose ethnic, racial, and gender programs. How deeply do these frameworks actually inform the ideas of those who organize routine social practice? As we shall show, the evidence suggests that although the critics of the right and the left refer to society-wide crisis and polarization, their theories and rhetorics neither penetrate nor reflect the routine politics of the nation, institutional activities at the grass roots, or the attitudes, cares, and interactions of the proverbial person in the street.

SOME PARADOXES, AND THE LOSS OF COMMON GROUND

In regarding the contemporary discourse of discontent as an ideology, we note some striking paradoxes. (In doing so, we move toward developing a political sociology of the cultural turn.) The first paradox concerns what might be called a contrast between culture and materiality. The current cultural framing of national crisis has occurred almost at the expense of traditional claims about economic injustice. During the two decades beginning in 1973, economic conditions for many Americans actually declined. The real wages of much of the country's labor force fell, and the distribution of income became more regressive. The interrelated social problems of poverty, homelessness, drug use, and crime also worsened during those decades. Yet, although these socioeconomic problems have remained the focus of substantial attention in government and in policy-oriented academic circles, they have been given little systematic attention in contemporary cultural debates.

A second, related paradox concerns the social status of the movement intellectuals themselves. The left, or "progressive," participants in this cultural complaint often represent groups that have experienced significant economic, status, and political gains in the past three decades. For women, working- and middle-class members of disadvantaged racial groups, and other traditionally stigmatized minorities these gains have been uneven and hard fought, to be sure, but they are real and have been documented in statistics about income, occupational mobility, intermarriage, and even to a modest degree residential segregation. In an oddly parallel fashion, conservatives often come from members of elite, high-prestige groups who have also experienced gains in income and wealth in the two decades of wage stagnation and more regressive distribution. The normal logic of class and status deprivation does not promise an adequate explanation for the discourse of discontent.

The most striking anomaly of the current situation is that it has made strange bedfellows on the left and the right. Those who have created the contemporary sense of cultural polarization find common ground in the claim that, in contemporary America, common ground no longer exists. Conservative ideologists launch an apocalyptic complaint that contemporary developments are destroying common values, and the critical left seems to agree.

Nowhere is this anomaly more striking than in the public controversies over multiculturalism. Rather than viewing claims for increasing recognition of diversity as responses to discrimination, inequality, and exclusion, conservative critics claim that such demands actually introduce divisions where none existed before. Thus, Arthur Schlesinger, Jr., former Kennedy liberal and cosmopolitan thinker, blames multicultural activists for reviving "ancient prejudices" (1991: 15). By "exaggerating differences," he writes, "the cult of ethnicity . . . intensifies resentments and antagonisms," producing "a nation of minorities [and] makes it appear that membership in one or another ethnic group is the basic American experience" (112). On this basis Schlesinger argues that multiculturalism has undermined the solidarity necessary for American democracy. "The cult of ethnicity," he laments, "has reversed the movement of American history," and he condemns it for "breaking the bonds of cohesion—common ideals, common political institutions, common language, common culture, common fate—that holds the republic together" (13). More strident neoconservatives denounce multiculturalism as itself a new form of racism, one directed against the white majority. D'Sousa denounces "the new separatism" and likens it to defending the South African apartheid regime (1992: 30). For Kimball, multiculturalism, "far from being a means of securing ethnic and racial inequality," is "an instrument for promoting ideological separatism based on . . . differences" (1992: 82). He asserts that "what we are facing is nothing less than the destruction of the fundamental premises that underlie . . . a liberal democratic polity" (65).

One might suppose that multicultural advocates would respond to such shrill and disparaging attacks by arguing that their approach does nothing of the kind but that multiculturalism merely articulates and extends long-standing American values of tolerance of diversity. The paradox is that they argue in an opposite way. Some of the most articulate and publicly visible multiculturalists argue that their movement is indeed destructive of the traditional concept of American community. In her influential philosophical treatise *Justice and the Politics of Difference*, Iris Marion Young (1990) proposes as her normative ideal a social system of insulated but equally empowered groups who, rather than experiencing some shared humanity and solidarity, simply grant one another the right to pursue their distinct and "different" lifestyles and goals. In her presidential address to the Modern Language Association in 1990, Catharine Stimpson, the well-known feminist literary scholar, described multiculturalism as "treating society as the sum of several equally valuable *but distinct* racial and ethnic groups (1992: 43–44; italics added). At the same meeting, the editor of the omnibus *Health Anthology of American Literature* defended his textbook's emphasis on race and gender by insisting, "I know of no standard of judgment . . . which transcends the particularities of time and place . . . of politics" (Kimball 1992: 75). In another scholarly presentation at the MLA, a Shakespearean scholar justified the need for a multicultural approach to literature by highlighting the boundedness of his own particular identity. Reading the work of a black woman author, he explained, "I do not enter into a transcendent human interaction but become more aware of my whiteness and maleness, social categories that shape my being" (Kimball 1992: 69). In another context, Molefi Kete Asante, chair of the Department of African American Studies at Temple University, justified Afrocentrism on the grounds that even for Black Americans, "our Africanity is our ultimate reality" (quoted in Schlesinger 1991: 65). "The idea of 'mainstream American'," he writes, "is nothing more than an additional myth meant to maintain Eurocentric hegemony" (305).

What emerges from these polarizing and mutually reinforcing discourses is a further weakening of the intellectual middle ground, of the possibility for finding a progressive but democratic "vital center" (a formula for politics advocated in an earlier era by Schlesinger [1949]) that can create grounds for ideological consensus and the resolution of political conflict in American public life. Such ideological fragmentation, of course, reinforces recent political developments. Liberal politicians and intellectuals were stigmatized throughout the 1980s and 1990s from the right during the Reagan and Bush administrations as being soft on family values, crime, drugs, pornography, and heterosexuality, all of which touch upon core American values. During this same period—and earlier—the same liberal intellectuals were attacked from the left by an ideology that viewed them as part of a hegemonic establishment, thus denying them the possibility of articulating authentic, progressive values and programs.

We can appreciate the powerful combination of social and intellectual forces that have driven some of the middle to the right and some to the left, yet we believe it is important to assert the continuing vitality of the middle ground. It is justified on normative grounds, because mutual understanding is the key to mutual respect, deliberative democracy, engaged debate, and affirming citizenship. The middle position is also justified on empirical grounds; our belief is that more common ground exists than protagonists of discontent allow. Both left and right have an unjustifiably "thin" (Walzer 1994) appreciation of what kind of solidarity is required in a highly differentiated, diverse, and inclusive civil society. From the right comes a hope for the regeneration of solidarity through the reassertion of common family, religious, and community values—a vision that reveals an impoverished sense of the richness and multiplicity of social institutions and attitudes that constitute civil solidarity. From the left comes a minimalist, procedural vision suggesting that democratic solidarity can be constituted by elaborating the sociological equivalents of what Isaiah Berlin called negative liberties—protection and tolerance of differences and the promotion of formal respect.

As if realizing the inadequacy of such visions of solidarity, both right and left, while scarcely denouncing democracy, sometimes advocate more coercive roads to solidarity. The right would implement a governmental program of cultural homogeneity, replete with media censorship and English-only language rules, and would supplement this cultural program with tough laws and sanctions against immigration, criminals, drugs, pornography, and sexual deviation. Some intellectuals on the left have also been drawn to direct forms of control, not only to hegemonic assertions of political correctness but also to legal restrictions on hate speech and pornography, and to "requirements" for diversity throughout the educational system. These temptations signify, to us, an uneasiness on both sides with the utopian visions of solidarity that each embraces.

In the remainder of this introduction we undertake to examine the adequacy of the culture of discontent according to traditional theoretical and empirical criteria of social science. This summary will suggest that social and cultural polarization is neither as unprecedented nor as dramatic as some discontented intellectuals and political figures believe. We will also advance the claim, based on documentation provided by the essays in this book, that there are good reasons to believe that a vital center persists in American society, both despite and because of the intensity of social change we continue to experience.

WHAT WE HAVE LEARNED IN THIS VOLUME

We may now confess to an initial sense of apprehension when we convened our conference on Common Values, Social Diversity, and Cultural Conflict. We feared that we and our participants would produce nothing new, that we would fall into the polarizations that the current cultural debates have produced, and that we would embrace the presuppositions and language of these debates rather than problematize them. In light of these initial fears, we were surprised at the degree of objectivity achieved, both from the causes and positions participants personally favored and from their feelings about those they opposed. We were even more surprised by the convergence if not consensus on the part of scholars gathered. We will now attempt to distill this convergence.

A Historical Glance at Contemporary Realities. It seems clear that the contemporary sense of decline of and anxiety about social cohesion is nothing new. From the beginnings of the Republic, institutional and social change has been constant, creating periodic crises of confidence and spasms of concern about national stability, social cohesion, and democracy itself. Immigration has been a continual sore spot, and the urban areas that have received immigrants have long been decried as sources of culturally threatening diversity, corruption, and immorality. Changing sexual mores and gender roles and the shifts in family structure they induce have been obsessions since at least the 1920s. Proclamations of religious decline have permeated American culture since the end of the seventeenth century. Claims that diversity has corroded the nation's schools, undermining their ability to provide a common culture, have been evident since the early nineteenth century.

The example of education underscores these points. Contemporary cultural critics are alarmed by what they see as pandering to particularism in American schools. These critics have forgotten that parochial education, now respectable, is itself a product of a social movement, begun more than a century ago, that contemporaries viewed as particularistic and threatening to Protestant American values and beliefs. Catholic parents withdrew from secular public schools so they could educate their children in a way more consonant with their religious values. Courts ruled that such particularism was constitutional. Lutheran, Baptist, Methodist, Seventh-Day Adventist, and Jewish educational institutions have been similarly protected.

This historical perspective on cultural discontent should moderate both contemporary alarm and contemporary hope, and caution us not to yield to the tempting assumptions that our times are unique and that history is not relevant. The nation does not seem to be at an unprecedented turning point.

The second thing we discovered is that common values are still a social reality. National surveys report that Americans continue to believe in democracy, in the opportunity for social mobility, and in the value of American life. In her chapter Zelizer (ch. 9) shows how an expanding commercialized popular culture—reflected in everything from musical hits and sports stars to fast food and afternoon talk shows—is a homogenizing cultural focus that pervades differences of region, ethnicity, and social class.

This sense of shared culture and tradition—whether authentic or ersatz—can be seen both in America's national symbolic icons and narratives and in specific institutional arenas. Those divorced still express support for marriage and typically remarry, and homosexual men and women legitimate their choices by stressing their ability to sustain stable monogamous relationships. Stepparents, separated parents, and other members of "affinal" family networks assert in words and deeds that their primary concern remains their children's well-being—hence the great variety of invented institutional arrangements that have emerged to provide for children's financial and emotional stability.

The desire for a common national education continues to be widely accepted. Teachers and parents believe that elementary schools should concentrate on both academics and democratic values, and surveys of students reveal that they continue to cite traditional heroes and heroines as the central figures in our national myths. Church attendance is on the upswing, and religious revivalism permeates majority and minority denominations alike. Although ethnic and racial minorities demand economic goods that reflect their particular lifestyles and tastes, these preferences are expressed as variations on mass-produced and widely consumed popular commodities. Immigrants continue to make learning English a primary goal, and they express a faith in the opportunity and openness of their adopted land that is often stronger than those who have been here for generations.

When opportunities for interaction arise, members of "majority" and "minority" groups are increasingly marrying one another—even African Americans and other groups—which historically has been the focus of the strongest and most intractable taboo. This is more than propinquity; social conventions have come to regard intermarriage as acceptable if not completely legitimate to a greater degree than ever before.

If the sense of crisis that critics argue Americans are experiencing has been more or less resolved at many earlier times in our national history, and if national and democratic values are still widely shared, we might ask what the problem is. Why is there a sense of cultural crisis, a sense that social change is out of control? In response to these questions the contributors to this volume have provided important insights.

Social Change and "Cultural Work." Deep and irreversible structural changes have been experienced in American society, changes that have created challenges to long-standing, traditional expectations and routines. Role structures, for example, have become more complex. New occupational categories have been produced and others eliminated, not only in the sphere of production (computer specialists have replaced typesetters) but in the service sector as well (professional mediators, addiction counselors, cultural sensitivity trainers have grown out of roles previously performed by lawyers, physicians, and teachers). As new roles form and old ones are threatened, groups emerge to advance them or to defend them, and new claims are made for social legitimacy. Another ongoing structural process involves the fashioning of new forms of social integration required to deal with growing complexity. New forms of mediation develop: citizenship becomes more elaborated, overarching values become more generalized and less particularistic, and new situational norms must be continually invented and applied. In the American case, the processes of complexity and integration are complicated by new levels of cultural diversity. Successive waves of immigration and emigration mean that traditional roles have new occupants, and expanded citizenship rights are expected to apply to people with different customs and backgrounds. When a society is continually changing with respect to both differentiation and integration, and when demands are made more complex by increasing cultural diversity, new sources of anomie are bound to emerge. These ambiguities stir up demands for cultural interpretation, accommodation, and recognition.

Structural changes of this sort are complex and open-ended. They do not move the society in one clear direction or another; they are multitracked rather than unilinear. They seldom produce unequivocal, totalistic effects. The cultural discourse of discontent, however, tends to go for single or either-or formulations, such as "loss of values," "fragmentation," "decline of community," "corrupt values," "irresponsible leaders," "hegemonic patterns," or "modernity vs. postmodernity." These formulations give us little insight into the specifics of these strains, either what caused them or what, if anything, can be done to resolve them.

The facts suggest that despite deep structural strains and cultural polarization, the contemporary American situation cannot realistically be read in either-or terms—whether there are common values or not, whether there is stability or chaos, whether there is tradition or modernity or postmodernity. Indeed, much social conflict in America today is characterized by reference to the *same* set of values. For example, both advocates for and opponents of affirmative action refer many of their arguments to the same value principle, equality of opportunity (Smelser 1998). Cohen (ch. 13: 276) articulates this point in noting that "contestation over past institutionalizations and struggles over cultural hegemony—over the power to name, signify, and interpret norms and national identity—are not necessarily signs of social disintegration, or moral decay." Rather, she argues, "open, public, even conflictual pluralization . . . can be a response to change" that has the aim of realizing or institutionalizing shared democratic principles.

The misunderstandings of contemporary social conflict rest on a theoretical confusion as well. What is missing from the discourse about cultural values is an understanding of the intermediate, mediating character of social norms. Values are very general statements of desirable social conditions or states of affairs. Norms "realize" values in the sense that they specify situations and contexts in which values apply and generate rules for conduct in those situations and contexts. This realization is always problematic, however, because there is always an element of ambiguity, or slippage, or interested disagreement about the links between values and norms. Is a rule or norm a legitimate interpretation of the values in the name of which it is implemented? Or, to put the question in a distinctively American context, is a given law (norm) constitutional (consistent with general principles)?

The ambiguous relations between values and norms raises questions about the nature of conflict and criticism. In many cases it is norms, not values, that are addressed. As Wuthnow (ch. 2: 25) observes about debates about the family, "it is more about how best to attain a certain value than about whether that value is worth attaining at all." Similarly, in his analysis of conflicts over sexuality, Seidman (ch. 8: 177) suggests that "the differences are usually quite specific and occur within a network of shared beliefs. . . . Divisions over abortion mostly pivot on disagreement over when life begins, not on a woman's right to have sex, not on the value of her life and the life of children, and not on broader social and sexual values such as the individual's right to choose to be sexual, the linking of sex to affection or love, [or] the importance of family."

In the face of profound structural changes, the most frequent challenge is to create new norms to bring the changed conditions under the umbrella of general values. However, we find little space for this pragmatic kind of response within the perspectives of either "traditional" intellectuals, who react against recent social changes, or "emancipated" intellectuals, who seek to legitimate them. On the contrary, by depicting changing social conditions as either-or, they suggest that traditional values must be affirmed, which allows little normative flexibility (the conservative position), or that traditional values should be discarded (the emancipated position), which denies that norms must be legitimized by cultural values. These polarized reactions obscure the principal fact that new forms of normative mediation evolve though cultural work, group negotiation, legal interpretation, and institutional experimentation.

Family and Sexuality. The intimate spheres of American life have experienced radical change. Women have entered the workplace and civil society; marriage is being postponed; sexuality is being separated not only from love but from gender ascription; parenting responsibilities are less tightly linked to procreation or kinship. As Seidman points out and Furstenburg's demographic data confirm, these are accelerations of a century of change; but "it was [only] in the 1960s and 1970s" that these shifts "emerged into public view and became the focus of major social conflicts" (ch. 8: 174).

Conservatives respond to these shifting patterns by demanding the restoration of the traditional, gender-divided, intact nuclear family. An outcry over the dissolution of family values, however, can have little effect on the broad patterns of family and affectual change. Concentrating on generalized values, moreover, leaves little room for legitimate forms of normative mediation. Radical, postmodern advocates of these emerging patterns seem equally wide of the mark. They argue that the very idea of the family should be abandoned, that society should organize intimacy and socialization in entirely different ways. Ignoring the need to link concrete practices with generalized values, their position also abandons the issue of normative mediation of social behavior and social change.

When one examines actual practices, one finds that the level of normative mediation is, in fact, both evident and important. Seidman's findings reveal that many actors participating in these new institutional arrangements have been employing what Seidman calls a "communicative ethic" to justify their nontraditional engagements by emphasizing the ideals of individual choice, responsibility, consensus, and toleration for pluralism and by recognizing the importance of a pragmatic approach to morality that looks to the contents of interaction rather than to dogmatic moral standards. Looking toward institutional practices, such an ethic has the flexibility to cover wide substantive differences. As Seidman (ch. 8: 184) suggests, "such an ethical standpoint legitimates a plurality of sexual practices and patterns of intimacy, including different kinds of families." While justifying divergent practices, however, the communicative norm also submits them to a set of ethical standards. Such explicit evaluation allows this emergent norm of intimacy to look toward general values as well. The idioms of this ethic about family and intimacy are drawn from the traditional American discourse about liberty, which idealizes democracy in a pragmatic, consensual, and pluralistic manner (Alexander and Smith 1992).

Immigration and Multiculturalism. For the first three centuries of American history, immigration was virtually a demographic necessity, an adaptation by a modernizing and aggressively expansive nation to a vast and underpopulated physical space. Similarly, the post-1965 immigration wave can be understood as a response to America's position in the global political economy, in which continent-spanning migration has become typical, economic organization has become more mobile, and the profitability of labor markets is evaluated internationally as well as locally. Not only are immigrants responding to less favorable home conditions but global economic restructuring has made America itself increasingly dependent on the motivation and social capital that new economic immigrants provide.

A similar point can be made about the demographic aspects of the new multiculturalism. Following four decades of low immigration—a midcentury pause that provided sustained opportunities for assimilation—the recent period has brought huge populations of mainly Latins and Asians into the United States. During this same period the effects of civil rights legislation and affirmative action have allowed historically displaced domestic populations the opportunity to enter mainstream institutions at unprecedented rates. As Higham (ch. 3) points out, because this extraordinary growth in heterogeneity has occurred within a compressed time frame, the capacity to "assimilate" in traditional ways is lessened. In separate essays Fischer (ch. 10) underscores the continuing power of the assimilative mode. Tienda (ch. 6), although not denying this power, stresses some evident strains and more threatening possibilities. Forces other than demographic are also involved in producing the multicultural alternative to assimilation. Since the 1960s a distinct "deprimordialization" of America's mainstream values has occurred. This cultural movement away from provincialism toward cosmopolitanism has made the ideals of homogeneity and ethnic deracination much less compelling. These are the underlying structural reasons for the turn to more multicultural criteria for incorporation.

Yet in their constructions of immigration and multiculturalism, conservative critics paint them as out-of-control social problems and present them not as structural processes but as the results of wrong values and threatening people. Defending their version of "classical republican" values (Cohen), these conservatives critically compare the new heterogeneity with a nostalgic version of a homogeneous American culture emptied of ethnic and racial difference. According to their map of the good society, consensually agreed-upon substantive values can and should control differentiated institutions and segmented interactions in a direct way. As we have noted, the positions of radical multiculturalists mirror the conservative arguments in important ways. Demanding that difference should be honored, they envision a society organized around separated yet mutually respectful segmented groups. Implying that normative standards of interaction can and should emerge from heterogeneity per se, this argument ignores not only the need for legitimization vis-à-vis cultural values but the fact that normative mediation itself must manifest an ethical intent.

When we look to empirical processes in the society we find, again, that many involved in disputes over immigration and multiculturalism are engaged in "normative work." As Farley (ch. 5) reminds us, it was the respecification of American values in law—not only the 1960s civil rights legislation articulating new definitions of voting rights, fair employment practices, and open housing, but also the Celler immigration act of 1965—that established the conditions for heterogeneity that are at the middle of the contemporary debate. Legal articulation and legitimization have continued to mediate and moderate immigrants' access to schools, education, welfare, and citizenship.

Important as legal mediation is in regulating the turmoil over "difference," however, the very qualities that make it a neutral arbiter—abstract universalism, emphasis on procedural regularities—also constitute its limitations. Legal rationality ensures continuity and flexibility for new institutional arrangements; it does not, however, legitimate them. This requires linking those arrangements to substantive values and ethical ideals.

Higham (ch. 3) describes how this sort of link was achieved in the double-sided response to earlier waves of American immigration. With the passage of the national origins law sharply restricting immigration in 1924, an "intensely racialized nativism" seemed triumphantly poised to primordialize national values. What happened, however, was different. On the one hand, many younger ideological leaders of the ethnic Protestant core group rejected their elders' particularism and moved to embrace the "deviant," denigrated cultural orientations of excluded ethnic and racial groups: "Young intellectuals, in rebellion against their own ethnic origins, were no longer guardians of the inherited culture[;] they were becoming its adversaries" (51). At the same time, new, more pluralistic and multiethnic constellations of American values emerged from the outgroups themselves. Noting the "enormous yearning on the part of the immigrants and their children to become Americans," Higham observes that from the 1920s onward "a common process drove people in many disparate ethnic enclaves to redefine themselves in more open and inclusive ways" (52). For example, "the small middle class of southern and eastern European derivation was expanding, receiving some civic recognition, and joining the movement from cities to suburbs." Within the immigrant working class, "ethnic nationalism correspondingly yielded to a common working class culture." The result was that "all of the institutions of ethnic culture weakened" and there was a "rebuilding and extending [of] the tradition of American universalism" (53).

We find some parallels in the ways immigration and incorporation are being mediated today. Many "mainstream" Americans and "white" intellectuals have abandoned the restrictive ethical orientations of their own ethnic and racial groups—orientations that were dominant only a generation ago. This shift can be seen, moreover, in the discourse of discontent itself. As Fischer (ch. 10: 217) remarks, "the nativist reaction to 'brown' and 'yellow' immigrants today is notably milder than nativist reactions were to 'white' immigrants in earlier eras." For their part, even in this multicultural age, recent immigrant ethnic and racial groups have shown a willingness to accept "Americanism" in exchange for their "particular" and "foreign" values. As Fischer observes, "the trend lines look similar to those of the [earlier immigrant] Europeans: increasing spatial dispersion away from enclaves, loss of language in later generations, and increasing intermarriage" (218).

Although the radical multicultural position advocated by many spokespersons for minority groups seems to contradict this connectivity, the actual political and social movements advocating multiculturalism consistently employ a civil-society discourse. This discourse presents particular claims for recognition as legitimate refractions of traditional American democracy itself. Hollinger (ch. 12: 256) remarks, moreover, that "a growing appreciation for the value of multiple identities and solidarities, especially those transcending color, has helped in the 1990s to stimulate a new engagement with civic nationality in the United States." Hollinger's empirical observation dovetails with Benhabib's (ch. 14: 293) plea for a new "sociological skepticism vis-à-vis group-differentiated rights claims." Suggesting that "the normative haste with which political philosophers have [sympathetically] responded to identity/difference politics has prevented us from analyzing the social dynamics of the politics of recognition," Benhabib argues that "the result has been, more often than not, a premature reification of group identities rather than a critical interrogation of their limits as well as illusions" (293).

Education, Religion, and Voluntary Organization. In education, too, polarized cultural rhetoric has obscured emergent processes of normative mediation. Tyack (ch. 4) shows that "school wars" in America are nothing new. American society has continually incorporated outgroups through a complex interplay between affirming traditional national values and expanding and hyphenating them. What is new is that the contemporary public confrontation between these contending positions is visible and evenly divided. Formerly dominated racial and ethnic groups and newly arrived immigrant groups fight against homogenizing school curriculum and pedagogy with an aggressive self-confidence that signifies continued involvement in these institutions and continuing faith in education itself. In response to these demands for new normative mediation between ethnicity and tradition, moreover, contemporary custodians of public and private education have assumed a open, ready-to-compromise stance.

With respect to religion, cultural critics argue that secularization and expressive individualism have privatized American spiritual life, creating fragmentation and egoism that exacerbate social conflict and erode moral integration. Warner (ch. 11) shows, on the contrary, that the increasingly open religious conflict in America reflects underlying structural shifts. These new conflicts should be viewed not as simple divisions but as new modes of religiosity, as outlets for expressing increasing social complexity and decentralization. American religion has, from this perspective, become more differentiated and segmented, but Warner stresses it has not, for all of that, become more private. True, demands for recognition of religious particularity seem to have displaced earlier efforts to articulate national statements about substantive religious consensus. Yet religious demonstrations of critical universalism and active citizenship—national values of a less substantive but equally democratic kind—have become more visible:

> Although religion's public face is less visible and less unifying at the national level today than a generation ago, local religious communities, individually or through local ministerial alliances, still make themselves felt to their neighbors. They promote char-

itable causes, from providing meals to elderly citizens to housing the homeless. They provide services, including resale shops, family counseling, after-school tutoring and courses in English as a second language. They host concerts and community meetings. They lobby city hall to collect the garbage, close down crack houses, and award development contracts to socially responsive builders. (ch. 11: 237)

The complaint about the disintegration of voluntary organizations provides a final illustration of this systematic overlooking of emerging levels of normative mediation. Because this complaint is framed within the Tocquevillian view of American civil society realized through local voluntary organizations, it has appealed to many. Nonetheless, as Cohen shows, the complaint ignores important dimensions of democracy articulated by other strands of civil-society theory, particularly the notions of "publicness," "legality," and "critical dialogue" by which the Pragmatic and Kantian traditions have highlighted the importance of expanded solidarity and equality. By ignoring these dimensions, the complaint about voluntary organizations ties itself to a defense of localism and focuses on the weakening traditional institutions such as the gender-divided family, the homogeneous community, and the consensus-building church.

We agree that long-term structural changes indeed have made local voluntary organizations of the traditional sort much less viable in contemporary American society. When women are in the work force, and when local institutions and neighborhoods are increasingly marked by heterogeneity and differentiation, there is neither local commitment nor personnel to sustain and staff unpaid voluntary associations. Does this mean, however, that the mediating role between state and economy that voluntary organizations performed has disappeared? Wuthnow's research demonstrates that the "independent sphere" in America has grown substantially, in the form of not-for-profit organizations run by paid professional staff. These nongovernmental agencies continue to perform many of the tasks administered by state bureaucracies in other democratic societies. In a word, the Tocquevillian specificity of American society remains in place, but it has been given a different structure. Cohen is right to suggest, moreover, that the group-specific ethical mediations between local groups and broader values—once effectively produced by voluntary organizations—are increasingly being formulated by national media that are themselves becoming more segmented and heterogeneous in the cable and computer age.

A Concluding Note

In the 1960s and 1970s, American society, reacting to long-term structural shifts in society, was shaken by a series of critical and defensive social movements that polarized the nation. Since the 1980s structural changes in society have been accelerated, if anything, but the nation has been divided more by tense cultural conflicts between left and right than by social movements themselves. In this introduction we have drawn on the contributions to this book to suggest an explanation for this cultural turn and to question the picture of polarization and crisis it depicts.

What we have found differs considerably from both the conservative and radical versions of the discourse of discontent. Beneath the shrill rhetoric of many intellectuals and opinion leaders, we have found a deep process of institutionalization at work. Despite the dire warnings of the right and the utopian claims of the left, the reformist projects of the movements of the 1960s have been realized to a great degree. Faced with the pressures of growing institutional complexity and cultural diversity, new forms of democratic integration have developed. Those working at the grass roots of American society have created new, normatively sanctioned organizational arrangements and new ways to negotiate conflicts. Traditional American values, rather than being fragmented or deconstructed, have not only provided a stabilizing anchor for these pragmatic responses but have stimulated them. As these normative innovations have developed, social polarization has lessened rather than increased, and a new consensus has been developing beneath the ideological surface. In identifying the misdiagnoses of both the left and the right we are far from claiming that "all is right with the world." But we are convinced that the assertions about the death of common values are premature at best.

NOTE

1. In doing this, we try to remove ourselves as much as possible from the concepts, language, assertions, and terms of debates employed by participants in these conflicts. This remove is demanded by our obligations as social scientists and by our broader intellectual and moral commitments to undistorted communication. Nevertheless, we make no claim to epistemological neutrality. As actors in the cultural and political realities of our time, we do not and can not aspire to a completely disembodied objectivity, and as social scientists we know that the very idea of such objectivity is escapist.

REFERENCES

Alexander, Jeffrey C., and Philip Smith. 1992. "The Discourse of American Civil Society." *Theory and Society* 22: 151–207.

D'Sousa, Dinesh. 1992. "The Big Chill? Interview with Dinesh D'Sousa." Pp. 29–39 in *Debating P.C.: The Controversy over Political Correctness on College Campuses*, edited by Paul A. Berman. New York: Dell.

Eyerman, Ron, and Andrew Jameson. 1991. *Social Movements: A Cognitive Approach.* Cambridge: Polity Press.

Geertz, Clifford. 1973a. "Thick Description: Toward an Interpretive Theory of Culture." Pp. 3–30 in *The Interpretation of Cultures*. New York: Basic Books.

———. 1973b. "Ideology as a Cultural System." Pp. 193–233 in *The Interpretation of Cultures*. New York: Basic Books.

Kimball, Roger. 1992. "The Periphery v. the Center: The MLA in Chicago." Pp. 61–82 in *Debating P.C.: The Controversy over Political Correctness on College Campuses*, edited by Paul A. Berman. New York: Dell.

Schlesinger, Arthur M., Jr. 1949. *The Vital Center*. Boston: Houghton Mifflin.

———. 1991. *The Disuniting of America*. New York: W. W. Norton.

Smelser, Neil J. 1999. "Problematics of Affirmative Action: A View from California." Pp. 169–92 in *Promise and Dilemma: Perspectives on Racial Diversity and Higher Education*, edited by Eugene Y. Lowe, Jr. Princeton, N.J.: Princeton University Press.

Stimpson, Catharine R. 1992. On Differences: Modern Language Association Presidential Address, 1990. Pp. 40–69 in *Debating P.C.: The Controversy over Political Correctness on College Campuses*, edited by Paul A. Berman. New York: Dell.

Walzer, Michael. 1994. *Thick and Thin*. Notre Dame: University of Notre Dame Press.

Young, Iris Marion. 1990. *Justice and the Politics of Difference*. Princeton, N.J.: Princeton University Press.

The Culture of Discontent

DEMOCRATIC LIBERALISM AND THE CHALLENGE OF DIVERSITY
IN LATE-TWENTIETH-CENTURY AMERICA

R O B E R T   W U T H N O W

AT THE END of the twentieth century, Americans' assessment of the nation's well-being is decidedly less than optimistic. Despite the United States' continuing prosperity in international markets and its virtually unrivaled military power, many of the nation's leaders express doubts about its resolve to address the ills that trouble it from within. In addition to such specific challenges as balancing the federal budget, fighting crime, curbing racism, and reforming the health care system, there is a clear sense that democracy itself may be in jeopardy. Questions have arisen about the extent to which the nation is being fragmented by tensions separating racial, ethnic, and religious groups, and about Americans' willingness to shoulder the difficult tasks of working together for the common good. Observers argue that passivity has overtaken the electorate, that civic engagement is declining, that self-interested individualism is rampant, that moral consensus is weak, and that communities are in disrepair. Surveys show that many Americans believe the nation is off course and that they can no longer trust their leaders or their fellow citizens. Many interpreters sense that Americans are neither maintaining their traditional values nor responding well to social diversity.

These concerns require thoughtful examination, for they reveal a great deal about the climate in which substantive policy debates are currently situated. An examination of these concerns, I shall argue, points to the serious degree to which the present culture of discontent is shaped by anxieties about the increasing level of diversity in the United States and the capacity of its institutions and traditions to accommodate this diversity. Yet it is equally apparent that diversity itself cannot fully account for the wider issues that are now being raised, especially in view of evidence that Americans remain committed to common values and are still exposed to common cultural experiences. A satisfactory account of these issues must therefore pay closer attention to the underlying changes in social conditions that have taken place during the past half century and to the rhetoric of reform to which these changes have given rise. An understanding of this rhetoric, I shall suggest, reveals several specific ways in which it will need to be revised if the ills to which many social observers have drawn attention are truly to be addressed.

THE DECLINE OF CIVIL SOCIETY

Current concern about the condition of civil society in the United States appears to be exceptionally widespread. Journalists, scholars, and civic leaders point to a number of specific problems: low voter turnout rates, negative campaigning and acerbic rhetoric in the public sphere, able leaders who either quit or refuse to run for public office, gridlock on important matters of legislation, the growing litigiousness of the society, declining levels of trust in neighbors and of confidence in the leaders of major institutions, diminishing participation in civic associations, apathy toward public issues, and a reduction of public values to questions of self-interest.

"It is no longer possible for us to speak to one another," writes Jean Elshtain in *Democracy on Trial*. "We, quite literally, inhabit our own little islands of bristling difference where we comport with those just like ourselves" (1995: xi). A similar argument has been advanced by Francis Fukuyama in his comparative study of trust. He observes: "The moral communities that made up American civil society at midcentury, from the family to neighborhoods to churches to workplaces, have been under assault, and a number of indicators suggest that the degree of general sociability has declined" (1995: 308). The indicators to which Fukuyama refers are those assembled by Robert Putnam (1995) in his widely cited article "Bowling Alone," including voter turnout, membership in secondary associations, participation in political activities, and expressions of "trust in people," all of which lead Putnam to conclude that "Americans' direct engagement in politics and government has fallen steadily and sharply over the last generation."

In the popular press, the perception that something has gone seriously awry is also voiced repeatedly. "There is no longer a serious question about whether much of our national project is unraveling," says William Bennett (1995). In his view, "Social pathologies have become a permanent feature of late-twentieth-century America." Emphasizing the roots of these pathologies in decadent moral values, Bennett observes that "we have become the kind of society that civilized countries used to send missionaries to" (quoted in Buckley 1994). But similar sentiments have been expressed by leaders with quite different views, such as Bill Bradley (1995) and Hillary Rodham Clinton (quoted in Murphy 1994). Indeed, the prevalence of such comments has prompted one pundit to observe that "after baseball, railing against the system is the great American pastime" (Lukas 1996).

To be sure, allegations of civic malaise are often couched in language that blames them on members of the opposite political party or that uses such allegations to boost interest in popular books and magazines. Yet it is revealing that so many criticisms and from such widely discrepant political and ideological perspectives have focused on the character of civil society itself. If it is "the system" that comes under attack so often, the meaning of this phrase is no longer simply "the establishment" or "the power elite" but something more deeply rooted in the character of American values and in the nature of social relations themselves.

Common to these concerns is the sense that shared national values are now in jeopardy. The central question is not about how best to realize prespecified aims in the most effective and efficient manner possible (such as reducing drug use or promoting foreign trade), or even about such perennial issues as crime, corruption in politics, or stagnation in the economy. It is rather about the mechanisms—and even the resolve—with which to engage in public debate about collective values and then to mobilize voluntary participation in such debate.

Thus, the present concerns about civil society need to be scrutinized carefully. Rather than assuming immediately that the culture of discontent is simply an accurate depiction of current problems, scholars need to ask why the "national funk," as some have called it, has become such a compelling perspective. Indeed, the appropriate role of scholarly debate, taking place as it does a step removed from the public arena itself, should be to examine the underlying assumptions in the debate about civil society, to raise contrarian points of view, and to subject popular truisms to theoretical and empirical criticism. The role of sociological investigation in this undertaking is to focus especially on the changing social conditions that may be reinforcing the current mood.

Civil society is an appropriate rubric in this context because it points to the connections between citizens and the nation's collective need for discussion of the common good. Civil society connotes the so-called free associations and public spaces in which citizens gather to discuss and to carry out collective purposes, either apart from the formal mechanisms of government or in cooperation with those mechanisms (Cohen and Arato 1992; Seligman 1992). It consists of the secondary associations and mediating structures that link individuals to one another and help them mobilize politically or resolve their problems apart from political means. The current debate has centered on these modes of association and the kinds of values they are capable of sustaining. Whether negative campaigning or declining civic involvement is at issue, the unifying element is a concern about the quality of public discourse and the willingness of citizens to work for the preservation of democratic government. Culture, both in the sense of values and symbols (as sociologists and anthropologists understand it) and as the "political culture" of norms and networks (as political scientists understand it), is central. But the debate about civil society has also taken several distinct directions.

One of the most common complaints focuses on questions of trust and cooperation. In this view, civil society breaks down when conditions favor individual rights at the expense of social responsibilities, especially the kinds of social obligations that encourage people to vote, join voluntary associations, and sacrifice their own desires for the common good (Etzioni 1993). Such conditions, say the proponents of this idea, have become increasingly evident in the United States in recent decades. The so-called rights revolution that has taken place since the 1960s has given each individual greater autonomy, thus undermining the ability of employers, priests, community leaders, and, for that matter, parents to evoke commitments from individuals (Fukuyama 1995: 283). The trust that sustains both markets and democratic social relationships also breaks down, resulting in a downward spiral in which individuals rationally pursue their own interests without taking into account the needs of others. What is necessary to correct this problem, say proponents of this view, is for the courts to back away from certain rights and entitlements and for individuals to pay greater heed to their civic responsibilities.

A related line of argument focuses on alienation from society and apathy toward the needs and interests of the nation. Although individuals are assumed to withdraw from civic participation, just as they are alleged to do in arguments about excessive emphasis on rights, this view attributes such withdrawal to a sense of disenchantment that comes with fearing one's efforts will be futile, even if one tries to exercise civic responsibilities (Dionne 1991). The key to this argument lies in its concern with the effect of special interests on the public life of a nation. When organized interests become too powerful, ordinary citizens allegedly withdraw from the field because they think there is little chance that their own voices will be heard. This argument is difficult to assess empirically, but it is consistent with surveys showing that many Americans believe labor unions, women's groups, fundamentalists, and other special interests exercise too much power in public life.

Yet another theme in the current debate emphasizes the growing privatization of moral convictions and their attendant irrelevance to public debate. The argument here is that a thin consensus emerges in a complex society such as the United States in which the deeper values and traditions that were once part of public debate are pushed increasingly into the realm of personal life (Walzer 1994). Order is maintained in civil society by encouraging people not to speak about their true beliefs. Tolerance depends on a tacit agreement neither to question others nor to voice one's own opinions. But such an agreement also reduces motivation for banding together, for organizing around deeply held values, and attempting to bring these commitments to bear on public issues. In religion, for example, beliefs are relativized as personal opinions that should be kept to oneself, rendering them irrelevant to civic deliberations (Carter 1993; Casanova 1994).

There is also an important aspect of the recent literature on civil society that stresses fragmentation (Taylor 1995). Here, the concern is not so much that people will withdraw from public life but that those who remain interested in civic issues will be unable to reach any agreement among themselves. One variant of this argument holds that growing numbers of Americans live in isolated enclaves, separated from other enclaves by racial or socioeconomic differences, and that the inhabitants of these enclaves may be willing to protect their own lifestyles but are unlikely to express interest in broader issues of national importance (Taylor 1992). Another variant asserts that fragmented, localistic groups may nevertheless come together occasionally to engage in "culture wars" that produce further dissension and separation rather than social cohesion (Hunter 1991).

These arguments are not mutually exclusive or exhaustive of the current culture of discontent, but they encompass its more important aspects. Other complaints generally have less to do with the character of society itself, focusing either on specific problems (such as declining SAT scores or teen pregnancies) or matters of moral character alone (such as cheating or promiscuity). Certainly, the problems of declining civic responsibility, alienation, privatization, and fragmentation deserve consideration for what they reveal about our perceptions of ourselves.

DIVERSITY AND DISCONTENT

Much of the recent anxiety about the condition of civil society points directly or indirectly to diversity as a major source of America's current problems. In some instances, ethnic and racial diversity, not to mention immigration, is specifically targeted as the underlying problem. For example, Peter Brimelow (1995) writes that "the country is coming apart ethnically under the impact of the enormous influx [of new immigrants]," and he adds that shared values are unraveling as a result. In other instances, the references to racial and ethnic diversity are oblique but sufficiently apparent to evoke concern. As Michael Walzer observes, the "contemporary dissatisfaction" leads to "dangerous desires" that run counter to the ideals of democratic liberalism, such as militant patriotism and exclusionary attitudes toward persons of different races or groups espousing nonconventional lifestyles (1992: 96). For these reasons, it is worth examining each of the arguments I have just summarized in order to see how it is conditioned by suppositions concerning diversity. My claim is not that diversity is *all* these arguments are about, but that it is a recurrent theme.

The rights revolution that is assumed to be undermining a sense of trust and civic responsibility is generally illustrated by pointing to various entitlement programs that have been advanced to protect minorities or the claims of other special populations. Although it is noteworthy that few observers criticize the civil rights movement itself, many who voice concern about rights focus on legislation that came into being as a result of discrimination suits or on court cases deemed to have arisen from affirmative action requirements or from environmentalists, immigrants, and other special interest groups. Indeed, discussions of excessive rights in the arenas of legislation, higher education, and partisan politics point implicitly to the demands of African Americans, Hispanics, women, and gays and lesbians as sources of a perceived retreat from common values and responsibilities (Fukuyama 1995: 295–306).

The argument about alienation also focuses attention on special interests, and these are implicitly taken to be more active as a result of the growing diversity of the population. Of course, some formulations of this argument resemble those of mass society theorists a generation ago, who, writing in the wake of World War II and during the cold war era, regarded overweening bureaucracy (or large, distant, impersonal institutions generally) as the source of alienation.

It is all the more interesting, therefore, that the argument about alienation has come in recent years to focus more on special interests. The trouble with these interests is not that they are bureaucratic (they may still be distant) but that they reflect the identity politics of particular racial and ethnic groups or of people who define themselves in terms of lifestyle or sexual preference.

The idea of a thin consensus, leading to a privatization of deeper values, has also emerged from considerations about how to promote civic order amid an ever-expanding array of diverse subpopulations. *Thin consensus* is an agreement to abide by procedural rules but to leave substantive values at home. Although thin consensus has been defended chiefly with arguments that arose in the seventeenth and eighteenth centuries in the aftermath of Europe's religious wars, it has been popularized in recent years by the idea that the United States is now facing pluralistic religious and ethnic loyalties that go beyond the Judeo-Christian consensus that embraced earlier waves of immigration (Rawls 1994). Critics of thin consensus worry that the new diversity will cause an unraveling of the social order as long as procedural rules are the only stitching holding it together. The preferable alternative, in many of their views, is to curb diversity either by restricting immigration or by promoting speedier assimilation.

Concerns about fragmentation raise the issue of diversity even more directly than do any of the other arguments, because it is particular racial, ethnic, language, and religious groups that compose the "fragments" into which civil society is said to have broken. Fragmentation is taken to be a problem in at least three ways. One is that diverse groups have so little in common that they are unable to come to agreement at all, and thus live as "islands of bristling difference." A second is that diverse groups can agree only on limited or single issues and thus perpetuate acrimony around these issues. The third is that some groups do not share a commitment to the wider society enough to participate in efforts to promote its larger aims (Taylor 1995: 211–12).

These concerns have of course been elevated by the fact that the United States is in many ways a more diverse society than it was a generation or two ago. Immigration in the past two decades has rivaled that of the first decades of this century and has brought more people to the United States from outside Europe than ever before. Assimilation has appeared more difficult to achieve because of large numbers of Muslims and Hindus as well as because of a sizable Spanish-speaking population. In addition, African American neighborhoods remain geographically and economically differentiated, and lifestyle diversity has increased, as has a religiously conservative segment of the population that appears intent on championing its own beliefs and values.

One interpretation of the current culture of discontent, therefore, is that it reflects the demise of a longstanding white Protestant, or at least white Judeo-Christian, understanding of civil society. As racial, ethnic, religious, and lifestyle minorities have increased in size and political prominence, the traditional culture has reacted, rightly sensing that its ways of life are threatened. In this interpretation, the recent diversity is too varied for any single group to be blamed (although new immigrants may be a vulnerable target), and so the *ef-*

fects of diversity on civil society have come to be the focus of attention. Whereas simplistic solutions would emphasize a reduction of diversity itself, the more complex debate about civil society recognizes that diversity is already a reality and attempts to identify the worrisome ways in which civic engagement has responded. Discussions of rights and responsibilities, alienation, privatization, and fragmentation should not be understood as euphemistic ways of lashing out against minority groups but as serious expressions of concern about the problems facing an enormously diverse society. If this interpretation is correct, diversity is placing American democracy in jeopardy because it is undermining common values and setting in motion centrifugal forces that lead people to distrust each other and withdraw from public participation.

COMMON VALUES

There is considerable evidence that American culture remains oriented toward a set of common values and that most Americans are unified by a common language and by common cultural experiences—enough so at least that the current concerns about civil society seem inexplicable in terms of diversity alone. Although values and the extent to which they are shared are always difficult to assess empirically, such evidence as is available can readily be interpreted to suggest widespread agreement on at least some of the basic aims and aspirations of human life. For instance, surveys consistently reveal that virtually the entire U.S. population places high value on family, freedom, and moral integrity (Wuthnow 1995). To the extent that conflict is evident on some of these issues (family, for instance), it is more about how best to attain a certain value than about whether that value is worth attaining at all.

Some of these values can easily be reconciled with concerns about civil society; for example, the public's emphasis on family can be taken as a kind of "amoral familism" or self-interested personalism that favors private life rather than public responsibilities. Similarly, high levels of commitment to self-sufficiency, freedom, and individual autonomy raise doubts about a commitment to working together for the common good. Nevertheless, the role of such values in *maintaining* social cohesion should not be underestimated. The secret of liberal democracy lies partly in giving individual citizens enough room to disagree so that they do not feel compelled to arrive at consensus on all levels. Moreover, individual freedom is a "decoupling" mechanism that allows people to work together despite different interests and convictions. More important, these are not the only values to which a high proportion of the public gives assent. Most Americans also value their country and take pride in it, believe it is good to participate in voluntary organizations, and say it is important to have social relationships and to contribute to the well-being of other people.

Common cultural experiences also supply a unifying dimension to American life. To be sure, some evidence points to communities of immigrants who expect to return to their countries of origin and who therefore have shown little interest in assimilating to U.S. patterns of life, and it is true that ethnic groups continue to practice religious rituals and to eat, dress, and speak in ways that are not shared by outsiders (LaMare 1981; Bouvier 1992: 178). Yet it is clearly the case that in an age of television and mass marketing, general patterns of consumption spread widely and create a kind of mass culture that transcends most ethnic and racial boundaries. Any consideration of what holds the nation together would have to include such widely known symbols as Mickey Mouse and Elvis Presley, Rice Krispies and Chevrolet, the Dallas Cowboys and the Chicago Bulls. Most children attend schools where they are taught to speak and read English, and most learn the values of honesty and kindness. Despite the criticisms that can rightly be directed toward television and the motion picture industry, most children also share a common culture that includes Snow White and the Seven Dwarfs, the Lion King, and various superheroes, and the characters in these stories often exemplify such virtues as caring, loyalty, and courage.

It would be naive to suggest that a high level of agreement in public opinion polls concerned with abstract values or general exposure to mass marketing is sufficient to prevent extreme and even violent social conflict (were it possible to conduct them, polls in Lebanon would undoubtedly show widespread agreement on the importance of family, for instance). The same public opinion polls show that many Americans are worried that our values are fraying and that the country has gotten seriously off track. Television and newspapers are also filled with stories of violence, indecency, and inhumanity. Indeed, it is often the decay of manners and mores that is more worrisome than the fraying of common values. Lawyers who make obscene gestures to judges while court is in session, reports of fistfights at town meetings, and highly publicized discussions of presidential underwear are among the indications that all is not well in civil society. But other unifying aspects of civil society must also be considered.

For all the concern it has generated, minimalist government has served the United States fairly well in recent decades. It has done so in no small measure because gridlock, acrimonious campaigns, and low voter turnout (not to mention actual shutdowns of government agencies) have not seriously undermined the functioning of an expanded government bureaucracy. As Paul Light's (1995) research on the federal bureaucracy has shown, layers of administration have grown consistently over the past several decades and have done so because of a number of incentives that perpetuate this growth. Bureaucracy of this kind is not without costs, both in high taxes and in inefficiency and a lack of accountability. Yet it is revealing that Americans engage in split-ticket voting as often as they do and seem to prefer bipartisan government to situations in which one party or the other controls both the White House and Congress. Some of the alienation that allegedly keeps Americans from voting in larger numbers is actually a sense that things are running about as well as can be expected, and much of the distrust evident in opinion surveys is directed toward the performance of specific leaders rather than reflecting deep misgivings about major institutions themselves.

Besides government, most other institutions also function fairly well and provide a stabilizing social force, despite widespread criticism of these institutions. The corporate world turns out products that consumers decide to purchase, and stockholders continue to invest large sums of money in corporate ventures. Nonprofit educational and service organizations have proliferated in recent years, enlisting volunteers in their efforts but also fulfilling many of the civic functions that used to be performed voluntarily and informally (Weisbrod 1988). Religious organizations continue to attract a larger share of the public than in virtually any other advanced industrial nation. For all its problems, the college and university system annually processes more students than ever before and does so with sufficiently high standards to attract record numbers of foreign students.

The publicity that special interest groups have attained suggests that there is nevertheless reason to be concerned about the fragmentation of civic life. It is in the nature of these groups, however, to focus on single issues, such as abortion or gay rights, and thus to be limited in the extent to which they can be regarded as harbingers of an all-out cultural cleavage. The conservative Christian Coalition, for example, purports to be concerned with a wide range of fundamental values but in reality is seldom able to elicit agreement from its constituents on issues other than abortion and homosexuality. In addition, many of the examples that are cited to support arguments about fragmentation turn out to be groups with quite limited followings or that are atypical of larger populations. For example, Hispanic separatist groups are sometimes cited, but no mention is made of the degree to which most Hispanic Americans have assimilated to wider cultural expectations.

As far as public opinion itself is concerned, there is little evidence to suggest either growing polarization on specific issues or a deepening rift around more fundamental world views. Studies of opinion polls conducted over the past two decades yield no evidence that more and more of the public is taking extreme positions on social issues, nor are opinions on various issues congealing into hardened ideological camps (DiMaggio et al. 1996). The variation in opinions does reflect some differences in such underlying orientations as belief in God or a commitment to absolute moral standards, but it is also attributable to social experiences that cut across some of these orientations.

Yet another reason for thinking that diversity itself cannot explain the current concern about civil society is that an important strand of this concern stems from arguments about individualism—arguments that pay little attention to diversity and, indeed, regard individualism as a common thread in American culture (Bellah et al. 1985). Some of these arguments suggest that individualism has simply gotten worse, perhaps as a result of some internal logic, or because of advertisers, teachers, or therapists who have inadvertently pushed it too far. In some arguments the antidote to individualism is said to be greater commitment to local communities and organizations, some of which would of course heighten the identities of diverse racial, ethnic, and religious groups.

Close consideration of the current discontent therefore necessitates looking beyond diversity itself as its source. Diversity is more aptly viewed as a challenge to the social order than as the main reason for being concerned about the future of civil society in the United States. It worries many observers because they are unsure that civic commitment is strong enough to face this challenge. Why there is so much concern about the character of civil society remains the issue to be understood.

Changing Social Conditions

The culture of discontent can be understood partly in terms of personal biographies (many upwardly mobile Americans who write about it may worry about what they have left behind), and it is perpetuated by public leaders who worry about why their party or movement may not be more successful than it is or who further their own interests by pointing out woes that can be blamed on their opponents (Lemann 1996). But the deeper source of Americans' sense that something is wrong lies in the loosening of social relationships that has taken place during the past half century. An appropriate way of understanding these relationships is to realize that people have not simply become atomized or fragmented into disillusioned interest groups but that institutions have become more *porous* as they have become more complex, permitting social ties to be broken more easily and yet requiring that they be maintained more flexibly and at greater distance as well.

Porousness is best understood by contrasting it with tightly bounded institutions. Such institutions restrict the flow of people, goods, information, services, and other social transactions. In social network terms, the density of relationships within institutions would thus be higher than the density of relationships among them. Normative barriers also function to set institutions apart, both explicitly through sanctions against interacting with outsiders and implicitly through distinctive languages and lifestyles. In contrast to such tightly bounded arrangements, porousness is characterized by permeable membranes. Social relationships can be established that transcend the boundaries of specific organizations or communities, and social norms facilitate such relationships. In a changing or uncertain social environment, porousness is an adaptive response that encourages looser and more functionally specific relationships (Taylor 1992: 63; Powell and DiMaggio 1991).

The clearest example of this loosening is of course within the family itself. For growing numbers of people, lifelong marital bonds have been replaced by patterns of divorce and remarriage. The number of people who remain single or who live alone has increased as well, but the largest impact of this change is that more and more people have complex relationships involving what are known as blended families (Cherlin 1992). Some relationships with ex-spouses, stepparents, half siblings, in-laws, former in-laws, and the like, remain, and these relationships form a loose set of familial connections. But apart from this much discussed example, familial relationships have loosened in a number of ways. Siblings do not live near one another, share babysitting, and work together in the family business, but they keep in touch by telephone. Parents do not live down the road and hold the mortgage to the family farm, but adult children visit them once in a while and perhaps depend on them in serious emergencies.

Neighborhoods, as territorially defined communities, also have porous boundaries that permit looser connections to be maintained. Spending social evenings with neighbors has declined in recent decades, but spending time socializing with friends outside one's neighborhood has increased. Easier transportation and a more mobile population are the reasons for this change. Most people report that they know people at work better than those in their own neighborhoods. Friendships can be formed around temporary or specialized interests, rather than being embedded in the neighborhood. Nations, too, have porous boundaries, happily encouraging tourism and foreign trade, and less happily being able to police their borders.

In religion, the so-called seeker phenomenon is the most visible example of loose connections (Roof 1993). While attendance at religious services has held fairly steady over the past half century, membership in religious organizations has declined significantly since the 1950s, and interest in nontraditional forms of spirituality, ranging from self-help groups to books about angels and near-death experiences, has increased. Fewer people belong to the same denomination or congregation as their parents did or expect to remain in the same religious organization as long as they once did. In the process, spirituality has not so much become privatized as personalized, meaning that individuals connect themselves loosely with a large number of traditions, groups, and spiritual networks.

Work and business have also come increasingly to be characterized by loose connections. Fewer people take jobs that were recommended to them by a parent or sibling, and fewer people work in their immediate neighborhoods. Most of the labor force changes jobs every few years, and a majority of American workers choose several different lines of work during the course of their working life (Wuthnow 1996). Growing numbers of people take up second careers after early retirement in one, and larger numbers of people work in temporary and adjunct positions or as independent consultants.

Business ideology has come increasingly to favor loose connections. Rather than modeling themselves as pyramidally constituted bureaucracies, businesses imagine themselves to be networks composed of smaller, flatter, less top-heavy organizations (Peters 1992). The shift from manufacturing to services and information is said to necessitate this newer form of organization. Service requires smaller, flexible units; information cannot be contained within a monopolistic structure and so must be exchanged freely: the organization with the largest number of weak ties wins. Service and knowledge workers retain more of their own cultural capital, so they must also be responsible for selling themselves and furthering their own interests. Market forces are said to work best in a complex system of this nature.

The extent to which porous institutions and loose connections have come to characterize American society should not be exaggerated. A majority of adults get married and live with their spouses over long periods of time, and they consider it desirable to settle into careers, neighborhoods, and jobs, even though it may be difficult for many Americans to realize these aspirations. Transaction costs deter continuous shopping, especially when goods and services depend on knowing whom to trust, having reliable friendships, or pursuing values that cannot be attained in the marketplace. Many of the loose connections that Americans slip into and out of so easily are anchored by the existence of more durable relationships and institutions. As with other short-term contractual relationships, these connections are possible because of a relatively dependable legal system, for instance. It is nevertheless the case that they are also encouraged by technological changes, especially telecommunications and computing, that facilitate contacts over greater distances and with greater rapidity.

Many of these changes are compatible with the American tradition of democratic liberalism. Loose connections are consistent with Americans' emphasis on personal freedom and with the value of being able to choose what one does, for how long, and with whom (Walzer 1990). Such ties are scarcely novel in a society that has always encouraged settlers to move on, to explore the open frontier, to seek new vistas. But these ties are also frighteningly fragile. They generate fears because they are constantly being renegotiated; there is less to depend on, especially when the magnitude of social problems itself seems to be increasing. Paradoxically, they are a response to economic uncertainty, but a response that generates additional anxiety when this uncertainty deepens. For instance, trust is harder to maintain when social relationships are more sporadic, and yet heightened economic uncertainty creates a desire for greater trust as a way of minimizing risk.

The link between loose connections and worries about civil society is evident in the language used to describe these worries. In qualitative interviews I have been doing as part of a research project on civic participation, people talk about "fragmentation," a lack of commitment, and a desire for connectedness. They deny feeling utterly isolated or lonely, explain that they have friends and are frequently in contact with people, and yet are worried that their communities are breaking up and that something has been lost compared with the ways their parents and grandparents lived. In academic discussions, similar language appears frequently. Scholars ask whether the center holds, point to the decline of associations based on long-term memberships, and acknowledge the rise of support groups and telecommunications but raise questions about the capacity of newer forms of sociability to promote a stable democracy.

THE RHETORIC OF REFORM

To make sense of these changes in social conditions, many discussions appear now to be resorting to a rhetoric of reform that is also deeply embedded in the American tradition of democratic liberalism. Rather than simply embracing the porous institutions we have created, we argue that these institutions must fundamentally be reformed. In seeking language in which to express these arguments, we are able to draw on rich traditions that in their very familiarity provide security.

Some of this rhetoric reflects the nation's religious traditions or secular variants of these traditions. For instance, biblical arguments about the importance of community have been rediscovered as ways of encouraging Americans to band together more tightly. Religious arguments also favor the idea of working together for common betterment, and although explicit conceptions of evil have not been as prominent, these arguments also suggest a need to avoid optimistic views of society. Other arguments assert that it is simply sensible for Americans to give up their emphasis on individual freedom and to attach themselves more loyally to their communities.

In academic and popular social science, therefore, one finds a good deal of hand-wringing about what is wrong with America, about the social problems that need further study, and about the failure of public officials to see how bad things really are and the unwillingness of ordinary people to get involved. The few writers who emphasize what is right with America are regarded by fellow academicians as being hopelessly naive. Indeed, pro-American boosterism (once more the domain of conservative academics) is now located almost exclusively in the literature of business and management consultants, whereas scholars in other fields appear compelled to distance themselves from this literature by suggesting ways in which the society can address its ills more effectively.

The brand of reform that Americans seem to favor is more in keeping with democratic liberalism itself, and with progressive and pragmatic orientations, than it is with either an authoritarian religious tradition or the more thoroughly secular philosophic arguments that emerged in western Europe after the Enlightenment. There is little in the current literature of discontent, for example, that reflects Nietzschean despair, or the pervasive nihilism of European treatments of mass society, or even the specter of totalitarianism set forth in the work of Hannah Arendt. Contemporary reform rhetoric in the United States is cautiously optimistic insofar as it suggests possibilities of reversing present social trends through good legislation and moral tutelage.

Although some reformers argue that the best solution to America's problems is to restrict immigration and otherwise curb diversity, most discussions show evidence of recognizing the deeper changes that are taking place in social relationships. It is true, for example, that blended families create situations in which neglect or abuse of children or diminished economic resources for educating children become more common, and thus proposals have emerged for legislation to address such issues as family-leave policies and paternal responsibilities for child support. The individual freedom that comes with porous institutions has led to various movements that aim to guide and support individuals in their decisions: self-help movements, antidrug campaigns, consumer advocacy movements, and renewed efforts to teach values in schools. With looser connections in families and neighborhoods, it also becomes easier for people to behave as free-riders, benefitting from the civic participation of others rather than contributing themselves. Efforts to promote civic involvement and volunteerism are responses to these conditions. The culture of discontent, therefore, is channeled repeatedly into positive proposals for reforming the society rather than being simply a dirge about the woes of America or even an antidiversity rhetoric that scapegoats outsiders for the more general fraying of tight-knit relationships.

RETHINKING THE ISSUES

The rhetoric of reform serves a positive function insofar as it promotes discussion of how to strengthen civil society, but it needs to be revised in several important ways to take account of the social realities that now characterize American society. In particular, arguments about social reform need to incorporate a multicultural perspective, reckon with the nostalgia on which reform is often based, shape specific proposals to be consistent with changing social conditions, and come to terms with the egalitarian strand of democratic liberalism.

Multiculturalism challenges progressive proposals that seek to heal civil society by reducing or eliminating diversity. All too frequently, the standard rhetoric of reform appears to be couched in terms that reflect the traditionally dominant position of the white middle class rather than the growing realities of a racially and ethnically diverse society. For example, civic participation is encouraged in organizations that are dominated by white middle-class people and that perform small acts of kindness for recipients who must show gratitude by conforming to the lifestyles of the middle class. True multiculturalism takes the position that diversity itself is of value and that genuine diversity respects the value of people's being able to live within their own communities and pass on their own traditions to their children (Raz 1994).

Rhetorics of reform are also legitimated by selective reconstructions of the past. In the present case, nostalgia has sometimes prevented observers from understanding the similarities between present social conditions and those of earlier times and places. When stylized versions of the American family are presented, they must be compared with historical evidence to determine whether they correspond to actual families or bear greater resemblance to the televised sitcom families of the 1950s (Coontz 1992). Similarly, nostalgic representations of the shtetl, the Lower East Side, South Philly, and Lake Wobegon need to be examined carefully to see the extent to which these images were the work of tourist bureaus, filmmakers, and politicians.

In addition, concrete efforts to energize civil society must be developed with a realistic view of the loose connections that characterize contemporary social relationships. Loose connections have become more common because they give the flexibility needed to move through life in a highly complex social environment. Few Americans would stand for legislation that banned divorce or that denied people the right to move from one community to another. In the future, fewer people may be inclined to express their civic sensibilities by joining male-dominated, hierarchical organizations such as Elks and Shriners or to bend their already complicated family schedules to make room for regular membership on the local bowling team. But there are alternatives. Volunteer organizations are finding ways of enlisting volunteers for fewer hours at a time and on shorter notice. Nonprofit organizations give growing numbers of Americans opportunities to contribute to the common good while earning a living, as well as a way to interact with volunteers and fellow staff members much like people used to do in their neighborhoods and service clubs. There are also innovative coalitions and partnerships that draw people from the community for special projects and that utilize existing networks among churches, human service agencies, schools, and corporations. Increasingly, strategic partnerships and alliances are replacing large bureaucratic service organizations. Neither the current culture of discontent nor the rhetoric of reform has paid much attention to these innovative forms of civic engagement.

The most serious challenge facing democratic liberalism is to reconcile its libertarian strands with the intervention required to ensure that its egalitarian ideals are also upheld. Curiously, much of the current rhetoric of reform emphasizes curbing the more libertarian aspects of American culture in the name of promoting the common good, and yet it is tacitly assumed that these restrictions will automatically generate greater equality as well, rather than simply protecting the interests of those with more abundant resources. Were more Americans to join Kiwanis and Elks as they did in the past, for example, whole communities would presumably be strengthened and not just the interests of white, upper-middle-class males; or stronger family values would go a long way toward eradicating poverty because the number of children being raised in single-parent households would thereby be reduced. Yet the flaws in these arguments are all too apparent.

In a worst-case scenario, the current debate about civil society simply deflects attention from the worsening problems of inequality and marginalization in the United States—problems that invariably increase when institutions become porous in a way that rewards people who already have resources and lets others slip through the cracks. Middle-class Americans can too easily devote their energies to overcoming their own individualism and alienation without having to look much beyond their own communities. As long as civic participation is assumed to depend mainly on voluntary commitment, the resources required for people to engage in civic activities can be overlooked. The fact that these resources have diminished greatly for low-income groups during the past decade and a half can simply be neglected.

Egalitarianism has always been the hardest aspect of democratic liberalism to preserve. It is not fully guaranteed by a strong emphasis on individual rights or by an abstract concern for communal responsibilities (Spragens 1995). Thin consensus needs to be amplified by traditional values, such as those embedded in religious conceptions of justice and mercy or in humanistic discourse about the realization of collective aspirations. Collective values must also take into consideration the need for government initiatives, taken in the name of equality itself, to maintain and expand the opportunities of all citizens to realize their ambitions.

In the final analysis, the current culture of discontent is both accurate and misleading. It is accurate insofar as it registers the public's perception that all is not well in the United States at the end of the twentieth century. It is misleading insofar as it fails to recognize that social conditions themselves are the source of this discontent, more so than some failure of nerve or penchant for passivity on the part of individual Americans. Coming to terms with the increasing porousness of social institutions is the first step toward recognizing that immigration and diversity are not the threats to American values they are sometimes depicted as being. It is also an essential step toward understanding that porous institutions allow new inequalities to develop that pose the most serious challenges to the nation's liberal democracy.

References

Bellah, Robert N., Richard Madsen, William M. Sullivan, Ann Swidler, and Steven M. Tipton. 1985. *Habits of the Heart: Individualism and Commitment in American Life.* Berkeley and Los Angeles: University of California Press.
Bennett, William J. 1995. "Moral Corruption in America." *Commentary* (November): 29.
Bouvier, Leon. 1992. *Peaceful Invasions: Immigration and Changing America.* New York: Free Press.
Bradley, Bill. 1995. "National Press Club Luncheon Speaker." *Federal News Service* (February 9): n.p.
Brimelow, Peter. 1995. "*Conservatism and Immigration.*" *Commentary* (November): 34.
Buckley, William F., Jr. 1994. "Let Us Pray? The Link between Excessive Church–State Prohibitions and the U.S.'s Increasing Problems." *National Review* 19 (October 10): 86.
Carter, Stephen L. 1993. *The Culture of Disbelief: How American Law and Politics Trivialize Religious Devotion.* New York: Basic Books.
Casanova, Jose. 1994. *Public Religions in the Modern World.* Chicago: University of Chicago Press.
Cherlin, Andrew J. 1992. *Marriage, Divorce, Remarriage*, rev. ed. Cambridge: Harvard University Press.
Cohen, Jean L., and Andrew Arato. 1992. *Civil Society and Political Theory.* Cambridge: MIT Press.
Coontz, Stephanie. 1992. *The Way We Never Were: American Families and the Nostalgia Trap.* New York: Harper Collins.
DiMaggio, Paul, John Evans, and Bethany Bryson. 1996. "Have Americans' Social Attitudes Become More Polarized?" *American Journal of Sociology* 102: 444–96.
Dionne, E. J., Jr. 1991. *Why Americans Hate Politics.* New York: Basic Books.
Elshtain, Jean Bethke. 1995. *Democracy on Trial.* New York: Basic Books.
Etzioni, Amitai. 1993. *The Spirit of Community: Rights, Responsibilities, and the Communitarian Agenda.* New York: Crown.
Fukuyama, Francis. 1995. *Trust: The Social Virtues and the Creation of Prosperity.* New York: Free Press.

Hunter, James Davison. 1991. *Culture Wars: The Struggle to Define America*. New York: Basic Books.

LaMare, James. 1981. "The Political Integration of Mexican-American Children: A Generational Analysis." *International Migration Review* 16: 173–82.

Lemann, Nicholas. 1996. "Kicking in Groups." *Atlantic Monthly* (April): 22–26.

Light, Paul C. 1995. *Thickening Government: Federal Hierarchy and the Diffusion of Accountability*. Washington, D.C.: The Brookings Institution.

Lukas, J. Anthony. 1996. "Thunder on the Hill." *New York Times Book Review* (May 5): 34.

Murphy, Ann Pleshette. 1994. "An Exclusive Interview with Chelsea's Parents." *Parents' Magazine* (May): 22.

Peters, Tom. 1992. *Liberation Management: Necessary Disorganization for the Nanosecond Nineties*. New York: Fawcett Columbine.

Powell, Walter W., and Paul J. DiMaggio, eds. 1991. *The New Institutionalism in Organizational Analysis*. Chicago: University of Chicago Press.

Putnam, Robert. 1995. "Bowling Alone: America's Declining Social Capital." *Journal of Democracy* 6: 65–78.

Rawls, John. 1994. *Political Liberalism*. New York: Columbia University Press.

Raz, Joseph. 1994. "Multiculturalism: A Liberal Perspective." *Dissent* (winter): 67–79.

Roof, Wade Clark. 1993. *A Generation of Seekers*. San Francisco: Harper.

Seligman, Adam. 1992. *The Idea of Civil Society*. New York: Free Press.

Spragens, Thomas A., Jr. 1995. "Communitarian Liberalism." Pp. 37–51 in *New Communitarian Thinking: Persons, Virtues, Institutions, and Communities*, edited by Amitai Etzioni. Charlottesville: University of Virginia Press.

Taylor, Charles. 1992. *Multiculturalism and "The Politics of Recognition."* Princeton, N.J.: Princeton University Press.

———. 1995. "Liberal Politics and the Public Sphere." Pp. 183–217 in *New Communitarian Thinking: Persons, Virtues, Institutions, and Communities*, edited by Amitai Etzioni. Charlottesville: University of Virginia Press.

Walzer, Michael. 1990. "The Communitarian Critique of Liberalism. *Political Theory* 18: 6–23.

———. 1992. *What It Means to Be an American: Essays on the American Experience*. New York: Marsilio.

———. 1994. *Thick and Thin: Moral Argument at Home and Abroad*. Notre Dame: University of Notre Dame Press.

Weisbrod, Burton A. 1988. *The Nonprofit Economy*. Cambridge: Harvard University Press.

Wuthnow, Robert. 1995. "From Religion to Spirituality: A New Basis for the Unum?" Pp. 191–202 in *Reinventing the American People: E Pluribus in the Nineties*, edited by Robert Royal. Grand Rapids, Mich.: Eerdmans.

———. 1996. *Poor Richard's Principle: Restoring the American Dream through the Moral Dimension of Work, Business, and Money*. Princeton, N.J.: Princeton University Press.

PART TWO

How Much Has Really Changed?

CHAPTER THREE

Cultural Responses to Immigration

JOHN HIGHAM

> Without the spirit of nationalism, or at least without the recognition of the
> unity of a people, it is hard to lay a sure foundation of democracy. . . .
> Nationality has no degrees. It is equal in the least and in the greatest.
> Therefore it makes the people one in a way that neither the finest nor the most
> pervasive culture can ever by itself assure.
>
> —*Robert McIver, The Web of Government*

The Immigrant Nation

IMMIGRATION, from the point of view of the individual, is a transitory and liminal state. No one remains an immigrant, in the full sense of the word, for very long. Acting one by one or family by family, immigrants have chosen America, whatever the compulsions that may have driven them from home. Neither an organized invasion, such as the original settlement of the English mainland colonies, nor an importation of slaves is an immigration in the usual sense of the word. Immigrants are celebrated in American myth and story for the choice they made and the individual act of will they displayed, at least if the deed was done some time ago.

As soon as they begin to find a place for themselves in the new country, the newcomers acquire collective identities that designate their supposed origins. The immigrants cohere as members of ethnic groups. Gradually they become less foreign—less "immigrant"—but their ethnicity endures into the next generation and beyond. An overall estimate of relations between immigration and American values will therefore have to deal not only with immigration as a process but also with the more persistent identities that the process engenders; and those identities will need some comparison with other identities that have entered into the making of America.

It used to be said that all Americans, with the possible exception of the Native American Indians, are immigrants or descendants thereof. Oscar Handlin took this powerful national legend about as far as it could go by declaring grandly in the introduction to *The Uprooted* his discovery "that the immigrants *were* American history," not a special aspect of it (1951: 3). Most historians have, I believe, quietly abandoned Handlin's claim. As a version of consensus history, it casts us all in the same mold, imposing on a heterogeneous society the particular type with which the author identifies. Yet there is a great truth that both the legend and its rejection obscure: more than any other large country, ours has been continuously shaped by migration from abroad and within.

But it is not sheer numbers that make the United States the preeminent immigrant nation. Canada's population in 1911 was 22% foreign-born. Nearly one-third of the population of Argentina was then foreign-born. In some provinces of both countries foreigners outnumbered natives by two to one. Buenos Aires was and is the immigrants' city in a way that even New York has never been. At the peak of immigration to the United States the proportion of the foreign-born in the total population was half as great as it was in Argentina (Higham 1984: 13–15).

The truly distinctive feature of immigration to the United States is its extraordinary and continuing diversification from the early eighteenth century to the present. Other immigrant-receiving countries have tended to draw from a few favored ethnic backgrounds: Argentina, from Italy and Spain; Australia, from the British Isles; Malaya, from China; Fiji, from India. Where the way of life of the predominant immigrant group contrasts markedly with that of the older inhabitants, as in Malaya and Fiji, a deep and lasting schism can split the receiving society. In contrast, the United States has continually attracted new groups and has thereby avoided a fixed division between an immigrant people and an older native population. As the country became more accessible to less familiar immigrant types, by fits and starts it made room for them. The gates have widened, so that the United States now receives a significant immigrant stream from every part of the world except Oceania (Fogleman 1996; Jasso and Rosenzweig 1990). Even that tiny migration has grown sufficiently in recent years to give some concern in the state of Hawaii.

By what means have Americans learned to cope with so vast a heterogeneity of origins? Three factors stand out.

1. *The Bounties of Nature.* The English mainland colonies were uniquely endowed with seemingly limitless fertile lands, with numerous rivers that penetrated the interior, with rich forests, and with a Calvinistically driven population intent on improvement and enrichment. The restraints on individual land ownership that weighed heavily on the lower classes in Europe and in other colonies overseas were largely absent. "The whole scale of life, the spaciousness, the scatteredness, the relative emptiness never failed to impress European travellers," a modern geographer tells us (Meinig 1986: 440). What was chiefly needed was labor. To ambitious men who were already uprooting themselves from their native localities in search of a better life in their own country, these circumstances spelled opportunity. Before non-English immigration had any significance, the mainland colonies were preparing for it by attracting from the English homeland an already mobile population.

2. *Political Access.* The creation of a decentralized republic added liberty to the lure of opportunity. Resting theoretically on principles that belong to everyone by right of a common humanity, the United States presented itself to the world as a universal nation, a home for all peoples. Here there would be no subordination to an ancient dynasty or a national church, no enclosure in a fixed and hallowed place. This American self-image was enormously magnetic. It implied that nationality was not exclusive, that citizenship could be widely available, and that class and ethnic boundaries would be soft and permeable. The invitation to newcomers (at first to white males only) to participate in political life on equal terms with other citizens gave outsiders some leverage in using the power of suffrage and the protection of courts. It encouraged white ethnic groups to organize, to make their weight felt, and so to use a system of liberty under law. Because no single group could overawe the rest, habits of sharing power and negotiating compromises flourished (Horowitz 1992; Fuchs 1990).

In this political framework the localization of power tended especially to defuse ethnic conflicts. Problems in one jurisdiction or region did not cause opposing factions to mobilize throughout the country. Instead, a pluralistic interplay of interest groups developed, and a proliferation of voluntary organizations—ethnic and otherwise—was encouraged.

3. *Geographic Mobility.* Capitalism and abundance laid the economic foundations for multiethnic immigration, then a decentralized republic built the political structures it needed. There was also a third precondition for continuous, substantial, and adaptive immigration: the country had to develop a fluid, uncongealed society. For that, America provided an essential solvent: geographic mobility. As immigrants by definition come from somewhere else, they are an unsettling force wherever they appear. But in America their arrival has commonly been less stressful than in other countries because here most of the older, supposedly settled population have themselves been engaged in an endless round of relocations. From east to west, from town to city, from city to suburb, from one city to another, and from one neighborhood to the next, Americans have always been an extraordinarily migratory people (Thernstrom and Knight 1970). More than any other nation, ours has been continuously shaped by geographic mobility, sometimes organized but mostly spontaneous and uncoordinated. An Anglo-Irish observer who lived in the United States during the 1840s put the migratory impulse of Americans in a comparative perspective:

> No one who buys a property [wrote Thomas C. Grattan] looks at it with the fondness of European possession. The respective owners only think of improving for the purpose of selling. . . . Each raises his house as the wild-bird makes its nest, conscious that when his brood is fledged its first impulse will be to fly. He knows nothing of the ties which bind the denizen of the Old World to the home of his fathers. Patriotism with the American is not a passionate regard for the soil and its associations. It is a mere abstract notion made up of personal interest, prejudice, and pride. (1859: II, 99)

One hundred and fifty years after Thomas Grattan sneered at the placelessness of American attachments, a young Vietnamese American repeated the Irishman's lament more gently:

> Recently on a trip to Vietnam I saw well-tended graves rising among the green rich rice fields. "Why are there so many graves on your rice fields?" I asked a young Vietnamese farmer on an oxcart making his way home. "They're my ancestors," he said. "They worked here and they died here. We pay them respect and their spirits in turn protect the land."
>
> The farmer, who had never seen a city, asked me if we in America invest as much sweat and blood in our land as he does. Not the same way, I told him. Americans live in towns and cities, and we move about, from city to city, restlessly. (*Baltimore Sun,* 21 Sept. 1991)

Is it any wonder that Americans democratized the automobile, or that their popular culture revels in images of speed, escape, and portability? Is it surprising that the liberating effects of exodus reverberate in classic American literature, from Walt Whitman's songs of the open road to Mark Twain's *Huckleberry Finn,* and in the entertainments of our own time, from *Easy Rider* to the Indy 500?

The amazing levels that internal mobility reached in the nineteenth century have declined in recent decades. Compared with the 1960 census, which showed that 12.2% of American homeowners had moved during the previous fifteen months, the 1990 census counted only 9.4% who had packed up and slipped away. Although the lowest level ever recorded, this movement still contrasts dramatically with the rootedness of home ownership in other developed countries (*New York Times,* 12 December 1994).

Transmitted to immigrants, these patterns explain why American ethnic groups have characteristically lacked even the memory of a secure territorial base. With certain interesting exceptions, descent groups in this country have been unable to hold (if indeed they ever had) an emotional tie to a place of their own, a locale they could remember as a source of their being and cherish as an ultimate defense against a depersonalized, cosmopolitan modernity. This has been the principal difference between the ethnic structure of the United States and that of other multiethnic nations.

In short, the nation's migratory urge has dispersed and Americanized immigrants and weakened ethnic groups in the process. But for millions of individuals, an ongoing migration has also redeemed the promise that led them to America in the first place. Old ties may loosen, but new and often less restrictive identities will form.

The openness of the American milieu has sometimes been beneficial for the survival and nourishment of the ethnic collectivity. In this vast land, groups can often locate where the weather and the countryside remind them of home. Until recent decades they could also choose locations that would avoid sharp competition with rival groups. Before the Civil War the practice of mutual avoidance diverted nearly all European immigrants from the South, because African

Americans did the heavy work there. In the North, from the eighteenth century onward, Germans and Irish tried to keep out of one another's way. The Irish seized New England and most of the mid-Atlantic area. The Germans predominated heavily in the Midwest, except for a belt of cities from Milwaukee to New York, where the two groups kept their distance in separate quarters of the city (Leach 1966: 137; Power 1836: 113–15; Gerber 1989). Even in the twentieth century, when ethnic clusters in big cities necessarily overlapped, people kept moving, partly to avoid too many unfamiliar or "undesirable" neighbors (Pacyga 1995).

Finally, America's love affair with mobility has enabled the immigrant to symbolize the meaning of America in the preeminent myth of national identity. Typically, a national myth glorifies both a place and a founder or group of founders. To later generations, place and founder become basic referents of collective identity. Although no single American place could fully satisfy the requirements of a foundational myth, in the nation's folk memory a founding of sorts emerged in the epic of migration westward.

Early American nationalism, born in the tumult of revolution, rested on a cosmopolitan ideology. It declared the country's independence from any specifically ethnic antecedents. But from the beginning there was a sense that something was missing—some solidarity as a people. Ideology by itself seemed a frail basis for national unity in the loose-knit society of the early republic. Talking obsessively about the need for a distinctive American literature, cultural elites as late as the 1850s worried about the incompleteness of a national character. The editor of the *Illustrated News*, for example, complained in 1853 that

> we have scarcely any really national instincts, tastes or ambitions; so mixed, incongruous and discordant are the parts which make up our population. There is indeed . . . a common enough demagogueism about equality and liberty; but we have not yet a clearly defined and fixed character as a people. ("The Last New Magazine"; Kammen 1978: 15–26)

Nevertheless, from the 1820s onward an answer to the problem of an American focus was found in the great story of a moving people (Welter 1975: 298–328; Smith 1950).

A comparison with Australia helps clarify the relative openness of what became the predominant American myth. It is well known that both the United States and Australia began in the nineteenth century to draw copiously on the image of the frontiersman as the national type. In story and legend the bush workers of Australia and the pioneers of the American West formed a model of national traits. The great difference between the two myths, in Russel Ward's classic interpretation, is that democracy meant class solidarity or "mateship" on the Australian frontier and self-reliance on the American (1978; Carroll 1982). A second difference—more relevant to my theme—has gone unnoticed, namely, the insularity of the Australian myth in contrast with the unboundedness of the American one.

In resisting the strong pull of the British connection, Australian national con-

sciousness posited a wholly endogenous type: a "nomad tribe," in Anthony
Trollope's telling phrase. Australia's frontiersmen belonged exclusively to the
interior. That was their homeland. They had no connection whatever with any
larger migration. The American frontiersman came from somewhere else. He
was, for example, *The Virginian* in the most famous of American cowboy
novels (Wister 1902). Characteristically, the American pioneer was seen not as
the autochthonous product of an empty land but as the spearhead of a continuous migratory process: a westward march of the people in all their multitudes,
which had formed the older parts of the country as well. Instead of repressing
the memory of earlier migrations, the American pioneer extended and fulfilled
them.

Here, for example, is Walt Whitman universalizing the American movement
westward in the poem "Pioneers! O Pioneers!":

> All the pulses of the world,
> Falling in they beat for us, with the Western movement beat,
> Holding single or together, steady moving to the front, all for us,
> Pioneers! O pioneers!
>
> Life's involv'd and varied pageants,
> All the forms and shows, all the workmen at their work,
> All the seamen and the landsmen, all the masters with their slaves,
> Pioneers! O Pioneers!
>
> (Whitman [1865] 1939: 204–5)

Thus, through a pervasive onward mobility, the legend of the pioneer blended
with the legend of the American as immigrant. In effect, a vision of *process*
provided a substantial (though not a complete) substitute for a vision of *place* in
the symbology of American identity.

The synergy between the westward movement and immigration arose from
their common promise of rebirth and renewal. By moving farther west, Americans repeatedly reenacted a ritual of deliverance, which for some had begun in
their original departure from the Old World; and the magic of hope buoyed
their movement onward. American national self-consciousness, Paul Nagel
(1982) has remarked, "has been mostly a spirit of anticipation." Although the
promise of a better life and an improved society was certainly grounded in the
political and religious ideas of the Revolutionary era, it acquired an everyday
reality and a deeply personal significance from the energies of geographic and
social mobility. As images of pioneers, immigrants, and other supposedly self-
made men fleshed out the ideology that Americans proclaimed in 1776, it flow-
ered into a myth of an unbounded society. America is the place where anything
is possible, where no one is irrevocably fenced in (Higham 1969: 5–15).

It is appropriate, therefore, that the frontier and the immigrant came to the
fore in American historical writing at almost the same time and in much the
same hands. Frederick Jackson Turner brought them together in 1893 by spell-
ing out the myth of American boundlessness with a new analytical clarity.

Turner's claim that "the immigrants were Americanized, liberated and fused into a mixed race . . . in the crucible of the frontier" placed immigration squarely on the agenda of professional scholarship (Milner 1989).

Turner's association of the European immigrant with a redemptive process of becoming American was linked with a sense of foreboding. Might not the passing of the frontier and the new stresses of an urbanized, industrial society weaken the myth of an open society? Had Turner realized that the frontier he loved and the immigrants he admired were only two specific dimensions of a far more pervasive, multifaceted mobility, he might have felt much more confident. The historians, intellectuals, and social scientists who came after him in the decades from 1910 to the 1950s probed the complexities and limitations of mobility more deeply. They were engaged in modernizing the American myth. On the whole, their work sustained a process-oriented and progressive vision of an open society.

That era, of course, is over, and when it ended national myths lost much of their credibility. Nevertheless, the immigrant remains in place as a national icon—both a link and a contrast between the United States and a larger world.

ETHNOCENTRISM AND NATIVISM

People of all sorts generally find the company, customs, and attitudes of others like themselves preferable to the habits of strangers. How they define "their own kind" varies of course with social conditioning, education, and personal taste. Even more variable is the intensity of their in-group feeling. Yet the phenomenon itself is so nearly universal that some scholars interpret ethnocentrism as an evolutionary mechanism that developed to unify our remote ancestors under threatening circumstances (Fox 1996).

In view of the virtual universality of we–they dichotomies, one would suppose that research on xenophobia and racism would have begun by examining the circumstances under which in-group feelings are either inflamed and absolutized or reconfigured and contained. Neither history nor sociology has taken that course, however. Ethnocentrism is rarely mentioned. Unfriendly intergroup behavior is perceived everywhere as culturally determined, ideologically deployed, and politically aggressive. It is *imposed*. I, too, in early writings on nativism, largely pursued that approach. I now believe, however, that in overemphasizing the extreme and fanatical manifestations of ethnic discord, scholarship has neglected quotidian experience. For the most part, ideology in America has worked in favor of immigrants, not against them. That is why this essay began with the predominant American ideology, which I have elsewhere called American universalism (Higham 1993). Its limits and contradictions bring us to a contrasting myth, in which ethnocentric rivalries and demographic pressures have played a large role.

Before the ideology of the Revolution was solemnized in Philadelphia in 1776 and then mythicized into a vision of a new and universal people, a more earthy and localized story of American origins was current. This tale often lurks behind or silently qualifies the official myth. It is an ethnocentric myth of exclusive possession that dates from the founding of Anglo-American colonies and was summed up in the *Federalist* in 1788:

> Providence has been pleased to give this one connected country, to one united people, a people descended from the same ancestors, speaking the same language, professing the same religion, attached to the same principles of government, very similar in their manners and customs. (Madison, Hamilton, and Jay 1788)

Before Americans learned to think of themselves or others as immigrants—before the very word existed—an incipient national consciousness celebrated the early English settlers who had staked out for themselves and their descendants a domain where their own particular way of life could be defended and perpetuated. The founders of the original colonies, created sporadically throughout the seventeenth century, had wanted simply to reproduce and enhance familiar communities. Without a twinge, they did whatever that purpose required, from enslavement to expulsion of the native inhabitants. This birth of white America was by expropriation and exclusive possession.

We find the myth of exclusive possession in religious as well as in secular contexts. It appears in the Hebraic side of Puritanism, from which early New Englanders derived assurance of being a chosen people whom God had endowed with a promised land. "Christ having made a covenant with us," John Cotton preached, "he gives the inheritance of the world to such as believe on him" (Miller 1939: 481). We meet a similar confidence of possession expressed in racial language by the colonial elites who, on the eve of the American Revolution, were defending against a corrupt regime what they viewed as their ancient English heritage. "The Americans," John Randolph declared in 1774, "are descended from the Loins of *Britons*, and therefore may, with Propriety, be called the Children, and *England* the Mother of them" (Savelle 1962: 912). At the very beginning of the quarrel with the home government, James Otis had pointed out that Americans were not "a compound mongrel mixture of *English*, *Indian*, and *Negro*, but . . . freeborn *British white* subjects" (Vaughan 1982: 936).

The formative importance of this restrictive, Anglophile myth was long overlooked. The idea of exclusive possession has attracted no great poets and few of our leading historians. The true founding, we are usually assured, took place at the climax of the Enlightenment, when the American was described, in Crèvecoeur's words, as a "new man" who left "behind him all his ancient prejudices and manners" (1976: 25–26). This second founding, however, never expunged the memory of the first. One was superimposed on the other. The contradiction between them has usually been minimized by emphasizing "liberty" as the predominant motive of the first founders as well as of the second.

A persistent myth of exclusive possession revives in every crisis in which a core population feels threatened by outsiders. Listen, for example, to an anonymous broadside published in Danvers, Massachusetts, in behalf of the patriot cause during the American Revolution:

> Now unto who belongs this Land?
> It was gain'd by our Fathers Hands:
> This Land they did their Children give,
> That they a free born Race might live.
>
> This Land they won themselves alone,
> The Blood shed for it was their own;
> They thank none that dwelleth around,
> For Help from them they never found.
>
> Now let us keep it as our own,
> For it belongs to us alone:
> And let us stand firm like a Tree,
> That never can removed be.
>
> (A Short Account, n.d.)

Is it significant, I wonder, that the anonymous author of these verses never identifies "us" and never attaches a name to "our Fathers," from whom title to the land descends? Even in Massachusetts in the late eighteenth century it must already have been difficult to specify by descent who the true Americans were. On a continental scale the lineaments of a founding group were still more uncertain. Not only did the first founders lack a territorial center; they were also separated from one another by religion, country of origin, local institutions, patterns of trade, and time of arrival. Although the cultures of the early English and Dutch settlements on the north Atlantic coast were actually fairly similar and grew more so during the eighteenth century, no coherent, overall image of those first founding fathers could crystallize. The private sponsorship and diverse antecedents of the original European colonies gave American history a pluralistic bent at the outset, and that has generally put the myth of exclusive possession at a disadvantage.

Every attempt in the nineteenth century to define an old American type, an autochthonous, prerevolutionary American, splintered on the rock of irreducible particularism. The lack of a suitably distinctive name is perhaps the best evidence of the amorphousness of an indigenous core population. In colonial Latin America and the Caribbean islands, people of European descent who were born in the colony became known as "creoles." The label declared their social preeminence, as descendants of conquistadors and early settlers, over the often more energetic or politically well-connected immigrants from the mother country (Góngora 1975: 81, 96–98, 162–64, 183–86). On the North American mainland, however, an explicit, invidious distinction between creole and immigrant was almost unknown. Only in Louisiana did the French usage of "creole" persist as a means of affirming the social preeminence of *l'ancienne population* over the Anglo-Americans who poured in after annexation to the United States in 1803 (Dominguez 1977: 589–602).

Again, Australia illustrates the relative breadth and openness of American myths. Australians have never celebrated the immigrant. As in Latin America much earlier, Australian nationalists in the late nineteenth century defined themselves as "natives," not as new men. An Australian Natives Association, founded in 1871 to combat the prevailing Anglophile spirit of the Australian colonies, promoted an unabashedly indigenous outlook; and after World War I a major political party, the Country Party, which shared in power for forty-three years, gained votes everywhere in Australia by glorifying the rural interior (Aitkin 1988). The United States never institutionalized an ideology of native birth and native character. In this country "native Americans" were (and are) generally understood to be Indians. The first powerful mobilization of native-born Americans in the nineteenth century was a midcentury movement that enemies disdainfully characterized as "nativist." But this secret, anti-Catholic crusade had little success in identifying "true" Americanism with a particular place of origin and actually made no consistent effort to do so. From the outset the American Party faced the charge that it was un-American. This was deeply embarrassing, for the Know-Nothings (as party members were also called) packaged their melange of prejudices and anxieties in the universalistic, libertarian ideology they shared with Republicans and Democrats. Their hero was George Washington (Gienapp 1987: 93, 415–435; Bennett 1988: 48–155; Bryan 1950).

Accordingly, the strength of the liberal strain in American nationalism—along with the contradictions in which it entangled the Know-Nothings—goes far toward explaining their swift collapse. The country wasn't ready for bitter religious and ethnic intolerance. Yet the power of the movement, brief as it was, also made clear the underlying intensity of xenophobia. In 1854–55 the American Party elected eight governors, more than a hundred congressmen, and the mayors of Philadelphia, Chicago, and Boston, along with thousands of other officials. For a while the Americans seemed on the verge of replacing the Whigs as one of the two major political parties. Mobs burned churches, tarred and feathered priests, and devastated foreign quarters in numerous cities. In Louisville, Kentucky, an election battle killed some twenty people and wounded forty more. For several days the entire German district in Cincinnati was under siege (Hutcheon 1971). Something baffling and perhaps momentous was happening.

Historians have offered many explanations for this upsurge. For our purposes they may be reduced to three.

1. *The Nation in Danger.* Nativists believed that Roman Catholicism, as a political force operating through swarms of alien voters, was undermining the freedoms of the American republic. This fixation on American freedom and on themselves as its true guardians aligned the Know-Nothings with both of the country's founding myths. They were the possessors of a special American heritage that someday would spread the blessings of liberty around the world, but only if they defended it against subversion. Accordingly, most of the Know-Nothings in the North were strongly antislavery and were vigorous proponents

of other Protestant reform movements such as temperance and public schools. Mixing liberal and reactionary nationalism, they perceived the Slave Power and the pope as similarly tyrannical enemies of the nation (Anbinder 1992). The Know-Nothings wanted a free society, but they also wanted to keep America for themselves by resisting the expansion of slavery and disqualifying immigrants from voting for 21 years.

2. *Protestant Possessiveness.* In 1847 a Presbyterian evangelist, articulating a relatively new and growing sentiment, declared: "Puritanism, Protestantism, and True Americanism are only different terms to designate the same set of principles" (Knobel 1986). The evangelist's implication that "true" Americans were exclusively Protestant descendants of Puritan founders postulated a strong ethnic and national boundary for a citizenry that had earlier been quite fragmented and loosely defined. Before the coming of the Irish in the 1840s, people who attended Protestant churches had thought of themselves chiefly as Christians or as belonging to particular denominations. Their identities inhered in the doctrines they subscribed to and over which they quarreled exuberantly. The arrival of a mass immigration from Catholic Ireland, however, solidified and ethnicized a Protestant identity, to which a more secular culture and a romantic worldview also contributed. In increasing numbers white Protestants came to see themselves as a people, the Americans *tout court*, and they celebrated their identity on the Fourth of July with picnics and firecrackers instead of the church services and the long political speeches of an earlier day (Higham 1994; Kammen 1978: 54).

This self-image, although certainly ethnocentric and nationalistic, did not necessarily produce a strictly nativist attitude of hostile exclusivity. Others could be Americans also, though perhaps not as fully. Nevertheless, the ethnic consciousness that arose from awareness of a differentness from Irish Catholics did give people of white Protestant descent some of the communal feeling, ethnic warmth, and territorial possessiveness that could easily spark a nativist movement.

3. *Numbers and Concentration.* When ethnic conflict erupts, historians routinely mention the numerical proportion between newcomers and the preexisting population. Yet this relationship is hardly ever given the salience it had for those who were involved. Mob attacks on newcomers tend to occur only when their proportion of the local population suddenly increases too rapidly to permit much assimilation, and the older inhabitants see themselves in danger of dispossession. The first great explosion of ethnic turmoil in American history—in the mid-1850s—took place at the peak of an enormous wave of immigration. The immigrants who arrived in the 1850s amounted to 12% of the antecedent population of the United States—a ratio between newcomers and residents unequaled before or since. In 1860 several leading American cities, including New York, Chicago, Milwaukee, and St. Louis, were half foreign-born. Baltimore, then the third largest American city, was divided into twenty wards,

only one of which had a native white majority. Immigrants were a majority in five (Carpenter 1927; Towers 1993: 286–88). In short, immigration from Ireland and Germany exploded in the early 1850s. It was highly concentrated on the principal cities, which a still-rural nation already regarded with deep suspicion. On just those cities the torrent of immigrants—many of them arriving in desperate straits—brought down huge problems of crime and dependency (Bennett 1988: 68, 72–76). It is hardly surprising that a great many northern Protestants felt that *their* country was breaking apart under the simultaneous threat of southern secession and immigrant invasion.

The only other nativist crisis on a comparable scale built up more gradually in the second decade of this century and reached a peak in the early 1920s. Once again the nation seemed in danger, although the source of danger was now more diffuse. What nativists saw behind the rampant disorder in American cities in the early twentieth century was less specifically Catholic than in the nineteenth. Instead, they observed a widening gulf between rich and poor, a general civic irresponsibility, and perhaps most especially, the immigrant masses' passionate involvement in the greatest wave of strikes the United States had yet known (Wolman 1924: 33, 85; Edwards 1981: 15–16; Montgomery 1974).

Additionally, nativists during this period argued that the so-called new immigration from southern and eastern Europe was racially inferior to the "old immigration" from northern and western Europe. It was therefore polluting the nation's bloodstream. To justify discrimination against the newer immigrants, elaborate pseudoscientific theories about the races of Europe were concocted. One cannot doubt that this "Nordic" racism was widely believed. Still, the obvious shallowness and sleaziness of nativist efforts to demonstrate the hereditary inferiority of the new immigration might suggest that race was a problem for nativists, not just a weapon. Surely their jerry-built racial theories, which the next generation of social scientists eagerly tore down, have received excessive emphasis in accounting for the drastic immigration restriction legislation of the early 1920s. At most, those theories could only loosely associate the sometimes blond peoples of eastern Europe with the color phobia—the grassroots racism—that was then reaching an unparalleled intensity in the American South and West (Williamson 1984; Higham 1955). Perhaps the notion of a racial danger was mostly a way of obscuring the rising class conflicts that were truly threatening the American faith in a mobile society.

Again, as in the 1850s, the sheer numbers and concentration of the newcomers, pushing against a jealous myth of exclusive possession, proved to be critical in the anger that peaked during and after the Great Red Scare of 1919. At the time of the First World War the foreign-born no longer constituted so formidable a mass as they had in 1860. But now the first and second generation together had reached an all-time high in proportion to the older population. Three-quarters of the population of New York, Chicago, Detroit, Cleveland, and Boston in 1910 consisted of first- and second-generation immigrants (Higham 1984: 14–15). The great industries relied on them absolutely. In the great cities the rise of an ambitious second generation was probably cutting into opportunities in white-collar jobs for native-born whites who were leaving the countryside in large numbers. The children of the immigrants were also deeply involved in a burgeoning popular culture in which hedonism, crime, and consumption played a large role.

Emerging in this setting, a new Ku Klux Klan (appropriating the name of vigilantes who had terrorized southern blacks in the 1870s during a struggle to restore white supremacy) became the most successful nativist fraternal organization in American history. Its lingering reputation as an aggressively race-baiting and alien-bashing organization is deserved but also misleading. Its object was essentially defensive. It wanted to shore up the solidarity of ethnic Protestants and so to preserve their hegemony in the nation. Over all the moral rearmament and struggles for power that the Klan undertook, over all its crimes and reforms, hung a sense of impending dispossession and of the urgency of closing ranks against invading forces (Higham 1994).

The greatest problem facing middle-class and lower-middle-class white Protestants after World War I was perhaps a loss of the kind of ethnic leadership that Theodore Roosevelt and Woodrow Wilson had given them. The intellectual and social elites on which Protestantism relied heavily were drifting away from the rank and file of the ethnic community. The Protestant Ascendancy, as Joseph Alsop (1992) has styled the northeastern upper class, was sealing itself off from the rest of society, including the Protestant middle class. Young intellectuals, in rebellion against their own ethnic origins, were no longer guardians of the inherited culture; they were becoming its adversaries. The leaders who had customarily spoken for the Protestant masses, and provided them with a model of aspiration and conduct, were giving way to faceless bureaucrats in the business world, cosmopolitan secularists in the universities, and corrupt politicians in both political parties. All in all, the *kulturkampf* of the 1920s was a struggle over who owned the nation.

The outcome was a shattering defeat for the Klan, the prohibitionists, and the larger body of ethnic Protestantism—a defeat from which none of them ever recovered. To simplify a complex scene of cultural conflict in the 1920s, it may be sufficient to say that the Klan was a desperate, last-ditch effort to reimpose by intimidation a Protestant moral code to which other Americans—including business elites, intellectuals, universities, and mass media—would no longer submit. In contrast to the Know-Nothing party, which was superseded by a stronger reform movement, the Klan was simply driven from the field by its own crimes and the superior strength of its enemies. In dozens of cities far more outrages were committed against the Klan than it succeeded in perpetrating. The country had spun out of the control of any single group (Coben 1994; Goldberg 1996).

In the midst of the *kulturkampf*, anti-immigrant legislators did succeed in enacting a stiff restriction law with a racist tilt against the new immigration and the Japanese. But for a decade or more the country had needed an effective numerical restriction to protect the living standards and the bargaining power of the American working class. In the passage of the "national origins" law of 1924 an intensely racialized nativism was an important factor but not the only one. The new law, for all its extravagant unfairness, was an essential building block in the slow construction of a welfare state.

Ironically, however, it did nothing to arrest the decay of an old-stock Protestant culture and society. It worked just the other way. The national origins quotas cut immigration so sharply that the fears and anxieties driving the immigration restriction movement subsided like a pricked balloon (Higham 1955: 324–30). Ethnic Protestants demobilized in the late twenties and gradually reopened themselves to the idea of an inclusive America.

LIBERAL NATIONALISM RENEWED

The collapse of nativism in the late 1920s revealed once again the importance of numbers in explaining the intensity of ethnocentrism in American history. The near embargo that the law imposed on immigration from southern and eastern Europe and from Asia was reinforced in the 1930s by the Great Depression and in the 1940s by World War II. The foreign-born population of the United States skidded from 14.6% of the total in 1910 to 5.4% in 1960 (Hacker 1983: 44). At the same time, a very rapid and widespread assimilation went forward. Although initially stimulated by government propaganda and pressure from employers, the loosening of Old World ties on the part of the "foreigners" (as they had called themselves) and their children arose mostly from an enormous yearning to become Americans.

A full story of how European and old-stock American ethnicities—and therefore ethnocentrism itself—weakened in the 1920s has never been told. It runs counter to today's academic preference for defiant victims and minority coalitions. But a recognition that ethnicity is a common inheritance of majorities and minorities alike enables us to see that, emerging from the cultural turmoil of the 1920s, a common process drove people in many disparate ethnic enclaves to redefine themselves in more open and inclusive ways. Although their immediate experience was often painful and disillusioning, in the end they were rebuilding and extending the tradition of American universalism.

An important essay by Henry May, "The Religion of the Republic," argues that what he calls America's national religion, "Patriotic Progressive Protestantism," collapsed in 1920 along with the millennial hopes that the war effort had raised (1983: 163–86). May's account of a tremendous religious failure is not very far from my interpretation of an equally shattering ethnic failure. The two theses suggest that the postwar disillusion of old-stock Americans matched a similar disillusion among ethnic minorities and created a space for wider identities on both sides. The aftermath of World War I unquestionably left many Americans of recent European descent with a sense of betrayal. For them, too, the war had raised vaulting expectations. Many had dreamed of and worked for a new day of freedom in their homelands. Others had eagerly expected a proletarian revolution. All needed some larger identity, either to replace or to anchor the one that had failed them. Grudgingly, in many cases, all moved toward a new sense that they could belong to a more inclusive America. Before World War I, for example, the Polish-American press in Chicago had always identified its readers as "We Poles" or "Poles in America." After the war the designation changed. "Poles in America" became "Polish-Americans." By the end of World War II they were "Americans of Polish descent" (Kantowicz 1975: 163–65).

As the numbers and concentration of the newer immigrants declined in the interwar years, defensiveness on both sides relaxed and affiliations multiplied. By the twenties the small middle class of southern and eastern European deriva- tion was expanding, receiving some civic recognition, and joining the outward movement from cities to suburbs. The ethnic neighborhoods were left to the working class (President's Research Committee 1934: 564; Zunz 1985: 64). Ethnic nationalism correspondingly yielded to a common working-class culture, which the mass media and the new industrial unions of the 1930s did much to forge (Cohen 1990). All the institutions of ethnic culture weakened. Lodges declined, ethnic ceremonies and theaters faded, saloons closed, and in their churches and newspapers a younger generation of priests and editors began to encourage a greater use of English. "Against Americanization there is no rem- edy," wrote a Slovenian editor in 1929. "That we are in the melting pot there is no question, but there is no sufficient reason why we go so fast" (*Amerikanski Slovenec* 1929; Nelli 1970: 204, 238–44; Fishman 1966: 38–67; Buczek 1976: 58–60).

Significantly, the melting pot was softening ethnic and local boundaries in the nonimmigrant population at the same time. It was forming a national com- munity in which group differences persisted, but ran together. Comparing weekly newspapers published in English and in Danish, Marion Marzolf (1979) found that local cultures were weakening right along with ethnic cultures. From a peak in 1914, both ethnic papers and local papers lost circulation and adver- tising fairly constantly. Tacitly acknowledging the new primacy of national me- dia, they abandoned divisive party politics and fell back on a common strategy of concentrating on their own localities (156, 210). Even among white south- erners, a group exhibiting an extreme degree of parochialism and bigotry in the twenties, the ethnic boundary eased somewhat. An exodus of blacks to the North (the "Great Migration") relieved racial tensions. Simultaneously, new networks of communication, such as national radio programs, national mer- chandising, good roads, and movies, began to turn the Southern mind away from its traditional emotional fixation on the black man. Only now, looking backward, can we see that an avant garde of middle-class blacks and whites, collaborating in the South in the 1920s, sowed early seeds of the modern civil rights movement (White 1969: 192–93; Egerton 1994).

Liberal scholars, myself included, have often observed a tendency for eco- nomic downturns to sharpen interethnic conflict. That did not happen in any major way, however, during the greatest depression in American history. It did not happen because immigration and internal ethnic migrations largely ceased.

Liberal nationalism, with its myth of an inclusive America, regained ascendancy. Strongly negative attitudes toward the world outside the United States certainly persisted in the 1930s and 1940s. Not until the civil rights movement crested in 1965 did the liberal persuasion gather enough momentum to take down the exclusionary structure of immigration restrictions erected in 1924. But meanwhile a major recasting of group relations within the country had been accomplished.

That the depression produced fascist movements and governments abroad while invigorating a democratic sense of commonality at home is hard to explain. I can point only to the underlying strength of the ideas of the second founding—specifically, the pervasive and unifying belief in America as a sanctuary for liberty and equality. The depression was so broadly devastating, so global, and so hard to comprehend that it lessened a sense of superiority among the strong and enhanced a sense of belonging among the weak.

Especially in the late thirties, as the threat of war loomed, the times called not for divisive stereotypes but for common heroes. The lazy black, the scheming Jew, the criminal Italian, and the villainous Chinese faded from movies and mass circulation magazines. In their place writers searched for a "usable past," and they found it in the great nineteenth-century embodiments of American democracy, especially Abraham Lincoln and the Statue of Liberty. The man and the monument emerged in the thirties as the foremost personifications of the nation (Weiss 1979; Jones 1971; Lee 1946: 145; Higham 1984: 76–79).

Two powerful forces gave the upsurge of liberal nationalism its leadership and its broad popular base. Working from the top down, a large body of intellectuals designed the images, goals, and arguments. Their ranks included the self-styled "young intellectuals" who had joined H. L. Mencken in hooting at America in the 1920s and now followed him again in rediscovering the country's amplitude and diversity. They included major painters whose intense fixation on American people and places attracted extensive coverage in popular magazines. They included the most widely read American historian, Charles A. Beard, whose books acclaimed the inexhaustible energies of American democracy and hinted at the coming of a democratic collectivism. Above all, perhaps, they included the sociologists and anthropologists who founded a sympathetic, nonjudgmental investigation of racial and ethnic relations in American cities. One outcome of these newly inclusive (but still predominantly white) perspectives was to make "intercultural education" a priority. The schools would seek to maintain the self-esteem of all children by respecting their various ethnic antecedents while also encouraging a common American culture (Alexander 1980: 152–91; Weiss 1979: 576–84).

A second force for liberal nationalism, rising from below, sprang from the Democratic Party. Always more sympathetic than Republicans to white minorities who were outside the traditional eastern-Protestant core of the nation, the Democratic Party had long served to defend immigrant and Catholic cultures from the authority of the socially dominant. From the late 1920s onward, this usually fractious potpourri of minorities became the vehicle for a mass movement—a movement that brought together the liberal intelligentsia, organized labor, and a vast population of second-generation immigrants who were claiming recognition and incorporation in a new America (Kelley 1977, 1979).

By the late 1930s egalitarian welfare and labor policies enabled the New Deal to win overwhelming support in the African American ghettos of the North. Few recognized at the time that pragmatic bread-and-butter politics were nudging American universalism beyond its Eurocentric limitations. But the imperatives of World War II fed the rising demand for universal civil rights and established the New Deal's agenda in the postwar years. With remarkable prescience and a touch of awe in his tone, a leading black journalist, George Schuyler, in 1937 summed up: "I am convinced that a revolution has taken place" (*Pittsburgh Courier*, 18 September 1937).

NEW CONDITIONS

The mid-1960s, when liberal nationalism reached an apogee, now seem far away. Much has changed, much is obscure, and much is beyond my ken as a historian. I can venture only some impressions of what remains of the social patterns and cultural responses I have reviewed. Let us look first at the immigrants themselves and then at the conditions they are encountering.

Partly because today's immigrants include more professionals and managers than those of a century ago, they are on average less poor and better educated than their predecessors. The great mass, however, seem much like the peasant-immigrants of the early twentieth century. Similar handicaps of social status burden them; the same ambition for betterment drives them; the same determination sustains them. To be sure, they look different from whites and African Americans. But the color and appearance of Asian and Latin American immigrants are far less offputting to native-born people than were the pseudoracial stereotypes of Irish and southern Europeans in the nineteenth century (Knobel 1986: 5). Moreover, the immigrants of today are a substantially smaller share of the entire U.S. population than were their predecessors in 1860 or 1920. Like those of the past, today's newcomers gather in cities. And in many ways the cities benefit from their presence.

What is most striking in the present scene—and substantially different from earlier times of crisis—are dense regional concentrations of a single immigrant group. Never before in a large American city has one immigrant nationality reached the numerical preponderance that Mexicans have attained in Southern California and Cubans in Miami. In 1990 one-third of the population of Los Angeles County was foreign-born, the vast majority of them Mexican. In a single decade the Hispanic population of the county had increased 62%. Still more overwhelming was the Cuban presence in Miami, where foreign-born islanders were a majority of the total population. Half of all the Mexican immigrants and 40% of the Cubans spoke English either poorly or not at all (Rumbaut 1994: 601–4; O'Hare 1992: 22–25). Among American minorities only the slaves in the Black Belt of the Old South have exceeded this degree of regional concentration.

In short, numbers and concentrated visibility in specific regions have reached a level at which our history should have warned us to expect serious trouble. No convoluted theories of racism are needed to explain the eruption of four major riots in Miami in the 1980s, or the immense upheaval in Los Angeles in 1992. Although both situations involved abusive police, the underlying anger stemmed in good measure from an alien invasion, which blacks perceived as a product of white favoritism and a portent of their own dispossession. The "browns" were taking over, underbidding blacks in the Los Angeles labor market, buying into their impoverished but familiar neighborhoods, and draining existing social services. There was no place for blacks to go but out, and many who took that route must have left with bitter hearts (*U.S. News and World Report* 1993; Navarro 1995; Johnson, Farrell, and Guinn 1996). Because Koreatown was also involved in the Los Angeles riot, it was the first major tri-racial upheaval. But that does not alter the basic upsurge in Los Angeles of the intense ethnocentrism that sudden, unregulated population movements have always aroused.

The problem will not be temporary. Previous overconcentrations of an immigrant group have gradually dissolved when extrinsic events, interrupting an incoming stream, have allowed time for the ordinary action of internal mobility to redistribute people. The Civil War abruptly cut off the torrent from Ireland, and after the war the Irish no longer emigrated in such large numbers. Throughout New England new migrations from French Canada and the Maritime Provinces replaced many of the Irish, who ventured westward. Similarly, World War I, together with the restrictionism of the twenties, provided an interlude for the immigrants of the early twentieth century to mingle, adjust, and move up.

No similar interruption seems likely today. The great Latino communities are on the border between the United States and Latin America. They are positioned for a closeness of association with the homeland—an indelible foreignness—that will be new in American experience. Their vitality may be expected to pull Latinos in other parts of the United States back to these ethnic centers instead of pushing them farther afield. The only other foreign-language group that has had such immediate access to the United States, and such a predisposition to stay close to the homeland, was the French Canadian. But as soon as Quebec industrialized, their emigration stopped. For the first time we may be creating enclaves of permanent minorities on a pattern familiar in other parts of the world, where a dominant ethnic group dwelling at the center of the country is surrounded by minorities on the periphery. A geographic pattern that produces bitter conflict from Quebec to Tibet is becoming possible in the United States.

To the spatial separation that is growing on the southern border of the United States, recent research by demographers at the University of Michigan adds a larger dimension. Across the country, they tell us, the major metropolitan areas where immigrants congregate no longer attract an equivalent number of domestic migrants. Instead, these largest metro areas are losing domestic migrants, especially those with limited education and poverty-level incomes. The latter are moving to smaller population centers in the Southeast and the Mountain West, where the immigrants are much less likely to go. The two migrations, traveling in opposite directions, are sharpening differences between regions with a distinctly immigrant character and those that are attracting an older American population (Frey 1996a, 1996b).

To some degree these regional transfers reflect the powerful territorial possessiveness that comes down to us from the first founding of America. As always, people are claiming a space for themselves. What may be troubling is not that today's immigrants are much different from earlier ones but that the integrative capacities of the larger society seem diminished. In the last several decades America has probably offered all but the best educated immigrants more limited opportunities than it did in the past. The widening distance between unskilled jobs and the technological complexity of better ones condemns most immigrant families to minimal social mobility and thus may deprive them of the hope that keeps the American system going.

The new American culture of our time poses another challenge to the traditional role of immigration. From the beginning, immigration was perceived as a crucial aspect of nation-building, mostly as a positive aspect but often as a detriment. Immigration was fundamental to the myth of American universalism, and it has figured as an obstacle in the myth of exclusive possession. Since the 1960s, however, nation-building has collapsed both as strategy and concern, particularly in the high culture of the academic world. Immigrants remain very popular there, but largely as members of victimized groups. Because the scholars who specialize in ethnic studies generally see nations as oppressive and cooptive, the relations of ethnic groups to a core culture do not interest them. Hyphenated identities are no longer richly problematic, as the current fashion of dropping the hyphen from terms like African American indicates.

The eclipse of liberal nationalism since the 1960s has deprived all the nation's minorities of a powerful means of affirming their fraternity with others and exploring their relations to a common Americanism. Are we experiencing, basically, an increasing indifference of people to one another, both within and between ethnic groups? If so, immigration may prove to be just an aspect of a wider social fragmentation.

REFERENCES*

Aitkin, Don. 1988. "'Countrymindedness': The Spread of an Idea." Pp. 50–57 in *Australian Cultural History*, edited by S. L. Goldberg and F. B. Smith. Cambridge: Cambridge University Press.
Alexander, Charles C. 1980. *Here the Country Lies: Nationalism and the Arts in Twentieth-Century America*. Bloomington: Indiana University Press.

* For particular references I thank Martin Grey and George Sanchez.

Alsop, Joseph W. 1992. *"I've Seen the Best of It:" Memoirs.* New York: W. W. Norton.

Amerikanski Slovenec. 1929. Chicago Foreign Language Press Survey, Reel 62, III E. Immigration History Research Center, University of Minnesota.

Anbinder, Tyler. 1992. *Nativism and Slavery: The Northern Know Nothings and the Politics of the 1850s.* New York: Oxford University Press.

Bennett, David H. 1988. *The Party of Fear: From Nativist Movements to the New Right in American History.* Chapel Hill: University of North Carolina Press.

Bryan, William A. 1950. "George Washington: Symbolic Guardian of the Republic, 1850–1861." *William & Mary Quarterly* 7: 53–63.

Buczek, Daniel S. 1976. "Polish Americans and the Catholic Church." *Polish Review* 21: 39–61.

Carpenter, Niles. 1927. *Immigrants and Their Children, 1920.* U.S. Bureau of the Census, *Census Monographs* 7: 25–26.

Carroll, John, ed. 1982. *Intruders in the Bush: The Australian Quest for Identity.* Melbourne: Oxford University Press.

Coben, Stanley. 1994. "Ordinary White Protestants: The KKK of the 1920s." *Journal of Social History* 28: 155–65.

Cohen, Lizabeth. 1990. *Making a New Deal: Industrial Workers in Chicago, 1919–1939.* New York: Cambridge University Press.

Crèvecoeur, Hector St. John. 1976. *Immigration and the American Tradition,* edited by Moses Rischin. Indianapolis: Bobbs-Merrill.

Dominguez, Virginia. 1977. "Social Classification in Creole Louisiana." *American Ethnologist* 4: 589–602.

Edwards, P. K. 1981. *Strikes in the United States, 1881–1974.* New York: St. Martin's Press.

Egerton, John. 1994. *Speak Now against the Day: The Generation before the Civil Rights Movement in the South.* New York: Knopf.

Fishman, Joshua. 1966. *Language Loyalty in the United States.* The Hague: Mouton.

Fogleman, Aaron. 1996. *Hopeful Journeys: German Immigration, Settlement, and Political Culture in Colonial America, 1717–1775.* Philadelphia: University of Pennsylvania Press.

Fox, Robin. 1996. *The Challenge of Anthropology: Old Encounters and New Excursions.* New Brunswick, N.J.: Transaction Publishers.

Frey, William H. 1996a. "Immigrants and Native Migrant Magnets." *American Demographics* 18 (November): 1–5.

———. 1996b. "Immigration, Domestic Migration, and Demographic Balkanization in America: New Evidence for the 1990s." *Population and Development Review* 22: 741–63.

Fuchs, Lawrence H. 1990. *The American Kaleidoscope: Race, Ethnicity, and the Civic Culture.* Hanover, N.H.: Wesleyan University Press.

Gerber, David A. 1989. *The Making of an American Pluralism: Buffalo, New York 1825–1860.* Urbana: University of Illinois Press.

Gienapp, William E. 1987. *The Origins of the Republican Party, 1852–1856.* New York: Oxford University Press.

Goldberg, David J. 1996. "Unmasking the Ku Klux Klan: The Northern Movement against the KKK, 1920–1925." *Journal of American Ethnic History* 15: 32–48.

Góngora, Mario. 1975. *Studies in the Colonial History of Spanish America.* Cambridge: Cambridge University Press.

Grattan, Thomas Colley. 1859. *Civilized America.* Vol. 2. London: Bradbury & Evans.

Hacker, Andrew. 1983. *U/S: A Statistical Portrait of the American People*. New York: Viking.

Handlin, Oscar. 1951. *The Uprooted: The Epic Story of the Great Migrations That Made the American People*. Boston: Little, Brown.

Higham, John. 1955. *Strangers in the Land: Patterns of American Nativism, 1860–1925*. New Brunswick, N.J.: Rutgers University Press.

———. 1969. *From Boundlessness to Consolidation: The Transformation of American Culture, 1848–1860*. Ann Arbor, Mich.: William L. Clements Library.

———. 1984. *Send These to Me: Immigrants in Urban America*. Baltimore: Johns Hopkins University Press.

———. 1993. "Multiculturalism and Universalism: A History and Critique." *American Quarterly* 45: 195–219.

———. 1997. "Ethnicity and American Protestants: Collective Identity in the Mainstream." Pp. 239–59 in *New Directions in American Religious History*, edited by Harry S. Stout and D. G. Hart. New York: Oxford University Press.

Horowitz, Donald L. 1992. "Immigration and Group Relations in France and America." Pp. 3–35 in *Immigrants in Two Democracies: French and American Experience*, edited by Donald L. Horowitz and Gérard Noiriel. New York: New York University Press.

Hutcheon, Wallace S., Jr. 1971. "The Louisville Riots of August, 1855." *Register of the Kentucky Historical Society*. Pp. 150–72.

Jasso, Guillermina, and Mark R. Rosenzweig. 1990. *The New Chosen People: Immigrants in the United States*. New York: Russell Sage Foundation.

Johnson, James H., Jr., Walter C. Farrell, Jr., and Chandra Guinn. 1996. "Immigration Reform and the Browning of America: Tensions, Conflict, and Community Instability." Paper presented at the conference "Becoming American/America Becoming," International Migration Program, presented by the Social Science Research Council, Sanibel Island, Fla.

Jones, Alfred Haworth. 1971. "The Search for a Usable American Past in the New Deal Era." *American Quarterly* 23: 710–24.

Kammen Michael. 1978. *A Season of Youth: The American Revolution and the Historical Imagination*. New York: Knopf.

Kantowicz, Edward R. 1975. *Polish-American Politics in Chicago, 1880–1940*. Chicago: University of Chicago Press.

Kelley, Robert. 1977. "Ideology and Political Culture from Jefferson to Nixon." *American Historical Review* 82: 531–62.

———. 1979. *The Cultural Pattern in American Politics: The First Century*. New York: Knopf.

Knobel, Dale. 1986. *Paddy and the Republic: Ethnicity and Nationality in Antebellum America*. Middletown, Conn.: Wesleyan University Press.

"The Last New Magazine." 1853. *Illustrated News* 1 (February 5): 86.

Leach, Douglas Edward. 1966. *The Northern Colonial Frontier, 1607–1763*. New York: Holt, Rinehart & Winston.

Lee, Alfred McClung. 1946. "The Press in the Control of Intergroup Tensions." *Annals of the American Academy of Political and Social Science* 244: 145.

Madison, James, Alexander Hamilton, and John Jay. 1788. *The Federalist* (no. 2).

Mann, Arthur. 1979. *The One and the Many: Reflections on the American Identity*. Chicago: University of Chicago Press.

Marzolf, Marion. 1979. *The Danish Language Press in America*. New York: Arno.

May, Henry F. 1983. *Ideas, Faiths and Feelings*. New York: Oxford University Press.

Meinig, D. W. 1986. *The Shaping of America*. Vol. 1, *Atlantic America, 1492–1800*. New Haven, Conn.: Yale University Press.

Miller, Perry. 1939. *The New England Mind: The Seventeenth Century*. Cambridge: Harvard University Press.

Milner, II, Clyde A., ed. 1989. *Major Problems in the History of the American West*. Lexington, Mass.: Heath.

Montgomery, David. 1974. "The 'New Unionism' and the Transformation of Workers' Consciousness in America, 1909–1922." *Journal of Social History* 7: 509–29.

Nagel, Paul. 1982. Review of Samuel P. Huntington's *American Politics: The Promise of Disharmony*. *American Historial Review* 87: 1149.

Navarro, Armando. 1995. "The Latinorzation of Los Angeles: The Politics of Polarization." Pp. 170–82 in *Multiethnic Coalition Building in Los Angeles*, edited by Eui Young Yu and Edward T. Chang. Claremont Calif.: Regina Books.

Nelli, Humbert. 1970. *Italians in Chicago, 1880–1930: A Study in Ethnic Mobility*. New York: Oxford University Press.

O'Hare, William P. 1992. "America's Minorities—The Demographics of Diversity." *Population Bulletin*. Washington, D.C.: Population Reference Bureau 47.

Pacyga, Dominic A. 1995. "Chicago's Ethnic Neighborhoods: The Myth of Stability and the Reality of Change." Pp. 604–17 in *Ethnic Chicago: A Multicultural Portrait*, edited by Melvin G. Holli and Peter d'A. Jones. Grand Rapids, Mich.: William B. Eerdmans.

Power, Tyrone. 1836. *Impressions of America*. Philadelphia: Carey, Lea & Blanchard.

President's Research Committee on Social Trends. 1934. *American Civilization Today: Recent Social Trends in the United States*. New York: McGraw Hill.

Rumbaut, Rubén G. 1994. "Origins and Destinies: Immigration to the United States since World War II." *Sociological Forum* 9: 583–621.

Savelle, Max. 1962. "Nationalism and Other Loyalties in the American Revolution." *American Historical Review* 67: 901–23.

A Short Account of the Troubles and Dangers our Fore-fathers met with to obtain this Land: Shewing the Right Their Children have to it at this Day . . . recommended to be preserved in the House of every true Friend to the Rights and Priviledges of America. n.d. Danvers, Mass. Ann Arbor, Mich.: William L. Clements Library.

Smith, Henry Nash. 1950. *Virgin Land: The American West as Symbol and Myth*. Cambridge: Harvard University Press.

Thernstrom, Stephan, and Peter R. Knight. 1970. "Men in Motion: Some Data and Speculations about Urban Mobility in Nineteenth-Century America." *Journal of Interdisciplinary History* 1: 7–35.

Towers, Frank Harold. 1993. "Ruffians on the Urban Border: Labor, Politics, and Race in Baltimore, 1850–1861." Ph.D. diss., Department of History, University of California, Riverside.

"The Untold Story of the L.A. Riot." 1993. *U.S. News and World Report*, May 31, 46–57.

Vaughan, Alden. 1982. "From White Man to Redskin: Changing Anglo-American Perceptions of the American Indian." *American Historical Review* 87: 917–53.

Ward, Russel. 1978. *The Australian Legend*. Melbourne: Oxford University Press.

Weiss, Richard. 1979. "Ethnicity and Reform: Minorities and the Ambience of the Depression Years." *Journal of American History* 66: 566–85.

Welter, Rush. 1975. *The Mind of America, 1820–1860*. New York: Columbia University Press.

White, Walter. 1969. *Rope and Faggot.* New York: Arno.

Whitman, Walt. 1939 [1865]. *Representative Selections*, edited by Floyd Stovall. New York: American Book.

Williamson, Joel. 1984. *The Crucible of Race: Black–White Relations in the American South Since Emancipation.* New York: Oxford University Press.

Wister, Owen. 1902. *The Virginian: A Horseman of the Plains.* New York: Macmillan.

Wolman, Leo. 1924. *The Growth of American Trade Unions 1880–1923.* New York: National Bureau of Economic Research.

Zunz, Olivier. 1985. "American History and the Changing Meaning of Assimilation." *Journal of American Ethnic History* 4: 53–71, 82–84.

Preserving the Republic by Educating Republicans

DAVID TYACK

FROM THE AMERICAN REVOLUTION ONWARD, political and educational leaders have argued that the survival and stability of the republic depended on the wisdom and morality of its individual citizens. "I know of no safe depository of the ultimate powers of the society but the people themselves," Thomas Jefferson wrote in 1820, "and if we think them not enlightened enough to exercise their control with a wholesome discretion, the remedy is not to take it from them, but to inform their discretion by education" (Ford 1892–1899, 10: 161). In 1822 Governor DeWitt Clinton declared that "the first duty of a state is to render its citizens virtuous by intellectual instruction and moral discipline, by enlightening their minds, purifying their hearts, and teaching them their rights and obligations" (Lincoln 1909, 2: 1100). "It may be an easy thing to make a Republic," observed Horace Mann in 1848, "but it is a very laborious thing to make Republicans" (Cremin 1957: 14).[1]

Jefferson, Clinton, and Mann believed that public schools should inculcate common republican values, becoming, in effect, a fourth branch of government. The educated character and trained mind of the individual was the foundation of public virtue, a small *imperium* in the larger *imperio* of the state, a better guarantor of civic behavior than whole regiments of constables. An untutored person was not a trustworthy custodian of individual rights and liberties, but a properly schooled person would recognize the bonds of obligation and principle that stabilize society and preserve freedom.

The pedagogy of civic republicanism was moral as well as cognitive, religious as well as political in inspiration. Public-school leaders drew on a belief system that John Higham has called a Protestant-republican ideology, one that believed that God had selected America as a redeemer nation. The prolific Noah Webster, whose spellers had sold over 20 million copies by 1829, devised a "Federal Catechism" to teach the proper republican principles to children. He warned them of the evils of monarchy, aristocracy, and direct democracy while praising the virtues of representative republics as embedded in the constitution of the nation and those of the individual states. He also inserted a "Moral Catechism" that stressed virtues such as obedience, moderation, truthfulness, frugality, and industry. Textbook writers endlessly praised statesmen like George Washington as exemplars of republican character (Webster 1798: 154–55, 145–52; Elson 1964).

The public philosophy of republican education resonated in the speeches of politicians and school leaders, in state constitutional debates, and in the text-books children read in school. Advocates of common schools differed some-what among themselves. Some feared anarchy and worried about protecting government from the people; others, more concerned about despotism, sought to protect the people from government. But in a nation roiled by partisan politi-cal battles, raw economic competition, and furious sectarian contests for church members and souls, crusaders for the common school thought it possible, none-theless, to discover and teach a common denominator of political and moral truths and civic virtue to future citizens who would seek the common weal because they were educated to do so. Political parties and religious sects, they thought, should stop their conflicts at the schoolhouse door.

This early public philosophy of education may seem quaint and naive today, a time when critics deride "government schools" as bureaucratic and coercive, when some say that social pluralism forbids the possibility of a common civic education, when "culture wars" resonate in political conventions and the groves of academe, when critics proclaim educational decline rather than a millennial future, when economic survivalism dominates the rhetoric of educational pur-pose, and when voucher advocates claim that education is a consumer good best chosen by parents in a competitive market of schooling. Indeed, individual "choice" has become for many a way to avoid the collective determination of common goods that was the goal of the earlier public philosophy of education. As Mann declared, it is indeed "a very laborious thing to make Republicans," perhaps never more so than now.

It is easier to deconstruct the ideas of the founders and followers of the pedagogy of civic virtue than to reconstruct the world view that made it seem plausible, indeed essential, to a wide swath of citizens. Amid the cultural con-flicts of the mid-nineteenth century there were many who dissented from a consensual civic education. Mann's religious and political foes, for example, claimed that his advocacy of nonsectarian morality and nonpartisan political instruction neatly fit his own values as a Whig Unitarian; they argued that he wanted not to find and teach common values but to use the state to teach his own (Messerli 1972). People who disagreed with Jefferson's science of politics thought he was politicizing that very "science" (Tyack 1966; James 1991).

Most of the leaders of the common-school movement were white, male, pros-perous, Protestant, and native-born Anglo-Americans. They believed their ver-sion of the republican ideology of education to be a self-evident common de-nominator of civic virtue. They shared similar millennial religious hopes and political fears about the republican experiment. They wanted a religious but "nonsectarian" foundation for morality. They wanted to strengthen the individ-ual character of citizens rather than to stress the primordial claims of kinship and ethnicity. And they believed that economic opportunity was open to the virtuous and industrious (Kaestle 1983: ch. 5).

Common-school crusaders sometimes assumed that certain groups of peo-ple—native-born, rural yeomen, Protestants, nonpoor—were more likely to be exemplars of worthy citizenship than, say, the Irish, who had four strikes against them, as most of them were foreign-born, poor, urban, and Catholic. Not surprisingly, when Irish Catholic leaders faced raw ethnic and religious prejudice, they opposed the common-school crusade. And all too often, African Americans and Asians were excluded altogether from the common school or segregated from whites (Kaestle 1983: ch. 7; Katz 1968).

Even if it is easy to find ethnocentrism and self-interest in the common-school crusade, that is only part of the story. It is hard to find another reform in American history that spread as fast as the common school, had such a persuasive rationale, and aroused so little dissent nationwide. In a society that offered few other government services, Americans created the most comprehensive system of public schooling in the world (Tyack and Hansot 1982: pt. 1).

Success in translating the blueprint of republican education into a nationwide institution called the common school is all the more surprising because most Americans from the Revolution to the end of the nineteenth century distrusted strong government and hobbled the powers of states. Citizens were ambivalent about giving powers to legislators and state school officials, for example, and sometimes even abolished the office of superintendent (this happened to Barnard and almost to Mann). In the middle of the nineteenth century there was a nationwide social movement to create public education and to foster common civic virtues, but because of this distrust of powerful central governments, both national and state, the common-school crusaders had to rely far more on exhortation in local communities—by reminding citizens of their duties—than on governmental command. American public-school governance was by far the most highly decentralized in the world, and the creation of the common school was largely a grassroots phenomenon. In most communities local people *chose* to have common schools and were able to shape directly what their children learned (Tyack and Hansot 1982; Farnham 1963).

Toward the end of the nineteenth century, however, conservative reformers began to succeed in using the state to reshape education and to enforce their ideas of political and moral orthodoxy. Perhaps the biggest impetus behind the coercive use of schooling came from panic about the need to assimilate the "new" immigrants. The federal government itself began to use schooling as a follow-up to war, beginning with attempts to "civilize" defeated native peoples and then in programs to educate colonial wards of the nation. As time went by, the rationale for and means of civic education in such circumstances became more coercive, but the public philosophy that schools must produce virtuous citizens remained strong.

At certain times, Americans became self-conscious about the civic values that the schools should teach. In such periods, implicit principles came into sharper relief because they were not taken for granted. I do not argue that crises produced new values. I suggest instead that cultural notions of civic republicanism remained remarkably durable in public education. What changed was not so much the concept of a uniform civic virtue as an increasing willingness to use the state to enforce those values in times when Americans worried about political challenges or increased social diversity. My interest here is more in the cultural history of those ideas than in actual practice in the schools. In this essay I briefly analyze a few such episodes:

- The founding of the nation, when educational theorists of the Revolutionary generation laid the ideological groundwork for common political values by asking what sort of schooling would build and preserve the new republic.
- The part that public education played in the creation of new states in the nineteenth century, when Congress and the territorial governments negotiated the educational clauses of state constitutions to make sure that each state would have "a Republican form of Government."
- The puzzling spread of roughly similar common schools across the nation in the nineteenth century despite America's practice of extreme decentralization of governance. A widespread ideology of local republican trusteeship helps to explain what became "common" about public education.
- The response of conservative educators at the turn of the twentieth century to the presumed challenge that "new" immigrants seemed to pose to traditional civic education and how they expanded the role of the state to enforce a common culture.
- The use of schooling by the federal government as a follow-up to war, which became for Native Americans, Filipinos, and Japanese Americans in World War II an extreme case of national control of political and cultural socialization.

Cultural struggles over political values—between uniform citizenship and social diversity, individualism and group identity, liberty and order, freedom from the state and freedom for the state to use its powers to socialize the young—run through two centuries of deliberation about a public philosophy of education. But it would be a mistake to focus only on dissent. In the past, there has also been substantial consensus on the common political values that should be taught to the young in public schools. And even today, despite heightened awareness of social diversity and despite a cottage industry of best-sellers lamenting lost common values, there may be more agreement than meets the eye. Or so I shall suggest.

The New Nation: A Republican Charter for Education?

Anxiety and hope about the fate of the republic marked the educational thought of the revolutionary generation. In 1811 Jefferson warned that "the eyes of the virtuous all over the earth are turned with anxiety on us, as the only depositories of the sacred fire of liberty. . . . our falling into anarchy would decide forever the destinies of mankind, and seal the political heresy that man is incapable of self-government" (Lipscomb and Bergh 1903, 10: 319, 13: 58). Benjamin Rush cautioned that "we have changed our forms of government, but it remains yet to effect a revolution in our principles, opinions, and manners so as to accommodate them to the forms of government we have adopted" (Butterfield 1951, 1: 388). Noah Webster proposed an "ASSOCIATION OF AMERICAN PATRIOTS for the purpose of forming a NATIONAL CHARACTER."

"Our national character is not yet formed," he explained, and it was imperative to "implant, in the minds of American youth, the principles of virtue and of liberty; and inspire them with just and liberal ideas of government" (Webster 1798: 3, 17–21, 23, 25). As soon as a child could speak, he should learn the history of his country and "lisp the praise of liberty, and of those illustrious heroes and statesmen who have wrought a revolution in her favor" (Warfel 1936).

How, asked Rush, could Americans stabilize freedom and preserve republican principles? His answer did not strike him as paradoxical: the *free* American individual was the *uniform* citizen. "I consider it as possible," declared Rush, "to convert men into republican machines. This must be done, if we expect them to perform their parts properly, in the great machine of the government of the state." A republic is adulterated by "monarchy or aristocracy that does not revolve upon the wills of the people, and these must be fitted to each other by means of education before they can be made to produce regularity and unison in government" (Rush 1786: 20–22).

Both Jefferson and the Federalist Judge Joseph Story hoped that by teaching the principles of government to the rising generation popular rule might be made safe. Story thought that a free republic was the most complicated form of government known to humanity, but he wrote a civics textbook to demonstrate that republican principles "admit of a simple enunciation, and may be brought within the comprehension of the most common minds" (Story 1835: 260, 264–65). Jefferson also believed that there were correct doctrines of government that schools should teach, though they differed from Story's. He tried to persuade the lay board of visitors of the University of Virginia to be "rigorously attentive to . . . [the] political principles" of its law professor. "There is one branch [of knowledge] in which we are the best judges," he wrote, "in which heresies may be taught, of so interesting a character to our own State, and to the United States, as to make it a duty in us to lay down the principles which are to be taught. It is that of government" (Cabell 1856: 339).

The republican educational theorists wanted to make sure that people considered themselves part of a larger polity to which they owed a larger loyalty, rather than giving their prime allegiance to class, sect, or ethnic group. They believed that schooling could create a new kind of citizen in the process of rooting out the vestiges of a prerepublican political order. They knew that everyday politics was an arena of contending interest groups and often bitter conflict, but they persisted in the dream that young Americans could be trained to seek the common weal and to detect demagoguery because they had absorbed republican principles.

Although revolutionary political theorists of education like Rush and Jefferson did not succeed in creating uniform public systems of education during their lifetimes, they did help establish the principle that in the new republic a vital purpose of schooling was to produce virtuous citizens. This notion became embedded in the constitutions of some of the original states and increasingly in the new states created out of the public domain. One of the most copied of the constitutional provisions on education was the clause in the Massachusetts Constitution of 1780, which held that virtue as well as knowledge was necessary "for the preservation of [the people's] rights and liberties." For that reason, the Commonwealth should "cherish the interests of literature and the sciences, and all the seminaries of them" and inculcate the civic republican virtues of honesty, industry, frugality, sincerity, and benevolence (Hough 1875: 49–51).

FORMING NEW STATES: THE ROLE OF PUBLIC SCHOOLING

The process of admitting new states to the Union offers insight into the relation of schooling to republican values. From the start, Congress used the national domain to support common schools. The Ordinance of 1785 declared that "There shall be reserved the lot No. 16, of every township, for the maintenance of public schools, within the said township" (*Journals of the American Congress* 1823: 520). Thus began a land-grant common-school system; over the next century Congress allotted three times more acreage to common schools than it did to the better-known land-grant colleges. In the Northwest Ordinance of 1787, which laid down the terms for creating new territories and states, the Congress included this clause: "Religion, morality, and knowledge, being necessary to good government and the happiness of mankind, schools and the means of education shall forever be encouraged" (U.S. Statutes 1845, 1: 52).

In Article 4, Section 4, the U.S. Constitution required Congress to guarantee that new states had "a Republican form of Government." The founding fathers worried about the coherence and stability of a continental nation composed of different states carved from the vast public domain (Wiebe 1984: 7–20). What assurance could there be that the citizens of those states would share not only a commitment to republican liberties and duties but also an allegiance to the nation based on those principles?

As time went by, both the Congress and territorial leaders who wrote constitutions for new states came to agree that public education was an essential feature of a republican government based on the will of the people. In 1826, for example, the U.S. House Committee on Public Lands declared that education "has directly in view the improvement of the minds and morals of the present generation, and of generations to come. It contemplates giving additional stability to the government, and drawing round the republic new and stronger bonds of union. We are indeed a peculiar people" (U.S. House of Representatives 1878: 939, 942, 944). Similar sentiments punctuated discussions in the constitutional conventions in the territories. Public education, said the president of the California convention in 1848, "is the foundation of our republican institutions; the school system suits the genius and spirit of our form of government." Most new states included preambles in their constitutions asserting the civic and moral purposes of schooling (Browne 1850: 18, 210).

After the Civil War, Congress demanded that the former Confederate states create systems of public education before they could be readmitted to the

Union. In 1867 the Radical Republican Charles Sumner explained why. He told his fellow Senators that they must prescribe universal education if they were to demand universal suffrage in the reconstructed Southern states. "In a republic," he said, "education is indispensable. A republic without education is like . . . a human being without a soul, living and moving blindly, with no sense of the present or the future. It is a monster. Such have been the rebel States. . . . But such they must be no longer" (*Congressional Globe* 1867: 166–67).

In 1889 Congress admitted six western states to the Union. In its enabling acts Congress became prescriptive, requiring the new states to have free, non-sectarian public schools open to all as a prerequisite for admission. "A high degree of intelligence, patriotism, integrity and morality on the part of every voter in a government by the people being necessary," said North Dakota's constitution, the state "shall make provision for the establishment and mainte-nance of a system of public schools which shall be open to all children . . . and free from sectarian control" (North Dakota 1889). By asserting that this require-ment was "irrevocable without the consent of the United States and the people of North Dakota," the delegates indicated not only a state commitment to edu-cation but a national one as well. Two state constitutions said that educating all children was "the paramount duty of the state" (Thorpe 1909).

As time passed, the constitutions of new states came to include more and more details of governance and finance, specifying how to select officials like state superintendents and boards and how to administer land grants and school funds. One should not assume, however, that Americans abandoned the tradi-tion of local control in favor of more central control. Distrust of distant state government persisted. As late as 1890, the average size of state departments of education was still only two persons, including the state superintendent, amounting to one state official for every 100,000 pupils (Blodgett 1893: 20).

Leaders at the state level complained throughout the nineteenth century about their inability to enforce legislation and even to gather accurate statistics. The federal government helped finance schools through land grants, but the Office of Education was tiny and had almost no direct influence. State constitutions helped establish the ideological case for public schools. They also created a legal structure and partial funding of schools. But the real action in educational finance and governance remained at the local level. There were more school trustees than teachers, and in 1890 American school committeemen were the most numerous class of public officials in the world (Tyack and Hansot 1982: pt. 1).

LOCAL TRUSTEES: THE AGENTS OF REPUBLICAN IDEOLOGY

In the nineteenth century, public schools were largely grassroots affairs, espe-cially in rural districts where a majority of citizens lived. Because control and finance was decentralized in locally elected school trustees, communities re-tained collective choices over schooling—who would teach, how much schools would cost, and what kind of instruction would be offered. This form of grass-roots democracy meant that most decisions about schooling were not decreed by a distant government but were made by local, elected representatives expected to be responsive to community opinions. If people disagreed with school trustees, they might be able to elect others (Fuller 1982; Gulliford 1984).

Under such radical decentralization one might expect great variety in schooling. Schools did differ according to community wealth and ethnic composition and region (the South was late in developing public education, for example). But as settlers moved across the continent, their schools were remarkably similar in institutional character and in the lessons they taught. This is a puzzle— why should this have been so?

One obvious answer is that families moving West wanted to reproduce what they had known in their old homes. School buildings in Oregon looked much like those in Maine or Indiana. But there was a deeper source of standardization: a powerful public philosophy of republican education articulated by national and state leaders and carried out by local notables—ministers, farmers, lawyers, teachers, and other citizens who served as trustees of the schools and guardians of its civic mission. They knew the script that national or state advocates like Horace Mann or John Pierce of Michigan had developed for public education: the chief purpose of public schooling was to train upright, self-sufficient citizens. A common ideology, more than governmental command or professional decree, was responsible for the croppinng up of similar schools at the grass roots. Crusaders like Mann and Pierce were not career state bureaucrats or professional educators. They were career reformers whose task was to remind local leaders to do their duty (Tyack and Hansot 1982).

Today, the creation of Christian day schools illustrates a comparable connection between a strong ideology and local institution-building. Christian day schools appear to be a paradigm of grassroots institutions, for local churches usually build them. But Christian fundamentalists are also inspired to create such schools by nationally televised evangelists. An ideology expressed by national leaders and coordinated by centralized agencies like the Association of Christian Schools International guides and reinforces local conformity of ideals and practices today (Kienel 1985).

The nineteenth-century common school, like the church, was expected to be (in Willard Waller's phrase) a "museum of virtue." When John Swett, the chief common-school crusader in California, advised teachers to give "Practical Lessons in School Ethics," he assumed that all citizens would agree with his list of virtues: self-knowledge, self-restraint, temperance, honesty, obedience, punctuality, conscientiousness, impartiality, gratitude, friendliness, kindness, patience, frankness, seriousness, firmness, cleanliness, and courtesy (Swett 1885, ch. 10). No one captured the common denominator of civic virtue better than the Reverend William Holmes McGuffey, whose school readers sold 122 million copies. The advertising blurb printed with his fourth reader in 1844 assured the public that "NO SECTARIAN matter has been admitted into this work" and

"NO SECTIONAL matter" (reflecting on slavery, for example) appeared (Tyack 1967: 178).

Underlying the political culture of the decentralized common school was a notion of trusteeship. The term school *trustee* is revealing: reformers argued that these elected representatives, heirs of the past, held in trust not only the education of all the children in the present but also the future of the society. School trustees, wrote Horace Mann (1891: 245–46), were responsible for the duties "of improving the young, of advancing the welfare of the state and of the [human] race." Mann argued that school committeemen should be aristocrats of character, exemplars of the values they sought to inculcate in the children. They "are more worthy than any other class of men, to be considered as the pilots, who are directing the course of the bark that contains all the precious interests of mankind, and steering it either for its rescue or its ruin."

Darwin Atwater was a school trustee and clerk of the common school in Mantua Village, Ohio, in 1841. He waxed philosophical as he pondered the meaning of the new school term. "The earth in its annual revolution," he wrote, prompts us to consider again "what has been done during the year that has past [*sic*] and what can be done during the year to come in the school in our neighborhood to forward the great enterprise of educating the human race." No task was more important than "to devise means to forward the education of our children who are soon to succeed us in active life and be our representatives for ages to come." To carry out that mission, however, required more than rhetoric. The school board also needed to levy local school taxes, to fix a leaky roof, to hire a teacher each term, and to make sure that the citizens cut firewood small enough to fit into the school's stove. Two years later Atwater himself taught the school for forty-three days at a salary of $14 per month (Turner 1940: 18, 91).

This mixture in Mantua Village of the mundane and the eternal, the local and the cosmopolitan, reflected the work of school trustees as the common-school movement spread across the nation. They were expected not only to see to the everyday details of running the school but also to mobilize collective choices and to negotiate a sense of the common good. Consensus on education was often tenuous and temporary, however, for every community had its factions.

In the nineteenth century, majority rule typically settled cultural conflicts in school districts. For the most part, local school boards rather than courts or legislatures adjudicated disputes over questions like Bible reading and instruction in languages other than English. When the common school was still an uncertain innovation dependent on the good will of citizens in local communities, state leaders were generally reluctant to legislate about value issues. The bitterest conflicts typically involved religious practices in the supposedly nonsectarian public schools. Some groups—Catholics were the largest—decided that the public-school system was so religiously biased and unresponsive that they must create their own alternative school system. But local trustees, operating under the influence of a common ideology of republican schooling, generally provided some scope for local accommodations to cultural groups. In ho-

mogeneous rural communities and in a number of cities, for example, powerful
ethnic groups like the Germans persuaded school boards to permit instruction in
their native tongues (James 1991; Tyack and Hansot 1982).

As the century drew to a close and the nation became more urban, industrialized, and ethnically diverse, however, more and more educational leaders
came to believe that a common ideology of republican education and local
control of schools by a multitude of school committees was not powerful
enough to meet the challenge of educating newcomers to be virtuous citizens of
one nation, speaking one language, and saluting the same flag. By the Progressive Era, many reformers agreed that it was time to employ an activist state and
schools of expanded functions to aid and assimilate the strangers, to "natural-
ize" the "aliens" through a new kind of civic education. Politically powerful
WASP groups organized to give their convictions the force of law and to enforce what the American Legion would later call "the Americanization of
America" (Pierce 1933: 35).

"NEW" AMERICANS AND CIVIC EDUCATION

In 1891 leaders in the National Education Association (NEA) declared that all
children should be compelled to attend schools taught in English. They feared
that "foreign influence has begun a system of colonization with a purpose of
preserving foreign languages and traditions and proportionately of destroying
distinctive Americanism." Demanding compulsory Americanization, one educator asserted that "when the people established this government they had a certain standard of intelligence and morality"; once Americans could assume "that
an intelligent and moral people will conform to the requirements of good citizenship." By the 1890s, he warned, this outlook could no longer be taken for
granted: "People have come here who are not entitled to freedom in the same
sense as those who established this government." It was unthinkable "to lower
this idea of intelligence and morality to the standard" of the newcomers. Such
people could not be trusted to come to a voluntary consensus on republican
values. Instead, republican orthodoxy should be inculcated by means such as
the Pledge of Allegiance, first employed in the New York City schools in the
1890s (National Education Association 1891: 393–403).

Already apparent in the NEA discussion were some central themes in the
nativist construction of ethnic difference that would dominate much discussion
about immigrant education for the next thirty years: that "foreign colonies"
were forming; that the newcomers were inferior in intelligence and morality to
those who preceded them; and that their children must be compelled to attend
school, learn English, and be deliberately inculcated with American political
and cultural values. To accomplish such purposes in cities dominated politically
by immigrant machines, reformers argued, school governance must be transformed so that small boards of elite citizens would control urban systems. The
older notions of representative local school governance gave way to new con-

ceptions of decision making based on scientific expertise and business efficiency (Tyack 1974: pt. 2).

By 1909, 58% of students in the thirty-seven largest American cities had foreign-born parents. No longer, thought reformers, could schools go about business as usual. It was necessary to pass effective compulsory attendance laws and to catch all the newcomer children in the net. The child was coming to belong more to the state and less to the parents, leading educator Ellwood P. Cubberley (1909: 63–64) believed, and the state's interest and duty was to educate the child to be an American. Although there was at least in theory a separation of church and state, there was to be no separation of ethnicity and state, no bill of rights for social diversity. Underlying most attempts at "Americanization," as Michael R. Olneck (1989) has pointed out, was a "symbolic delegitimation of collective ethnic identity," and this became deliberate state policy. A powerful ideology of individualism undergirded reformers' efforts. The true American had no competing group loyalties, no hyphens in his or her identity.

Reformers disagreed not so much about the goal of assimilation as about the best means of accomplishing it. Some urged a sharp-edged intervention: in order to assimilate such a motley collection of humanity, schools should drive a wedge between students and the parental culture and language, thereby assimilating the second generation. Humanitarian reformers who knew immigrant families firsthand—for example, settlement house workers and child labor inspectors—recognized the pain this confrontational strategy could bring. They wanted to give children health care, free lunches, and counseling, and they sought to match schools better to the cultural backgrounds of immigrants so that assimilation could be transitional rather than abrupt (Covello 1936; Roberts 1920).

The outbreak of World War I brought to a boil nativist anxiety about "foreign colonies" and a potential fifth column of unassimilated aliens within the nation. "By 1916," writes John F. McClymer (1982: 96–116), "cultural diversity had come to be defined as a national crisis." The Red Scare and nativist organizations kept paranoia alive well into the 1920s. Employers, churches, federal and state bureaus, patriotic associations, and many other organizations joined forces with public schools to ensure that children were superpatriots (for an attack on hyperventilating nationalism, see Dewey 1916: 183–89).

Groups like the American Legion, the American Bar Association, and the Daughters of the American Revolution pressed dozens of states to pass laws prescribing the teaching of American history and the Constitution and sometimes dictating the content of such courses. Whereas in 1903 only one state required the teaching of "citizenship," by 1923 thirty-nine did so. The National Security League lobbied to ban the teaching of German and to prescribe superpatriotic instruction. Thanks in part to its efforts, thirty-three states mandated that all teachers pass a test on the Constitution in order to be certified. By 1923 thirty-five states had enacted legislation that made English the only language of instruction in public schools. In Oregon in 1922 the Ku Klux Klan, which had made the little red schoolhouse a symbol of Americanism, lobbied successfully for a law mandating that all children attend public schools (Flanders 1925).

Anything foreign was suspect. In New York City, schoolchildren who went into the tenements to sell war bonds were instructed to report adults whose loyalty was dubious. The campaign to define "American" in a narrow conservative mold and to enforce conformity of thought and deed among immigrants outraged many ethnic leaders, much of the ethnic press, and a number of native-born liberals (Brumberg 1990; McClymer 1982).

In reaction to these hard-edged Americanizers, a few writers called for ethnic self-preservation. In 1924, for example, Horace M. Kallen (1924: 139, 121–24) proposed "a democracy of nationalities" in which all groups would enhance "the selfhood which is inalienable in them, and for the realization of which they require 'inalienable' liberty." Kallen thought that culture was "ancestrally determined" rather than an interactive and constantly changing set of practices. But the policies of total ethnic preservation or total assimilation bore little relation to the everyday lives of immigrant families, whose cultural practices blended the old and the new in kaleidoscopic ways (for a critique of Kallen's proposals, including his racist attitudes, see Sollors 1986).

The frenzy of nativism during World War I and its aftermath turned Americanization into yet another pedagogical specialty, especially for writers of civics texts and for adult educators. Public schools became accountable by law for producing patriots. A good proportion of the experts in Americanization, however, deplored paranoid ideology and harsh methods. After laws in 1921 and 1924 restricted immigration, educators could go about assimilating the second generation at a less frenetic pace. Social scientists began to portray assimilation as a long-term and complex intergenerational process. "In the eyes of many liberals," Nicholas V. Montalto (1982) writes, "the Americanization movement epitomized all that was wrong in the American attitude and policy toward the immigrant: the bankruptcy of racism and chauvinism, the tendency to blame the immigrant for domestic social problems, and the failure of coercion."

These liberal professionals, many of whom were second-generation immigrants, believed that attacks solidified ethnic groups rather than dissolved them. Denigrating the language and cultures of students' parents, they argued, split families and created an alienated second generation that was neither foreign nor American. Increasingly these liberal educators argued that a more tolerant, slow-paced approach would produce better results than high-pressure assimilation. They still thought that the public schools should Americanize pupils, but they wanted transitional programs that taught tolerance for diversity and preached the doctrine that the United States was a composite of the contributions of many nations (Smith 1939).

Michael Olneck (1989: 147–74) has observed that most educators—the hardline Americanizers and the interculturalists alike—distrusted collective ethnic identities. In civics texts and the writings of the interculturalists, he has identified an underlying ideology of individualism and an ideal of including all people, as individuals, in a greater unity called American society. The cure for group conflict was understanding and appreciation; over time this would result in the inclusion of members of all groups in the mainstream of society as autonomous individuals. Separate ethnic identity was to be dissolved, but as painlessly as possible.

Hannah Arendt (1958) has argued that in the United States "education plays a different and, politically, incomparably more important role than in other countries." One reason is simply the diversity of its population, the fact that it has been a land of immigrants in process of becoming citizens. But American citizenship has had a special, even universal, resonance apart from this fact, she has claimed, as revealed in "the motto printed on every dollar bill: *Novus Ordo Seclorum*, The New Order of the World." There were those who believed that American doctrines of civic virtue could redeem even enemies, the classical "other." The activists who sought under the aegis of the federal government to remake the vanquished in their own image by turning them into republicans echoed themes that stretched back to Benjamin Rush's "republican machines."

PACIFICATION BY PEDAGOGY: SCHOOLING AS A FOLLOW-UP TO WAR

To pessimists about the future of the republic the migrants from strange shores have been a threat to the American "New Order." But the depth of the optimistic, if sometimes draconian, American faith in the power of civic education becomes apparent when one looks at the repeated attempts to Americanize former enemies and colonial wards. A cartoon of 1900 in *Judge* magazine captured this belief in coercive transformation by education. Truant officer Uncle Sam is rounding up an American Indian, a Puerto Rican, a Filipino, a Cuban, and a Hawaiian while the teacher, Miss Columbia, stands outside her little red schoolhouse ringing her bell (*Judge* 1901).

When schooling became a follow-up to war, its political functions were not merely taken for granted or superficially celebrated; instead they stood out in bold relief. At such times, the federal government used schooling to Americanize former enemies and colonized wards of the state. It defined and enacted policy relatively free from the constraints of local control and from the habitual American distrust of centralized authority in education. Unlike local operations of a democratic politics of education, in which action typically required persuasion, the federal government was able to translate American beliefs in the power of education more or less directly into policy.

Three examples illustrate this point: (1) the attempt to solve the "Indian problem" by developing the Bureau of Indian Affairs (BIA) schools in the half century after the Civil War (Szasz 1974: ch. 1), (2) the campaign to transform Filipino children into citizens in the years following the Spanish-American War (Suzuki 1990), (3) the move to "democratize" Japanese Americans incarcerated in camps during World War II and to impose what Toshio Nishi calls "unconditional democracy" on Japan after the war (James 1987; Nishi 1982).

The three episodes of pacification by pedagogy were by no means unconnected. Soldiers who began their careers fighting and teaching Indians on the Great Plains ended up battling and instructing Filipino insurgents in the jungles of Luzon. Policy makers concluded that it was cheaper and more humane to educate Indians and Filipinos than to kill them. Many of the administrators of the U.S. detention centers for Japanese Americans had been educators in the BIA. A former teacher in the Philippines became head of education in the BIA during the Eisenhower years. Sometimes the role of soldier-teacher ran in families: Douglas MacArthur grew up on the Indian frontier, where his father, Arthur, was an Army officer. Arthur went from fighting Filipino guerillas to setting up schools for them, and Douglas dictated the terms of democratic education in postwar Japan. The similarities of policies and personnel in the three cases are not coincidental. In each case the federal government applied lessons learned in dealing with one former foe to assimilate the next (though it often did not learn from defects in earlier policies) (James 1987).

The federal government had little control over mainstream public schools within the United States, but when it came to former foes, colonial subjects, or wards of the national state, military and federal officials had authority to define and enforce Americanization. They did not conceive of this as inventing new goals or institutions; rather, they believed that they were expressing an American consensus. But in seeking to transform "the other," the former enemy or colonial ward, into an acceptable citizen, they became self-conscious about education's role in political and social formation.

People outside the federal government also did much to shape this common formula of Americanization. A yearly conference of "Friends of the Indian" at Lake Mohonk near New Paltz, New York, for example, brought together white reformers with an interest in Indian affairs: members of associations devoted to Indian rights, soldiers, editors, educational leaders (largely from universities), members of the unpaid Federal Board of Indian Commissioners, and officials in the Indian Bureau. Through formulating and publicizing proposals and lobbying Congress and federal officials, this group had a large impact on Indian policy and helped shape educational programs for Filipinos as well. Likewise, in the Philippines and in Japan commissions of nongovernmental lay experts and reformers—many of them academics—gained considerable influence over the policies adopted by the federal government (Prucha 1973; Adams 1988).

Sometimes the policy statements of the federal officials and lay advisers betrayed doubt about the assimilability of the conquered. For the most part, however, they revealed faith in the power of education to transform the "savage" into a "civilized" citizen, the "little brown brother" into a modern man, and a once-hated Japanese foe into a good democrat. The participants at Mohonk, the members of the commissions, the army officers—these were typically Anglo-American native-born men, prosperous, well-educated, Protestant, and with the self-confidence that comes from having one's opinion count.

In the early stages of education of Native Americans the leaders were optimistic about how rapidly they could accomplish the aim stated by the founder of the Carlisle School, Richard Henry Pratt (1973: 260–61): "Kill the Indian in him and save the man." Native Americans need not vanish, said the Commissioner of Indian Affairs in 1890 (Adams 1979: 341), for they could be educated "to become absorbed into the national life, not as Indians, but as Americans." If enough "schools were established to give each youth the advantages of three to five years of schooling, said the Secretary of the Interior in 1883 (Eastman 1935: 95), "the next generation will hear nothing of [the Indian problem] and we may leave the Indian to care for himself." No need for troops or welfare doles. Armies might subdue Indians, but only educators can eradicate Indianness.

Common themes emerged when these policy makers spoke about the relation of education to citizenship. They agreed about the importance of individualization, of divorcing the Indian from the tribe, the Filipino from the "feudal" system of the Spaniard, or the Japanese from the tyranny of emperor worship. Before wards could become "free" they first had to become individuals taught to exercise their rights and liberties responsibly. Schooling was designed to break the hold of the group over the person, to create a new-modeled "community," and to link individuals to an idealized version of an open society and republican political system.

These "individuals," however, had to become culturally alike in certain respects. The education of Native Americans illustrated this concept. Reformers spared no details in their campaign to transform outsiders into citizens. They attended to dress, athletics, vocational training, learning English, and traits like punctuality, industry, and discipline. Typically they saw such customs and values not as culturally specific but as universals held by "civilized" people. Pratt (1964) regarded his students as blank slates easily inscribed. They would soon forgo their past and embrace the latest stage of Euro-American civilization. A missionary to the Sioux described in 1901 the cavalier faith that schooling by itself would create uniform republican persons from many native peoples: "Uncle Sam is like a man setting a charge of powder. The school is the slow match. He lights it and goes off whistling, sure that in time it will blow up the old life, and of its shattered pieces he will make good citizens" (Adams 1988: 3).

In his instructions to BIA educators on "inculcation of patriotism in Indian schools," Commissioner Thomas Jefferson Morgan (1890: clxvii) insisted that Indian students should acquire a new past on the way to a new future: "special attention should be paid . . . to the instruction of Indian youth in the . . . lives of the most notable and worthy historical characters. While in such study the wrongs of their ancestors cannot be ignored, the injustice which their race has suffered can be contrasted with the larger future open to them, and their duties and opportunities rather than their wrongs will most profitably engage their attention." In the process of "exciting . . . ambition after excellence in character," the teachers, he said, "should carefully avoid any unnecessary reference to the fact that they are Indians." He apparently forgot his own advice when he spoke to Indian students in a chorus at Hampton Institute: "As I sat here and listened with closed eyes to your singing, you were not Indians to me. You sing our songs, you speak our language. In the days that are coming there will be nothing save his color to distinguish the Indian from the white man" (Adams 1979: 350).

Although the eventual goal was to integrate the former foe or ward into the larger society, well socialized, the federal government often segregated them: Indians in boarding schools or in day schools on the reservation, Japanese Americans in detention camps, and Filipinos in garrison towns protected by the military from rebels who did not want their children to become Americanized. It is not coincidental that the most famous of the boarding schools for Indians, the Carlisle School, originated as an educational program for a group of intractable Indian warriors. Pacification by pedagogy sought to destroy one identity and impose another, a campaign notable for its illusory optimism and draconian arrogance and yet similar in its assumptions to the campaign to Americanize the new immigrants from the Old World.

COMMON VALUES AND SOCIAL DIVERSITY IN SCHOOLS TODAY

Whether relying on exhortation or coercion, reformers have turned repeatedly in times of political and social stress to the schools to preserve the Republic. Once again this is happening, though policies are now perhaps more sharply contested than ever before in our history. Groups previously excluded from the debate over the teaching of values have sought to align instruction in public schools with the pluralistic character of the American people, to redefine the meaning of "American" in both the past and the present. Ronald Takaki (1995: 31) describes this aspiration: "In the sharing of our varied stories, as Americans of diverse groups, we create a community of a larger memory." But veneration of earlier, more monocultural, versions of patriotism and virtue is hardly dead. Not long ago ninety-nine U.S. Senators voted not to accept a new set of national standards in American history because, some said, they were not suitably deferential to the founders.

Historian Michael Frisch (1989) of the University of New York at Buffalo has found that the traditional American heroes are alive and well in the memories of his students. In eight different years from 1975 to 1988 he asked them to "write down the first ten names that you think of in reponse to the prompt, 'American History from its beginning through the end of the Civil War.'" And what were the names most frequently mentioned? In order, Washington, Lincoln, Jefferson, Franklin, and a list of other political and military figures. The only woman to appear in the top twenty-four was Betsy Ross, who weighed in as number 15. When students were asked to make a second list—excluding presidents, generals, and statesmen—Betsy Ross came in first by a large margin, ahead of Paul Revere, Harriet Tubman, and Lewis & Clark (elided as one historical figure). In the free associations of these students the myths of the founders were vivid, as Frisch observes: "If George is the Father of the Country—of the nation, of all the American sons and daughters—then surely Betsy Ross exists symbolically as the Mother, who gives birth to our collective symbol."

Another revealing study of the persistence of traditional values in the schools is a survey of public school teachers reported by Public Agenda (Farkas and Johnson 1996). A majority of both teachers and the general public believed that teaching common-core moral values was more important than teaching academics. Noah Webster and John Swett would not have been surprised that 95% of teachers thought honesty an essential lesson to teach; 90%, punctuality and responsibility; and 83%, industriousness. About three-quarters of teachers thought that studying American history and learning "habits of good citizenship such as voting and caring about the nation" were "absolutely essential." Seventy-two percent believed that schools should stress "that democracy is the best form of government" (27–31, 42–43).

Teachers strongly supported toleration of social differences but thought at the same time that the duty of the school was to acculturate children to a common pattern. Ninety-six percent said they believed in "Teaching respect for others regardless of their racial and ethnic background." Eighty-five percent said that if students teased a child about race, they would not only stop the teasing but teach students that it was wrong. Nine out of ten teachers wanted "kids from all backgrounds taught in the same public schools [rather than in separate schools] so that they learn to get along with one another." Three-quarters thought that the public schools should "help new immigrants absorb language and culture as quickly as possible, even if their native language and culture are neglected." Relatively few teachers (6 to 13%) wanted to introduce divisive issues into their classrooms, such as "arguing that racism is the main cause of the economic and social problems blacks face today," "bringing in a speaker who advocates black separatism," or "bringing in a guest speaker who argues that the Holocaust never happened." Mann and McGuffey would have understood their aversion to controversy.

If what Frisch and the Public Agenda survey found can be generalized, it may be that there is a considerable gap between the hyperventilated debate between what Takaki calls "ardent assimilationists and shrill separatists" and what is taught in schools. My hunch is that elements of multiculturalism have been gradually layered onto the previous and durable teaching of traditional political and moral values. Civic instruction in 1996 has changed from that of 1950, but slowly and in ways that seem more evolutionary than abrupt. The politics of pluralism in education has expanded the canon of public culture, and this is long overdue, but the national iconography has been enlarged rather than abandoned.

The culture wars may make good copy for media and politicians, and academics may write improbable best-sellers on the subject, but the extreme positions of the assimilationists and the separatists are neither accurate as descriptions nor trustworthy as normative guides. It is true that some leaders have tried to use the state to create a monocultural society. It didn't work. Ethnic pride did not destroy patriotism, either. The Italian-American Legion post in Beverly, Massachusetts, may make no sense to the total assimilationist who wants to abolish hyphenated citizenship or to the separatist scornful of nationalism, but it makes good sense to the legionnaires. Total assimilation (as some English-*only* folk would have it) and total preservation of ethnic differences (as if cultures were heirloom tables to polish) are neither possible nor desirable. Governments should tread lightly in such terrain. We never have been and never can be monocultural. Ethnic identities can be good social nuclei, but it is not the business of government to police ethnic boundaries. Today, as in the past, cultural interactions have altered both the newcomers and the native-born, for in social groups with permeable boundaries, cultural influences have moved in every direction (on the distinction between ethnic nuclei and boundaries see Higham 1974).

Much policy talk about assimilation or separatism polarizes discussion today in fruitless and divisive ways. Relishing the extreme example and absolute principle, this exaggerated discourse has not been serious. As the memories of Frisch's students and the beliefs of the teachers in the Public Agenda poll suggest, there has probably been more continuity in teaching traditional values than one might suspect. Some pluralism has entered the cultural canon, but it has often been celebratory and superficial. Some talk about multiculturalism has verged on a cultural relativism that denies the value, even the possibility, of finding a common ground of civic values.

If public schools today strive to promote a sense of common civic purpose and engagement, it will not happen if we simply attend to traditional icons. If they seek to foster cultural democracy, the task involves far more than an eclectic celebration of social diversity. I believe Americans can negotiate a public philosophy of education that is more generous, tough-minded, and pluralistic than in the past, one less averse to controversy, but one that still builds on a long tradition that inextricably linked the welfare of the Republic to the education of each successive generation. At its best, debate about educating the next generation has always been, and still is, deliberation about the kind of common future citizens wish to create.

NOTE

1. Two central works on the political philosophy of American education are Welter 1962 and Curti 1935.

REFERENCES

Adams, David Wallace. 1979. "Schooling the Hopi: Federal Indian Policy Writ Small, 1887–1917." *Pacific Historical Review* 48 (August): 335–52.

———. 1988. "Fundamental Considerations: The Deep Meaning of Native American Schooling, 1880–1900." *Harvard Educational Review* 58: 1–22.

Arendt, Hannah. 1958. "The Crisis in Education." *Partisan Review* 25: 493–513.

Blodgett, James H. 1893. *Report on Education in the United States at the Eleventh Census: 1890.* Washington, D.C.: GPO.

Browne, Ross J. 1850. *Report of the Debates in the Convention on the Formation of the State Constitution in September and October, 1848.* Washington, D.C.: GPO.

Brumberg, Stephan F. 1990. "New York City Schools March Off to War: The Nature and Extent of Participation of the City Schools in the Great War, April 1917–June 1918." *Urban Education* 24: 440–75.

Butterfield, Lyman, ed. 1951. *Letters of Benjamin Rush.* Princeton, N.J.: Princeton University Press.

Cabell, Nathaniel F., ed. 1856. *Early History of the University of Virginia as Contained in the Letters of Thomas Jefferson and Joseph C. Cabell.* Richmond: J. W. Randolph.

Congressional Globe. 1867. 40th Congress, 1st Session, March 16.

Covello, Leonard. 1936. "A High School and Its Immigrant Community—A Challenge and an Opportunity." *Journal of Educational Sociology* 9: 331–46.

Cremin, Lawrence A., ed. 1957. *The Republic and the School: Horace Mann on the Education of Free Men.* New York: Teachers College Press.

Cubberley, Ellwood P. 1909. *Changing Conceptions of Education.* Boston: Houghton Mifflin.

Curti, Merle. 1935. *The Social Ideas of American Educators.* New York: C. Scribner's Sons.

Dewey, John. 1916. "Nationalizing Education." *NEA Addresses and Proceedings, 1916.*

Eastman, Goodman. 1935. *Pratt: The Red Man's Moses.* Norman: University of Oklahoma Press.

Elson, Ruth Miller. 1964. *Guardians of Tradition: American Schoolbooks of the Nineteenth Century.* Lincoln: University of Nebraska Press.

Farkas, Steve, and Jean Johnson. 1996. *Given the Circumstances: Teachers Talk About Public Education Today.* New York: Public Agenda.

Farnham, Wallace D. 1963. "The Weakened Spring of Government: A Study in Nineteenth-Century American History." *American Historical Review* 68: 662–80.

Flanders, Jesse K. 1925. *Legislative Control of the Elementary Curriculum.* New York: Teachers College Press.

Ford, Paul L., ed. 1892–1899. *The Writings of Thomas Jefferson.* New York: G. P. Putnam's Sons.

Frisch, Michael. 1989. "American History and the Structures of Collective Memory: A Modest Exercise in Empirical Iconography." *Journal of American History* 75: 1130–55.

Fuller, Wayne. 1982. *The Old Country School: The Story of Rural Education in the Middle West.* Chicago: University of Chicago Press.

Gulliford, Andrew. 1984. *America's Country Schools.* Washington, D.C.: Preservation Press.

Higham, John. 1974. "Integration v. Pluralism: Another American Dilemma." *Center Magazine* 7: 67–73.

Hough, Franklin B. 1875. "Constitutional Provisions in Regard to Education in the Several States of the American Union." *Curricular of Information No. 7.* Washington, D.C.: Bureau of Education.

James, Thomas. 1987. *Exile Within: The Schooling of Japanese Americans, 1942–1945.* Cambridge: Harvard University Press.

———. 1991. "Rights of Conscience and State School Systems in Nineteenth-Century America." Pp. 117–53 in *Toward a Usable Past: Liberty Under State Constitutions,* edited by Paul Finkelman and Stephen E. Gotlieb. Athens: University of Georgia Press.

Journals of the American Congress, 1785. 1823. "An Ordinance for Ascertaining the Mode of Disposing of Lands in the Western Territory," May 20, 1785. Washington, D.C.: GPO.

Judge. 1901. "The American Policy." April 20.

Kaestle, Carl F. 1983. *Pillars of the Republic: Common Schools and American Society, 1780–1860.* New York: Hill and Wang.

Kallon, Horace M. 1924. *Culture and Democracy in the United States: Studies in the Group Psychology of the American Peoples.* New York: Boni and Liveright.

Katz, Michael. 1968. *The Irony of Early School Reform: Educational Innovation in Mid-Nineteenth-Century Massachusetts.* Cambridge: Harvard University Press.

Kienel, P. A. 1985. *Why Christian Schools Are Good for America.* Whittier, Calif.: Association of Christian Schools International.

Lincoln, Charles Z., ed. 1909. *State of New York: Messages from the Governors.* Albany: J. B. Lyon.

Lipscomb, Andrew, and Albert E. Bergh, eds. 1903. *The Writings of Thomas Jefferson.* Washington, D.C.: GPO.

Mann, Horace. 1891. "Duties of School Committees." In *Educational Writings of Horace Mann.* Boston: Lee, and Shepard.

McClymer, John F. 1982. "The Americanization Movement and the Education of the Foreign-Born Adult, 1914–1925." Pp. 96–116 in *American Education and the European Immigrant: 1840–1940,* edited by Bernard J. Weiss. Urbana: University of Illinois Press.

Messerli, Jonathan. 1972. *Horace Mann: A Biography.* New York: Knopf.

Montalto, Nicholas V. 1982. "The Intercultural Education Movement, 1924–41: The Growth of Tolerance as a Form of Intolerance." Pp. 142–160 in *American Education and the European Immigrant: 1840–1940,* edited by Bernard J. Weiss. Urbana: University of Illinois Press.

Morgan, T. J. 1890. "Instructions to Indian Agents in Regard to Inculcation of Patriotism in Indian Schools." *Fifty-Ninth Annual Report of the Commissioner of Indian Affairs to the Secretary of the Interior.* Washington, D.C.: GPO.

National Education Association. 1891. *Addresses and Proceedings of the NEA.*

Nishi, Toshio. 1982. *Unconditional Democracy.* Stanford, Calif.: Hoover Institution Press.

North Dakota. 1889. Constitution of 1889, Article 8.

Olneck, Michael R. 1989. "Americanization and the Education of Immigrants, 1900–1925: An Analysis of Symbolic Action." *American Journal of Education* 98: 398–423.

Pierce, Bessie L. 1933. *Citizens Organizations and the Civic Training of Youth.* New York: C. Scribner's Sons.

Pratt, Richard Henry. 1964. *Battlefield and Classroom: Four Decades with the American Indian, 1867–1904,* edited by Robert M. Utley. New Haven, Conn.: Yale University Press.

————. 1973. "The Advantages of Mingling Indians with Whites." Pp. 255–62 in *Americanizing the American Indians: Writings by the "Friends of the Indian," 1880–1900,* edited by Francis Paul Prucha. Cambridge: Harvard University Press.

Prucha, Francis Paul, ed. 1973. *Americanizing the American Indians: Writings by the "Friends of the Indian," 1880–1900.* Cambridge: Harvard University Press.

Roberts, Peter. 1920. *The Problem of Americanization.* New York: Macmillan.

Rush, Benjamin. 1786. *A Plan for the Establishment of Public Schools and the Diffusion of Knowledge in Pennsylvania; to Which Are Added Thoughts about the Mode of*

Education, Proper in a Republic. Addressed to the Legislature and citizens of the state. Philadelphia: Thomas Dobson.

Smith, William C. 1939. *Americans in the Making.* New York: Arno.

Sollors, Werner. 1986. "A Critique of Pluralism." Pp. 250–79 in *Reconstructing American History,* edited by Sacvan Berkovitch. Cambridge: Harvard University Press.

Story, Joseph. 1835. "On the Science of Government as a Branch of Popular Government." In *The Introductory Discourse and the Lectures Delivered Before the American Institute of Instruction in Boston, August 1834.* Boston: American Institute.

Suzuki, Mary Bonzo. 1990. "American Education in the Philippines, the Early Years." Ph.D. diss., University of California at Berkeley.

Swett, John. 1880. *Methods of Teaching: A Handbook of Principles, Directions, and Working Models for Common-School Teachers.* New York: Harper & Brothers.

Szasz, Margaret. 1974. *Education and the American Indian: The Road to Self-Determination, 1928–1973.* Albuquerque: University of New Mexico Press.

Takaki, Ronald. 1995. "The Unities in Pluralism," *A National Conversation on American Pluralism and Identity: Scholars' Essays.* Washington, D.C.: National Endowment for the Humanities.

Thorpe, Francis N. 1909. *The Federal and State Constitutions, Colonial Charters, and Other Organic Laws of the States, Territories, and Colonies Now or Heretofore Forming the United States of America.* Washington, D.C.: GPO.

Todd, Helen M. 1913. "Why Children Work: The Children's Answer," *McClure's Magazine* 40: 68–79.

Turner, Lewis C. 1940. "School-Board Minutes of One Hundred Years Ago." *American School Board Journal.* 100 (June): 17–19.

Tyack, David. 1966. "Forming of the National Character: Paradox in the Educational Thought of the Revolutionary Generation." *Harvard Educational Review* 36: 37–41.

————. 1967. *Turning Points in American Educational History.* Waltham, Mass.: Blaisdell.

Tyack, David, and Elisabeth Hansot. 1982. *Managers of Virtue: Public School Leadership in America, 1820–1980.* New York: Basic Books.

U.S. House of Representatives, Committee on Public Lands. 1878. "Report on Educational Land Policy," February 24, 1826, as published in *Barnard's American Journal of Education* 28.

U.S. Statutes at Large. 1845. Boston: Little, Brown.

Warfel, Harry R. 1936. *Noah Webster: Schoolmaster to America.* New York: Macmillan.

Webster, Noah. 1798. *A Collection of Essays and Fugitive Writings on Moral, Historical, Political and Literary Subjects.* Boston: I. Thomas and E. T. Andrews.

Welter, Rush. 1962. *Popular Education and Democratic Thought in America.* New York: Columbia University Press.

Wiebe, Robert. 1984. *The Opening of American Society: From the Adoption of the Constitution to the Eve of Disunion.* New York: Knopf.

Racial Issues: Recent Trends in Residential Patterns and Intermarriage*

REYNOLDS FARLEY

INTRODUCTION

THE CIVIL RIGHTS REVOLUTION of the 1960s marked a turning point in how Americans viewed the racial practices of this country, especially the discriminatory policies that excluded blacks from most desirable opportunities. Although many organizations, including the National Association for the Advancement of Colored People (NAACP), had a long history of suing for equal opportunities for African Americans, the system of racial exclusion and segregation that evolved from slavery and was ratified by federal courts in the late nineteenth century continued to thrive after World War II. We defended our democracy and defeated German and Japanese dictators with Jim Crow armed forces. During and after that war, blacks migrated to the North and West, where neighborhoods, schools, and jobs were segregated by race, just as in the South. Jim Crow moved north rapidly, continuing the centuries-old practices of excluding African Americans.

This situation was challenged in the 1960s. Dr. Martin Luther King, Jr., led an effective movement, capped by the historic March on Washington on August 28, 1963. The next year, Congress enacted and President Johnson signed one of the most important laws of this century, the Civil Rights Act of 1964, which sought to end the exclusion of blacks from good job opportunities. Twelve months later, after bloody marches in Selma, Alabama, caused three deaths, Congress passed the Voting Rights Act—a law that finally made the Fifteenth Amendment operative in all states, thereby ending the exclusion of blacks from southern voting booths. That year, Congress passed another civil rights law: the Immigration Reform Act. It terminated our century-long history of racially discriminatory immigration policies that closed our doors to Asians, Africans, and eastern and southern Europeans. Following the murder of Dr. King in Memphis in April 1968, Congress approved the fourth major civil rights act of that

---

* This paper was prepared for presentation at the conference "Common Values, Social Diversity, and Cultural Conflict," held at the Center for Advanced Study in the Behavioral Sciences; Stanford, California; October 17–19, 1996.

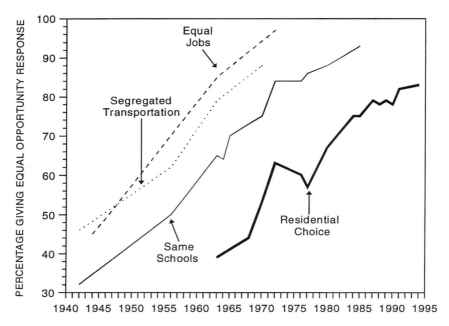

FIGURE 5.1. Percentage of Whites Giving the Equal Opportunity Response to Questions about Principles of Racial Equity: 1942 to 1994

Questions:

(Same Schools): Do you think that white students and (Negro/Black) students should go to the same or to separate schools? (Percentage saying "same schools").

(Equal Jobs): Do you think Negroes should have as good a chance as white people to get any kind of job, or do you think white people should have the first chance at any kind of job? (Percentage saying "as good a chance as white people").

(Segregated Transportation): Generally speaking, do you think there should be separate sections for Negroes in streetcars and buses? (Percentage saying "no").

(Residential Choice): Which statement on the card (showing four responses from agree strongly to disagree strongly) comes closest to how you yourself feel? White people have a right to keep blacks out of their neighborhood if they want to, and blacks should respect that right? (Percentage disagreeing).

Sources: Schuman, Steeh, Bobo, and Krysan, 1997: Table 3–1; National Opinion Research Center, 1996, Items 127–36.

decade—the Fair Housing Law—an act that was intended to overturn practices that excluded blacks from white neighborhoods.

White Americans who had accepted a system of racial stratification based on white dominance came to endorse the ideals of American democracy. Figure 5.1 summarizes trends in white attitudes about principles of equal racial opportunity. The graph shows the percentage of nationally representative samples of whites who gave the "equal racial opportunity" answer to questions about racially integrated schools and public transportation and about equal opportunities for African Americans in the labor and housing markets. (For further details, see Schuman, Steeh, and Bobo, 1985: ch. 3.)

Two generations ago, only three whites in ten endorsed the principle that blacks and whites should attend the same schools. The majority of whites also rejected the idea that both races should have the same chances to fill jobs that became available. The overwhelming majority of whites endorsed the system of segregated transportation that Rosa Parks helped overturn when she sat in the front of a Montgomery bus on December 5, 1955. During World War II and for years thereafter, whites generally accepted the principle of racial exclusion. But by the 1960s, attitudes had liberalized, and, for the first time, a majority of whites supported the principle of equal racial opportunities. The liberalization trend continued despite claims that there would be a backlash, and by 1980 more than nine whites in ten favored equal opportunities for blacks in the job market and in education. The civil rights revolution brought a thorough shift in white attitudes; racial discrimination is now seen as morally as well as legally wrong.

Three decades have passed since President Johnson signed the civil rights laws. Much has changed. Most Americans no longer support the flagrant practices of discrimination that kept our sports teams all-white, that kept blacks home on election day, and that once steered most black women into domestic service and black men into manual labor. By 1996, forty African Americans were serving in Congress, four had been selected by President Clinton for his first cabinet, one had retired from and one was serving on the Supreme Court, and a black man, Colin Powell, had been briefly considered as a leading contender for the presidency by the Republicans.

But blacks and whites have not achieved equality of status, and racial discrimination has not disappeared. If we focus on many of the indicators of educational attainment and almost all the important indicators of economic status, we find extremely large and persistent black–white gaps.

RACIAL ECONOMIC TRENDS

A capsule summary of black–white racial differences in economic status should focus attention on two different periods. Between 1940 and the energy crisis in 1973, we had high rates of economic growth and a rapid expansion of employment. As a result, millions of men—black and white—who had high school educations or less shifted from poor-paying jobs in the agricultural sector to good jobs in the industrial sector, jobs that often included generous fringe benefits along with a strong union to protect their interests. Since 1973 we have seen a new emphasis on labor productivity, new norms and policies regarding employment, and, generally, much weaker unions. During the earlier period, both before and after the civil rights revolution, blacks gradually "caught up" with whites on most indicators of earnings, income, and poverty. Since 1973, however, these black–white gaps have neither widened nor contracted.

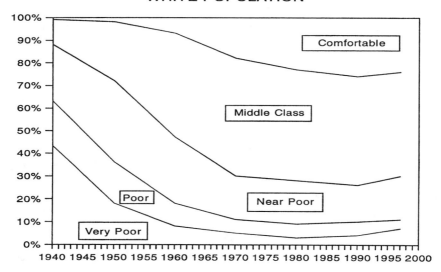

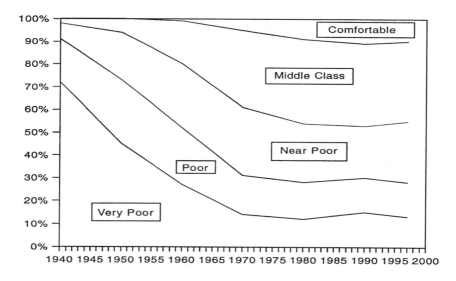

FIGURE 5.2. Economic Status of the Black and White Populations: 1940 to 1997

Sources: U.S. Bureau of the Census, Public Use Microdata Samples from the censuses of 1940 to 1980 and the March 1993 Current Population Survey.

Note: **Very Poor:** Below 50% of poverty line; **Poor:** 50% to 99% of poverty line; **Near Poor:** 100% to 199% of poverty line; **Middle Class:** 200% to 499% of poverty line; **Comfortable:** 500% or more of poverty line.

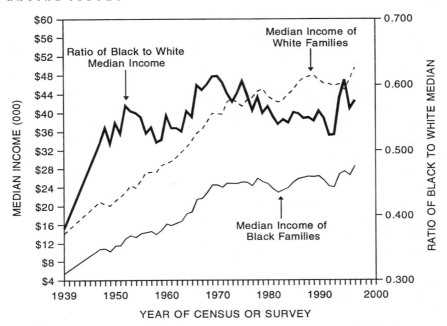

FIGURE 5.3. Median Income of Families and Ratio of Black to White Median: 1939 to 1997. (Amounts in constant 1997 dollars)

Note: Information for whites before 1972 includes data for Spanish origin whites; thereafter Spanish-origin whites are excluded. Data for 1939 refer to wage and salary earnings of family members as reported in the census of 1940; data for subsequent years include all sources of income tabulated by the statistical system.

Figures 5.2 and 5.3 illustrate the economic changes. Figure 5.2 shows the distribution of the black and white populations according to their relationship to the poverty line from 1940 to 1997. Those classified as very poor lived in households with pretax cash incomes below half the poverty line, which was $16,400 for a family of four in 1997. Those classified as economically comfortable or prosperous lived in households with incomes five or more times the poverty line; that is, they had cash incomes of more than $75,500 for a family of four.

At the outset of World War II, more than 90% of the black population was impoverished, living in households with cash incomes below the poverty line. But the tremendous economic growth in the next thirty years greatly reduced poverty. These economic trends and many favorable governmental policies, including the GI Bill and federal housing programs after World War II, produced a nation in which 70% of whites could be termed economically middle class by 1970. Although those trends substantially lessened poverty among blacks, the majority of blacks have never had incomes twice the poverty line. *Throughout our history, the majority of blacks have lived either in cash-poor households or in households with incomes less than twice the poverty line.*

What has happened since 1973? The story is much the same for blacks and whites: the growth of the middle class stopped. It is not that poverty has greatly risen; rather, the beneficent era during which the middle class grew steadily year after year came to an end. To be certain, as the white and black populations increase, the number of middle-class households goes up slowly, but the middle class as a share of the total population has not changed since the resignation of President Nixon. Among blacks, as among whites, the income distribution has polarized: the number of black millionaires has increased. In many metropolises, it is likely that a black athlete is now the highest paid salaried employee. The percentage of black families with incomes exceeding $50,000 (in constant dollars) went up from 10% in 1967 to 26% in 1997. Among white families, the change was an increase from 27% to 50% (U.S. Bureau of the Census 1998: table B-4). The Gini Index of Income Inequality went up among African American families from 40 in 1967 to 44 in 1997, whereas the index among whites changed from 35 to 42; that is, income became more polarized among both races and is now less equitably distributed among black families than among white ones. This change led to a larger number of prosperous and prominent blacks, but it should not be mistaken for a great expansion of the black middle class.

When most economic indicators of the status of blacks vis-à-vis whites are considered, we find modest improvement from 1940 through the early 1970s but not much change since then: neither a deterioration in the status of blacks relative to whites nor much improvement. Figure 5.3 graphs information about the median incomes of black and whites families from 1939 to the present. Trend lines show changes over time for black and white families, and the bold line traces the ratio of the black median to the white. At the time of the 1940 census, the average income of black families was less than 40% of whites'. World War II and the ensuing economic boom—along with new racial policies—changed this ratio, and by the early 1970s, the median income of black families was 60% that of white families. But there has been no further improvement in the relative income of black families.

Despite the stagnation on many economic indicators, there were several favorable developments for blacks in the 1980s, suggesting that we may hope for further racial progress. I believe there has been a gradual breakdown in the traditional practices that excluded blacks from desirable opportunities. First, findings from attitudinal surveys show that whites increasingly—now almost universally—endorse the ideals of equal racial opportunities—ideals that the majority of whites rejected at the start of the 1960s. As younger generations complete school and become voters, workers, and home owners, they bring their egalitarian racial attitudes with them and they replace older people who completed their schooling long before the *Brown* decision and who typically hold less egalitarian racial ideas.

Second, the long-term trend toward a racial convergence of educational attainment through high school continued in the 1980s and 1990s. Thanks to innovative programs that keep teenagers in school and to the General Education Development (GED) certificate now obtained by about half a million people each year, when birth cohorts reach their late twenties, roughly equal proportions of blacks and whites report high school diplomas or GED certificates (U.S. National Center for Education Statistics 1995: table 100).

Third, the census of 1990 revealed an extensive pattern of small declines in black–white residential segregation throughout the country, with large declines recorded in quite a few areas (Farley and Frey, 1994). Blacks are somewhat less excluded from white neighborhoods than in the past.

Finally, racial intermarriage increased fairly sharply between 1980 and 1990, although this is still a rare occurrence. Growing proportions of young black men are increasingly marrying white women.

RACIAL RESIDENTIAL SEGREGATION

It does not require much study of the urban landscape to realize that blacks and whites generally live in different neighborhoods. As Douglas Massey and Nancy Denton (1993) argue in their convincing book *American Apartheid*, segregation is the norm throughout this nation and has been ever since blacks moved to cities in great numbers during World War I. It is less well known that in the 1980s black–white segregation declined moderately in most metropolises and quite a bit in other places. Indeed, although segregation is still common and few neighborhoods can be labeled integrated, racial segregation seems to be waning, thanks to the civil rights revolution and the changes in attitudes and policies it produced.

History and Trends Before the 1960s

At the turn of this century, blacks and whites were not highly segregated in cities of either the North or the South. Many southern cities had neighborhoods with largely black populations, but other blacks lived side by side with whites. In the North, most blacks were poor and lived with other impoverished immigrants in neighborhoods that we would call urban slums, but slums that were racially and ethnically mixed because of the presence of eastern and southern Europeans.

In the first three decades of this century, social values and policies built the first racial ghettos. Several strategies were used. When blacks came to southern cities in large numbers, city ordinances sought to specify where they might or might not live, a practice seemingly in keeping with the 1896 *Plessy* (163 U.S. 537) decision but one that the Supreme Court overturned in 1917 in *Buchanan v. Warley* (245 U.S. 60) on the grounds that it abridged property rights. That is, the Supreme Court ruled that municipalities lacked the power to mandate that only blacks could live on some blocks and only whites on others (Johnson

1943: ch. 8). When blacks arrived in northern cities during World War I, the type of segregation Massey and Denton identify as American Apartheid became common.

Violence was frequently used to deter blacks who moved into largely white neighborhoods. The investigators of the great Chicago racial riot of 1919—Charles Johnson and Robert Park—described fifty-eight firebombings of blacks who dared to enter white neighborhoods (Chicago Commission on Race Relations 1922). The most famous racial trial of the 1920s involved Dr. Ossian Sweet, a black doctor in Detroit who moved into an attractive residence on that city's northeast side. When his home was attacked by neighborhood whites, police officers stood by, but Dr. Sweet and his brother defended themselves with their guns, leading to the death of one white man. Although Sweet was charged with first-degree murder, Clarence Darrow eventually won an acquittal for him by asserting Sweet's right to defend his property (Canot 1974). Nevertheless, the great violence directed toward middle-class blacks who moved into white areas in the post–World War I era helped maintain segregation.

Those who wished to preserve neighborhood segregation did not have to resort to violence. By the 1920s it had become common for property deeds to include a restrictive covenant specifying that the land could not be owned or occupied by blacks, Jews, Asians, or some other undesirable minority for a long span such as ninety-nine years. The Supreme Court in 1926 in *Corrigan v. Buckley* (271 U.S. 323) upheld the legality of such private agreements, and thus they became a tool in bolstering America's color line. President Truman's Committee on Civil Rights (1947) estimated that by the 1940s, 80% of the residential land in Chicago was covered by restrictive covenants preventing its occupancy by blacks.

The Depression and World War II curtailed the construction of new homes or apartments, but from the end of that war until 1980, 29 million new housing units were added to the nation's housing stock (which totaled only 37 million units in 1940). In this period, the nation invaded and conquered a "crabgrass frontier" (Jackson 1985). The housing boom offered an opportunity for a diminution of the residential exclusion that isolated blacks from whites and kept black and white children in separate schools. But the opportunity was lost when the nation created a second ghetto in the years after World War II. In many older and larger metropolises, this meant a white suburban ring surrounding a majority black central city—hence the song heard on soul music stations a couple of decades ago: "Chocolate City, Vanilla Suburbs" (Farley et al. 1978).

How was the second ghetto built? Three specific techniques contributed. First, mortgage lending practices were discriminatory. Because of innovative federal programs, families of moderate or low income could buy homes for the first time in the nation's history after World War II, but redlining was enforced by the federal lending agencies. When the government first insured mortgages during the Depression, administrators developed a systematic procedure for ranking the creditworthiness of neighborhoods. Color-coded maps indicated whether the homes were likely to retain their value, go up in value, or lose their

worth. According to the assumptions of the real estate industry and urban planners of the 1930s, it was presumed that any neighborhood undergoing racial
change or likely to undergo racial change in the future—and often the in-migration of Jews was defined as racial change—would see home prices plummet.
Such a neighborhood was colored red on appraisal maps. It is not so much that
lenders and the federal agencies refused mortgage applications from blacks.
They did not, as long as the blacks bought housing in segregated neighborhoods. Consistent with this practice were codes of ethics for real estate brokers,
which called for the maintenance of segregation and censured brokers who
introduced minorities to all-white neighborhoods.

Second, in the North and East, and in some major metropolises in the West,
dozens or hundreds of independent suburbs surround the largest cities, many of
them with histories dating from the nineteenth century. After World War II, the
suburbs often competed for central city residents, because the construction of
new housing complexes and shopping centers ensured suburban prosperity. Almost without exception, these individual suburbs indicated that only white residents were welcome. We have complete documentation about both the subtle
and flagrant policies used to signal that a suburb was for whites only for Parma,
Ohio—involved in a long federal court suit (*U.S. v. City of Parma* 1981; 494 F.
Supp. 1049)—and for Dearborn, Michigan (Good 1989), where Mayor Hubbard used his police to keep blacks out for more than three decades. Very few
blacks risked the violence and hostility they knew they would face if they dared
enter the white-only suburbs that boomed after World War II.

Third, federally sponsored public housing kept large cities segregated. When
first designed in the 1930s, public housing was to provide temporary shelter for
poor families as they worked their way into the middle class. By the early
1960s, however, public housing became the home of last resort for problem
families, especially those headed by black women with children (Rainwater
1970). Federal urban renewal monies razed old neighborhoods occupied by
blacks, especially in eastern and midwestern cities. Instead of dispersing this
population to the edges of central cities or to burgeoning suburbs, local and
federal policies intentionally concentrated the displaced African Americans into
all-black public housing projects built almost exclusively in already black
neighborhoods.

These three policies—discriminatory lending, the racial specialization of
suburbs, and public housing policies—along with the intimidation of blacks
who moved into white neighborhoods, kept segregation levels very high
(Hirsch 1983).

The Civil Rights Revolution and Reductions in Segregation

Racial residential segregation is now declining, although there is no likelihood
that inner-city black ghettos will soon disappear. Four main factors are now
reducing segregation. First, there have been changes in federal housing policy
reflecting, I believe, an increased endorsement of the ideal of equal racial op-

portunity. Throughout this century the NAACP and Jewish groups have fought discriminatory housing policies, winning a major victory in 1948 when the Supreme Court in *Shelly v. Kraemer* (334 U.S. 1) ruled that restrictive covenants could not be enforced. They continued to be written into deeds, but courts could not enforce them.

The Fair Housing Law was the most significant achievement of civil rights groups in this field. It had languished in Congress for several years until James Earl Ray shot Dr. Martin Luther King, Jr. Four days later, Congress passed legislation outlawing racial discrimination in the sale or rental of housing units, legislation that was promptly upheld by the Supreme Court in 1968 in *Jones v. Alfred H. Mayer* (329 U.S. 409). Although enforcement by federal agencies was often lax at the start, the open housing movement was bolstered by subsequent developments focused on discrimination by lenders. After newspaper investigators and academics reported racial discrimination in housing finance, Congress, in 1975, passed the Home Mortgage Disclosure Act (HMDA), which proved to be a potent "freedom of information" tool. It required that federally chartered fiscal institutions report exactly where they made or denied loans. The law was subsequently strengthened to require additional information from applicants about their race and financial capabilities, making it easier to detect practices that denied blacks home-owning opportunities granted to ostensibly similar whites (Yinger 1995). Then, in 1977, urban development groups succeeded in getting Congress to enact the Community Reinvestment Act (CRA), which mandated that federally chartered banks and savings institutions meet the credit needs of the entire metropolis they serve, not just the prosperous white suburbs. As we switched from the traditional system of state banks to national banks in the 1980s and 1990s, CRA took on much greater significance because interstate bank mergers gave advocacy groups an excellent opportunity to demonstrate that banks failed to meet the credit needs of low-income and minority communities in their service area.

Another important change in federal housing policies flowed from a decision involving public housing in Chicago (*Hills v. Gautreaux* 1976; 425 U.S. 284). As a result, federal dollars are no longer used to construct public housing that concentrates minorities into segregated neighborhoods. Indeed, there has been some emphasis on scattered-site publicly financed housing and limited federal support for both vouchers and rent supplements that allow low-income people to shop for their own housing.

Second, residential integration depended on changes in the racial attitudes of whites and changes in behavior as a result of the more egalitarian attitudes. There have been such changes. At the start of the civil rights decades, 60% of national samples of whites agreed with the statement that "White people have a right to keep blacks out of their neighborhoods if they want to, and blacks should respect that right." By the early 1990s, only 20% agreed with that principle of racial segregation. In the late 1950s, a Gallup survey found that 44% of a national sample of whites said they might or definitely would leave if a black moved next door. When that question was asked in 1997, only 2% said the arrival of a black neighbor would trigger their flight from the neighborhood (Schuman et al., 1997: table 3.3).

Changes in the racial attitudes of whites during and after World War II facilitated enactment of the civil rights laws of the 1960s. Those statutes—along with many Supreme Court decisions upholding them—encouraged a further liberalization of the attitudes of whites. Thus, in the 1990s, whites almost universally support the principle of equal opportunities for blacks in the housing market and overwhelmingly report a willingness to accept black neighbors.

A third change encouraging more integration is the continued high rate of new housing construction. Investigations in the 1960s reported that high rates of home building in a metropolis were associated with high levels of segregation, because whites left central cities where blacks and whites lived near one another and moved into exclusively white suburbs. Since the Fair Housing Law of 1968 became effective, new construction has been associated with decreases in black–white segregation. Many older central city neighborhoods and the suburbs built just after World War II are well known for their extreme hostility to blacks. But newly built areas had to comply with the Fair Housing Law, and, at the outset, new neighborhoods probably did not have strong reputations for racial hostility. Open housing advocates often checked to determine that new developments were complying with the law. Since 1972, regulations of the Department of Housing and Urban Development mandate that developers using government-backed loans advertise affirmatively, meaning that advertisements must be placed on soul music stations or in black-oriented newspapers.

Finally, the growth of the black middle class contributes to a decline in racial residential segregation. The black middle class is still small compared with the white middle class, but there has been numerical growth and a more rapid expansion of the black financial elite. Undoubtedly, some of these people look for prosperous black enclaves, but many others seek the housing amenities sought by comparable whites. They quite often find them in integrated areas, and because of their own financial capabilities, they may not trigger the exodus of the whites already living there.

These four developments—changes in federal housing policies, liberalization of white attitudes, substantial new housing construction, and a modest growth of the black middle class—set the stage for declining segregation.

Racial Residential Segregation Trends in the 1980s

Segregation has most often been assessed with the index of dissimilarity using data showing racial composition for census tracts or block groups. This index takes on its maximum value of 100 in a situation of total apartheid; that is, every block group is exclusively black or exclusively white, and no block group simultaneously houses blacks and whites. The index approaches its minimum of zero when individuals are randomly assigned to their places of residence, as might happen in a college dormitory or military barracks.

Using data for block groups—census-defined areas with about 200 housing units—we measured black–white segregation in 1980 and 1990 for those 232 metropolitan areas in which either 3% of the population was black in 1990 or there were 20,000 black residents in that year. We found a pervasive pattern of modest declines. The average index of dissimilarity fell from 69 in 1980 to 65 in 1990. Black–white residential segregation declined in 194 of the 232 metropolises, and in 85 of them the decrease was 5 points or more. In 1980, 14 metropolises had indexes exceeding 85, whereas ten years later only 4 metropolitan areas were so thoroughly segregated by race. In 1980, 29 metropolises could have been classified as moderately segregated, meaning they had a segregation score of less than 55. The number of moderately segregated places more than doubled to 68 in 1990. These measures pertain to blacks and whites. (For an analysis of the residential segregation of Asians and Latinos, see Frey and Farley 1996.)

Table 5.1 lists the 15 most and least segregated metropolises in 1980 and 1990. Of the 15 most segregated in 1990, 11 were old midwestern industrial centers, and 2 were retirement communities in Florida. A decade earlier, the most segregated areas included seven midwestern places but also seven retirement centers in Florida. Five of those seven areas in Florida disappeared from the most segregated list as their population grew and they became less segregated, thanks, in large part, to new construction.

The list of least segregated metropolises was dominated by areas whose economic base was the armed forces: Anchorage, Alaska; Clarksville, Tennessee; Fayetteville, North Carolina; Jacksonville, North Carolina; and Lawton, Oklahoma, appeared on the list both years, and Cheyenne, Wyoming; Fort Walton Beach, Florida; Honolulu, Hawaii; and Killeen, Texas, were on the 1990 list. The university towns of Lawrence, Kansas, and Charlottesville, Virginia, also had low levels of segregation; Columbia, Missouri, was among the least segregated a decade earlier. Low levels of black–white segregation are not restricted to small places: Honolulu, Hawaii, and Tucson, Arizona, with populations over 500,000; San Jose, California, with 1.5 million, and Anaheim, with 2.5 million residents, were among the least segregated areas in 1990.

Several factors were linked to levels of black–white residential segregation in 1990 and changes during the 1980s. First, region was important. Segregation levels were lowest in the West and were lower in the South than in the Northeast and Midwest. The upper panel of Figure 5.4 shows the levels of segregation by region and the average percentage change in segregation during the decade.

Regional differences in segregation are not the outcome of regional differences in racial attitudes nor in the enforcement of open housing laws. Rather, they primarily reflect regional differences in the history of cities and their suburbs. Older central cities in the Northeast and Midwest are surrounded by many independent suburbs, but in the South many government activities—including the public schools—are organized on a countywide basis. A white resident of a northern city seeking to avoid racial change in the neighborhood or integrated schools typically could choose among many all-white suburbs, but his or her

TABLE 5.1

Indexes of Dissimilarity for the Fifteen Most Segregated and Least Segregated
Metropolitan Areas: Blacks vs. Whites; 1980 and 1990

1980		*1990*	
Metropolitan Area	*Index of Dissimilarity*	*Metropolitan Area*	*Index of Dissimilarity*
Most segregated			
Bradenton, Fla.	91	Gary, Ind.	91
Chicago, Ill.	91	Detroit, Mich.	89
Gary, Ind.	90	Chicago, Ill.	87
Sarasota, Fla.	90	Cleveland, Ohio	86
Cleveland, Ohio	89	Buffalo, N.Y.	84
Detroit, Mich.	89	Flint, Mich.	84
Ft. Myers, Fla.	89	Milwaukee, Wis.	84
Flint, Mich.	87	Saginaw, Mich.	84
Ft. Pierce, Fla.	87	Newark, N.J.	83
West Palm Beach, Fla.	87	Philadelphia, Pa.	82
Ft. Lauderdale, Fla.	86	St. Louis, Mo.	81
Naples, Fla.	86	Ft. Myers, Fla.	81
Saginaw, Mich.	86	Sarasota, Fla.	80
Milwaukee, Wis.	85	Indianapolis, Ind.	80
St. Louis, Mo.	85	Cincinnati, Ohio	80
Average	88	Average	84
Least segregated			
El Paso, Tex.	49	Charlottesville, Va.	45
Columbia, Mo.	49	Danville, Va.	45
Victoria, Tex.	49	Killeen, Tex.	45
Charlottesville, Va.	48	San José, Calif.	45
Clarksville, Tenn.	48	Tucson, Ariz.	45
Colorado Springs, Colo.	48	Honolulu, Hawaii	44
San José, Calif.	48	Anaheim, Calif.	43
Anaheim, Calif.	47	Cheyenne, Wyo.	43
Honolulu, Hawaii	46	Ft. Walton Beach, Fla.	43
Fayetteville, N.C.	43	Clarksville, Tenn.	42
Lawton, Okla.	43	Lawrence, Kans.	41
Anchorage, Alaska	42	Fayetteville, N.C.	41
Danville, Va.	41	Anchorage, Ala.	38
Lawrence, Kans.	38	Lawton, Okla.	37
Jacksonville, N.C.	36	Jacksonville, N.C.	31
Average	45	Average	42

Note: These indexes are based on block group data and pertain to persons reporting white or
black as their race.

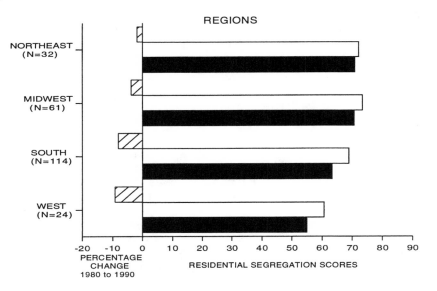

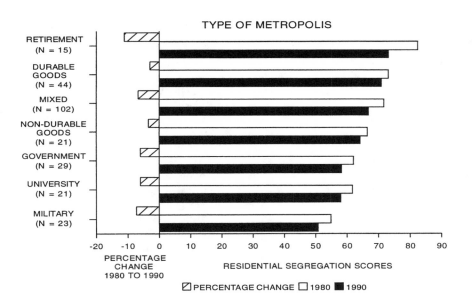

FIGURE 5.4. Black–White Residential Segregation Scores, 1980 and 1990, for Metropolises Classified by Region and by Functional Specialization

counterpart in a southern city could do so less often. In addition, southern and western cities are more likely than those in the Midwest to have a third or fourth major demographic group: Asians or Latinos. Data from the census of 1990 reveal that the presence of a third or fourth group had the independent effect of slightly reducing the residential segregation of whites from blacks (Frey and Farley 1996).

Functional Specialization

Metropolises differ in their economic bases, and this specialization, in turn, influenced the kinds of people who lived there, their attitudes, and levels of segregation in 1990. The housing stock of a university or military center differs in important ways from the housing stock in an older manufacturing center in the Midwest. The educational level of a metropolis is strongly influenced by the type of economic activity sustaining it.

Metropolitan areas are classified into seven types:

retirement communities where the principal economic activity involves the older population; that is, retirement checks, Social Security payments, and Medicare serve as the economic base, e.g., Ft. Myers, Fla.

durable goods manufacturing communities that specialize in the production of cars, steel, or other manufactured products, e.g., Flint, Mich.

nondurable goods manufacturing communities where many workers are employed in making chemicals, food products, textiles, and other such products, e.g., Greensboro, N.C.

government communities, including many state capitals, where much of the employment is civil service; e.g., Washington, D.C.

university communities where the major employer is a university or several colleges

military communities centered around a large military complex

diversified communities where there are several major economic activities and no specialization in a particular one.

The lower panel in Figure 5.4 shows the level of black–white segregation in each type of community in 1980 and 1990 as well as the percentage change (the bars to the left of the vertical line). There is an interesting pattern here. Retirement communities were the most highly segregated in both census years. Few retired blacks have the savings to move into such areas, so the elderly population is largely white. Many of the residents have moved south from metropolises where racial conflict was frequent. Blacks in those places tend to be much younger than whites and to live in different neighborhoods. These retirement centers are located in the South and grew rapidly in the 1980s, so their segregation levels declined on average by 12%.

Durable goods communities also were highly segregated. Of the 44 such metropolises, 41 are located in the Midwest or North, including Flint, Gary, and Saginaw. Nevertheless, segregation levels fell in the 1980s even in these metropolises, although the rate of decline was minimal.

The populations of government, university, and military communities dif-fer—especially in educational attainment and occupation—from those of manufacturing centers. Many residents of university and military communities spend only a few years there, so their attachments to their neighborhoods may be ephemeral. Persons living in dormitories, barracks, or homes on a military base may have been assigned to their places of residence, and the military insists on nondiscrimination in the housing markets near bases. Thus in 1990 the segregation levels were low in governmental and university metropolises generally, but at a minimum in places centered around a large military installation.

Age of the Metropolis

The age of a metropolitan area is quite strongly linked to its segregation level. Older places in which central city neighborhoods were built well before the Depression and most of the suburban ring in the years just after World War II were more segregated than metropolises whose growth spurt occurred in the last two decades.

To classify metropolises by age, we determined when the central city first reached 50,000—a demographic development that occurred in Baltimore, Phil-adelphia, New York, and New Orleans before the Civil War. At the other end are new areas such as Daytona Beach and Anchorage where the central city reached that size during the 1980s.

Figure 5.5 presents information about metropolises classified by their age and indicates that the older the location, the greater the segregation. Those 29 metropolises whose central city reached 50,000 more than a century ago had average black–white segregation scores of 72 in 1990, whereas places whose central city first had 50,000 residents after 1970 had average scores of 57. Seg-regation levels declined in all age categories, but the decreases were, on aver-age, greater in younger metropolises than in older ones. Social practices such as the color coding of neighborhoods, and economic patterns maintain segregation in the older metropolises, but rapid population growth in new areas lowers segregation.

New Construction

Metropolitan areas differ greatly in the proportion of their housing stock built after the Fair Housing Act of 1968 became effective. A few examples will illustrate how differential rates of growth influence the housing stock and, in turn, segregation. In booming Orlando, just under half of the homes and apart-ments enumerated in the census of 1990 were built in the last decade; in Phoe-nix the comparable figure was 40%, and in Atlanta 37%. At the other extreme are places where the population stagnated or declined, and thus few new homes or apartments were built in recent decades. In the Buffalo, Pittsburgh, and

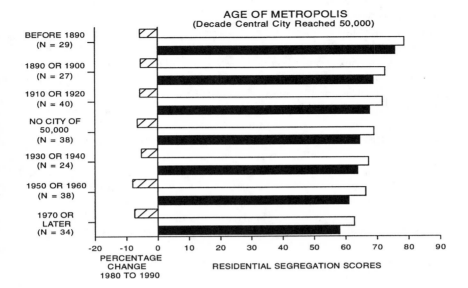

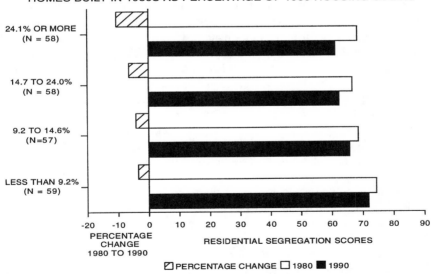

FIGURE 5.5. Black–White Residential Segregation Scores, 1980 and 1990, for Metropolises Classified by Age and by New Housing Construction in 1980s

New York metropolitan areas, less than 9% of the housing stock of 1990 was erected in the previous decade.

The Fair Housing Law may be encouraging more racial integration, because metropolitan areas with a high proportion of their housing stock recently built were, in 1990, considerably less segregated than places where there was little new construction, as illustrated in the lower panel of Figure 5.5. Here, metropolises have been classified by the percentage of their housing stock built during the 1980s. The average segregation score for places with roughly one-quarter or more of their housing stock built in that decade was 58 in 1990; in places where fewer than 10% of the homes were constructed recently, the average segregation score was 73. And although segregation declined in all types of metropolises, the proportionately greatest declines occurred in the places that grew most rapidly, offering hope that the new pattern of black migration revealed by the census of 1990—that is, black out-migration from the traditional urban centers (e.g., Chicago, Detroit, and Cleveland) and into the newer and rapidly growing metropolises—will eventually lead to less segregation. Multivariate analyses show that region, functional specialization, and new construction had independent effects on changes in black–white segregation in the 1980s (Farley and Frey 1994: table 3).

Blacks, Asians, and Hispanics

There is no ambiguity about what occurred during the 1980s. There was a clear pattern of declining black–white residential segregation. To be certain, the drops were very modest in the older manufacturing centers of the Midwest, but in smaller metropolises of the West and South—especially those dependent on the military, universities, and government agencies for employment—declines were more substantial. In addition, some of the larger metropolises that are now serving for the first time as magnets for black internal migration, including Dallas and Orlando, saw large drops in racial residential segregation.

Despite the extensive pattern of declines, blacks remain much more segregated than the two other minority groups now arriving in U.S. cities in great numbers: Hispanics and Asians. Two-thirds of the Asians in this nation in 1990 were born abroad, as were about four in ten Hispanics. But when these groups move to metropolitan areas and select places to live, they find themselves less residentially segregated than blacks.

Information about this phenomenon is reported in Figure 5.6. The graphs show the distribution of segregation scores in 1980 and 1990 and compare each of the three minority groups with all other persons. The number of metropolises differs, as there were 232 places with sufficient numbers of blacks to carry out this analysis but only 153 locations with sufficient Hispanics and 66 with enough Asians. The average segregation score comparing blacks with nonblacks dropped from 69 to 64, as indicated by the index of dissimilarity, which would take on its maximum value of 100 were apartheid enforced. For Hispanics, there was no change in the average segregation level in the 1980s, but

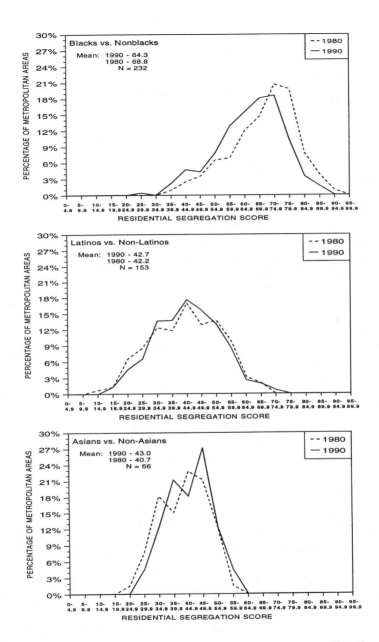

FIGURE 5.6. Frequency by Residential Segregation Score: U.S. Metropolitan Areas, 1980–1990

Source: Farley and Frey (1994) from 1980 and 1990 Census Summary Tape Files, 1A.

Note: Metropolitan areas for each minority group comparison include those in which the minority has a 1990 population of greater than 20,000 or represents at least 3% of the total population of the area.

their average score—42 in both years—was much less than that for blacks. Among Asians there was a small increase in segregation, undoubtedly reflecting the concentration of many newcomers in the Asian neighborhoods of ports of entry. Nevertheless, the index measuring the segregation of Asians from all others in 1990 was 43, or a much lower level of segregation than that for blacks.

Increasing Interracial Marriage: Is it Symbolic of a Declining Significance of Race?

When Gunnar Myrdal (1944: 60) studied race relations in the United States more than 50 years ago, he concluded that when white southerners were asked about types of discrimination, they consistently listed as most important the bar against intermarriage and sexual intercourse between black men and white women. Indeed, Myrdal used the white man's rank order of discrimination—with intermarriage at the top of that list—as the organizing principle for his *An American Dilemma*. In his view, the foundation for racial discrimination throughout American society was an antiamalgamation doctrine that was implemented by laws against intermarriage and enforced by the use of violence, sometimes lynching, against black men who dared to have sexual intercourse with white women.

Would Myrdal be surprised at the situation today? Although it is still rare for white men to marry black women, more than 5% of the black men who married during the 1980s married white women. Census data permit us to analyze trends in intermarriage over time. They reveal substantial increases.

There are two notes of caution. First, race is self-reported on the census, but in most households, one individual filled out the census schedule for all persons, listing his or her own race as well as that of the spouse and children. Thus we lack information about intermarriage derived from an independent reporting of race by spouses.

Second, we focus on people who married recently, but a troubling problem in such analyses is defining a pool of potential marriage partners. It is plausible to think of metropolitan areas as labor markets or housing markets, as most residents can get to jobs or search for housing throughout one metropolis. It is more difficult to define the pool of candidates from which a spouse is selected. In other words, it is not easy to determine whether there is more intermarriage in California than in North Dakota because California is a more racially diverse state or because people in California have more liberal racial attitudes than North Dakotans.

Miscegenation: Ideologies, Laws, and Observations

Many writers have described interracial sexual practices in the American colonies and the United States; their works range from scholarly analyses of laws to prurient and licentious descriptions of what actually happened. Most histories of race include discussions of the persistent efforts of civic and moral leaders to ban interracial sex and proscribe interracial marriages, but these are immediately followed by long descriptions of how frequently white men had black concubines or black wives along with a recounting of the very large mulatto or mixed-race population that has been here since the early seventeenth century. As the Walt Disney Studio reminded us in *Pocahontas*, some—perhaps many—of the early settlers from England married American Indians.

In three distinct periods authorities sought to ban interracial sex, principally between blacks and whites. Winthrop Jordan (1968), in his authoritative history of the emergence of the American racial system, points out that demographic pressures encouraged a mulatto population because most Europeans arriving here were men. The American marriage market from which they selected partners disproportionately included African and American Indian women. But the existence of a large mixed-race population—especially the offspring of black–white unions—raised problems for the developing system of slavery. Were all children of black women to be enslaved, or were those who had a white father and black mother to be included with the free white population even if their physical features signaled their African heritage? And what about the children of white women who married or cohabited with black men? Were they to be free or enslaved? To prevent such ambiguities, colonial legislatures as early as 1660s prohibited interracial fornication and marriage. These ordinances also sought to protect public morals, because there was a widespread view that interracial sex most often occurred outside marriage. Such laws established a precedent for legislation that continued to deny blacks and whites the right to marry until the civil rights decade.

Following the American Revolution, southern states gradually passed anti-miscegenation laws. As Myrdal (1944) points out, throughout the era of slavery some, perhaps many, white men had black women as regular sexual partners for long periods of time. Some masters took special care of and provided opportunities for the numerous children they fathered, even when their features marked them as mixed race. Cash (1941), in his *Mind of the South*, contends that in the era of slavery white boys on plantations almost inevitably began their sexual activity with enslaved women and accepted this pattern as natural, leading them to continue these sexual liaisons long after they married white women. Despite the frequency of this practice, southern states enacted measures prohibiting interracial marriage. Northern states including Massachusetts also banned black–white marriages in the early 1800s (Litwack 1961: 106).

In the two generations following the Civil War, Social Darwinism became the dominant perspective. It condemned miscegenation because interracial marriages were thought to produce offspring with traits of the weaker race. During Reconstruction, southern states rewrote their legislation and passed new laws banning interracial marriage; the northern and western states followed. By early this century, thirty of the forty-eight states had laws against black–white marriages.

Eventually, eighteen states forbade Asian–white marriages, using many definitions for Asians, and five states prohibited Indian–white marriages (Cox 1948: 445). California's law, dating from 1880, prohibited "intermarriage of white persons with Chinese, negroes, mulattos, or persons of mixed blood, descended from a Chinaman or negro from the third generation, inclusive" (Chen 1991). This law was twice amended to outlaw marriages of whites with Japanese or with Filipinos. The amendments also illustrate a fundamental problem that led state legislatures frequently to rewrite these laws. This country has a long history of a mixed-race population, and many ostensibly white Americans found they had a distant relative who was black or Indian. Thus legislation, especially that written in the South, had to define specifically who was black. At the start, a one-quarter rule was used in many states, but as Social Darwinism became the dominant philosophy, states shifted to the one-sixteenth black criterion or, as in Virginia, the one-drop rule: a person with any African American ancestor was defined as black. An extraordinary amount of legal effort went into laws dealing with interracial marriage and sex. New Orleans, for instance, mandated racial segregation of commercial sex workers, but courts eventually overturned this ordinance as a violation of civil rights (Johnson 1943: 170).

In the era of Social Darwinism, it was presumed that visual inspection would easily permit classification by racial origins, and thus mulatto and octoroon became categories used by the federal statistical system. Before the 1890 census, enumerators were given the following instructions:

> Be particularly careful to distinguish between blacks, mulattos, quadroons, and octoroons. The word "black" should be used to describe those persons who have three-fourths or more black blood; 'mulattos' those persons who have three-eighths to five-eighths black blood; 'quadroon' those persons who have one-fourth black blood; and 'octoroon' those persons who have one-eighth or any trace of black blood.

Census returns for that year reported there were 6.3 million blacks, just under 1 million mulattos, and 100,000 quadroons, but only 70,000 octoroons. Census officials knew the classification procedure was flawed and stated: "These figures are of little value. Indeed, as an indication of the extent to which the races have mingled, they are misleading." Nevertheless, mulatto remained a racial category in the census until the count of 1930 (U.S. Bureau of the Census 1918: 207).

A different perspective on interracial sex developed in the latter decades of the nineteenth century, linked to the rise of lynching in the South and to even more deliberations about laws concerning interracial sex. A common stereotype that many whites held about blacks posited not only their lack of intellectual abilities but also their unrestrained sexuality and the large size of black men's sex organs. In the era of slavery, whites could more or less forcefully control blacks and thereby protect white women from black men, but with freedom, new controls were needed. One justification for the laws banning interracial sex and marriage—and Myrdal emphasizes it as the principal justification—was the desire to protect the purity of southern white women and, hence, the purity of the entire white race. The justification for some lynchings was the need for white men to deter black men from having sex with white women by killing those who did so.

There can be, of course, another interpretation of the same racial and sexual dynamics. That is, influenced by the stereotypes of their age, perhaps white southern men thought that white women would find greater sexual satisfaction with black males as partners. Therefore, to protect their own access to white women, white men threatened their rivals with death if they so much as made an inappropriate advance to white women. (For a different interpretation, see Cox 1948: ch. 19.)

Although such ideas are discredited by most academics, they are still repeated. Herrnstein and Murray (1994: 642) cite the observations of Philippe Rushton that blacks and whites differ in genital size, rate of sexual maturation, and frequency of sexual intercourse. And one of the nation's popular black authors states:

> A lot of white women who date black men say the black men treat them better than white men do. . . . The other thing, of course, is that white women get into relationships with black men because they think THE SEX IS GOING TO BE BETTER. (Rodman 1996: 142. Rodman's emphasis)

At first glance, one might think that the Fourteenth Amendment and the Civil Rights Act of 1866 prohibited antimiscegenation laws because they granted to blacks the legal prerogatives of whites. But this matter was litigated often, and for 84 years, the 1883 *Pace v. Alabama* (106 U.S. 583) ruling upheld a state's right to ban interracial marriages. Just after Reconstruction, Alabama's legislature passed a law prohibiting all fornication, but interracial fornication was more severely punished than fornication between individuals of the same race. The Supreme Court upheld this statute, claiming that it did not violate the Fourteenth Amendment because it applied equally to blacks and whites. Numerous challenges to antimiscegenation laws were turned back on this principle.

In the same year that Congress enacted the most encompassing civil rights act of this century—1964—the Supreme Court upheld a Florida law that prohibited unmarried interracial couples from living together but included no such ban on couples of the same race. The civil rights revolution eventually ended such prohibitions. In June 1958, a white Virginia man, Richard Loving, married a black Virginia woman, Mildred Jeter. Knowing that Virginia would not grant them a marriage license, they wed in the District of Columbia but later returned to Virginia. They were arrested, convicted, and sentenced to one year in jail. The merciful judge agreed to suspend their sentence if Richard Loving and Mildred Jeter would stay out of Virginia for 25 years. They moved to Washington, but in 1963, perhaps prompted by the racial ethos of that era, they filed a motion to vacate their conviction. The litigation percolated through federal courts for four years. The Supreme Court eventually ruled that Virginia's ban on interracial marriages involved an invidious racial classification prohibited by the Fourteenth Amendment, thereby invalidating laws that then remained on the books in fourteen states (*Loving v. Virginia* 1967; 388 U.S. 1).

Racial Intermarriage: What the Census Tells Us about Recent Trends

Censuses provide us with data about the race of spouses in married couples. Presumably this information is more accurate for recent counts, as forms are now filled out by the individuals enumerated, not by census takers.

Using these data, I classified husbands and wives into the following categories, categories I will call races, although the definition is social or statistical, not biological.

- Hispanic—These persons may be of any race, although 52% of them in 1990 said they were white by race, and another 47% wrote in a Spanish-origin term on the race question (such as Andalusian, Catalonian, or Nicaraguan).
- Non-Hispanic Whites—shown as whites in the figures
- Non-Hispanic Blacks—shown as blacks in the figures
- Non-Hispanic American Indians, including those few people identified as Aleut or Eskimo by race—shown as American Indians in the figures
- Non-Hispanic Asians and Pacific Islanders—shown as Asians in the figures

First-generation immigrants to the United States—those born abroad—are much more likely to marry within their racial group than are people born in the United States of immigrant parents. For that reason two of the tables separate the native- and foreign-born Hispanics and Asians. The census of 1990 reported that 40% of the Spanish-origin population and 67% of the Asian were born outside the United States.

This analysis is restricted to couples who were married and living together at the time of the census of 1990 or 1980. I use the term *marrying out* to refer to people who married outside their racial group. Asians and Hispanics are considered to have married within their own racial group when they married another Asian or Hispanic, be the spouse native-born or foreign-born.

Information from the census of 1990 was graphed in Figure 5.7, which shows substantial racial differences in out-marriage and suggests a trend toward more out-marriage. Individuals are classified by their age in 1990, that is, by their birth cohort. The panel to the left shows the percentage of husbands who married outside their group, and the panel to the right presents similar data for wives.

Those identifying themselves as American Indians are distinguished by their high rate of out-marriage. Even among the grandparents of the baby boomers—those born before World War I and typically marrying before World War II—the majority of American Indians entered interracial marriages. Note that these are cross-sectional data, and although most of the older population are now in marriages contracted decades ago, not all of them are, so caution is needed in interpreting changes in intermarriage rates from one period to the next.

Over time an increasingly large proportion of native-born Asians and native-

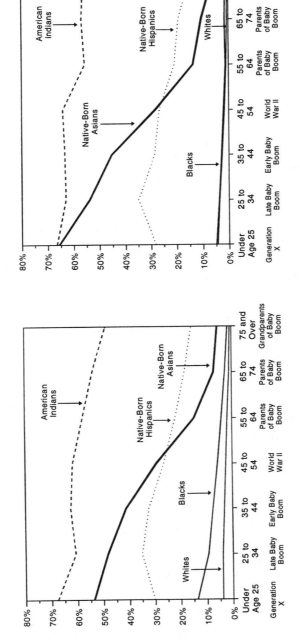

PERCENTAGE OF HUSBANDS MARRYING OUTSIDE THEIR RACE

PERCENTAGE OF WIVES MARRYING OUTSIDE THEIR RACE

FIGURE 5.7. Percentage of Husbands and Wives Who Married Outside Their Group, for Birth Cohorts

Source: U.S. Bureau of the Census, *Census of Population and Housing: 1990.* Public Use Microdata Sample.
Note: Native-born Hispanics who married foreign-born Hispanics and native-born Asians who married foreign-born Asians married within their group.

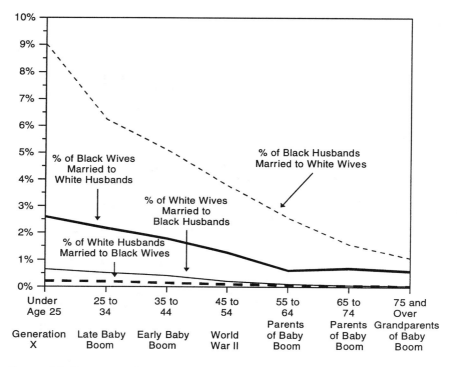

FIGURE 5.8. Percentage of Black and White Husbands and Wives Marrying Opposite Race: Black–White Comparison for Birth Cohorts

Source: U.S. Bureau of the Census, *Census of Population and Housing: 1990.* Public Use Microdata Sample.

born Hispanics have married outside their group. The majority of baby boom Asian women born in this country married non-Asian husbands; just about half of Asian men married Asian women, and the other half, non-Asian women.

Blacks and whites are distinguished by their relative low rates of intermarriage. Myrdal (1944: 55) observed that even in the North, where interracial marriage was not outlawed, it occurred rarely because mixed-race couples were punished by almost complete social ostracism. Perhaps fewer than 1% of whites and 2% of blacks who married before 1960 married outside their racial group (Myrdal 1944: 1208–9). Nevertheless, for both races there has been an increase in interracial marriage. More than 10% of the black men born after the start of the civil rights decade who marry will marry women who are not black, implying a substantial change from earlier periods when fewer than 2% of black men married out.

The type of interracial marriage most frequently prohibited involved blacks and whites. One of the important changes flowing from the shift in the racial paradigm after the civil rights revolution is a rise in the frequency with which blacks and whites marry. Trends over time are shown in Figure 5.8, again using information from the census of 1990, but this time restricted to marriages involving blacks and whites. Among the parents of baby boomers, fewer than 1% of black husbands married white wives, but among those most recently arriving at the typical ages of marriage—Generation X—more than 8% of black men married white wives. A similar, albeit slower, rise is shown in the percentage of black wives who married white husbands. These trends are consistent with Kalmijn's (1993) observation that black–white intermarriage increased rapidly after the Supreme Court lifted the ban.

This figure seems to suggest a fairly sharp rise in the proportion of blacks marrying whites but a more modest change in the proportion of whites marrying blacks. The relative size of the two populations comes into play. The number of black men marrying white wives necessarily equals the number of white women marrying black husbands. But a switch from 2% of black husbands marrying white wives to 8% shows up as a larger change in this figure for blacks than for whites because the black population is much smaller than the white population. The proportionate change over time in the rate of interracial marriage will be roughly the same for black men as for white women.

Appendix Table 1 shows the percentage who out-married for specific types of young—aged 25 to 34 in 1990—Latinos and Asians. Two-thirds of those who wrote "Spaniard" for Spanish origin married out, but among those who wrote the word "Hispanic," fewer than one-sixth married out. Among Asians, Filipinos were the most and Japanese the least likely to marry non-Asians.

Who Marries Whom?

Previous figures suggest a secular trend toward higher proportions of every racial group marrying out. Figure 5.9 and Table 5.2 give more detail about the specific types of marriages. In brief, marriages pairing Hispanics and whites or pairing American Indians and whites occur relatively frequently, but marriages where one spouse is white and the other black are still rare. These figures are based on married couples in which both spouses were between 25 and 34 years old in 1990, so with very few exceptions, these are marriages contracted during the 1980s.

As Figure 5.9 illustrates, whites and blacks have uniquely low rates of out-marriage. Young American Indians, on the other hand, married whites just about as often as they married other American Indians, and native-born Asian wives were just about as likely to marry white men as Asian men. (For a further analysis of racial intermarriage and the racial identity of children whose parents differ in race, see Harrison and Bennett 1995: fig. 4.4 and table 4.4.)

Figure 5.9 also implies that an assimilation process occurs across the generations, because the out-marriage rates for native-born Hispanics and native-born Asians are much higher than out-marriage rates for those born abroad. Nevertheless, foreign-born Hispanics and foreign-born Asians had higher out-marriage rates than whites or blacks.

Table 5.2 refers to young people who married in the 1980s and shows the racial distribution of spouses. For example, the first panel reports that 96% of

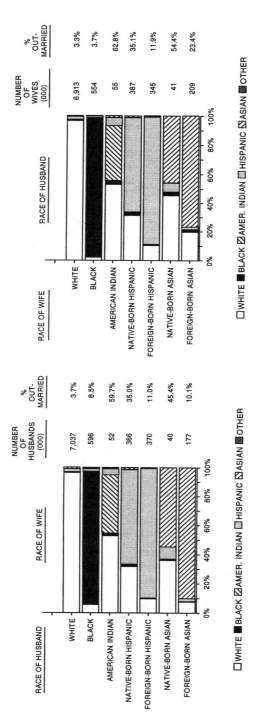

FIGURE 5.9. Race of Spouse for Married Persons Aged 25 to 34 in 1990

Source: U.S. Bureau of the Census, *Census of Population and Housing: 1990.* Public Use Microdata Sample.

Note: These data refer to people aged 25 to 34 in 1990 who were married-spouse-present at the time of the census. Thus almost all of them had married in the 1980s.

TABLE 5.2
Race of Wife by Race of Husband for Married Couples with Both Spouses Aged 25 to 34 in 1990, and Ratio of Actual Odds of Marrying Someone of a Specific Race to Expected Odds

	WHITE HUSBANDS		BLACK HUSBANDS		NATIVE-BORN HISPANIC HUSBANDS		NATIVE-BORN ASIAN HUSBANDS		AMERICAN INDIAN HUSBANDS	
	Race of Wife	Ratio of Actual to Expected Odds	Race of Wife	Ratio of Actual to Expected Odds	Race of Wife	Ratio of Actual to Expected Odds	Race of Wife	Ratio of Actual to Expected Odds	Race of Wife	Ratio of Actual to Expected Odds
White	96.3%	6.05	5.6%	0.01	31.7%	0.11	36.0%	0.13	52.9%	0.26
Black	0.2	0.02	91.6	154.23	1.2	0.18	0.6	0.09	1.6	0.24
Hispanic	2.2	0.24	1.7	0.19	65.1	19.75	8.4	0.97	4.2	0.46
Asian	0.9	0.29	0.8	0.26	1.3	0.44	54.7	36.86	1.0	0.33
American Indian	0.4	0.67	0.3	0.38	0.7	0.98	0.3	0.47	40.3	101.60

TABLE 5.2 (Continued)

	WHITE WIVES		BLACK WIVES		NATIVE-BORN HISPANIC WIVES		NATIVE-BORN ASIAN WIVES		AMERICAN INDIAN WIVES	
	Race of Husband	Ratio of Actual to Expected Odds	Race of Husband	Ratio of Actual to Expected Odds	Race of Husband	Ratio of Actual to Expected Odds	Race of Husband	Ratio of Actual to Expected Odds	Race of Husband	Ratio of Actual to Expected Odds
White	96.7%	6.55	2.2%	<.01	31.4%	0.10	45.1%	0.19	53.9%	0.26
Black	0.4	0.06	96.3	354.73	2.0	0.28	2.2	0.31	2.5	0.35
Hispanic	2.1	0.23	1.1	0.12	65.0	20.15	6.7	0.73	5.4	0.62
Asian	0.4	0.15	0.2	0.06	1.1	0.42	45.5	32.54	1.0	0.40
American Indian	0.4	0.65	0.2	0.26	0.5	0.82	0.5	0.75	37.2	96.63

Source: U.S. Bureau of the Census, Census of Population and Housing: 1990. Public Use Microdata Sample.

Note: The first column of percentages in each panel of data shows the racial distribution of spouses for the group identified in the heading above the columns. It sums to 100. The second column shows the ratio of the actual odds of marrying someone from a specific race to the expected odds. For example, 96.32 percent of white husbands aged 25 to 34 married white wives, meaning that the odds that a white husband married a white wife were 26.17:1. White wives made up 81.22 percent of all wives married to men aged 25 to 34, meaning that the expected odds of a white man marrying a white wife if race were of no import were 4.32:1. Thus the ratio of actual odds of marrying a white wife to expected odds were 6.05. Ratios of greater than unity indicate that marriages of the specific type occurred *more* frequently than expected were race to make no difference in the marriage market. Ratios of less than unity report that marriages of a specific type occurred *less* than expected were race to make no difference in the marriage market.

Nativity of spouse is not considered here. That is, native-born Asians married to foreign-born Asians are considered to be married to Asians.

white husbands married white wives, and just over 2% of white husbands married Hispanic women. The data should be read going down the columns. Looking at these data reveals a considerable degree of racial endogamy; for most groups, the modal spouse was from the same race. Young American Indians, however, were more likely to marry whites than were American Indians, and native-born Asian women married white men as often as they married Asian men.

As an index of the degree of exogamy, Table 5.2 also lists the ratio of actual odds of marrying a spouse from a specific race to the expected odds of marrying someone from that race, assuming that race made no difference in mate selection. Ninety-six percent of white men, for instance, married white wives, meaning that the odds that a white man would marry a white woman were roughly 24 to 1. But white women made up about 80% of the young women who married in the 1980s. If race made absolutely no difference in the marriage market, we might expect that only 80% of white husbands would marry white women, so the expected odds that a white husband would marry a white wife would be roughly 4 to 1. The ratio of actual odds, 24 to 1, to expected odds, 4 to 1, is shown in Table 5.2; that is, a relative odds ratio of roughly 6 to 1.

These odds ratios reveal a pattern of racial endogamy, but the extent of this varies by race. Blacks make up a rather small fraction of the population, so we would expect many blacks to marry spouses from other races, but out-marriage occurs much less frequently than expected. The ratio of actual to expected odds is very high for blacks marrying other blacks: a higher index of endogamy than for other races. Even though the majority of American Indians marry out, we would expect many more to do so in light of the very small size of the Indian population. Therefore, the ratios of actual to expected odds are very elevated for Indians. In some sense, racial endogamy is greatest for blacks and higher among Indians than among Asians, Hispanics, or whites.

These ratios also provide suggestive indicators of a racial order of the groups. Whites, for example, married Hispanics, Indians, and Asians less frequently than expected. Recall that the ratio of actual-to-expected odds would be 1.00 if whites married another group in proportion to their representation in the population. But white–black marriages occurred very seldom relative to expectations, that is, the relative odds ratio was exceptionally low for whites marrying blacks. And although blacks did not frequently marry Hispanics, Indians, or Asians, they married whites even less frequently, relative to what one might expect were race to have no salience. And, relative to what one might expect, Asians married Hispanics and Indians much more frequently than they married blacks or whites.

Determinants of Out-Marriage

Censuses provide information suggesting how marriage markets may be operating, but they do not allow us to model the mate selection process precisely. Presumably, individuals search for a spouse using a variety of techniques, but even in this era of "personals" advertisements in newspapers, most search-ing is likely done within a pool of friends, classmates, co-workers, or other potential partners well known to an individual or to his or her friends and relatives. Presumably, in the past many people decided that their search had to be exclusively within their own racial group, and undoubtedly many people still rule out all potential partners who differ in race or skin color.

When census data are examined, three demographic characteristics stand out for their strong link to out-marriage among those who married in the 1980s: educational attainment, place of residence, and military service. All these fac-tors tap some aspect of the pool of potential partners from which spouses are selected, but they may also indicate attitudes about willingness to cross the racial line when selecting a spouse.

Panels to the left in Figure 5.10 (see p. 118) refer to young husbands in four major racial groups: whites, blacks, native-born Hispanics, and native-born Asians. (The American Indian population is too small to permit similar anal-ysis.) The net effects of schooling are shown at the top of each panel as five educational levels. The bars represent net relative odds ratios resulting from a logistic regression equation with the odds of out-marriage as its dependent vari-able. The odds of out-marriage for a specific category of a variable are pre-sented relative to the odds for a baseline category: high school diploma as the baseline category for the educational variable, Midwest for place of residence, and no military service for the armed forces variable.

Consider the panel of data for young white husbands. Men with a postgradu-ate degree were about 1.2 times as likely to marry out as those with a high school diploma when the effects of place of residence and military service were controlled. White husbands living in California in 1990 were more than six times as likely to marry out as those in the Midwest, and those who served in the armed forces during the 1980s were 2.3 times as likely to marry out as those who had not served.

With regard to educational attainment, Figure 5.10 shows that white men with college or postgraduate degrees were somewhat more likely to marry out than those with high school educations, but among black husbands out-marriage increased sharply with education. This finding may reflect the pool of potential partners, as secondary schools are, for the most part, more thoroughly segre-gated than colleges or professional schools. Increases in education also go hand-in-hand with more liberal racial attitudes, including a greater willingness to date and marry across racial lines. Among Hispanic husbands, the positive link between education and out-marriage was even sharper than among blacks, but among native-born Asian men the reverse was true. In particular, Asian husbands with postgraduate degrees were least likely to marry non-Asians. This result may also reflect marriage pools, as it is likely that Asian men in profes-sional schools have a higher density of Asian classmates than do Asian men in high school. Asians constitute only 3% of the total population but 16% of the enrollment in the nation's graduate and professional schools. Appendix Table 2 reports the actual percentages who married out for men and women in each of the categories of the variables shown in Figure 5.10.

Racial intermarriage occurs more frequently in Pacific Rim states than in other parts of the nation, but the pattern varies by racial group. In this analysis, data are analyzed for eight geographic divisions and for California. Thus the odds ratios in these panels report the net likelihood of out-marriage relative to that for men in the Midwest.

Among white husbands, men living in California stood out for their elevated rates of out-marriage, whereas men in Alabama, Mississippi, and Tennessee—the East South Central states—rarely married out. The pool of potential black wives is large in those states, but centuries-old prohibitions may hold social power long after their legal power has died. The pattern was similar for black husbands, with those living in Mountain and Pacific states more than three times as likely to marry a nonblack as those living in the Midwest. These rates are strongly influenced by demographic patterns; the highest density of blacks is in the South Central states, and there the out-marriage rates of blacks were lowest. Similarly, among Asian husbands, the out-marriage rates were exceptionally low in the states with Pacific shores including Hawaii, the only state with an Asian majority—63 percent Asian in 1997. Asian men find it least challenging to search for Asian wives along the West Coast. Or, stated differently, if an Asian man in the Dakotas searches in the local marriage market, he will find few Asian women.

The U.S. military is the most racially integrated major employer and social institution in the country (Moskos and Butler 1996). It may also be the nation's leading matchmaker. The census reports that people who served in the armed forces were much more likely to marry outside their own racial group than those who did not. That is, the census ascertained whether a person had served in the military and, if so, when. Here we categorize persons by whether they served since 1980 and found that for all groups—except Asian husbands—military service had a strong net effect on interracial marriage. White and black husbands who served were more than twice as likely to marry out as white and black men who did not serve, net of schooling and place of residence. Presumably, the military presents young men and women with a pool of potential marriage partners that is much more racially diverse than the pools they find at home in high schools, churches, or workplaces. Additionally, the armed forces' emphasis on equal racial opportunity may subtly encourage young people to minimize race as a selection criterion when they enter the marriage market.

Similar data for wives are shown to the right in Figure 5.10. Educational attainment had the net effect of increasing the probability of out-marriage except for native-born Asians, but the effect was much stronger among blacks and Hispanics than among whites. The net effects of place of residence were also much the same among wives as among men. Net of other factors, white women in California were more than six times as likely to marry nonwhites as white women living in the Midwest. At the other extreme were the low relative odds

INFORMATION ABOUT WIVES

INFORMATION ABOUT HUSBANDS

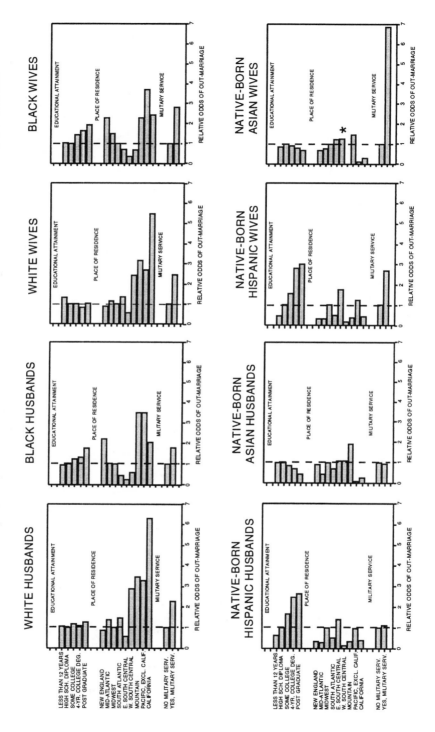

WHITE HUSBANDS

BLACK HUSBANDS

WHITE WIVES

BLACK WIVES

NATIVE-BORN HISPANIC HUSBANDS

NATIVE-BORN ASIAN HUSBANDS

NATIVE-BORN HISPANIC WIVES

NATIVE-BORN ASIAN WIVES

EDUCATIONAL ATTAINMENT
- LESS THAN 12 YEARS
- HIGH SCH. DIPLOMA
- SOME COLLEGE
- 4-YR. COLLEGE DEG.
- POST GRADUATE

PLACE OF RESIDENCE
- NEW ENGLAND
- MID-ATLANTIC
- MIDWEST
- SOUTH ATLANTIC
- E. SOUTH CENTRAL
- W. SOUTH CENTRAL
- MOUNTAIN
- PACIFIC, EXCL. CALIF.
- CALIFORNIA

MILITARY SERVICE
- NO MILITARY SERV.
- YES, MILITARY SERV.

RELATIVE ODDS OF OUT-MARRIAGE

FIGURE 5.10. Relative Odds Ratios Showing Net Effects of Educational Attainment, Place of Residence, and Military Service on Likelihood of Marrying Outside One's Racial Group; Husbands and Wives Aged 25 to 34 in 1990

Source: U.S. Bureau of the Census, *Census of Population and Housing: 1990.* Public Use Microdata Sample.

Note: This figure shows net effects parameters from a logistic regression model with the odds of marrying out of one's racial group as the dependent variable and categorical variables measuring educational attainment, place of residence in 1990, and military service since 1980 as independent variables. Separate models were run for each of the four racial groups. Native-born Hispanics and native-born Asians marrying foreign-born persons of the same group were considered as marrying within their racial group. The percentages of spouses marrying outside their race for this age group in 1990 were as follows:

White husbands:	3.7%	White wives:	3.5%
Black husbands:	8.5%	Black wives:	8.4%
Native-born Hispanic husbands:	35.0%	Native-born Hispanic wives:	34.5%
Native-born Asian husbands:	45.4%	Native-born Asian wives:	44.0%

The baseline groups for the relative odds comparisons were high school for educational attainment, Midwest for region, and no military service.

*Not ascertained because of the small number of native-born Asian women living in West South Central states.

ratios for Hispanics in the West South Central states—that is, Hispanic women in Texas could easily select mates from the large pool of Hispanic men in the Lone Star state, just as Asian women along the Pacific Rim had a relatively large pool of potential Asian husbands. And women who served in the military, like men, were very much more likely to marry someone from another race.

Determinants of White–Black Intermarriage

Educational attainment, place of residence, and military service are linked to the rates at which America's racial groups out-marry, perhaps by defining the pool from which mates are selected. Black–white marriages have been the most censured by law and social custom. Do those same demographic characteristics influence the likelihood that blacks and whites will marry each other?

Figure 5.11 uses a familiar format to demonstrate the net effects of education, place of residence, and military service on black–white marriages, once again focusing on couples who married in the 1980s. Turning first to white men who married black wives—and only 2 white husbands per 1000 did so—we find that increases in education were generally matched by increases in the likelihood of marrying an African American: college men were more likely to marry black women than were high school graduates. White men with post-graduate degrees were less likely to do so than men with four-year degrees, perhaps reflecting the racial composition of those who now attend graduate or professional schools.

White men living along Pacific shores were much more likely to marry black wives than those living elsewhere, and, as we expected, military service in the 1980s greatly increased the probability that white husbands would marry black wives. Men who served in the armed forces were two and a half times as likely to marry a black woman as men who had never served.

The percentage of black men marrying white wives is much higher than the percentage of white men marrying black wives; that is, 56 African American husbands per 1000 had white spouses. The effects of education are strong for black men; more years of schooling had the clear net effect of increasing the likelihood of marrying a white woman, presumably reflecting both racial attitudes and the racial composition of the pool from which highly educated African American men find wives. Place of residence and military service had net effects for black men similar to those they had for whites.

The lower panels in Figure 5.11 present similar information for white and black wives. White women are distinguished for the small effect education had on their net likelihood of marrying a black man. There is little evidence that advanced education is associated with an increased probability of marrying black husbands. Whether this finding indicates something about the interaction of racial attitudes, racial preferences, and gender or reflects the demographic composition of the pool of potential spouses for highly educated white women is not clear from these data. White women who continue their education beyond a bachelor's degree will likely attend class more frequently with Asian than

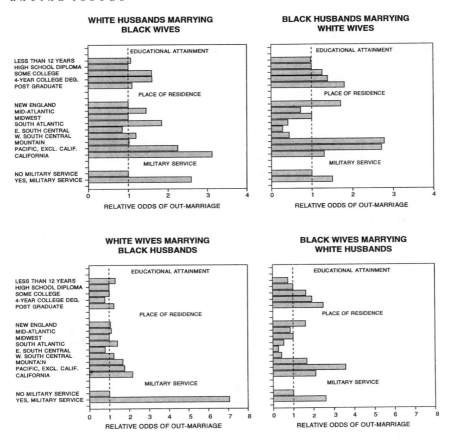

FIGURE 5.11. Relative Odds Ratios Showing Net Effects of Educational Attainment, Place of Residence, and Military Service on Likelihood of Blacks Marrying Whites and Whites Marrying Blacks; Married Persons Aged 25 to 34 in 1990

Source: U.S. Bureau of the Census, *Census of Population and Housing: 1990.* Public Use Microdata Sample.

Note: This figure reports relative odds ratios showing the net effects of educational attainment, place of residence in 1990, and military service since 1980 on the odds of a white man marrying a black wife and a black man marrying a white wife. Similar data are shown for wives. These models are limited to men aged 25 to 34 in 1990. The percentage of white husbands married to black women was 0.2; that is 2 per 1000. The percentage of black husbands married to white women was 5.6%. The percentage of white wives married to black husbands was 0.4; that is, 4 per 1000. The percentage of black wives married to white husbands was 2.2%.

with black men, as Asian men account for 19% of male enrollment in graduate and professional schools, black men only 6%. The pool of potential African American husbands for highly educated white women may be small. Place of residence and military service had the expected net consequences for white women. Indeed, white women who served in the armed forces in the 1980s and then married were seven times as likely to have African American husbands as those who had no military service.

For black women, increased educational attainment was linked to interracial marriage. Those with postgraduate training were about three times as likely to marry white men as those who stopped with a high school diploma. Region had a net effect, with black women in the South—where the density of blacks is greatest—least likely to marry white husbands. And, just as for white women, serving in the military had a large net effect on the likelihood of out-marriage, in this case the marriage of a black woman to a white man. *The net effects of military service on interracial marriage are larger for women than for men.*

A Summary of Findings about Interracial Marriage

The census of 1990 allows us to draw several conclusions about contemporary racial intermarriage.

First, when the adult population is divided into five racial groups (whites, blacks, American Indians, native-born Asians, and native-born Hispanics) we find large differences in rates of intermarriage. A majority of American Indians have married outside their racial group throughout this century. In recent years, a majority of native-born Asians have also married outside their racial group, but out-marriage occurs much less frequently among blacks and whites.

Second, over time there have been increases in the proportion who marry out for all five racial groups and for both men and women. In particular, the proportion of blacks who marry whites and whites who marry blacks has gone up since the civil rights revolution (Kalmijn 1993).

Third, gender makes a difference in rates of out-marriage. Native-born Asian women in recent years have out-married at a higher rate than native-born Asian men, but the out-marriage rate is substantially higher for African American men than for African American women.

Fourth, there are important regional and educational attainment differences in out-marriage. Out-marriage occurs with greater frequency in California and Hawaii than in other states. And for many groups, especially for black men, out-marriage is strongly linked to educational attainment. This analysis is unable to determine whether these differences result from differences in racial attitudes and the willingness to cross racial lines or if they come about because of demographic differences in the pools of potential marital partners.

Fifth, recent service in the armed forces greatly increased the likelihood that men and women in every racial group would marry outside their own racial group. Net of other characteristics, white men who served in the military were about three times as likely to marry black wives as white men who had never

served. White women with armed forces experience were seven times as likely
to marry black husbands as white women with no military service.

CONCLUSION

The ancestors of today's African Americans were forcefully included in the
colonies because of the low cost and self-replacing labor they supplied to European settlers. The first Asians were also included to meet a need for labor,
namely, contract laborers were imported from south China to build the railroad
east from Sacramento across the Sierra Nevada. But after arriving in America,
racial minorities found themselves excluded from political opportunities and
denied the legal rights and economic options granted to whites. The laws cited
in this paper prevented interracial marriage, thereby helping to preserve the
racial caste system. Two centuries later, when blacks began moving to cities in
large numbers—in the South this was around the turn of this century and in the
North at the time of World War I—a new system of residential exclusion developed. By the third decade of this century, all cities with numerous black and
white residents had Jim Crow neighborhoods along with their progeny, Jim
Crow schools.

The civil rights revolution of the 1960s sought to overturn the traditional
denial of opportunities to minorities with the encompassing law of 1964 banning discrimination in the labor market and specifying that race could no longer
be used to discriminate in public accommodations. The Voting Rights Act of
the next year sought to overturn the exclusion of blacks from polling stations in
the South, and the Fair Housing Act of 1968 provided racial minorities, in
theory, with the same opportunities in the housing market as whites—a change
some presumed would be followed by the gradual disappearance of Jim Crow
neighborhoods and schools. The denial of the right to marry whomever one
chose was among the last of the exclusionary prohibitions overturned by the
Supreme Court.

Although black–white gaps on most indicators of economic status changed
little after 1973, there is evidence from the 1980s of a diminution of the exclusion of blacks from white neighborhoods and from marrying whites. There was
a pervasive pattern of modest decreases in black–white residential segregation,
with larger declines recorded in southern and western metropolises, in those
that grew rapidly, and in those specializing in governmental, university, or military employment (Farley and Frey 1994). Although the American apartheid
system is not disappearing, the 1980s were the first years in which there were
unambiguous decreases in black–white residential segregation. The new pattern
of migration may hasten declines as blacks move away from the most highly
segregated older industrial metropolises and into the less segregated booming
metropolises of the South and West.

When describing a model of racial assimilation that would eventually characterize the United States, Robert Park (1914) argued:

There is a process that goes on in society by which individuals spontaneously acquire one another's language, characteristic attitudes, habits, and modes of behavior. There is also a process by which individuals and groups of individuals are taken over and incorporated into larger groups. Both processes have been concerned in the formation of modern nationalities. The modern Italian, Frenchman, and German is a composite of the broken fragments of several different racial groups. Interbreeding has broken up the ancient stocks, and interaction and imitation have created new national types which exhibit definite uniformities in language, manners, and formal behavior.

We no longer think of the Anglos and the Saxons; we think of English. We no longer speak of Ligurians, the Piedmontese, and Sicilians; we speak of the Italians. Are we now witnessing a process of assimilation as a result of increasing rates of racial exogamy in the marriage market? Will the American Indian population become increasingly difficult to identify as the majority of young American Indians marry spouses from other races? In the short run, the Asian population will continue to grow very rapidly thanks to immigration, but in the longer run, will the future descendants of Asians identify themselves merely as Americans because such a high proportion of young Asians marry outside their race? And though black–white intermarriage remains rare, the change in its frequency since the civil rights revolution seems substantial. At present, perhaps 10% of young black men marry nonblacks, and perhaps 5 or 6% violate the social norm that Myrdal perceived as the bulwark for our racial caste system by marrying white women. Will part of the solution to the continuing problem of black–white racial confrontations and hostility—perhaps a major part of the solution—be the emergence of a racially mixed population resulting from the now more frequent marriages of blacks and whites?

APPENDIX TABLE 1

Percentage of Husbands and Wives Out-Marrying for Specific Groups of Native-Born Spanish-Origin and Asian Persons Identified on the Census of 1990; Husbands and Wives Aged 25 to 34

	Percent of Husbands Out-marrying	Percent of Wives Out-marrying
MAJOR SPANISH-ORIGIN GROUPS		
Spanish-Origin Group		
Spaniard*	65	66
Columbian*	60	54
Cuban	57	52
Spanish*	53	53
Other Spanish Not Specified	41	41
Mexican*	33	35
Dominican*	33	25
Mexican American*	27	21
Mexican	27	27
Puerto Rican*	27	26
Puerto Rican	23	22
Spanish American*	18	22
Hispanic*	15	18
MAJOR ASIAN AND PACIFIC ISLANDER GROUPS		
Asian or Pacific Islander Group		
Filipino	57	51
Guamanian	56	46
Korean	52	36
Hawaiian	50	50
Chinese	36	29
Samoan	35	34
Asian Indian	30	44
Japanese	26	20

Source: U.S. Bureau of the Census, *Census of Population and Housing: 1990*. Public Use Microdata Files.

Note: This analysis is limited to groups in which there were 2500 or more native-born husbands and 2500 or more native-born wives aged 25 to 34 in the census of 1990. Out-marriage refers to marrying a non-Spanish-origin person for Hispanics, and marrying a non-Asian for Asians. Nativity of spouse is not considered.

*These are terms indicating a Spanish-origin written on the census enumeration form by the respondent. The other Spanish-origin terms appeared on the census enumeration form as a circle the respondent might check.

APPENDIX TABLE 2

Percentage of Men and Women 25 to 34 in 1990 Out-Married by Education, Place of Residence, and Military Service

	White		Black		American Indian		Native-Born Hispanic		Foreign-Born Hispanic		Native-Born Asian		Foreign-Born Asian	
	Men	Women	Men	Women	Men	Women	Men	Women	Men	Women	Men	Women	Men	Women
Total	4%	3%	8%	4%	60%	63%	35%	35%	11%	12%	45%	54%	10%	23%
					EDUCATIONAL ATTAINMENT									
< 12 Years	3%	4%	6%	3%	50%	52%	21%	18%	5%	3%	47%	50%	5%	20%
12 Years	3	3	7	3	57	61	31	31	12	14	46	54	9	32
Some College	4	4	10	4	66	66	42	42	20	25	47	53	16	30
College, 4 Years	4	3	10	5	76	78	52	56	32	35	45	55	11	18
College, > 4 Years	4	3	13	6	70	81	56	57	25	28	38	58	7	15
					PLACE OF RESIDENCE									
New England	2%	2%	19%	8%	90%	86%	34%	31%	23%	28%	68%	72%	10%	25%
Middle Atlantic	3	2	10	5	70	70	31	32	14	17	52	74	6	14
Midwest	2	2	10	4	72	75	61	58	18	17	74	80	12	23
South Atlantic	3	3	5	3	62	63	49	46	21	21	67	84	13	36
East South Central	1	1	3	1	75	71	71	72	64	62	79	100	18	45
West South Central	5	5	6	2	67	69	18	21	7	8	76	83	13	29
Mountain	7	6	30	9	24	31	34	34	13	14	86	87	19	43
Pacific, Excluding California	6	5	32	14	62	70	61	62	28	25	25	32	16	35
California	12	10	20	9	84	85	39	38	6	7	44	53	8	18
					MILITARY SERVICE AFTER 1980									
Yes, in Military	8%	9%	14%	10%	76%	81%	43%	66%	33%	51%	51%	92%	24%	75%
No Military Service	3	3	7	3	58	62	34	35	10	11	45	54	10	23

Source: U.S. Bureau of the Census, *Census of Population and Housing: 1990. Public Use Microdata Sample.*

REFERENCES

Canot, Robert. 1974. *American Odyssey*. New York: Bantam.

Cash, Wilbur Joseph. 1941. *The Mind of the South*. New York: A. A. Knopf.

Chen, Susheng. 1991. *Asian Americans: An Interpretive History*. Boston: Twayne Publishers.

Chicago Commission on Race Relations. 1922. *The Negro in Chicago: A Study of Race Relations and a Race Riot*. Chicago: University of Chicago Press.

Committee on Civil Rights. 1947. *To Secure These Rights: Report of the Committee on Civil Rights*. Washington, D. C.: Government Printing Office.

Cox, Oliver C. 1948. *Caste, Class and Race*. New York: Modern Reader Paperbacks.

Farley, Reynolds, Howard Schuman, Suzanne Bianchi, Diane Colasanto, and Shirley Hatchett. 1978. "Chocolate City, Vanilla Suburbs: Will the Trend Toward Racially Separate Communities Continue?" *Social Science Research* 7: 319–44.

Farley, Reynolds, and William H. Frey. 1994. "Changes in the Segregation of Whites from Blacks during the 1980s: Small Steps toward a More Integrated Society." *American Sociological Review* 59(1) (February): 23–45.

Frey, William H., and Reynolds Farley. 1996. "Latino, Asian, and Black Segregation in U. S. Metropolitan Areas: Are Multi-Ethnic Areas Different?" *Demography* 33(1): 58–99.

Good, David L. 1989. *Orvie: The Dictator of Dearborn. The Rise and Reign of Orville L. Hubbard*. Detroit, Mich.: Wayne State University.

Harrison, Roderick, and Claudette Bennett. 1995. "Racial and Ethnic Diversity." Pp. 141–210 in *State of the Union: America in the 1990s*. Vol. 2, edited by Reynolds Farley. New York: Russell Sage.

Herrnstein, Richard J., and Charles Murray. 1994. *The Bell Curve: Intelligence and Class Structure in American Life*. New York: The Free Press.

Hirsch, Arnold R. 1983. *Making the Second Ghetto: Race and Housing in Chicago: 1940–1960*. Chicago: University of Chicago Press.

Jackson, Kenneth T. 1985. *Crabgrass Frontier: The Suburbanization of the United States*. New York: Oxford University Press.

Johnson, Charles S. 1943. *Patterns of Negro Segregation*. New York: Harper.

Jordan, Winthrop P. 1968. *White over Black: American Attitudes toward the Negro: 1550–1812*. Chapel Hill: University of North Carolina Press.

Kalmijn, Matthijs. 1993. "Trends in Black/White Intermarriage," *Social Forces* 72(1) (September): 119–46.

Litwack, Leon F. 1961. *North of Slavery: The Negro in the Free States, 1790–1860*. Chicago: University of Chicago Press.

Massey, Douglas, and Nancy A. Denton. 1993. *American Apartheid: Segregation and the Making of the Underclass*. Cambridge: Harvard University Press.

Moskos, Charles C., and John Sibley Butler. 1996. *All That We Can Be: Black Leadership and Racial Integration the Army Way*. New York: Basic Books.

Myrdal, Gunnar. 1944. *An American Dilemma: The Negro Problem and Modern Democracy*. New York: Harper and Row.

National Opinion Research Center. 1996. *General Social Surveys, 1972–1996: Cumulative Codebook*. Chicago: University of Chicago National Opinion Research Center.

Park, Robert E. 1914. "Racial Assimilation in Secondary Groups with Particular Reference To the Negro." *American Journal of Sociology* 19 (March): 606–23.

Rainwater, Lee. 1970. *Behind Ghetto Walls: Black Family Life in a Federal Slum*. Chicago: Aldine.

Rodman, Dennis. 1996. *Bad as I Wanna Be*. New York: Delacorte Press.

Schuman, Howard, Charlotte Steeh, Lawrence Bobo, and Maria Krysan. 1997. *Racial Attitudes in America. Trends and Interpretations*, rev. ed. Cambridge: Harvard University Press.

U.S. Bureau of the Census. 1918. *Negro Population in the United States: 1790–1915*. Washington, D.C.: GPO.

—————. 1993. *Census of Population and Housing: 1990*. Public Use Microdata Sample.

—————. 1993. Current Population Survey, March. Public Use Microdata Sample.

—————. 1995. *Current Population Reports*. Series P-6, no. 188 (February).

—————. 1998. *Current Population Reports*. Series P-60, no. 200.

U.S. National Center for Education Statistics. 1995. *Digest of Education Statistics: 1995*.

Yinger, John. 1995. *Closed Doors, Opportunities Lost: The Continuing Costs of Housing Discrimination*. New York: Russell Sage Foundation.

CHAPTER SIX

Immigration, Opportunity, and Social Cohesion

MARTA TIENDA

INTRODUCTION

To MOST IMMIGRANTS, the United States represents a meritocracy, where as-cribed characteristics, such as birthplace, race, or national origin, are irrelevant for social position. This presumes that on admission all newcomers can com-pete fairly for social and economic rewards, and that opportunities are roughly equivalent, if not identical, for immigrants and the native-born. This was cer-tainly the social mood of the 1960s, when it appeared that equal opportunity was a realistic goal; that social mobility and comfortable lifestyles were possi-ble for all who put forth reasonable effort; and that both the War on Poverty and the civil rights movement would yield high social dividends toward the twin goals of reducing inequality and promoting racial and ethnic integration.

But times have changed. Recent social indicators and new social welfare legislation suggest that, as a society, the United States has drifted away from commitments to equal opportunity professed during the 1960s. Racial and eth-nic inequality has been rising, support for affirmative action has been eroding, and anti-immigrant sentiment has been intensifying. Although not unprece-dented, the most recent upsurge in immigrant-bashing is problematic for social cohesion because the underlying rejection is tied to legislation that denies the privileges of citizenship and legal resident status retrospectively; because chil-dren of immigrants have become the targets of exclusion from opportunities that permit, if not guarantee, social mobility; and because future economic op-portunities will favor those from advantaged family backgrounds even more so than in the past (Mare 1995; Farley 1996). Unskilled recent immigrants will confront particularly harsh economic futures if the social climate toward immi-grants continues to erode as their numbers increase, particularly in selected high-immigrant-receiving destinations.

Hindsight reveals that several undercurrents began to thwart the engines of economic growth after 1973 in ways that would threaten and even undermine the social and economic gains achieved during the 1960s. These include: (1) a gradual rise in wage inequality driven by the fall in demand for unskilled labor; (2) changes in the international competitiveness of U.S.-produced goods; and (3) rising income returns for higher education, which widened the wage gap between high-school- and college-educated workers (Danziger and Gottschalk 1993, 1995; Farley 1996). In addition, several demographic trends contributed to economic inequality by operating on labor supply: (1) a dramatic rise in female employment since 1960, which was accompanied by a gradual drop in men's labor force participation; (2) the entry of the baby boom cohort into the labor market; and (3) substantial growth in the volume and diversity of immigrants seeking work in the United States (Chiswick and Sullivan 1995; Farley 1996). In other words, after 1973, economic and demographic trends evolved in ways that maintained or exacerbated inequality, despite the fact that average levels of education rose and differentials in schooling levels narrowed for many demographic groups (Mare 1995).

Against this backdrop I submit that immigration will pose new challenges for the future contours of inequality, and thereby social cohesion, for several reasons. First, changes in the race and ethnic composition of immigrant cohorts since 1960 have favored Asian and Latin American source countries, visibly altering the racial and ethnic landscape of the United States. Second, immigrants are residentially concentrated in a few states. Concentration heightens their visibility and, more important, creates a distributional "problem" between their (federal) tax contributions and their (state and local) social consumption costs. Third, large shares of recent immigrants are unskilled, so they are in direct competition with other disadvantaged population groups, notably women and minorities, but also immigrants who arrived in earlier times. Fourth, highly educated Asian immigrants have fostered resentment among native-born populations who feel "crowded out" of their own social hierarchies (especially higher education). Fifth, rising shares of immigrants from non-English-speaking countries have accentuated divisions between native- and foreign-born residents, fueling old tensions about the merits of Anglo conformity assimilation versus cultural pluralism. Finally, distorted public perceptions about the racial and ethnic diversity of the U.S. population exaggerate the demographic, economic, and social impacts of immigration (both legal and illegal flows).

To develop these arguments, I first provide a brief substantive and historical background by outlining recent trends in the volume and composition of immigration and mapping these against trends in economic inequality. I argue that public tolerance for diversity is waning relative to the 1960s partly in response to misperceptions about the economic consequences of immigration. Finally, I consider how immigration threatens the value of equal opportunity as a societal goal. My general thesis is that in the current economic and political environment, the volume and diversity of recent immigrant streams challenge social cohesion by deepening and reinforcing distinctions among the social contracts of citizens, legal residents, and illegal residents; by tightening the link between group membership and social standing; and ultimately by undermining the social commitment to equal opportunity. In part, social cohesion is challenged because the tolerable limits and dimensions of inequality have never been clearly defined nor divorced from macroeconomic trends; because the commitment to equality and democratic ideals has always been highly contingent on economic and political interests; and because color has always circumscribed social and economic opportunity in the United States.

OLD GAME, NEW RULES

Three sets of circumstances are pertinent to understanding how contemporary immigration undermines social cohesion. First, immigrants have changed. Not only have the ethnic origins of recent immigrants shifted toward Asia and Latin America, away from their historically (white) European origin countries, but so too has the education (skill) composition of new arrivals shifted relative to the host society. Recent cohorts exhibit a close correspondence between region of origin and educational attainment, with the most educated immigrants arriving from Asian, African, and European countries, and the least educated from Latin America. Trends in the education and national origin composition of recent arrivals are germane for appreciating how the "new" immigration strains social cohesion because they define the association between group membership and socioeconomic inequality over time.

Second, opportunities for earning a living and for achieving upward mobility have changed dramatically over the past quarter century. Compared with demands for unskilled labor in prior eras of heavy immigration (most notably at the turn of the century), the current needs have been shrinking. These changes in economic opportunities are important not only for immigrants, who historically have occupied low-status positions as a way of gaining a foothold in the U.S. economy, but also for unskilled U.S. natives, who have experienced diminished income and employment opportunities precisely at a time that immigration flows have expanded.

Third, U.S. reception factors have changed. The 1980s and 1990s represent a period of national retrenchment in social obligations to U.S. citizens, but even more so to immigrants. This is evident in the term limits on welfare benefits included in recent welfare reform legislation, the exclusion of legal immigrants from access to means-tested health benefits and income transfers, and the provisions of the antiterrorist legislation authorizing deportation of legal immigrants ever convicted of a felony. Anti-immigrant hostility has been fueled by political scapegoating that often blames immigrants for the declining fortunes of U.S. citizens. The growing consensus that immigrants are a net benefit to the U.S. economy becomes meaningless when public perceptions and media messages convey the opposite. Next, I elaborate each of these master trends and indicate how each bears on questions of social cohesion amid growing diversity and rising inequality.

The Changing Face of Immigration

Changes in the volume and composition of U.S. immigrants since 1960 are well documented (Tienda and Liang 1994; Rumbaút 1996), hence the salient contours should suffice to frame a discussion of how immigration challenges or promotes social cohesion. First, in 1990 the foreign-born population numbered just under 20 million, making the United States host to the largest immigrant population in the world (Rumbaút 1996). In relative terms, immigrants composed approximately 8% of the 1990 U.S. population, far below the historic high of nearly 15% foreign-born enumerated in 1910. Nevertheless, the residential concentration of immigrants in just a few states, and especially in a few large cities, heightens their visibility and makes diversity potentially problematic.

Although immigrants are found in all 50 states, the vast majority reside in six: California, Texas, New York, New Jersey, Florida, and Illinois. California, the state where most of the recent anti-immigrant (and anti-affirmative action) legislation was initiated, housed nearly one-third of the 1990 foreign-born population, compared with 19% for New York and New Jersey combined, and 8% for Florida.

Spatial distribution of immigrants has important implications for social cohesion because it heightens awareness of differences while *potentially* slowing the process of cultural and social integration. It is unclear to what extent immigrants' residential segregation results from socioeconomic exclusion and to what extent it results from the emergence of ports of entry that allow newcomers to begin their adjustment in somewhat familiar environs. Nevertheless, spatial concentration of linguistically, racially, and ethnically diverse populations provides the demographic foundation for social cleavages; direct competition for scarce resources (especially jobs) determines whether and how the fault lines will break. Not only is the residential concentration of contemporary immigrants unusually high by historical standards, but the past confirms that concentrated visibility can be and has been associated with rising ethnic tensions (Higham, ch. 3).

Second, the volume of immigration rose appreciably during the period of moderating income inequality, from 1 million during the decade of the 1940s (of whom more than 85% arrived following the war's end), to 2.5 million during the 1950s, and in excess of 3.3 million during the 1960s. Legal immigration reached 4.5 million during the 1970s, and 7.4 million during the 1980s. The latter cohort rivaled the 1900 cohort of 8.8 million.[1]

That two-fifths (44%) of the foreign-born population enumerated in the 1990 census arrived during the 1980s is relevant for questions about how immigration strains social cohesion, because the "diversification" of the U.S. population appears to be *temporally* as well as *spatially* concentrated, and because the rise in immigration coincided with a period of widening wage and income inequality. Thus the coincidence of two trends—growing income inequality and rising immigration—has fostered (or reinforced) beliefs (fueled by the popular media) that immigration is at least partly responsible for the declining economic fortunes of native citizens.

A third feature of contemporary U.S. immigration that has direct implications for social cohesion and the long-term integration prospects of the foreign-born is the great diversity of recent cohorts in legal status, national origins, educational attainment at the time of arrival, and gender and age composition. Although contemporary U.S. immigrant cohorts represent over 140 different countries, *two-thirds of all immigrants originate in just 13 nations* (Rumbaút 1996: 28). The primacy of Mexicans among U.S. immigrants is evident in both stock and flow statistics. Mexican immigrants account for approximately 22% of the foreign-born population (stock) enumerated in 1990, and nearly one-quarter of all immigrants admitted (flow) during the past two decades. Moreover, they are highly concentrated in California, and to a lesser extent in Texas and Illinois. Filipinos are the second most numerous immigrant group, but they composed less than 5% of the 1990 foreign-born population. They, too, are residentially concentrated in California.

Had the structural relationship between productivity and income growth after 1945 remained unchanged after 1973, the gradual increase in the ethnic diversity of the U.S. population might have gone unperceived, whether it stemmed from natural increase or immigration. Unfortunately for the large number of citizens and legal resident aliens who lack training beyond high school, either because they could not afford college during adolescence or young adulthood, or because they made schooling investment decisions when the premium to postsecondary schooling was low, the future looks quite bleak. For all U.S. residents who left school before or just after completing high school, the rules for securing economic rewards were changed in the middle of the game.

The educational composition of recent immigrant cohorts acquires heightened importance for understanding future social and economic prospects because, more than any single attribute, it sets the ceiling for rates of social mobility within and between generations (Mare 1995). Although average educational levels of specific groups have changed very little, shifts in the source countries of recent immigrants have altered the aggregate educational composition of the foreign-born (Chiswick and Sullivan 1995: table 5.6). But average trends conceal as much as they reveal, because recent cohorts are educationally bifurcated by national origins. The educational distribution of the foreign-born population is bimodal, with highly educated immigrants from Asia, Africa, and Europe in one mode, and unskilled immigrants from Central and South America in another mode.[2] About 60% of immigrants from Mexico completed less than eight years of graded schooling, contrasted with Asian immigrants, whose educational attainment at the time of arrival is relatively high. Nearly two-thirds of Asian immigrants completed twelve to sixteen years of graded schooling, and an additional 15% completed postcollege education; overall, Asians compare favorably with U.S. natives in educational attainment, but less so in income attainment. The bifurcated ethnic and skill distribution could encourage social cohesion if skill groups become complements in production, and race/ethnic background does not become a source of division. Alternatively, the skill distribution could become the edifice on which interethnic tensions are predicated, especially if the high residential concentration levels characteristic of contemporary immigration persist—that is, if geographic mobility precludes social mobility and vice versa.

The large influx of poorly educated immigrants during the 1970s and 1980s, although not historically unprecedented, is important for appreciating the contemporary backlash against immigrants for at least two reasons. First, it under-scores the importance of evaluating differences in *relative* terms. It bears em-phasizing that the relevant comparison is not with the waves of immigrants who arrived at the turn of the century, when opportunities for earning a living were much different, but rather with the native-born and earlier immigrants with whom new arrivals will compete for social and economic rewards. Second, the educational composition of contemporary immigration brings into focus the changing terms of competition along skill lines (Danziger and Gottschalk 1993). Historically, a seemingly bottomless pool of low-wage jobs gave immi-grants a foothold in the U.S. economy. At the turn of the century, geographic and social mobility were inextricably linked to the ideology of nationalism (Higham, ch. 3 in this vol.). This era has clearly passed. Moreover, as the demand for unskilled labor has shrunk, as it has since the mid-1970s, the lowest steps of the social escalator have become more crowded. Thus it is not only the absolute size and high residential concentration of the most recent immigrant cohorts that will shape their short- and long-term prospects for economic mo-bility and social integration but also the skill composition of recent cohorts relative to the demand for unskilled labor in the United States. In other words, not only did immigrants change, but so too did opportunities for earning a living, as I elaborate next.

Changes in Opportunities for Earning a Living

According to Frank Levy (1995), U.S. economic history since World War II can be divided into four periods: (1) 1947–1973 represents a quarter century of sustained earnings growth and moderating income inequality; (2) 1974–1979 marks a transition period when earnings growth slowed and income inequality began to rise; (3) the 1980s were a period of rising income inequal-ity coupled with slow earnings growth; and (4) the 1990s opened with a re-cession in which job losses and wage declines extended to white-collar work-ers, particularly older, college-educated men. Since 1993, leading economic indicators have been more encouraging, but the demand for unskilled workers has not increased. Analysts of rising inequality generally agree that industrial restructuring in response to declining international productivity was largely responsible for the wage erosion of unskilled workers; unionization, immigra-tion, and international trade played minor roles (Murphy and Welch 1993; Freeman 1993).[3]

These macrostructural trends in the demand for skilled and unskilled labor have direct implications for the integration prospects of immigrants because they denote very different opportunities for economic mobility and social inte-gration even if the ethnic, racial, and skill composition of the foreign-born population had remained unchanged. In the main, nativity dimensions of rising inequality have been subsumed under the broad rubric of skill groups. For ex-ample, Blackburn, Bloom, and Freeman's (1990) analysis of declining earnings among less educated men is confined to whites. Burtless (1990) analyzed unemployment effects on earnings inequality, paying special attention to the influence of the large baby boom generation on unemployment and wage rates but little mind to the coterminous growth of immigration and female labor force participation during the period when the baby boomers entered the labor market.

Analyses conducted by minority scholars (e.g., Mincy 1990 and Enchautegui 1992) at the mainstream research institutes, and a few mainstream scholars, emphasize the racial and ethnic underpinnings of inequality but seldom include comparisons of the native- and foreign-born. Karoly's (1993) study of trends in inequality among families, individuals, and workers ponders a broad spectrum of race and ethnic differences but does not dwell on the economic prospects of immigrants. Mare's (1995) analysis of educational differences by birthplace acknowledges the future disadvantages of recent immigrants from Central and South America, particularly Mexico, but does not consider whether the significance of ascribed traits also has changed. A highly plausible hypothesis is that the social and economic significance of ascribed traits, and immigrant status in particular, may have increased as competition for relatively fewer low-skill jobs intensified. If unskilled immigrants admitted after 1973 have experienced limited or no wage mobility since their arrival, it is highly conceivable that the economic fortunes of immigrants have been further slowed by the growing volume of unskilled new arrivals. If so—and there is mounting evidence that immigrants compete directly with themselves and less with domestic workers— then nativity itself becomes a stratifying variable and is increasingly relevant for understanding social cohesion. For this purpose, nativity is not a binary category but rather a hierarchy defined by both skills and period of arrival.

If fundamental questions are not raised about whether and how the allocative influence of ascribed traits may have changed relative to new income and employment opportunities, the default interpretation that income and wage inequality reflects group differences in educational attainment is tacitly accepted (Mare 1995; Harrison and Bennett 1995). To be sure, the educational disadvantages of recent immigrants are important for understanding their current and future labor market prospects (Borjas and Tienda 1993; Tienda and Singer 1995), but persisting anomalies such as higher employment and wages of unskilled immigrants relative to African Americans with higher levels of education challenge simple human capital explanations of wage and income inequality (Tienda and Stier 1996). That minority men holding college degrees *lost* ground relative to whites raises fundamental questions about why returns to education still differ along race and ethnic lines and whether being Asian *and* immigrant, for instance, will cheapen the value of schooling more than either attribute alone.

Another contentious economic issue surrounding the immigration debates during the past two decades or so has revolved around alleged labor market displacement of native-born workers by immigrants—that is, the nature and extent of job/wage competition between immigrants and domestic workers. If foreign- and native-born workers compete for jobs and wages, and if immigrants displace domestic workers, then immigration arguably could be characterized as a demographic force that directly undermines social cohesion. Yet a spate of econometric studies of labor market competition between immigrants and various groups of domestic workers that were conducted during the 1980s and early 1990s essentially concluded that immigrants were not substitutes in production and, if anything, exerted modest positive effects on the wages and employment of the foreign-born (White 1992; Borjas 1994; Greenwood and McDowell 1993). Moreover, the preponderance of empirical evidence about the complementarity and substitutability of immigrant and domestic labor indicates that foreign-born workers compete more with one another than with U.S.-born workers (Greenwood and McDowell 1993; McDowell 1997).

But this finding is irrelevant if domestic workers *perceive* that their economic well-being depends in some fashion on the presence of immigrants. For understanding whether and how labor market processes undermine social cohesion, the *actual* forces driving erosion of real wages and contraction of job opportunities are less important than *perceptions* about the terms of competition—whether they are deemed fair or whether some groups are perceived to receive preferential treatment or advantage.

This leads to a third important implication for social cohesion of the trends in immigration and economic opportunities, namely, that *perceptions* are highly decisive in shaping future attitudes and actions toward immigrants—perhaps even more than facts, unfortunately. In other words, the belief that immigrants are a net, albeit modest, economic benefit for the U.S. economy is less important than is the popular perception that the foreign-born (and their children) drain public coffers (mainly school, medical, and welfare budgets) and compete with U.S. workers.[4] These perceptions, I argue, have rekindled intolerance for diversity, epitomized by immigration, and deflected attention from the foundations and promises of a meritocracy.

Tides of Intolerance: Immigrant Reception Amid Scarcity

Reception factors represent a third element that circumscribes the implications of immigration for social cohesion. Reception factors include general acceptance of newcomers but also more concrete circumstances, such as the availability of language instruction, employment training, and social programs to ease adjustment, and the opportunities to settle in communities similar to those left behind. Recent years provide harsh lessons that perceptions of immigrants directly influence how they are treated on arrival.

In depicting contexts of immigrant reception, Portes and Rumbaút (1990: ch. 3) distinguish among three official government reception postures toward immigrants: *exclusion*, as was practiced toward immigrants from Asia for many years; *passive acceptance*, which absolves governments of responsibility for immigrant adaptation to the host society; and *active encouragement*, which involves direct efforts to facilitate resettlement. The last mentioned stance has been particularly developed with respect to refugee populations; passive acceptance represents the dominant stance toward legal (and in some periods also illegal) immigrants. Exclusion describes official government posture toward the foreign-born in recent years, which has shifted from benign neglect to disparate treatment. Unequal treatment of foreign-born populations is not novel in the United States, but the rising numbers of benefit exclusions represent a strong and decisive erosion of the social contracts extended after the 1965 amendments to the Immigration and Nationality Act were passed. Moreover, in the future there may be even greater disparities in amenities provided to immigrants because the devolution of fiscal authority over federally funded welfare and medical benefits to states allows the high immigrant destinations even more discretion in legislating divisions by nativity status.[5]

It is highly relevant for a discussion of how immigrant reception has evolved that the post–World War II rise in immigration and refugee flows occurred in the context of an expanding welfare state, which witnessed the birth of Medicaid and Medicare programs and the expansion of SSI benefits, AFDC, and food stamp programs (Rumbaút 1989). The cold war environment was also conducive to the development of special resettlement programs for refugees fleeing communist regimes. That similar social benefits were not extended to immigrants admitted under the preference system resulted in a two-tiered social contract for post–World War II immigrants and refugees, a point highly relevant for understanding how immigration can undermine social cohesion. The highest rates of welfare dependence occur among refugee populations, yet immigrants who arrive legally under the preference system appear to be the main targets of exclusion from social welfare benefits (Tienda and Liang 1994).

Immigration accounts for approximately one-third of U.S. population growth in recent years and is largely responsible for the race and ethnic diversification of the U.S. population. Census counts for 1990 revealed that the U.S. population composition is approximately 12% black, just under 10% Hispanic, 3% Asian, and 75% white. But, the average white *perceives* quite a different society. According to a recent survey conducted by the Kaiser Family Foundation and Harvard University, whites reported that 24% of the U.S. population was black, 15% was Hispanic, and nearly 11% was Asian! The same survey showed that nearly 60% of white respondents believed blacks were as well off as or better off than the average white person in occupation and education, and that 40 to 45% of whites believed that blacks were as well off as or better off than the average white person in housing and income.

That this is far from the truth is beside the point. Sociologist W. I. Thomas long ago instructed us that if people believe phenomena are real, they are real in their consequences. By zero-sum reasoning, if the economic fortunes of whites have declined, someone—maybe blacks or immigrants—must be better off. More generally, these gross distortions reveal how the majority population perceives itself vis-à-vis minority populations, and immigration is presumed to be largely responsible for the declining economic fortunes of domestic workers.

Perceptions of immigrants vary appreciably by region and across major cities, but recent years have witnessed an increase in anti-immigrant sentiment, precisely in cities where immigrants are concentrated. Even if contemporary fears about immigration are expressed less overtly than in the past (Simon 1985), they are similar in their underlying sentiments. Historical ambivalence notwithstanding, opposition to immigration has been rising. In fact, recent Gallup polls indicate that the majority of the U.S. population (67%) now favors *decreased* levels of immigration (NAS 1997). There is only limited evidence, however, that states with high densities of immigrants are more likely to harbor negative attitudes toward immigration (Texas is a notable exception: 80% of Texas respondents indicated that immigration should be decreased). As important as the hardening of attitudes toward immigrants is evidence that underlying anti-immigrant sentiment signals rising intolerance for difference and, more consequentially, an erosion of a societal commitment to equality of opportunity. It bears repeating that in drawing this inference, the relevant comparisons are not the experiences of turn-of-the-century immigrants but rather the great watershed symbolized by the civil rights era.

Nowhere is the intolerance for immigrants more evident than in California, where the most recent assault on immigrants' rights (and affirmative action policies) was launched. Nor is it coincidental that California also receives the lion's share of immigrants. The Los Angeles riots following the first Rodney King verdict increased Koreans' awareness that they were unwelcome immigrants, despite their striving to become American (Min 1996). One consequence of the attack on Korean businesses was an intensification of ethnic resilience among Koreans, which works against the social cohesion amid diversity that most newcomers assumed was forthcoming for those who played by the rules (Min 1996). Portes and Bach (1985) similarly documented how Mexican immigrants accentuated their ethnic differences as a response to discrimination and rejection by the host society.[6] In recent years anti-immigrant sentiment has also manifested itself in the spate of referenda to assert the primacy of English (Portes and Schauffler 1996), to limit legal immigrants' access to social benefits (Tienda and Liang 1994), and most recently, to deny access to education and health services to all undocumented immigrants and to reduce benefits to legal immigrants. Intolerance for diversity is also evident in recent legislative acts to "manage diversity" by setting aside visas for immigrants from Europe.

California's infamous Proposition 187, perhaps one of the most egregious pieces of anti-immigrant legislation proposed in recent history, not only conveys the strong anti-immigrant mood of the country (because other states have attempted similar referenda) but also challenges the premise that immigrants and natives share a common social contract. Proposals to deny education to U.S.-born children of undocumented immigrants not only undermine the basic premises of equal protection but also (and perhaps more fundamentally) tighten the link between ascription and social standing. Stated differently, the most pernicious aspect of this and similar proposals from the standpoint of diversity and social cohesion is that they virtually guarantee that children of immigrants will be socially and economically disadvantaged by virtue of their conditional acceptance *before* birth. Although its constitutionality remains questionable,

Proposition 187 will stand as a historical testimony about the rising tide of anti-immigrant sentiment in California and other favored immigrant destination states that attempted similar referenda.[7]

The recent welfare reform bill and the Antiterrorism Act signed into law by President Clinton further underscore the different rules for immigrants, especially recent arrivals and legal residents who have not become naturalized citizens, compared with those for U.S. citizens, and represent another facet of the quiet policy revolution against immigrants. I use the term *quiet revolution* because immigration policy has become increasingly more diffuse as provisions that directly undermine rights of the foreign-born are divorced from admission criteria per se and instead are factored in as subcriteria of various national policies. For example, the new antiterrorism act includes a provision to deport any and all immigrants who were ever convicted of a felony, even after they have made appropriate retribution. And under the provisions of the recently enacted welfare reform, even long-standing legal residents who have abided by the law, but have not become U.S. citizens, stand to lose access to most forms of public assistance. So far-reaching are the proposed cuts in the benefits currently enjoyed by immigrants that approximately 40% of the projected $55 billion in welfare savings is expected to come from denying public assistance benefits to legal immigrants.[8] Even more revenue savings will accrue if the large immigrant states decline the option to provide Medicaid benefits to legal immigrants after five years of U.S. residence.

Summary

To recapitulate, in this section I argued that three sets of circumstances are critical for understanding the implications of immigration for social cohesion. I stressed changing labor market conditions because jobs are essential for immigrants to earn a livelihood; because the dramatic decline in the availability of unskilled jobs in the United States has direct consequences for recent immigrants' economic futures; and because there appears to be a growing mismatch between the skills demanded by the U.S. economy and the skills supplied by recent arrivals.

That inequality rose more among minority than among nonminority groups suggests that the association between minority group membership and economic status has been strengthened rather than weakened. This is exactly the opposite of what should occur in a meritocracy, especially one where social policies have been designed precisely to uncouple the links between ascribed traits and social rewards. Or were they? Were we ever seriously committed to principles of equity? Did we ever settle the tolerable limits of inequality in a just society, or do these move on a sliding scale, depending on the health of the economy? And are racial and ethnic economic inequalities more socially destructive than the growing divisions between college- and high-school-educated workers?

Whether the outcome is due to prior discrimination or to radically different opportunities confronting new generations, the harsh reality is that *not* everyone in the race for economic fortunes begins at the same starting line. Some immigrants have been falling behind in the queue for socioeconomic rewards. In particular, immigrants from Mexico and South America enter the U.S. meritocracy with severe educational handicaps that, in the current economic and political climate, may prove difficult to surmount in a generation or two, as was the case for previous waves of immigrants. But immigration was virtually halted after the high tide of the European influx at the turn of the century, and some have argued that turning off the immigration spigot was the key to the newcomers' successful integration. Is it necessary to stop immigration to appreciate the promises of a meritocracy? More generally, when does equal opportunity start for those who are not in line when the race begins? I consider these issues in the final section.

EQUAL OPPORTUNITY AND IMMIGRATION: AN ILLUSIVE GOAL?

Given that the U.S. population has become more ethnically and racially diverse in recent decades, a major societal challenge for the future is to ensure that diversity—broadly defined—is not the main correlate of inequality. A related and long-standing challenge is how to provide equal opportunity without compromising individual freedom. That inequality varies directly with ascribed characteristics, notably race, ethnicity, gender, and, increasingly, immigrant status, raises questions about whether diversity will necessarily undermine the foundations of our fragile meritocracy.

The optimist in me believes that diversity need not divide, but the pragmatist in me warns that unless the current policy trends are reversed, it can, because the social scientist in me sees all too clearly the "social metabolism" reproducing inequality along color lines. Especially important for the future coloring of economic inequality are differences in educational attainment along race and ethnic lines, and between immigrants and their native-born counterparts. Educational differentials imply lifelong differences in socioeconomic welfare, particularly at times when the returns to schooling are rising rapidly. Although parents' education constructs a floor below which offspring are not likely to fall, for immigrant minority populations with extremely low levels of education, parents' education also represents a potential ceiling for achievements of subsequent generations. This underscores one of the great dilemmas of equal opportunity, namely, that family background remains decisive in shaping individual opportunity beyond what is objectively possible via economic growth. It is not diversity that divides but rather unequal opportunity.

Although discrimination has been legally outlawed, there is ample and convincing evidence that it remains a pervasive force reproducing inequality among immigrant and native minority populations (Fix and Struyck 1993). Waning public support for the social props of the Great Society signals a greater willingness to accept higher levels of poverty and income inequality and thinner safety nets for the needy than was true in the past. The push to repeal affirmative action policies in educational institutions and in government contracting on the grounds that they create unfair advantages is a forceful testimonial that reducing inequality is not a collective goal. Presumably, such programs violate the very foundations of a meritocracy, which requires *fair* competition. The attempt to eliminate affirmative action as an ideal, if not a satisfactorily implemented, policy represents a marked departure from the commitments of the Great Society era.

With the benefit of hindsight, affirmative action and equal opportunity programs were feeble attempts to weaken the link between ascriptive traits and social position. Affirmative action policies attempted to *go beyond* the simple prohibition of disparate treatment on grounds of race, national origin, and sex by making jobs, promotions, and admission to educational programs available to individuals from groups that have historically experienced barriers in accessing these positions. Legislative and program behavior was governed by the questionable premise that it is possible to legislate equal opportunity in a society with high levels of inequality and an ambivalent love-hate stance toward immigrants. Although the gains achieved through the institutionalization of affirmative action programs and equal opportunity practices are not likely to be completely undone, for racially diverse immigrants with limited skills on entry, the process of becoming American may require an extra generation or two.

The problem resides not in the philosophy or intent of affirmative action and equal opportunity but rather in the interpretation of what it means "to go beyond" outlawing discrimination and what constitutes equal opportunity in a highly stratified society. Essentially, the problem resides in the fundamental incompatibility of liberty and equality in social pursuits. This question is often asked when we contemplate steps to reduce inequality. Laissez-faire advocates oppose all forms of government intervention to achieve justice or fairness (that is, equal opportunity) on the grounds that this interferes with individual freedom to pursue self-interest. Traditional liberals, on the other hand, consider government intervention both appropriate and necessary to ensure a greater level of aggregate freedom at the expense of individual freedom, provided that it yields a greater level of equality.

In the abstract, these positions are difficult, yet their inherent contradiction is clear enough. A widely shared view is that equal opportunity exists when individuals of similar ability and talents have comparable prospects for success. In fact, most assessments of prospects for success measure actual outcomes rather than opportunities by accepting the questionable assumption that unequal outcomes imply unequal opportunities. But it is not obvious what must be equal for opportunity to be equal. Nor are there common understandings about the meaning of a "fair chance," which makes it possible to change the rules as circumstances change. Whose freedom must be compromised for whose opportunity? Is it possible to create a more just society without compromising someone else's economic freedom? If inequality compromises freedom, will reducing inequality ensure more freedom of opportunity? These concerns, while highly relevant for broad questions about diversity and inequality, acquire special relevance for recent immigrants, whose conditional acceptance appears to pose formidable handicaps to successful integration.

James Fishkin (1988) posed a trilemma that virtually precludes equal opportunity. He identified three conditions that must be met in order for there to be equal opportunity: First, there should be widespread procedural fairness in the evaluation of qualifications for positions. Second, there should exist equality of life chances. This means that social and economic prospects should not vary systematically with arbitrary characteristics, such as race, birthplace, and gender, that are irrelevant for achievement. Third, the autonomy of the family should not be interfered with except to ensure for the children the essential prerequisites for adult participation in the society.

The trilemma arises because, under conditions of prior inequality, implementing any two of these principles precludes the third. The autonomy of the family allows privileged families to confer their advantages on their children, enabling them to compete in a meritocracy strictly defined. But the equality of life chances for those from advantaged backgrounds precludes similar outcomes for those from less privileged backgrounds, thus reproducing the structure of inequality. Based on the trends in educational composition of recent immigrant cohorts, it seems obvious that the increasing diversification of the foreign-born population will further divide the U.S. population. This follows because, in the main, Asian immigrants confer on their offspring the advantages of educational achievement, whereas Latin American immigrants transmit their educational underachievement. And Asians stand to gain appreciably by the elimination of affirmative action, whereas blacks and Latinos stand to lose opportunities conferred by differential consideration of race and national origin in the interest of diversity.

As a past response to the dilemma of fair chance in an unequal society, affirmative action programs bring into sharp relief Fishkin's trilemma. This is because giving preferential consideration to disadvantaged members of society is perceived to limit the chances of those who believe unqualified competitors are taking positions they would receive were it not for affirmative action. In other words, affirmative action redefines the rules of equal opportunity at least by modifying the autonomy of the family, but perhaps also by modifying the terms of merit. Affirmative action has become highly controversial not because it contradicts a central objective of traditional liberalism and the U.S. civil rights movement, that is, special consideration of individuals on the basis of their race, national origin, or sex, but because opportunities for earning a living and for social mobility have been shrinking overall.

Against the economic backdrop I outlined above, it is not surprising that immigration and affirmative action policy have stirred so much controversy in recent years, when economic uncertainty has clouded the achievement of coveted social rewards. If values such as liberty and equality cannot be traded off or balanced against each other without violating the fundamental nature of the values themselves, then equality of opportunity will remain an illusive goal.

Concluding Thoughts

This essay conveys considerable pessimism about what immigration, and race/ethnic diversity more generally, portends for future social cohesion. I predict that race and ethnic inequality will most likely increase further by the turn of the century because equality of opportunity is an impossible goal; because anti-immigrant sentiment has been rising, and recent legislation that bears directly on the well-being of immigrants will generate even greater inequality along nativity and national origin lines; and because as a society, we lack the political will to implement and enforce policies that dismantle the racial and ethnic foundations of inequality. The last consideration—which is most forcefully illustrated by the current assault on affirmative action—is presaged by the ever more narrow interpretations of the equal protection clause of the fourteenth amendment.[9]

I submit that as long as economic opportunity expands, it is possible to maintain social cohesion while achieving some measure of social and economic integration of racially and ethnically diverse immigrant groups. That these conditions have not been met during the past quarter century is central for understanding how contemporary immigration streams threaten to undermine social cohesion by fostering divisions along race and ethnic lines. Although diversity need not divide, it does so when the economic pie shrinks and changes the terms of competition among social groups. But the terms of competition have been further disequilibrated by recent legislative acts that render immigrants vulnerable to exclusion and even deportation, whereas citizens are protected by the U.S. Constitution.

My purpose in raising these issues is not to lament past societal policy failures but rather to ponder and reflect about whether—assuming there is a social desire to do so—it is possible to legislate greater social equity; about what must be equal for opportunity to be equal; and about whether it is possible to manage the conflict between equality and liberty in a manner that reduces rather than increases inequality along race and ethnic lines. This is an important consideration, given the educational disadvantages with which at least half of recent immigrants arrive.[10] Against the backdrop of rising inequality, the problem of diversity in a meritocracy becomes even more challenging.

Notes

1. INS data indicate that 7.3 million immigrants were admitted during the 1980s, whereas census data reveal that 8.7 million immigrants arrived during the 1980s. The discrepancies between the INS data and the census data stem partly from the differing periods used to delineate cohorts (1981–1990 for INS versus 1980–1989 for census) and the different practices for reporting the legalized population. That is, INS does not count the legalized population among immigrants admitted until the final stage of the legalization process is completed, whereas individuals whose status change was either in process

or nearly complete at the time of the 1990 census most likely self-reported themselves as legal immigrants during the 1980s (see Rumbaút 1996).

2. There are, of course, notable exceptions to these generalizations. Proportions of Laotian, Cambodian, Italian, and Haitian immigrants who completed high school and college degrees fell below the U.S. averages, whereas Peruvian, Cuban, Colombian, and Nicaraguan immigrants attained high school and college graduation rates comparable to the U.S. average (Portes and Rumbaút 1990: table 4). Immigrants from Mexico, who average seven and a half years of graded schooling, exhibit the lowest education levels of all immigrants (Chiswick and Sullivan 1995: table 5.6). Other Latin American immigrants as a group averaged eleven years graded schooling, compared with thirteen or more for immigrants from Asia, Africa, or Europe (Chiswick and Sullivan 1995: table 5.6).

3. Industrial restructuring involves a myriad of strategies, including moving firms to sites where labor costs are lower; downsizing production sites through consolidation; upgrading production equipment; retaining fewer, more highly skilled workers; and closing altogether.

4. The general consensus is that the U.S. economy benefits, on balance, from immigration, even its current composition (Borjas 1995; NAS 1997). Nevertheless, the aggregate national benefit comes at a cost that has significant regional, demographic, and social dimensions. In a nutshell, the benefits from tax revenues largely accrue to the federal government, whereas state and local governments in jurisdictions where immigrants reside bear a disproportional share of the costs (especially schooling and health, but also incarceration costs).

5. California will have especially large incentives to restrict immigrants' access to means-tested income transfers, as well as schooling opportunities for children of immigrants, because fiscal impact calculations reveal a large deficit from undocumented immigrants (Clark et al.1994).

6. They dubbed this reaction "ethnic resilience," a process whereby immigrant ethnics use ethnicity as a basis for facilitating their integration in the host society by relying on co-ethnics for their social and economic needs.

7. Proposition 209, which repealed consideration of race and national origin as criteria for college admissions, is another example of an eroding social commitment to economic parity of disadvantaged minority groups. Even if unconstitutionality leads to its demise, the message will have been conveyed nonetheless.

8. The congressional budget estimates that by 2002, more than one-quarter million elderly legal immigrants will lose Medicaid benefits as a result of the recent changes in the welfare law.

9. This is illustrated by the recent legal case *Hopwood et al. v. University of Texas*.

10. I also want to caution against using the term *diversity* so loosely that it becomes divorced from inequality and economic disadvantage. This is because differentiation need not be a social problem, but racial and ethnic inequality certainly is if produced by unequal treatment.

REFERENCES

Blackburn, McKinley L., David E. Bloom, and Richard B. Freeman. 1990. The Declining Economic Position of Less Skilled American Men. Pp. 31–76 in *A Future of Lousy Jobs?* edited by G. Burtless. Washington, D.C.: The Brookings Institution.

Borjas, George J., and Marta Tienda. 1993. "The Employment and Wages of Legalized Immigrants." *International Migration Review* 27 (4): 712–47.

Borjas, George J. 1994. "The Economics of Immigration." *Journal of Economic Literature* 32: 1667–717.

————. 1995. "The Economic Benefits for Immigration." *Journal of Economic Perspectives* 9 (2): 3–22.

Burtless, Gary. 1990. Introduction and Summary. Pp. 1–30 in *A Future of Lousy Jobs?* edited by G. Burtless. Washington, D.C.: The Brookings Institution.

Clark, Rebecca L., Jeffry S. Passel, Wendy N. Zimmerman, and Michael E. Fix. 1994. *Fiscal Impacts of Undocumented Aliens: Selected Estimates for Seven States.* Washington, D.C.: The Urban Institute.

Chiswick, Barry R., and Teresa A. Sullivan. 1995. The New Immigrants. Chap. 5 in *State of the Union*, Vol. 2, edited by Reynolds Farley. New York: Russell Sage Foundation.

Danziger, Sheldon, and Peter Gottschalk. 1993. *Uneven Tides: Rising Inequality in America.* New York: Russell Sage Foundation.

————. 1995. *America Unequal.* New York: Russell Sage Foundation.

Enchautegui, M. 1992. "Work and Wages of Puerto Rican Men During the Eighties." Washington, D.C.: The Urban Institute. Unpublished paper.

Farley, Reynolds. 1996. *The New American Reality.* New York: Russell Sage Foundation.

Fishkin, James. 1988. "Do We Need a Systematic Theory of Equal Opportunity?" Pp. 15–21 in *Equal Opportunity*, edited by Norman E. Bowie. Boulder, Colo.: Westview.

Fix, Michael, and Struyk, Raymond J., eds. 1993. *Clear and Convincing Evidence: Measurement of Discrimination in America.* Washington D.C.: The Urban Institute Press.

Freeman, Richard B. 1993. "How Much Has De-Unionization Contributed to the Rise in Male Earnings Inequality?" Chap. 4 in *Uneven Tides: Rising Inequality in America*, edited by Sheldon Danzinger and Peter Gottschalk. New York: Russell Sage Foundation.

Greenwood, Michael J., and John M. McDowell. 1993. "The Labor Market Consequences of U.S. Immigration." Unpublished report submitted to the U.S. Department of Labor, Bureau of International Labor Affairs, Division of Immigration Policy and Research. Boulder: University of Colorado.

Harrison, Rodrick J., and Claudette E. Bennett. 1995. "Racial and Ethnic Diversity." Chap. 4 in *State of the Union*, Vol. 2, edited by Reynolds Farley. New York: Russell Sage Foundation.

Karoly, Lynn A. 1993. "The Trend in Inequality among Families, Individuals, and Workers in the United States: A Twenty-Five Year Perspective." Chap. 2 in *Uneven Tides: Rising Inequality in America*, edited by Sheldon Danzinger and Peter Gottschalk. New York: Russell Sage Foundation.

Levy, Frank. 1995. "Incomes and Income Inequality." Chap. 1 in *State of the Union*, Vol. 1, edited by Reynolds Farley. New York: Russell Sage Foundation.

Mare, Robert D. 1995. "Changes in Educational Attainment and School Enrollment." Chap. 4 in *State of the Union*, Vol. 1, edited by Reynolds Farley. New York: Russell Sage Foundation.

McDowell, John M. 1997. *Economic Impacts of Mexican Immigration to the United States.* Unpublished report submitted to the United States Commission for Immigration Reform: Mexico–U.S. Binational Migration Study. Tucson: University of Arizona.

Min, Pyong Gap. 1996. "The Entrepreneurial Adaptation of Korean Immigrants." Chap. 23 in *Origins and Destinies: Immigration, Race, and Ethnicity in America*, edited by Silvia Pedraza and Rubén G. Rumbaut. Belmont, Calif.: Wadsworth.

Mincy, R. 1990. "Work Force 2000. Silver Bullet or Dud?: Job Structure Changes and Economic Prospects for Black Men in the 1990s." Washington, D.C.: The Urban Institute.

Murphy, Kevin M., and Finis Welch. 1993. "Industrial Change and the Rising Importance of Skill." Chap. 3 in *Uneven Tides: Rising Inequality in America*, edited by Sheldon Danzinger and Peter Gottschalk. New York: Russell Sage Foundation.

National Academy of Sciences (NAS). 1997. *The New Americans: Economic, Demographic, and Fiscal Effects of Immigration*. Report from the Panel on the Demographic and Economic Impacts of Immigration, edited by James P. Smith and Barry Edmonston. Washington, D.C.: National Academy Press.

Portes, Alejandro, and Robert Bach. 1985. *Latin Journey: Cuban and Mexican Immigrants in the United States*. Berkeley: University of California Press.

Portes, Alejandro, and Rubén Rumbaut. 1990. *Immigrant America: A Portrait*. Berkeley: University of California Press.

Portes, Alejandro, and Richard Schauffler. 1996. "Language Acquisition and Loss among Children of Immigrants." Chap. 32 in *Origins and Destinies: Immigration, Race, and Ethnicity in America*, edited by Silvia Padraza and Rubén G. Rumbaut. Belmont, Calif.: Wadsworth.

Rumbaút, Rubén G. 1989. "The Structure of Refuge: Southeast Asian Refugees in the United States, 1975–1985." *International Review of Comparative Public Policy* 1: 97–129.

———. 1996. "Origins and Destinies: Immigration, Race and Ethnicity in Contemporary America." Chap. 2 in *Origins and Destinies: Immigration, Race, and Ethnicity in America*, edited by Silvia Pedraza and Rubén Rumbaút. Belmont, Calif.: Wadsworth.

Simon, Rita. 1985. *Public Opinion and the Immigrant: Print Media Coverage, 1880–1980*. Washington D.C.: Lexington Books.

Tienda, Marta, and Zai Liang. 1994. "Poverty and Immigration in Policy Perspective." Pp. 330–64 in *Poverty and Public Policy*, edited by Sheldon H. Danzinger, Gary D. Sandefur, and Daniel H. Weinberg. Cambridge: Harvard University Press.

Tienda, Marta, and Audrey Singer. 1995. "Wage Mobility of Legalized Immigrants," *International Migration Review* 29 (1): 112–38.

Tienda, Marta, and Haya Stier. 1996. "The Wages of Race: Color and Employment Opportunity in Chicago's Inner City." Chap. 31 in *Origins and Destinies: Immigration, Race and Ethnicity in America*, edited by Silvia Pedraza and Rubén Rumbaut. Belmont, Calif.: Wadsworth.

White, Michael J. 1992. "Immigrants, Cities, and Equal Opporunity." Chap. 8 in *Urban Labor Markets and Job Opportunity*, edited by George Peterson and Wayne Vroman. Washington, D.C.: The Urban Institute Press.

CHAPTER SEVEN

Family Change and Family Diversity

FRANK F. FURSTENBERG, JR.

INTRODUCTION

FUTURE HISTORIANS of the family will undoubtedly look upon the final decades of the twentieth century as a time of upheaval, when a major shift occurred in the form and function of the Western family. During the last third of the century, the nuclear family built around durable conjugal ties and a distinct division of labor based on gender has given way to a multiplicity of kinship types. This new (or some would argue renewed) diversity of family forms has provoked considerable commentary and controversy on the consequences of these changes for producing basic civic values required for social order.

In this paper I first examine the transformation that has taken place and the reasons why it came about. Then I consider some implications of the changes in family structure for the quality of family life, especially as viewed from the vantage point of children. I shall explore, though surely not resolve, the question of whether the deterioration of the nuclear family form is compromising the future stability of American society, as so many observers believe to be the case. This issue cannot be addressed without considering the roiling public debate over family values that has been generated by political and policy differences over how to address the "problems" created by the decline of marriage, or at least the decline of marriage "as we have known it."

WHAT HAS CHANGED

By any historical standard, the changes that have occurred in the family over the past several decades have been truly remarkable. It can be fairly said that in no comparable era outside of wartime have we seen such a rapid shift in the shape of households and in the behavior of families. No doubt, these changes are highlighted by the fact that several decades ago one family type predominated as never before: the vast majority of Americans were living or aspired to live in nuclear families, a form of the family that now ironically is referred to as the "traditional" American family. In some sense this attribution is not inappropriate, because American families had always assumed a nuclear form; it nonetheless rings hollow to those able to recall that when this family form was in its heyday, many observers were bemoaning the disappearance of more extended and complex family forms and fearing that the nuclear family was becoming isolated from the network of kin and the larger community.

In the 1950s and early 1960s, before the revolution in gender roles occurred, complaints were commonly voiced about the headlong rush to early marriage, the segregation of women in the suburbs, the excessive dependency of children on their parents, the overindulgence of the young, and the number of marriages empty of emotion (Bell and Vogel 1968; Coser 1964; Winch 1963). These features of the nuclear family were said to contribute to the growing problem of delinquency, premarital sex, and school dropout among youth. When the revolution did occur, the emotionally charged character of the nuclear family was said to be a contributor to the discontents of youth in the late 1960s and 1970s (Flacks 1971; Slater 1970). These criticisms of the family seem almost quaint by contemporary standards, but they were experienced as very real by scholars and social critics at the time. Whether or not the complaints had merit, the hegemony of the nuclear family was viewed as a mixed blessing and was associated with many of the problems of growing up in American society (Friedan 1983; Friedenberg 1964; Goodman 1960).[1]

As we now know, the nuclear family in the 1950s was poised to become the "postmodern" family in the next several decades or, as Edward Shorter (1975) stated in his widely read book *The Making of the Modern Family,* to chart a course "straight for the heart of the sun." The term *postmodern family* has no precise meaning but generally designates a movement away from or delegitimation of patriarchal authority and a growing emphasis on personal autonomy of household members. Indeed, the term *family* itself is now culturally contested, a process that Peter and Brigitte Berger (1983/84) referred to as "the family wars." More than a few scholars have suggested that *family* as a singular is no longer appropriate; instead, by pluralizing the word to speak of American families, we encompass the new realities of American kinship. At least several well-known family sociologists have taken an even stronger position and advocate abandoning the word in scientific discourse altogether (Scanzoni et al. 1989). I do not think that semantic debates are likely to resolve the issues, though as I will point out later, the discussions of what constitutes family have important ramifications for family law and public policy.

How we conceive of marriage, family, and kinship has been reshaped or perhaps even shattered by a configuration of economic and social changes that broke apart a tightly prescribed pattern of kinship (Farber 1973; Goode 1963; Parsons 1951; Schneider 1980). In a matter of thirty years, we have gone from a time when nearly everyone married, usually in late adolescence or early adulthood, to a time when a growing minority will never wed, and most postpone marriage until their midtwenties or later. Marriage is no longer the master event that orchestrates the onset of sexual relations, parenthood, the departure from home, or even the establishment of a household. These events have become more independent of one another—discrete moments in the life course (Modell 1989; Modell, Furstenberg, and Hershberg 1976; Furstenberg 1982).

Many family scholars have pointed out that we are not so much creating a new life course as reclaiming a former one that prevailed until the twentieth century. It is certainly true that in the past, family careers were disorderly; events such as severe economic downturns that disrupted the supply of eligible partners, migration patterns that produced unbalanced sex ratios, or disabling diseases and death that removed partners and parents created family instability. Sharp regional, class, and ethnic differences distinguished patterns of family formation (Coale and Watkins 1985; Hareven 1981). Until well into the twentieth century, no standard form of "the American family" existed even though Americans always preferred to live in independent family units and were committed to strong conjugal bonds: however, the boundaries of family membership were highly permeable and often included related kin, servants, and boarders. Home life was often more chaotic than we frequently imagined it to have been. In all but the small stratum of wealthy families, children were required to justify their existence by economic production or were required to seek employment elsewhere. It was not uncommon for parents to give their children up to orphanages, foster care, or employment as a means of managing precarious economic circumstances (Bellingham 1988).

In a recent book, John Gillis (1996) argues that the family as a sacred and protected institution is a relatively recent cultural invention. Notions of privacy, intimacy, and elaborate family rituals emerged only because religious and local community institutions receded, yielding greater symbolic power to the family. And the nationalization of these standards occurred only during the middle of this century in the postwar era, when family life became more accessible and affordable to all.

The era of high domesticity was brief, and its demise swift. Between 1965 and 1995, marriage became both less accessible and less affordable to a growing number of Americans. Working-class Americans who frequently had been propelled into marriage by a pregnancy at midcentury began to consider options other than a shotgun wedding. Middle-class youth who confidently married and began families in or shortly after college extended their educational careers. Women stayed in school and entered the labor force, expecting to work for a period before parenthood. Men became less confident that they could sustain a middle-class life on their earnings alone.

Rising rates of divorce shattered the ideal of life-long monogamy. The premium placed on marital satisfaction rose, creating higher standards for intimacy, sexual gratification, and shared domestic duties. Individuals viewed marriage as ever more daunting and hesitated to make permanent commitments so lightly. Temporary partnerships and cohabitation became alternatives to early marriage and, for a small minority, to matrimony itself (Bumpass 1990; Cherlin 1992).

These patterns were not evenly distributed in American society. African Americans experienced a virtual collapse of early marriage beginning in the early 1960s as a growing number of pregnant teenagers who would have married chose instead to become single parents. No doubt, some also resorted to abortion, but its legal availability was still a decade away. Despite the greater selectivity of those blacks who entered wedlock, black marriages also became less stable (Cherlin 1992). By 1970, only 42% of black women in the population were married compared with 60% of white women (Espenshade 1985).

In part because these changes were so dramatic and because patterns of family formation among whites were slower to change, social scientists believed that changes in the black family were anomalous and distinctive (Rainwater and Yancey 1967). However, it seems increasingly evident that many of these changes were not confined to African Americans. Puerto Ricans have experienced almost identical patterns, and recently it appears that a growing proportion of lower-income white Americans are retreating from marriage as well (Farley 1995).

WHY THE CHANGES OCCURRED

It seems almost pointless to determine whether these changes resulted from economic events, social transformations, or cultural shifts in the importance placed on marriage. Large institutional changes rarely occur unless a confluence of conditions takes place. Individuals begin to reconsider their options when old solutions become unworkable. Tolerance for alternatives grows as more individuals engage in novel forms of behavior. Sanctions are weakened and new patterns become accepted even though they may be deemed less desirable accomodations to current realities (Gerson 1985). So it was with the rise of premarital sex, cohabitation, out-of-wedlock childbearing, and divorce. The model of the nuclear family became less attainable—not so much because people believed in it less, but because more and more people were unable to fulfill the demands required for behaving in the familiar way.

"Value stretch" is the term one sociologist used to describe how lower-class individuals begin to depart from mainstream practices (Rodman 1963). It is an appropriate way of understanding how individuals come to behave in ways that at least initially they do not entirely believe in or even actively disapprove of. As values are stretched, sanctions lose their grip, and more people talk openly about behaving in ways that were previously thought unacceptable. So it was with a host of family behaviors in the 1960s and 1970s. To be sure, people had for some time engaged in sexual relationships before marriage, lived together in informal arrangements, and had children outside of wedlock, but such events were not discussed in polite company—much less paraded in newspapers or television without the distinct scent of scandal. Publicizing such actions was an occasion to deplore them, and so these not-so-uncommon behaviors were carried out underground. The 1960s and 1970s broke down this state of "pluralistic ignorance."

Ironically, just before this transformation, a leading authority on family, William J. Goode (1963), described the sweeping changes in family systems that were occurring worldwide and predicted that the "conjugal based" family of the West would become more widespread. Goode's prediction was based on the idea that family and economy must "fit" for effective production and reproduction. Goode argued that the nuclear family was ideally suited to the demands of an industrial economy, with the requirements of a flexible labor market demanding geographic mobility, gender specialization, and autonomous youth loosely attached to the household.

In retrospect, an argument could have been made just as easily for the bad fit of the conjugal family with the industrial economy, especially as it began to draw women into the labor force. The ideal of a close-knit small family unit anchored by a strong and enduring marriage became increasingly difficult to achieve as the gender-based division of labor rapidly gave way to a dual-worker family system. Gender specialization within the family began to make less sense as women moved from being homemakers to paid workers in the economy. The model of marriage that prevailed at midcentury—two joining together as one—became less persuasive as a design for ordering relations between men and women. Moreover, the highly differentiated patterns of parenting became less appropriate as well. The absent father—whether inside or outside the home—came to be seen as a problem not just for women who were bearing a disproportionate share of the household load but also for children who, it seems, missed the presence of males as caregivers and role models.

Throughout the 1970s, the ideal of the nuclear family was attacked by many feminists, progressives, gays, and scholars of color who promoted the viability, if not the superiority, of alternative kinship arrangements. The rhetoric assault perhaps reached a peak in 1978 when the Carter administration was forced to cancel the White House Conference on the Family because it threatened to be politically embarrassing to the president if the deep ideological divisions over the family were permitted to surface. The public discussion actually contributed to the changes that were taking place concurrently (Lasch 1977; Tufte and Myerhoff 1979). No doubt it helped rationalize and perhaps legitimate the growth of varied family forms. Nonetheless, it seems likely that most of the change would have taken place had public discussion focused exclusively on the demise of the family and the costs to children, as it has in the 1990s. Indeed, the changes that have occurred from the 1980s to the present have taken place in a very conservative political climate. At least from the early Reagan years (and some might say starting with the Carter administration), calls for restoring family values were issued with increasing volume. However, the effect of these appeals appears to be quite limited, at least judging from demographic trends over the past two decades.

Sexual behavior among the young continued to increase during the 1980s despite a "just say no" campaign for premarital chastity promoted by the Reagan administration. Trends in teenage childbearing seem similarly unaffected by a continuous stream of public information campaigns to discourage young men and women from having children early in life or prior to marriage (Hayes 1987; Luker 1996). Cohabitation has been steadily on the rise and has become virtually institutionalized as a stage of courtship or, for some, a de facto marriage (Bumpass 1990).

Efforts to curb divorce and single parenthood have been equally unsuccess-ful. As far back as the middle 1980s, scholars began to sound the alarm that high rates of marital dissolution were jeopardizing the welfare of children and the stability of society (Blankenhorn, Bayme, and Elshtain 1990; Popenoe 1988; Wallerstein and Blakeslee 1989). Today, there are widespread calls for the tightening of divorce regulations. In fact, divorce rates have not risen since the late 1970s. What has occurred is a widespread postponement of marriage in favor of informal unions or solo living. These trends are largely responsible for the sharp growth of nonmarital childbearing (Morgan 1996). Fertility has risen among unmarried women, no doubt in part due to the declining attractiveness of marriage as a solution to prenuptial conception. Evidence suggests that the Murphy Browns—middle-class women who deliberately plan to become single parents—are still relatively rare (Alan Guttmacher Institute 1994). The ranks of never-married solo parents are largely filled by women who inadvertently be-come pregnant, reject the option of abortion, and see little gain to entering a union that is perceived to be fragile from the start (Furstenberg 1995a).

Marriage remains a privileged status. By this I mean that most Americans regard marriage as a preferred arrangement, especially when children are in-volved. However, couples frequently delay marriage as a hedge against the possibility that the union will not survive. Thus, marriage has increasingly become less the pledge of permanent commitment than a conditional commit-ment to remain together so long as both parties are willing and able. This cultural understanding has been reluctantly incorporated in the law and even in marriage rituals that speak less of permanent bonds and more of the impor-tance of equality, mutual respect, and intimacy—the cornerstones of a con-temporary relationship.

The meaning of marriage has also changed with the shifting of gender roles occasioned by women's entrance into the labor force—especially married women with children. In the course of several decades, labor force participation of married women with preschool children went from being a rarity (18.6% in 1960) to being the prevailing pattern (61.7% in 1994). Little wonder that ob-servers began to notice the disappearance of the Ozzie and Harriet form of the family (Blankenhorn, Bayme, and Elshtain 1990). In fact, no prevailing form of the family exists today that represents the typical family such as existed in the middle of this century when radio listeners and then television viewers were introduced to Ozzie and Harriet, Leave It to Beaver, and Father Knows Best.

As I stated earlier, the tightly orchestrated movement into marriage and childbearing with its highly segregated roles for men and women has all but collapsed. Individuals now typically live in many different families during the life course (Buchman 1989). A couple may cohabit, marry with both partners working, raise children while the wife works part-time, separate and co-parent before one or both remarry—themselves forming new families and perhaps beginning a cycle of further differentiation. Previously, it was relatively easy to distinguish between people who were doing it the right way (even if they cheated a little by having sex and perhaps getting pregnant prior to marriage) and those who were not—those living in sin, unmarried mothers, or divorcees. Now with family forms so diverse, it is nearly impossible to draw such sharp distinctions between the right and wrong ways of organizing families. In this sense as Judith Stacey (1993) argues, "the" family as a hegemonic cultural construct has been delegitimized.

A good deal of public opinion data support Stacey's argument. Although individuals continue to think that living in formal and durable marriages is ideal, most Americans tolerate, if not endorse, alternative family forms (Chadwick and Heaton 1992). To be sure, Americans continue to disagree—often heatedly—over these questions, as evidenced by the cultural wars openly waged at the 1992 Republican Convention and by the controversy over gay marriage that has surfaced since Hawaii began to consider changing its marriage statutes to permit members of the same sex to form legal unions. Nonetheless, the very discussion of these values would not and probably could not have occurred several decades ago. Divided opinion on what constitutes legitimate forms of the family itself represents a remarkable social fact.

Whether this division of opinion necessarily implies that "family practices"—how we live in families—have been weakened, particularly in ways that compromise the interests of children, remains an open question. I realize that for many observers and even for many social scientists, this matter seems settled: most believe the family has become less important and less effective during the final third of this century (Popenoe 1988; Uhlenberg and Eggebeen 1986). However, part of the evidence cited for the decline of the family typically refers to the demographic data on the deinstitutionalization of marriage and increases in nonmarital fertility. In a certain sense, that evidence begs the question because it neatly sidesteps the issue of whether variation in the kinship forms represents a weakening of the family (Condran and Furstenberg 1994).

The Consequences of Family Change

Have Americans become less committed to the importance of family? This is not an easy question to answer with the available data. The family continues to remain the institution most highly valued by Americans (National Commission on Children 1991). To be sure, Americans worry about family disintegration, but they remain committed to families and convinced that their own families are in good shape. I can find no evidence to suggest that parents are sacrificing less for their children. Indeed, a strong case can be made that parents feel more compelled than ever before to invest in their children's welfare—in both their material and psychological well-being (Furstenberg 1995b).

Admittedly, the data are sparse, but I suspect that were we able to monitor private household expenditures, investment per child is probably rising. The flow of resources that once went from children to parents has virtually stopped except perhaps in the parents' extreme old age. Many parents continue to support their children well into early adulthood by providing allowances and housing supplements (Lye 1996).

A great deal of data suggests that children continue to rely on their parents' advice and respect their opinions as they move through adolescence and into early adulthood (Modell 1989; National Commission on Children 1991). True, fathers who have lived apart from their children typically play an ancillary and often marginal role in these continuing patterns of support. This has certainly harmed children's interests. Step- and surrogate fathers have taken up some of the slack, but most research suggests that while stepparents may improve children's material position, on average children do not benefit by their presence in the home (Cherlin and Furstenberg 1994; White 1993).

It is also not easy to assemble evidence on time investment by parents. Clearly, the entrance of women into the labor force has meant less time available to spend with children in the home (Larson and Richards 1994; Rossi and Rossi 1990). Yet, comparisons over time frequently ignore the number of children in the household and competing obligations of parents in earlier times. At least some time studies suggest that monitoring and care of children has not decreased over the past half century even if mothers spend less time in the household (Robinson 1990). Again, the data are more ambiguous for fathers. When present in the home, it appears that they spend more time providing direct child care, but a higher proportion live apart from their children.

Grandparents remain a strong presence in children's lives. Fewer children grow up residing with grandparents in the home, but a greater number have contact with more of their grandparents. Because of increasing longevity of grandparents and modern means of transportation and communication, the older generation can often enjoy closer contact with their children and grandchildren than was possible earlier in this century. Moreover, declining rates of fertility imply that fewer children will receive the attentions of a greater number of grandparents. Indeed, most children report extensive contact with at least some of their grandparents. The attenuation of paternal links with children means that children are more likely to maintain contact with their mothers' kin, giving a slight matrilineal tilt to our kinship system (Johnson 1988). Yet, it also appears that to some extent stepgrandparents may pick up the slack (Cherlin and Furstenberg 1986).

I conclude two broad lessons from the admittedly incomplete evidence on kinship patterns. First, children may be less exposed to the continuous and stable influence of two parents. Nonetheless, kinship bonds remain strong and omnipresent for most children. Second, greater variability exists in the kinship system than was present at midcentury. The absence of standardized patterns may be destabilizing the family, but it may also signify a realignment of kinship away from the conjugal patterns toward greater reliance on lineage, especially matrilineage.

It is essential to keep in mind the centrality of the "isolated" nuclear family is a relatively recent development in Western history (Parsons 1951). Some scholars argue that we may be returning to the status quo ante when children were less exclusively supervised by parents and were more the shared responsibility of extended kin and members of the community. If this shift is indeed occurring, it is not surprising that Americans, especially, would find this change disturbing. By international standards, this nation has always been committed to a highly privatized nuclear family system (Bellah et al. 1985). American families, it has been said, were born modern: that is, from colonial times, our culture has promoted a conjugal family form.

In the early decades of the nineteenth century, foreign travelers took note of the strength of the domestic unit, the relative intimacy of marital relationships, the absence of hierarchy, and the democratic quality of parent–child relationships in American families (Furstenberg 1966; Hiner and Hawes 1985). The shrewdest of these observers, Alexis de Tocqueville (1835), noted that American families, buttressed by local institutions—religious and voluntary community organizations—helped protect individuals from possible intrusions of the state. An ample supply of farmland and a distant frontier also contributed to the flourishing of independent households and strong conjugal ties. Far earlier than citizens of other nations, Americans embraced the importance of "romantic love" as a basis for marriage and egalitarian family relationships (Rothman 1984). And compared with people of other Western nations, Americans married exceptionally young and were more geographically mobile. Community and extended kinship ties remained strong throughout the nineteenth century but were probably less accentuated than in Europe. Both economic conditions and a strong political distrust of state powers helped foster the ideal of the conjugal family and probably hindered the growth of the welfare state.

Moreover, this view of the family as a protector against state interference, a "haven in the heartless world," (Lasch 1977) is an idea that grew in response to the harsh demands of early industrialization and continues even today as economic institutions exert control over family life (Coser 1964). The relegation of women and then children into the domestic sphere helped foster the notion that working men could find refuge and relief from excessive work demands at home. This belief created a common understanding in American culture that a household consisting of a working father and a nonworking mother is the most "natural" way of raising children, a concept that would elude many cultures in the world (Murdock 1949; Schneider 1980). In the 1950s and early 1960s, a good deal of the sociology of the family was devoted to explaining how this form of the family arose from functional requirements of societies, especially advanced industrialized societies (Bell and Vogel 1968). For a relatively short span of time—from the end of the nineteenth to the middle of the twentieth century—it thus became "natural" for women to specialize in domestic and child care and for men to work outside the home. The single-wage-earner family went out of style fairly quickly but not without a certain amount of cultural resistance. Married women, who had first entered the labor force during the Depression from necessity and during World War II out of patriotism, were pressured to return to the home to make room for the returning vets. The huge government subsidies provided for education, housing, and employment helped sustain the single-wage-earner family throughout the 1950s and promoted an era of domestic mass production. However, the pressures of supporting the children of the baby boom enticed married women back into the labor force in steadily increasing numbers. At the same time, rising levels of divorce pushed mothers with young children to seek employment even when they preferred to remain at home. Throughout the 1950s and 1960s, the number of working mothers steadily increased, and the age at which women returned to the labor force declined. By 1980 a majority of married women with dependent children were gainfully employed outside the home, and by 1990 a majority of those with children under age six held jobs outside the home (U.S. Bureau of the Census 1996: 399).

Public opinion clearly favored keeping mothers in the home, and only as change occurred in the gender composition of the work force did views begin to shift and even then only reluctantly (Virginia Slims 1995). Again, it seems likely that the behavior of families stretched social norms in ways that legitimated the practices post facto. In the 1960s social scientists were divided on the effects of working mothers on children's development, but fairly soon a consensus emerged that the general impact was negligible. Many Americans continue to believe that children are better off if mothers remain in the home (National Commission on Children 1991; Virginia Slims 1995). Nonetheless, as the 1996 Welfare Reform Act attests, public support for mothers working in their households—at least if they are poor—has largely evaporated (Skocpol and Wilson 1994).

A spate of research linking employment patterns of mothers to the development and well-being of children searched in vain for evidence demonstrating the superiority of families with full-time housewives (Belsky and Eggebeen 1991; Menaghan and Parcel 1990; National Research Council 1993). The results of these studies have been quite consistent in showing no overall differences based on the working status of mothers. Employment, it seems, affects child rearing patterns differently depending on how parents regard their jobs and the desirability of working as well as what kinds of support exists for working parents and their children. By now most investigators have stopped looking for a general effect of employment and have begun to ask more sophisticated questions about how work is managed by families involving both the link between workplace and home, the availability and quality of child care, and the internal routines that arise inside the family in response to work demands. It is widely assumed that influences of work on children operate indirectly through these sorts of mechanisms but that it is difficult to identify any "direct" effects of work on children's welfare because so much variation exists in work patterns and their consequences for family life.

Interestingly, researchers often resist adopting a similar logic when it comes to assessing the impact of other features of family change discussed earlier in this paper. For example, many investigations of the effects of divorce and nonmarital childbearing continue to focus on the dichotomy between nuclear and nonnuclear families rather than trying to understand when and under what circumstances the family's form affects children. The broad comparisons between two-biological-parent households and other arrangements has diverted attention away from how parents successfully manage the demands of childbearing and childrearing whatever their marital status. It is as if parents who live together are more or less assured success, and those who do not are guaranteed to fail despite the considerable evidence to the contrary (Furstenberg and Cherlin 1991; McLanahan and Sandefur 1994).

Most studies show that children are more likely to thrive when they receive continuous care from parents, when parents invest in the relationship by providing time and material resources, when parents provide appropriate control of the child's impulses and actions according to his or her age, and when parents display warmth, concern, and confidence in the child's ability. All these qualities, no doubt, benefit from the presence of two parents. Whether these parents need be biological parents is still unsettled. We do not know whether adopted parents, gay parents, or a single parent and grandmother or a single parent by him or herself does as well as two biological parents when such arrangements come with stability, material resources, and skillful practices.

The presence of more than one parent generally confers added benefits to children for reasons other than the obvious ones of providing more time and resources. When they share common values and concerns, parents can reinforce each other's practices and monitor their results. In effect, the family as a cohesive social system generates social capital by creating a common culture and routines. Family-based social capital will arise when parents successfully collaborate and when they are embedded in a larger network of kin (Bott 1971). Relatively little research has addressed how social capital within the family is built and sustained or, for that matter, how it may be dissipated by conflict within the household or across the generations. It seems also likely that divorce and remarriage are events that can destroy existing social capital if it has not already been dissipated by marital conflict.

Parents—whether residing together or apart—can ally with other institutions outside the family as ways of garnering social capital that may enforce their standards. Beyond the circle of kinship, they are most likely to rely on religious institutions to embed their children in a community of like-minded individuals. A long tradition of research has shown that religiosity is associated both with family stability and successful outcomes for children (Blood and Wolfe 1960; Thornton, Axinn, and Hill 1992). Of course, more than one reason may explain this result, including self-selection. However, it seems likely that immersion in religious institutions builds social capital, as Coleman (1988) and others have argued.

Arguing as I do that children will generally do better when they have two (or perhaps more) parents does not lead me to conclude that such arrangements are invariably preferable or that most children cannot thrive in single-parent families. The evidence suggests otherwise. Family structure explains a relatively small amount of the variation in key outcomes of success such as educational attainment, mental health, or problem behavior, especially when single-parenthood does not expose children to poverty, conflict, and instability. Yet, we cannot gainsay the fact that in American society, where economic and social support for families of all types is meager, children are more likely to be disadvantaged when they grow up in a single-parent household. The reverse is just as true: children are more likely to grow up in a single-parent household when they are disadvantaged. Mounting evidence suggests that disadvantage breeds family instability by undermining confidence in marriage, necessitating improvised and impermanent arrangements, and restricting access to good neighborhoods, schools, and social services.

This circular causality has been at the center of policy debates about welfare, family structure, and the well-being of children, with conservatives claiming that economic incentives have made single parenthood more attractive than work, and liberals insisting that the absence of work is to blame for the erosion of marriage and family life. Chicken or egg?—both arguments oversimplify the transformation in the family; neither prescription—eliminating welfare or creating jobs—is likely to reverse the trends of the twentieth century, which have their roots in multiple and interrelated cultural, political, demographic, and economic forces. The ideological conflicts that dominate public discussion about family values are curiously reminiscent of other moments of social dislocation in American history. We are no more likely to restore the conjugal family rooted in the ideal of premarital sexual chastity, early and lifelong monogamy, and a sharply drawn division of labor between men and women than we are to bring back the family farm.

Yet, the presumption that families can and should be self-sufficient remains a powerful image in American society—so much so that even the African proverb that "it takes a village to raise a child" has become a source of controversy when employed by Hillary Rodham Clinton (1996) to generate public support for children. Although safeguarding the ecological system is a well-accepted policy premise when it comes to the natural environment, the idea of extending this notion to children and families continues to be politically contentious, suggesting as it does that the family is not completely self-sufficient and that parents are not entirely autonomous.

As mentioned earlier, Americans, when compared with citizens of other nations with advanced economies, are committed to a highly privatized notion of the family. We are inclined to regard efforts to build supportive institutions that share child-care responsibilities with parents as state intrusions upon the natural rights of parents. Over the past several years, "parents' rights" legislation has been introduced in many states as a corrective to what its proponents believe are efforts to undermine the authority of parents. Although most Americans do not subscribe to such an extreme idea of parental autonomy, we distrust state institutions and favor voluntary, local systems of support. Tocqueville understood America political culture well when he identified the central importance of mediating institutions that reduce the power of the government over individuals, and foremost among these mediating institutions was the democratic family.

When Tocqueville visited America, we were still an agrarian nation and remained so throughout the nineteenth century. The agrarian ideal of a largely self-sufficient family supported by local civic institutions has survived this century, though its credibility is being stretched to the breaking point as we head into the next century. We continue to rely on the family as the major, if not exclusive, mechanism for allocating resources to children, knowing full well that it generates extreme inequalities in income and opportunities, not to mention cultural and social capital. Correcting these inequalities remains a major challenge if American society is to adhere to its tenets of equality of opportunity and meritocracy.

Parents increasingly share the responsibility for preparing their children for economic and civic roles with other institutions, but parents are granted authority for "subcontracting" training to those institutions: schools, churches, voluntary organizations, and the like. Management or oversight of the child's involvement in these institutions has become a major activity of parents, probably of no less importance to the child's success in later life than in-home child-rearing practices. Yet, many parents differ enormously in their knowledge and access to institutions outside the home that affect the child's life chances. Differences by class, race, and ethnicity compound and magnify parents' individual differences in ability to manage the external world. No doubt, too, these status differences could be linked as well to parents' belief in their capacities to invest in institutions outside the home. And whatever their sense of "personal efficacy," a large number of parents simply do not have the means to live in the right neighborhoods, send their children to the right schools, or pay for quality child care, afterschool activities, and summer camp.

Our commitment to helping parents remains largely rhetorical in the form of exhorting parents to spend more time with their children and take better care of them. This rhetoric is not without its effect. The vast majority of citizens believe that American parents spend too little time with their children, are lax in their discipline, and are less willing to make sacrifices in their behalf. However when queried about the state of their own families, parents are much more upbeat in their evaluations. While feeling pinched for time, most parents are very positive about the quality of their family life. Moreover, children generally concur with their parents' assessments though, not surprisingly, adolescents are slightly more critical of parental practices. Still, it is obvious that most families think that it is the other folks who are not living up to their end of the bargain (Furstenberg 1995b).

This belief is likely to be especially pronounced when the other folks are the poor and minorities. Despite evidence to the contrary, most Americans believe that the poor hold different aspirations for their children and are less capable and competent parents. Ethnic minorities regardless of class, perhaps blacks especially, are likely to engender similar suspicions from the public at large, and these suspicions have been unscrupulously exploited by elected officials. Diversity has increasingly become a codeword to many Euro-Americans for a challenge to the American way of life, including the so-called traditional family.

Americans, and perhaps social scientists as well, may overestimate the significance of family change in accounting for changes in the well-being of children. Although rising levels of family instability surely contribute to the ill-being of children, they are not the exclusive and probably not the primary explanation for changes in the welfare of children. I come to this judgment for several reasons: First, the vast research literature on the immediate and long-term effects of marital disruption on children provides a consistent view that divorce has moderate to large effects in many realms of behavior. However, some portion of that effect is due to the family environment before disruption occurs and to the types of individuals who are predisposed to divorce or to single-parenthood. After taking account of these differences, the impact of the single-parenthood itself is reduced.

Second, macrolevel trends in children's ill-being as measured by such indicators as school dropout, drug use, delinquency, and teenage childbearing do not track well with trends in family change measured by either the level of single-parenthood or women in the labor force. The latter have risen more or less continuously, whereas the former have fluctuated from decade to decade. Children's welfare appears to reflect what demographers refer to as period effects, that is, immediate temporal influences resulting more from economic, political, and cultural conditions or exposure to media than from cohort effects that birth groups carry with them over a lifetime. This observation is supported by international data as well: there seems to be little correlation between levels of problem behavior and the amount of family change. Northern European nations have witnessed astoundingly high levels of family change in the past several decades with no large apparent impact on levels of problem behavior among youth. At least at a superficial level changes in the family and the conditions of youth seem to be weakly correlated if they are correlated at all.

Interestingly, too, the rhetoric of a decline in family values is much more pronounced in Anglo than in northern European countries. This may reflect the greater or more exclusive role that the family is expected to play in determining the child's fate in these nations. Of course, in the Scandinavian countries, the welfare state also plays a more prominent role in mitigating the impact of family change by allocating resources to children according to their needs, rather than relying on the family as the main source of material well-being or institutional access. Thus, it seems that appeals to strengthening family values are likely to be sounded in nations that regard the family as a protective institution against the potential intrusion of the state.

PROSPECTS FOR THE FUTURE

I have discussed several interconnected themes that have implications for the future of the family. First, I argued that the direction of change in the family that has produced a weaker conjugal system and destabilized the ideal of the nuclear family has not resulted, strictly speaking, from a shift in cultural preferences but a host of concurrent trends undermining the viability of this kinship arrangement. These trends have occurred in nearly all highly developed economies. In virtually all Western nations, women have been brought into the job economy, marriage occurs later, fertility has declined, and divorce and single-parenthood have increased. These patterns are not likely to disappear in the near future or to be altered by rhetoric appeals to traditional values.

Class and ethnic differences, in the short run at least, are likely to grow rather than diminish, exacerbating the differences between the preferred family patterns of the affluent and the adaptive kinship arrangements of the dispossessed. It is entirely possible that in another quarter of a century we may look back on the family of today nostalgically. Family systems are likely, even for the well-off, to become more complex and less predictable, as they have over the past several decades. This means that many more children are likely to grow up with more rather than less family instability. Even stable two-parent families will continue to feel the pinch of balancing work and domestic responsibilities.

This condition puts a demand on the state to pick up some of the slack by providing child care, medical insurance, preschool programs, afterschool services, summer activities, and so on to ease the burdens placed on parents who do not have the means to arrange for these services privately. As we have seen in the past two decades, Americans have become ever more resistant to using public funds to support the family, presumably because we are reluctant to intrude on "parents' rights." Our commitment to the privatized family, sheltered from state interference, arouses fears of government intrusion in this country more than in most other industrialized nations. "Socializing" children, in theory, is up to parents, not to state-supported, let alone state-run, institutions and services. But this ideology protects the privileged and conceals the obvious fact that parents cannot shoulder so much of the burden of investing human capital in children. The arrangement that worked well enough in an agrarian economy and in the early stages of industrialization is simply insufficient to equip children for the twenty-first-century economy. To take an obvious example, we cannot rely on the family to expose children to computer literacy, a skill that is becoming increasingly important to children in the educational system.

Our cherished notions of the family may be getting in the way of providing adequately for children who do not have the benefit of family resources. No doubt we would be better off if all children were able to grow up in stable and harmonious two-parent families. However, this prospect is unrealistic. In any event, this expectation still places an increasingly high burden on low- and middle-income parents who cannot provide adequately for the growing requirement of college and beyond. Privately, many families have accommodated by greater personal sacrifice. As one low-income parent told me: "It really requires four jobs to achieve a decent standard of living." However, this same woman admitted that she and her partner rarely saw each other and had contemplated splitting up. The paradox is that we seem to be undermining families that we purport to protect by our peculiarly American-style relationship between the family and state. We need to think intelligently about a way of resolving this public/private dilemma lest we undermine the family in the interests of saving it and put our nation's children in even greater jeopardy in the future.

NOTE

1. For excellent commentaries see the recent histories of the 1950s by May (1988), Modell (1989), Skolnick (1991), Coontz (1992), etc.

REFERENCES

Alan Guttmacher Institute. 1994. *Sex and America's Teenagers*. New York: Alan Guttmacher Institute.
Bell, Norman W., and Ezra F. Vogel, eds. 1968. *A Modern Introduction to The Family*. New York: Free Press.
Bellah, Robert N., R. Madsen, William M. Sullivan, Ann Swidler, and Steven M. Tipton. 1985. *Habits of the Heart: Individualism and Commitment in American Life*. Berkeley: University of California Press.
Bellingham, Bruce. 1988. "The History of Childhood since the Invention of Childhood: Some Issues in the Eighties." *Journal of Family History* 13: 347–58.
Belsky, Jay, and David Eggebeen. 1991. "Maternal Employment and Young Children's Socioemotional Development." *Journal of Marriage and the Family* 53: 1083–98.
Berger, Brigitte, and Peter L. Berger. 1983/1984. *The War over the Family*. Garden City, N.Y.: Anchor Books.
Blankenhorn, David, Steven Bayme, and Jean Bethke Elshtain, eds. 1990. *Rebuilding the Nest: A New Commitment to the American Family*. Milwaukee, Wis.: Family Service America.
Blood, Robert, O., and Donald M. Wolfe. 1960. *Husbands and Wives*. New York: The Free Press.
Bott, Elizabeth. 1971. *Family and Social Network*, 2d ed. New York: Free Press.
Buchmann, Marlis 1989. *The Script of Life in Modern Society*. Chicago: University of Chicago Press.
Bumpass, Larry L. 1990. "What's Happening to the Family? Interactions between Demographic and Institutional Change." *Demography* 27: 483–90.
Chadwick, Bruce A., and Tim B. Heaton, eds. 1992. *Statistical Handbook on the American Family*. Phoenix, Ariz.: Oryx.
Cherlin, Andrew J. 1992. *Marriage, Divorce, Remarriage*, rev. and enlarged ed. Cambridge: Harvard University Press.
Cherlin, Andrew J., and Frank F. Furstenberg, Jr. 1986. *The New American Grandparent: A Place in the Family, a Life Apart*. New York: Basic Books.
———. 1994. "Stepfamilies in the United States: A Reconsideration." *Annual Review of Sociology* 20: 359–81.
Clinton, Hillary Rodham. 1996. *It Takes a Village: and Other Lessons Children Teach Us*. New York: Simon and Schuster.
Coale, Ansley J., and Susan Cotts Watkins, eds. 1985. *The Decline of Fertility in Europe: The Revised Proceedings of a Conference on the Princeton European Fertility Project*. Princeton, N.J.: Princeton University Press.

Coleman, James S. 1988. "Social Capital in the Creation of Human Capital." *American Journal of Sociology* 94 (Suppl. 95): S95–S120.

Condran, Gretchen A., and Frank F. Furstenberg, Jr. 1994. "Are Trends in the Well-Being of Children Related to Changes in the American Family? Making a Simple Question More Complex." *Population*, 6 (Nov–Dec): 1613–38.

Coontz, Stephanie. 1992. *The Way We Never Were: American Families and the Nostalgia Trap*. New York: Basic Books.

Coser, Rose L., ed. 1964. *The Family: Its Structure and Functions*. New York: St. Martin's Press.

Espenshade, Thomas J. 1985. "The Recent Decline of American Marriage: Blacks and Whites in Comparative Perspective." Pp. 53–90 in *Contemporary Marriage*, edited by Kingsley Davis. New York: Russell Sage Foundation.

Farber, Bernard. 1973. *Family and Kinship in Modern Society*. Glenview, Ill.: Scott, Foresman.

Farley, Reynolds, ed. 1995. *State of the Union: America in the 1990s*. Vols. 1 and 2. New York: Russell Sage Foundation.

Flacks, Richard. 1971. *Youth and Social Change*. Chicago: Markham.

Friedan, Betty. 1983. *The Feminine Mystique*. New York: Norton.

Friedenberg, Edgar Z. 1964. *The Vanishing Adolescent*. Boston: Beacon Books.

Furstenberg, Frank F., Jr. 1966. "Industrialization and the American Family: A Look Backward." *American Sociological Review* 31 (3): 326–37.

———. 1982. "Conjugal Succession: Reentering Marriage after Divorce." Pp. 107–146 in *Life Span Development and Behavior*. Vol. 4, edited by Paul B. Baltes and Orville Gilbert Brim. New York: Academic Press.

———. 1995a. "Fathering in the Inner-City: Paternal Participation and Public Policy." Pp. 119–47 in *Fatherhood: Contemporary Theory, Research and Social Policy*, edited by William Marsiglio. Thousand Oaks, Calif.: Sage Publications.

———. 1995b. "Family Change and the Welfare of Children: What Do We Know and What Can We Do about It?" Pp. 245–57 in *Gender and Family Change in Industrialized Countries*, edited by Karen O. Mason and An-Magritt Jensen. Oxford: Clarendon.

Furstenberg, Frank F., Jr., and Andrew J. Cherlin. 1991. *Divided Families: What Happens to Children When Parents Part*. Cambridge: Harvard University Press.

Gerson, Kathleen. 1985. *Hard Choices*. Berkeley: University of California Press.

Gillis, John R. 1996. *A World of Their Own Making: Myth, Ritual, and the Quest for Family Values*. New York: Basic Books.

Goode, William J. 1963. *World Revolution and Family Patterns*. New York: Free Press.

Goodman, Paul. 1960. *Growing Up Absurd: Problems of Youth in the Organized System*. New York: Random House.

Hareven, Tamara K. 1981. *Family Time and Industrial Time: The Relationship between the Family and Work in a New England Industrial Community*. New York: Cambridge University Press.

Hayes, Cheryl D., ed. 1987. *Risking the Future: Adolescent Sexuality, Pregnancy, and Childbearing*. Washington, D.C.: National Academy Press.

Hiner, N. Ray, and Joseph M. Hawes, eds. 1985. *Growing Up in America: Children in Historical Perspective*. Chicago: University of Illinois Press.

Johnson, Colleen L. 1988. *Ex Familia: Grandparents, Parents, and Children Adjust to Divorce*. New Brunswick, N.J.: Rutgers University Press.

Larson, Reed, and Maryse H. Richards. 1994. *Divergent Realities: The Emotional Lives of Mothers, Fathers, and Adolescents*. New York: Basic Books.

Lasch, Christopher. 1977. *Haven in a Heartless World: The Family Besieged*. New York: Basic Books.

Luker, Kristen. 1996. *Dubious Conceptions*. Cambridge: Harvard University Press.

Lye, Diane. 1996. "Adult Child–Parent Relationships." *Annual Review of Sociology* 22: 79–102.

May, Elaine T. 1988. *Homeward Bound: American Families in the Cold War Era*. New York: Basic Books.

McLanahan, Sarah, and Gary Sandefur. 1994. *Growing Up with a Single Parent*. Cambridge: Harvard University Press.

Menaghan, Elizabeth G., and Toby L. Parcel. 1990. "Paternal Employment and Family Life," *Journal of Marriage and the Family* 52: 1079–98.

Modell, John. 1989. *Into One's Own: From Youth to Adulthood in the United States, 1920–1975*. Berkeley: University of California Press.

Modell, John, Frank F. Furstenberg, Jr., and Theodore Hershberg. 1976. "Social Change and Transitions to Adulthood in Historical Perspective." *Journal of Family History* 1: 7–32.

Morgan, S. Philip. 1996. "Characteristic Features of American Fertility: A Description of Late Twentieth Century U. S. Fertility Trends and Differentials." *Population and Development Review* 22 (Suppl): 19–63.

Murdock, George P. 1949. *Social Structure*. New York: Macmillan.

National Commission on Children. 1991. *Beyond Rhetoric: A New American Agenda for Children and Families*. Washington, D.C.: National Commission on Children.

National Research Council. 1993. *Losing Generations: Adolescents in High-Risk Settings*. Washington, D.C.: National Academy Press.

Parsons, Talcott. 1951. *The Social System*. New York: Free Press.

Popenoe, David. 1988. *Disturbing the Nest: Family Change and Decline in Modern Societies*. New York: Aldine De Gruyter.

Rainwater, Lee, and William L. Yancey. 1967. *The Moynihan Report and the Politics of Controversy*. Cambridge: MIT Press.

Robinson, John. 1990. "The Time Squeeze." *American Demographics* 12: 30–33.

Rodman, H. 1963. "The Lower-Class Value Stretch." *Social Forces* 42 (3): 205–15.

Rossi, Alice S., and Peter H. Rossi. 1990. *Of Human Bonding: Parent–Child Relations across the Life Course*. New York: Aldine de Gruyter.

Rothman, Ellen K. 1984. *Hands and Hearts: A History of Courtship in America*. New York: Basic Books.

Scanzoni, John, Karen Polonko, Jay Teachman, and Linda Thompson. 1989. *The Sexual Bond: Rethinking Families and Close Relationships*. Newbury Park, Calif.: Sage Publications.

Schneider, David M. 1980. *American Kinship: A Cultural Account*, 2d ed. Chicago: University of Chicago Press.

Shorter, Edward. 1975. *The Making of the Modern Family*. New York: Basic Books.

Skocpol, Theda, and William J. Wilson. 1994. "Welfare As We Need It." *New York Times* 9 February.

Skolnick, Arlene. 1991. *Embattled Paradise: The American Family in an Age of Uncertainty*. New York: Basic Books.

Slater, Philip. 1970. *The Pursuit of Loneliness*. Boston: Beacon.

Stacey, Judith. 1993. "Good Riddance to 'the Family': A Response to David Popenoe." *Journal of Marriage and the Family* 55(3): 545–47.

Thornton, Arland, William Axinn, and Daniel Hill. 1992. "Reciprocal Effects of Religiosity, Cohabitation, and Marriage." *American Journal of Sociology* 98: 628–51.

Tocqueville, Alexis De. 1835/1996. *Democracy in America*, translated by George Lawrence. New York: Harper & Row.

Tufte, Virginia, and Barbara Myerhoff. 1979. *Changing Images of the Family*. New Haven, Conn.: Yale University Press.

Uhlenberg, Peter, and David Eggebeen. 1986. "The Declining Well-Being of American Adolescents." *The Public Interest* 82: 25–38.

U.S. Bureau of the Census. 1996. Statistical Abstract of the United States, 116th ed. Washington, D.C.: GPO.

The 1995 Virginia Slims American Women's Opinion Poll. 1995. A poll conducted by Roper Starch Worldwide, Inc.

Wallerstein, Judith S., and Susan Blakeslee. 1989. *Second Chances: Men, Women and Children a Decade after Divorce*. New York: Ticknor and Fields.

White, Linda K. 1993. "Stepfamilies over the Life Course: Social Support." Paper presented at the National Symposium on Stepfamilies. State College, Penn.

Winch, Robert F. 1963. *The Modern Family*, rev. ed. New York: Holt, Rinehart and Winston.

CHAPTER EIGHT

Contesting the Moral Boundaries of Eros

*A PERSPECTIVE ON THE CULTURAL POLITICS OF SEXUALITY
IN THE LATE-TWENTIETH-CENTURY UNITED STATES*

STEVEN SEIDMAN

IT HAS BECOME COMMONPLACE to observe that sex, as much as the economy or education, is a political battleground. Whether our focus is nineteenth-century conflicts in the United States around masturbation, sodomy, women's sexuality, prostitution, and the free-love movement, or recent conflicts over reproductive rights, gay marriage, pornography, child abuse, and sex education, these aspects of personal life are, as feminists have insisted, indeed political. Moreover, as queer theorists have similarly insisted, sexuality is not only a personal issue that is politicized but is itself a social force. Whatever sexuality might mean for the individual, it functions as a social code, normative framework, and principle of social organization or, simply put, a way of defining, regulating, and organizing bodies, selves, and populations that produces identities, solidarities, and relations of domination. Hence sexuality may be approached as an analytically autonomous sphere of individual and social determination—a site of desire, identity, social organization, and politics.

But how are we to interpret conflicts over sexuality? At a minimum I suggest distinguishing two levels of sexual politics. First, there are conflicts over rights, resources, and representations. For example, Americans are divided over sex education, civil rights for homosexuals, funding for family planning, and the legitimacy of public sexual representations. Such divisions point to a sexual stratification system in the United States—for example, a system that socially privileges heterosexuality, marriage, two-parent families, romanticized sexuality, monogamy, and the privatization of sexuality. Such sexualities and intimacies receive social benefits, juridical-administrative recognition, symbolic esteem, social legitimacy, and a normalized, morally valued social status. Much of sexual politics involves struggles to alter and maintain this sexual hierarchy through battles around rights, resources, and representation.

These conflicts have been analyzed in the language of social movement literature—in terms, say, of resource mobilization, social interests, the formation of social and political organizations, grassroots and elite support, and the role of the the media. A key site of conflict, however, is at the level of sexual-intimate meanings and morality. For example, at the very center of the politics of sex education are contrasting views of the meaning of sexuality, clashes over whether sex education is or should be a private or public responsibility, and, most fundamentally, a conflict over sexual values, that is, over what sex means, what norms are appropriate to guide sexual behavior, and how to fix the place of sex in personal and public life.

I aim to analyze sexual conflicts at the level of the politics of meanings and morality. Such cultural conflicts bring into relief divisions that bear on basic, core aspects of American culture—for example, disagreements about how to establish moral boundaries with regard to sexual behavior and representations in public life, divisions with regard to interpreting and assessing sexual meanings and norms, and conflicts over what counts as a family. Although divisions over sexual-intimate meanings will likely remain contested and unsettled for some time (for example, it is hard to imagine a resolution to disagreements over whether sex is fundamentally about pleasure, procreation, or love), norms, rules, and conventions still must be established to govern intimate and public life. How are such normative conflicts to be settled? How in fact do Americans justify their sexual and intimate practices? What "moral logics" operate in this realm? These cultural and normative disputes are the main focus of my paper, as they underlie not only struggles over rights and resources but point to broader societal divisions and potentially far-reaching sociocultural shifts.

I argue that Americans are divided with regard to the moral logics they deploy to authorize sexual norms, to delineate the moral boundaries of legitimate and illegitimate intimate arrangements, and therefore to establish hierarchies of sexual and intimate practices. On the one hand, Americans appeal to a substantive sexual ethic or what I call a "morality of the sex act" that assumes that sexuality has an inherent meaning, social purpose, and moral status. Some sexual and intimate practices are said to be intrinsically right, good, normal, and healthy, whereas others are unnatural, abnormal, wrong, and immoral. On the other hand, more recently, especially with the rise of the counterculture and its evolution into a new age and human potential culture, and with the formation of feminist, lesbian and gay, bisexual, and sadism/masochism (S/M) movements, there has appeared a moral logic that does not assume that particular sex acts and intimacies have intrinsic social and moral meaning. Such a "communicative sexual ethic" holds that social agents make sex meaningful, and ethical judgment is to be determined by the moral qualities of the social exchange or communication. The two moral logics do not collapse into a simple political or ideological binary. For example, a morality of the sex act is often used not only to condemn but to justify homosexuality (by the claim that it is natural and therefore, given the folk culture of America, morally good). Although a morality of the sex act can legitimate sexual-intimate differences, its logic of natural/unnatural and normal/abnormal inevitably produces classes of "deviant" or outsider sexualities. In contrast, a communicative sexual ethic breaks from the logic of natural/unnatural and normal/abnormal. It still functions, of course, as a regulatory force, by providing general normative guidelines, not moral imperatives. Such an ethic permits a wide range of sexual choice, tolerance, and affirmation of intimate differences while also producing fewer deviant identities.

I suggest, moreover, that to the extent that a communicative sexual ethic is becoming part of the public culture of the United States, it renders the clash over sexualities and intimacies much more divisive and socially charged. This is so because a communicative ethic legitimates a range of choices and practices that challenge currently dominant modes of organizing sexual and intimate life, for example, normative heterosexuality, marriage-based families, families based on blood ties, romanticized sexuality, and intimacies organized around shared residence. Indeed, to the extent that substantive sexual and intimate values and practices such as normative heterosexuality, marriage, and nuclear families, have defined American national identity, these cultural clashes take on the weight of struggles over the very meaning of America.

Consider, for example, the politics of homosexual rights. Whether posed in terms of the debate over homosexuals in the military, gay marriage, or antisodomy legislation, the conflict over homosexual rights is at the center of U.S. public life. But how should we interpret this political conflict? At one level, it is surely about the politics of individual choice and social inclusion. Hence, advocates and opponents of homosexual rights argue over which sexual choices and practices are legitimate and which sexual identities should be accorded full citizenship rights. At another level, the debate can be interpreted as addressing the character of America's societal community. Thus, some advocates argue that granting homosexual rights will strengthen national unity while denying such rights will weaken it by fomenting social discontent. In contrast, some critics maintain that granting homosexual rights legitimates a "lifestyle" that undermines a heterosexual-based marital-familial institution that is said to be the basis of American national community.

I want to underscore two fundamental points. First, Americans defend or oppose homosexual rights by arguing over the meaning and morality of sexuality. Thus advocates speak of the naturalness and normality of homosexuality, interpret sexuality as having multiple purposes beyond procreation, appeal to the consensual character of same-sex intimacies, and emphasize the role of homosexuality today as a social identity providing personal coherence and social solidarity. In contrast, opponents of homosexual rights often justify their position by appealing to the perverse or unnatural and pathological nature of homosexuality, its uncoupling from procreation and a concept of family based on marriage and blood ties, and its immoral, promiscuous lifestyle. In short, the struggle over homosexual rights is engaged on the terrain of sexual meanings and values. In the end, to the extent that the clash of sexual meanings and values cannot be resolved discursively (there has been no resolution to the dispute over whether homosexuality is natural or unnatural, normal or abnormal), this ongoing discursive division evolves into a conflict over moral logics or principles that are appealed to in order to legitimate social norms. The second point I wish to emphasize is that the homosexual rights debate is about more than which "groups" or populations deserve rights or state protection from discrimination and harassment; it is about which social practices are legitimate, what kinds of intimacies and families are valued, what is the place of new sexual communities in public life, what range of behaviors is to be covered under privacy laws, and what kind of community and nation America imagines itself to be.

I shall map out key conflicts around sexuality in the late-twentieth-century United States. Initially I provide a historical perspective that describes some of the major changes and patterns of sexual diversity in the United States. Based on this perspective, I argue that although conflicts over rights, resources, and political and cultural representation are important, these clashes evidence struggles over "foundational" or core sexual beliefs and norms, over the logics that establish the moral boundaries of sexuality, and the status and social role of sexual identities and communities that are even more significant as indicators of social division and cultural conflict in contemporary America. Moreover, in the emergence of a communicative sexual ethic that assumes that practices have no intrinsic sexual meaning or moral status but that these emerge in social exchanges, I see the beginnings of both a new perspective viewing sexuality as a principle of social organization and a new politic contesting this organizing principle. I take this development to be the most radical impulse of current sexual politics—an impulse issuing from the social periphery but finding powerful articulation in critical knowledges and in social movements. For example, the rise of a queer and transgendered movement politicizing the sexualization of bodies, contesting essentialized constructions of identity and the organization of selves around the binaries of male/female sex, masculine/feminine gender, and heterosexual/homosexual sexuality, and challenging the normative regulation of self in terms of the binary of normal/abnormal, anticipates a major reorganization of American intimate culture.

In the concluding part of this essay I consider some of the ethical-political implications of these cultural conflicts. In particular, in the shift to a communicative sexual ethic, I highlight possibilities for the depolitization of many intimate choices. Such an ethic suggests approaching many sexual choices in the language of aesthetic preference or in a language involving ethical judgments that would be less normalizing and therefore would produce fewer deviant or outsider sexual-intimate practices. In part, the depoliticizing of intimate choices, of sexual and gender practices, is in my view an integral aspect of a democratizing sexual politic for late-twentieth-century America. Of course, there are still many spheres of intimate life such as sex education, family planning and funding, child care support, and antiviolence legislation where expanded state intervention should remain a vital component of a democratic sexual politic.

The "New Sexual Pluralism" in Historical Perspective

The mid-nineteenth century United States will serve as a historical baseline. My comments draw on research focused very broadly on white middle America and angled toward the Northeast and urban, nonimmigrant populations (Seidman 1991). I have no reason to think that my observations on sexual-intimate patterns in this century are not relevant to broader populations, but I would not want to preclude the possibility that certain nonwhite, non-middle-class populations exhibit somewhat different patterns and sites of sexual conflict.

Historians tend to agree that the core of the social organization of mid-nineteenth-century intimate life in the United States was marriage (e.g., D'Emilio and Freedman 1988). As proscriptions in popular medical and advice literature against masturbation, fornication, adultery, youth sexuality, premarital sexuality, and sodomy make abundantly clear, marriage was the only legitimate institution for sex. Moreover, within marriage a procreative ideal was normative. To be sure, erotic pleasure was expected to accompany procreative behavior, but valuing sex for its sensual pleasures was considered demeaning to the ethical-spiritual essence of a love-based marriage. The dominant contrasts in mid-nineteenth-century America were between marriage and nonmarital sexualities, between procreative and erotic behavior, and between ethical-spiritual love and a sensual, animal-like desire. The range of proscriptions in this normative literature point to a world of lived sexual difference—from the sexualities of youth and single Americans to the underworld world of pornography and prostitution that flourished in the major cities. These differences, though, lacked social legitimation.[1]

Elsewhere (Seidman 1991, 1992), I have described two major changes that occurred in American culture in the course of the twentieth century: the "eroticization of sex," which was linked to the "sexualization of love," and the rise of a "new sexual pluralism" connected to the making of a culture of sexual identities. I would today add a third development: the rise of movements challenging the very "system of sexuality" that took shape in the last two centuries.

As many historians have recently argued, our Victorian ancestors were not against sex or sensuality (Gay 1986; Lystra 1989; Rothman 1987). They disapproved of sexual pleasure as an end in itself and were convinced of the undesirable consequences of such pleasures. The power of sex was such that sensuality threatened to engulf marriage in a sea of lust and animal desire, thereby debasing its spiritual core. The seductive power of sensual pleasure required a social regime that channeled the "sexual instinct" into a reproductive imperative organized around a marital ideal of ethical-spiritual companionship.

The sexualization of love signaled the end of this aspect of Victorian culture. Relying on popular medical literature, novels, and autobiographies, I traced a shift in the meaning and normative role of sex (Seidman 1991; cf. D'Emilio and Freedman 1988). In particular, nonprocreative notions of sex became central to normative concepts of love and marriage. Moreover, as sex was approached as a legitimate way to sustain love and marriage its erotic or expressive-sensual aspects became the focus of social interest and value. In a word, the giving and receiving of sexual pleasure became a legitimate way to express love. This facilitated the making of a culture organized around the cultivation of the erotic aspects of sex. Sexualized love gave birth to a culture of eroticism that by the 1960s, ironically, staked claims to legitimacy by virtue of its individualizing and communicative aspects independent of love and marriage. As an expressive, pleasurable, and communicative practice, sex became an autonomous value sphere.

One major consequence of these changes is that sex has become a site of multiple meanings and conflicting social norms. Although some Americans criticize this culture by appealing to an ethical-spiritual ideal of sex and love, few oppose eroticized sex. Social dissension revolves around the balance of the erotic and nonerotic aspects of sex and love, around the individualizing versus the communitarian aspects of eroticism, and around the social form of sexual expression, for example, marriage, cohabitation, and committed or casual relationships.

The American culture of eroticism contributed to the rise of sex as a basis of self-identity. As sex was valued for its expressive, pleasurable, and communicative aspects apart from marriage and love, individuals were able to focus on particular sexual pleasures. This made possible the fashioning of new sex-based identities around specific sexual practices such as S/M or homosexuality. In fact, historians have argued that in the early decades of the twentieth century a national culture was taking shape that made sexuality into a basis of social identity. This is the second major change I wish to briefly address, as it made possible a "new sexual pluralism."

As I mentioned earlier, the dominant contrasts in mid-to-late-nineteenth-century middle America were between marital and nonmarital sex, procreative and nonprocreative sexualities, and between ethical-spiritual love and sensuality. Although these oppositions have retained a cultural resonance for subsequent generations of Americans, the legitimation of sex outside marriage (even if this is still contested), of nonprocreative sex (even if the issue of which nonprocreative sexualities are acceptable remains contested), and of eroticism (even if its role in intimacy and society is contested) has made these tensions peripheral. The major sexual dramas in postwar America pivot around the normal/abnormal and heterosexual/homosexual binaries. The shift in the site of tension indicates a reorganization of American sexual culture, with questions of identity and normality moving into the center of social conflict.

Historians have made a compelling case that in the nineteenth-century United States sexuality was not a category of social identity. For example, the concepts of heterosexuality and homosexuality were absent (Duberman 1986; Faderman 1991; Katz 1983; Rotundo 1989; Seidman 1991; Smith-Rosenberg 1975). The closest approximation to a category of sexual identity was sodomy, which encompassed a multiplicity of sexual acts, including bestiality, masturbation, fornication, and anal or oral sex. Sodomy gained its coherence in contrast to procreative sex within marriage. The sodomite was not an autonomous sexual identity but a person convicted of violating a social norm or law. Moreover, all Americans were considered potential sodomites. Sodomitic behavior was interpreted as a weakening of self or social control, perhaps a flaw in character or a momentary surrendering to temptation. It did not reveal a distinctive sexual identity.[2]

Jonathan Katz (1995) has proposed that it was not until the twentieth century that "heterosexuality" was invented. Previously, Americans organized intimacies around opposite-sex affections, but heterosexuality, as it evolved initially in medical-psychiatric discourses and later in popular culture, referred to a unique complex of ideas: the assumption of two distinct sexes, sex uncoupled from reproduction, the normality of opposite-sex desire, and opposite-sex desire as the basis of an exclusive sexual identity. What seems indisputable is that homosexuality, as a category of personal identity, did not become part of American society until the early decades of this century (Chauncey 1994; D'Emilio 1983; Faderman 1991; Katz 1983). This event points up a far-reaching change in U.S. intimate culture: particular sexual desires are now organized as the basis of primary social identities.

Although we cannot trace the history here, in the course of this century, sex moved from an act to an identity delineating, in many instances, the fate of the individual. It was as if the exotic catalog of sexual personages that occupied the pages of Krafft-Ebing, Havelock Ellis, and Sigmund Freud stepped onto the stage of history. This century witnessed the public appearance of a virtual parade of new sexual identities: the heterosexual, homosexual, pedophile, fetishist, sadist, masochist, and so on. Henceforth, sexual conflict would revolve around the meaning and social regulation of sexual identities.

Recent scholars have told a complex story of sexuality in America involving a cast of characters, from the vice squad, scientists, psychiatrists, lawyers, and news reporters, to the new sexual subjects themselves (D'Emilio and Freedman 1988). A leading motif of this story is that the new sexual subjects who stepped into public view in the first half of this century eventually mobilized to achieve a normalized moral and social status. The paradigmatic case is that of the homosexual. Vilified and made into a deviant, pathological figure by medical-scientific-juridical practices, positioned on the margins but periodically exposed to reinforce the norm of heterosexuality, the homosexual fought back, deploying the tools of the oppressor—science and the appeal to normality. One consequence of this politicization is that today the homosexual is no longer just a personage but a social identity (D'Emilio 1983). As the story of the homosexual goes, so goes the tale of the bisexual, the hysterical female, the sadomasochist, and the like. Many of the very sexual identities that were scandalized by medical-scientific discourses are now claiming legitimacy, in part, by using a revised version of the discourse of their oppressors. Sexual conflict is today centered around identities and the clash of communities.

Let me try to clarify the implications of these social developments for the question of sexual diversity. I suggest that sexual conflicts in contemporary America be approached along at least three interrelated dimensions. First, the shift from a Victorian culture organized around a procreative marital norm to a culture based on the legitimacy of nonprocreative and nonmarital sexualities has produced societal conflicts around sexual meanings and values. How do we fix the boundaries of legitimate sexual expression in a society where sex has acquired multiple meanings and social roles? Second, sexual conflict occurs around the issue of identity. How do we determine which sexual identities are legitimate? Moreover, to the extent that sex-based identities have been elaborated into cultural communities, should they be recognized in their differences in public and institutional policy? Third, conflicts focus on the system or regime of sexuality itself—with its sexualization of bodies, typologies of sexual identities, and norms of normality and health. What are the impulse and implications of movements that imagine an order of bodies, desires, and intimacies beyond sexuality?

THE CONFLICT OVER SEXUAL ETHICS

Sexual conflicts are not new to contemporary America. As the proliferation of purity campaigns, and struggles around prostitution, age of consent laws, abortion, and pornography indicate, sex was a site of considerable social tension in the nineteenth century. Nevertheless, at least among the white, nonimmigrant middle classes, as evidenced in the normative literature but also in diaries, memoirs, and in the few available surveys of sexual beliefs and practices, there was a general consensus that sex had its proper place in marriage and that its principal role was reproductive. Sexual pleasure may have been an acceptable consequence of procreation, but it was not valued in itself. Indeed, even by the turn of the century, as love was sexualized and sensuality legitimated, sex was still valued only in marriage. It was only gradually in the course of this century that love was legitimated apart from marriage, and sex acquired value apart from marriage and love.

It was in the 1960s and 1970s that this century-long change fully emerged into public view and became the focus of major social conflicts. The language of sexual revolution in this period captured less a reality of an abrupt shift than a gradual reorganization of intimate culture in America. Moreover, although public conflict was often riveted on issues of rights (e.g., reproductive or gay rights), underlying these important political struggles were conflicts over the very meaning and social role of sex. In other words, once sex was no longer exclusively tied to a procreative marital or romantic norm, social division surfaced around determining its moral and social coordinates. Battlelines were drawn, for example, between those who defended a tight alignment of sex, love, and marriage and defenders of a slippage between not only sex and marriage, but between sex and love. Moreover, if sex carried multiple legitimate meanings, how were its social parameters to be defined? What range of interactions, with what social and moral characteristics, legitimated sexual expression? And what was to be the appropriate public interest in sex, as it was no longer tightly linked to marriage and love—a question that has become more urgent in light of the AIDS epidemic, the rise of single-parent households, and the sexualization of youth culture.

Although these diverse sexual conflicts have been analyzed as struggles over individual rights and "group" social interests (e.g., in the case of the women's movement, struggle for reproductive rights), this political struggle also goes on at the level of "sexual ethics." Thus the struggle over reproductive rights is in part a struggle by women to be sexually autonomous, which includes the right to uncouple sex from procreation, marriage, and indeed, for some women, from love. Whether the site of conflict is reproductive rights, gay rights, or youth sexuality, one aspect concerns the meaning and normative regulation of sex.

How do we characterize this normative conflict over sexuality? At one level, Americans are divided over the very meaning of sex. Is reproduction, love, pleasure, self-expression, health, or communication the essential meaning of sex? Available evidence suggests that although some Americans continue to assign a primarily reproductive meaning to sex, many more view sex as an expression of love (see Seidman 1991). And although there is much evidence that Americans overwhelmingly value sex as a way to express love (which itself is the site of conflicting meanings), there is division over whether sex is also to be valued as a practice of pleasure, self-expression, or communication apart from love. To simplify this picture, I think the basic conflict in this regard is between Americans who believe that the essential meaning of sex is as an expression of romantic love and others who hold that sex carries multiple meanings. This conflict becomes especially consequential when we consider its normative implications. If sex is defined primarily as an act of love, only relationships that exhibit the culturally specific social characteristics of being "loving" will be normative, even though what is an appropriate relationship for "love" is itself in dispute. By contrast, if sex has multiple meanings, social norms will be defended that allow for sex in varied social arrangements, including those that are nonmarital and nonromantic.

This is not the place to try to map out the range of normative sexual conflicts. Instead, I wish to comment on one aspect of this conflict that is at the core of American sexual politics.

My thesis is that there is a division around the moral or justificatory logics that ground sexual ethics. This division refers less to a value conflict, for example, the conflict between sexual autonomy and social welfare, than to the logic of authorizing social norms. Specifically, Americans are divided between what I shall call a "morality of the sex act" logic and a "communicative sexual ethic." In the former, sex acquires a determinate moral and social meaning as part of a cosmology, which may be understood in the language of religion, natural law, or secular reason. From this perspective, sexual practices have an inherent moral significance that determines their appropriate social status. An example of this moral logic would be a perspective that justifies sex only as a procreative or loving act in a heterosexual marriage, while proscribing nonprocreative, nonloving, nonheterosexual, and nonmarital sex, by appealing to a Christian cosmology. Another example of the logic of a morality of the sex act is a psychiatric perspective that appeals to a scientific model of normal psychosexual development to justify norms of heterosexuality and a love-centered marital or quasi-marital arrangement on the grounds of what are taken to be universal standards of normality and health. By contrast, a communicative sexual ethic assumes that sex acts have no inherent meaning but gain their moral coherence from their interactive context. It is the qualities of the social interaction that are appealed to as ethical standards. This justificatory strategy judges sex practices by considering, say, the consensual, responsible, caring, reciprocal, and mutually respectful aspects of the social interaction.

To illustrate the difference in these two moral logics, let us consider the issue of lesbian and gay rights. From the vantage point of the logic of a morality of the sex act articulated in a Christian framework, homosexuality might be considered inherently sinful or immoral. Hence, extending rights to homosexuals to protect them against job or housing discrimination would be opposed on the grounds that society has an interest in protecting itself against an immoral practice. An alternative Christian perspective might hold that homosexuality is just another divinely created form of human expression. These Christians might oppose discriminatory practices by insisting that the only issue of moral significance should be "responsible behavior," that is, can an individual do his or her job and pay the rent. From this communicative ethical standpoint, an individual's "sexual orientation" would be irrelevant for establishing social norms.

As this example suggests, we have two different moral logics at work in authorizing sexual norms. Each standpoint has its own language, logic of justification, and metatheory that gives it coherence and ethical force. Moreover, each logic has its own stress points. The appeal to an "order of things" or a transcendent foundation to ground sexual ethics is subject to the suspicion that today surrounds "foundational" claims in general—namely, that they conceal particular interests and values or express a metaphysic or world view of a particular tradition or community. Although such a moral logic might have propped up a liberal intimate culture at one time, today it seems at odds with the multicultural character of the United States. The communicative sexual ethic exposes weaknesses relating to its formalism and minimalism. Not only can the general values it appeals to such as choice or consent be contested (e.g., in the feminist debates over consent), but such values (e.g., responsibility and respect) are so general that they often cannot provide guidance on specific disputes. For example, invoking the general value of individual choice, providing it does not involve coercion, to justify tolerance toward homosexuality may be effective for establishing certain "negative freedoms," (e.g., protection against job discrimination), but it does not necessarily provide guidance in determining "positive freedoms," such as whether homosexual marriages should be legalized or whether homosexuality should be taught as a valued lifestyle choice. These are matters of substantive social values and ideals for which a minimalist language of choice, consent, and responsibility does not provide much, if any, guidance.

To the extent that conflicts over sexual ethics are metatheoretical or pivot on contrasting world views, I don't imagine a resolution. It seems fanciful, moreover, to anticipate that an overarching or integrative moral logic will emerge from this division. The differences of moral logics will continue to be part of sexual politics. My sense is that conflict at this normative level has ambivalent social and political significance. On the one hand, these conflicts are typically local in two ways. First, the focus of conflict rarely leads to broader social divisions or alignments, and therefore to global civic polarization. For example, the field of conflict over pornography is not necessarily mirrored in divisions over, say, abortion or homosexuality (witness the feminist critique of pornograpy). Thus, many sexual conflicts are issue-specific and limited as sources of social division. Second, even within these issue-specific conflicts, the differences are usually quite specific and occur within a network of shared beliefs, values, norms, and argumentative styles and rhetorics. For example, divisions over abortion mostly pivot on disagreement over when life begins, not on a woman's right to have sex, not on the value of her life and the life of children, and not on broader social and sexual values such as the individual's right to choose to be sexual, the linking of sex to affection or love, the importance of family, or considerations of public or social welfare. On the other hand, these conflicts, especially along their outer edges, evidence a division over the legitimate boundaries of sexual expression and the standards guiding rule-making decisions. This conflict is potentially socially polarizing, as it may involve a clash of ultimate values, norms, and institutional forms of sexual-intimate life, and contrasting visions of national identity. It is especially when such normative conflicts get connected to clashes between social groups that they acquire enhanced societal importance.

THE CONFLICT BETWEEN SEXUAL COMMUNITIES

It would be misleading to assume that the division in moral logics reflects an ideological division between conservatives and liberals. Indeed, the meaning of conservative and liberal in the sphere of sexual politics is unclear, especially in light of the feminist sexuality debates (Ferguson 1989; Seidman 1992). Moreover, as we have seen, a morality of the sex act can be deployed to oppose or support gay rights. Thus, advocates often justify gay rights by appealing to a psychiatric model that defines homosexuality as normal. Similarly, critics might utilize a communicative sexual ethic by arguing that it is precisely the qualities of "the homosexual lifestyle," its "promiscuity," "pleasure-seeking," and "transient relationships," that warrant social repression. Although there is no one-to-one logical correspondence between moral logic and political ideology, it is nevertheless the case that historically the communicative sexual ethic has been closely aligned with movements defending sexual pluralism, while the morality of the sex act logic has often been used to resist such movements. It is this linkage of moral logics to social movements that has made this normative division into an important source of social tension.

I have already commented on the limits placed on the expression of legitimate sexual differences in nineteenth-century America. However, in the course of the present century the links among sex, love, and marriage loosened, and a wider range of sexual practices acquired legitimacy. Moreover, sex became the basis for establishing social identities. Some of these new sexual figures responded to their deviant status by creating quasi-ethnic communities akin to the European immigrant communities established in the first half of the twentieth century. The paradigmatic case is the homosexual community, but parallels are to be found in feminist communities, and more recently in communities that have evolved around S/M, bisexuality, and sex workers. In the remainder of this section I consider some of the implications of these new sexual communities for the issue of social diversity.

My comments will focus initially on the lesbian and gay community, as this is the most organized sex-based community. I assume a vast historiography and sociology of the making of these communities (e.g., Adam 1987; Chauncey 1994; D'Emilio 1983; Faderman 1991). I shall overlook the many differences within these communites and focus on some very general normative and political divisions.

Let me state the obvious. The mainstream of the lesbian/gay movement is in the social mainstream of America. Whether struggling against discriminatory laws, antigay violence, or media and popular stereotypes, the chief agenda of this movement has been social integration, which includes gaining equal civil rights, equality of opportunity, and freedom from harassment from the state and citizens. Moreover, the social values of the chief organizations (e.g., National Lesbian and Gay Task Force, Human Rights Campaign) mirror mainstream America. For example, the struggle for domestic partnership legislation or lesbian/gay marriage, as Andrew Sullivan and Bruce Bawer rightly insist, endorses a quasi-marital, familial social norm. I would argue that it is precisely the integration of many lesbian/gay Americans in every way but their homosexuality that is the chief pathos driving this movement. To justify an agenda of social inclusion this movement has typically deployed the morality of the sex act logic—for example, defending the normality of homosexuality by appealing to "modernized" medical-scientific knowledge.

A "mainstream" however makes sense only in relation to an "opposition." Thus, as much as the mainstream agenda aims at social inclusion by asserting the normality of homosexuality, and by trying to normalize a national identity that includes homosexuals, movements of opposition to both the straight and lesbian/gay mainstream have favored a communicative sexual ethic. In particular, individuals whose sexual-intimate values depart from mainstream culture, or for whom their homosexuality is only one way their sexual-intimate lives are rendered deviant, have preferred a communicative sexual ethic. Moreover, efforts to legitimate their sexual differences have often meant contesting the social norms that regulate sexuality. In other words, as unique sexual values and patterns have evolved in the lesbian/gay community, reflecting, among other considerations, a history of marginalization and oppression and the same-sex basis of their communities, there has emerged an oppositional sexual politic contesting the moral boundaries and hierarchies of sexual and intimate life.[3]

I present two brief examples to support my thesis.

- Sadomasochism is hardly unique to lesbian/gay culture. What is distinctive is the development of a public S/M community, with its own organizations, publications, knowledges, and styles of self presentation (Califia 1982). The practices and identities of individuals who are part of an S/M community are typically defined as deviant—pathological or perverse—by the heterosexual and often by the homosexual mainstream. Although some advocates appeal to the naturalness and normality of S/M for legitimation, such normative strategies have limited plausibility given the tight moral association of sex with affection and love exhibited in gentle and tender behaviors. Accordingly, it is not surprising that S/M practitioners prefer a communicative sexual ethic that appeals to, for example, the consensual, mutually responsible, respectful, and pleasurable qualities of this social practice (e.g., see Seidman 1992).
- The practice of having multiple sex partners is again hardly unique to the gay community. In a society in which sex acquires an independent value as a medium of pleasure, self-expression, and communication, multiple sex partner practices are to be expected. Nevertheless, even during the height of sexual liberalization in the 1960s and 1970s, the evidence was clear: gay men exhibited patterns of having multiple sex partners that suggested a unique social formation (Seidman 1991). In the era of AIDS, there has been some alteration in specific sex practices (e.g., less anal intercourse and more nonpenetrative practices) and perhaps a reduction in the number of sex partners, but the general pattern of having multiple sex partners among gay men has not significantly changed (Martin 1986; Turner 1989). Given this population's high-risk status for sexually transmitted disease, this pattern further supports the notion of a somewhat unique gay male sexual-intimate culture. Parenthetically, in light of the institutionalization of this pattern, and discourses that give it moral coherence and value, it is hardly plausible to dismiss its moral credibility by interpreting it as a pathological symptom of oppression. For gay men who have adopted this pattern, even if for a limited period of their lives, claims to its moral legitimacy ultimately invoke its "communicative" aspects, for example, individual choice or its consensual and responsible behavioral qualities. The legitimation of this practice, like the legitimation of S/M, involves contesting the logic (morality of the sex act) and the specific rules that now govern the social organization of sex in America.

Of particular importance in these two examples is that normative conflict is not simply among individuals, experts, or social elites, but among sexual communities. Conflict is driven by the demand of historically emergent oppressed sexual communities to have their particular nonconventional or different social practices recognized by society. This entails contesting the dominant sexual order—indeed, renegotiating the rules that govern establishing normative boundaries or rules and the system of sexual hierarchy itself. Thus, in the case of S/M communities, contesting moral boundaries and rules involves struggles at the level of sexual meanings (e.g., to legitimate consensual pleasure-centered sex while aestheticizing judgments of specific sex acts), struggles at the level of moral logics (e.g., against a morality of the sex act), and struggles at an institutional level (e.g., to change laws and cultural representations).

The Conflict over the System of Sexuality

It is but a small step, though of huge significance, to trace this struggle over moral logics, boundaries, and hierarchies to conflicts around the system of sexuality itself. In order to explain the full import of this social event, I need to clarify the broader analytical and historical perspective on sexuality that underpins this discussion.

For the past decade or so, a scholarly archive has accumulated that contests the conventional view, still dominant in public and academic discourses, that defines sexuality as a natural fact. Although sexuality may be said to vary historically with regard to the meaning and social form of its practices, the conventional view still leaves intact the assumption of a human sexual nature. Scholarship in this field supports the view that sexuality is to be understood as a sociohistorical event. This does not mean that the understanding of the nature of sexuality is a recent historical event. Nor does it imply a recognition that social forces shape human sexuality. Instead, the idea of sex as a natural order is understood as a historical event. Moreover, what creates this notion of sex is sexuality, which is viewed as a social organizing principle. If sex can be said to be universal, sexuality is a mode of social organization to be found only in some societies.

A more or less conventionalized version of this perspective proposes that sexuality emerged as a social organizing principle only in some European nations in the eighteenth and nineteenth centuries. Scholars argue that before "modernity" there were sex acts, intimacies, prohibitions, and regulations but not sexuality, which is said to refer to a historically unique social organization of sex. There was sodomy and sodomites but not homosexuality and homosexuals (Bray 1995; Foucault 1978; Goldberg 1992; Katz 1983; Weeks 1977), opposite-sex intimacies but not heterosexuality (Brown 1988; Katz 1995; Laqueur 1990), marriages and intimate unions, including same-sex unions, but not romantic love (Boswell 1994), and violators of moral boundaries who were punished but not deviant sexual identities such as the homosexual or the pedophile (Foucault 1978). Many historians claim that modernity gave birth to sexuality as an imagined unity of desires, acts, and sexual types and as an order with a developmental logic exhibiting normal and aberrant developments. Sexuality is then approached as a social organizing principle creating identities and social hierarchies, regulated by normalizing social norms enforced by the state and social institutions, and contested by movements of sexual affirmation and rights.

To elaborate this perspective, I turn to Foucault (1978), who, more than anyone else, has linked a historicizing argument regarding the making of sexuality to a non-Whiggish sociology of sexuality. Foucault speaks of a shift in Euro-

pean societies in the seventeenth and eighteenth centuries in their social structure and mechanisms of power from the "deployment of alliance" to the "deployment of sexuality." The former refers to a type of society in which kinship
is crucial in determining social roles, status, and the organization of wealth.
Accordingly, marriage and procreative behavior, as practices pivotal to the organization of kinship, are the focus of an elaborate system of laws and social
norms. All intimacies outside of marriage, and all desires within marriage that
exceed a procreative imperative, are subject to a host of prohibitions and punish-
ments. In such a society, power operates through the authority of sovereigns
(patriarchs, kings, nobles) to stabilize kinship systems, and thereby the political
economy, by enforcing a procreative marital norm by means, ultimately, of their
power to take life. The shift to the deployment of sexuality involved a change
from a form of social organization centered on the rules governing marriage and
kin relations to rules governing sex everywhere but especially outside marriage—
for example, among children, between men and women—and focused on peripheral sexualities such as obsessions and fetishes. In the course of the nineteenth
century, sex became an object of knowledge and basis of social regulation. A
system of sexuality emerged within which a range of particular excitations, pleasures, and acts were constructed as manifestations of "sexuality." Every conceivable form of sexual desire and practice was classified; clearly marked boundaries
were fixed between normal and abnormal sexuality; new sexual figures were
invented—the hysterical woman, the pervert, and the homosexual; new authorities were charged with knowing and regulating the sex of its citizens (e.g., doc-
tors, lawyers, state administrators, criminal justice personnel, and psychiatrists).
The deployment of sexuality involved a shift in the chief mechanisms of power
from juridical to disciplinary power. Thus rather than power operating through
the authority of sovereigns to take and give life, disciplinary power operates to
manage life. It is centered on the body and the sex of the individual (anatomo-
politics) and species (biopolitics). Power works not through denial or censorship,
but through the production, administering, and optimization of the utility of
bodies, and their subjection to normalizing social controls.

According to Foucault, the shift to the deployment of sexuality reflects the
new importance of the body and sex in a society where the productivity of labor
and the fertility and health of a huge, mobile population become key national
concerns. One effect of the deployment of sexuality is the creation of the idea
of sex as a unitary force, as the ground of the self and society, and as the basis
of national well-being. For those of us whose lives are organized by the deployment of sexuality, we are compelled to know our sexuality, announce our sexual
identity, and fulfill its nature. Whatever other effects are produced by this sexual self-assertion, we are operating within the logic of the system of sexuality
(Foucault 1978: 157).

Approaching sexuality as a sociohistorical event and an organizing social
force offers a distinct analytical vantage point from which to critically examine
issues of sexual diversity and conflict. For example, instead of assuming "sexuality" as a natural or sociological fact, this perspective offers an account of the

very possibility of a politics and discourse of sexuality by explaining the socio-historical transformation of bodies, desires, and intimacies or "sex" into "sexuality." If we understand sexuality as a social regime in this sense, simple-minded ideas of sexual progress will give way to analyses of the kinds of differences such a regime allows. This perspective makes it possible to ask what kinds of emotional-sensual-intimate differences are suppressed and indeed superseded by "sexuality," with what consequences for the lives of individuals and communities.

Approaching sexuality as a principle of social organization points a double edged critical vantage point. This perspective suggests the limits of the politics of sexual rights, pluralism, and liberation. To the extent that movements of sexual affirmation—from those that assert an ideal of orgasmic sexuality, to feminist struggles to affirm women's sexuality—assume the deployment of sexuality and articulate its grammer and logic, they contribute to its enforcement. For example, as important as the lesbian/gay rights movement is for expanding tolerance and social inclusion, this movement reinforces the system of sexuality—for example, by isolating an order of sex out of a field of feelings, desires, excitations, actions, and intimacies, by assuming that same-sex affections mark out a distinct sexual and social identity, by framing sexual identity in terms of the hetero/homosexual binary, and by assuming that sexual identity reveals the hidden truth of the self. The legitimation of lesbian/gay rights, moreover, does not end power over the homosexual but transfers it from scientifc-medical-juridical institutions to the lesbian/gay community or to those who construct normative and normalizing models of lesbian/gay identity.

Likewise, this perspective makes it possible to recognize the critical potential of movements that challenge the deployment of sexuality and imagine an order "beyond sexuality." This was the critical standpoint that Foucault seemed, at one point, to advocate. "It is the agency of sex that we must break away from, if we aim . . . to counter the grips of power with the claims of bodies, pleasures, and knowledges, in their multiplicity and their possibility of resistance. The rallying point for the counterattack against the deployment of sexuality ought not to be sex-desire, but bodies and pleasures" (1978: 157). Writing in the early 1970s, Foucault was directing his remarks, in part, to gay liberationism, a movement that he valued for its normalizing of homosexuality and criticized precisely because this normalization reinforced the deployment of sexuality. From the vantage point of the 1990s, it is possible to see in movements such as Queer Nation and ACT UP, in the transgendered and S/M movements, in the emergence of postmodern or hybrid models of identities, intimacies, and families, in the shifts from a morality of the sex act to a communicative sexual ethic, and in feminist deconstructions of the sexualization of the body, self, and intimacy, developments that are troubling to the deployment of sexuality, to use Foucault's terms. To the extent that such developments contest the reduction of sexuality to gender preference, challenge a bipolar hetero/homosexual grid as master categories of sexual and social identity, challenge the tight alignment of sex, gender and sexuality, and contest normalizing norms that classify desires into normal/abnormal, they point to an order beyond sexuality.

Two brief examples serve to illustrate my point: the rise of queer politics and the appearance of a transgendered movement.

Although Queer Nation came and went in a virtual flash, a queer politics—perhaps more as an impulse than an organized movement—remains a vital presence in lesbian/gay communities. Queer politics pivots around an opposition to sexuality as a system for producing, organizing, and disciplining selves that operates through the power of normalizing social norms and knowledges. While acknowledging the gains of sexual liberalization in postwar America, including the importance of homosexual rights, a queer perspective argues that such developments have reinforced a system of sexuality. Queers contest this sexualizing and disciplining of bodies and selves by challenging normalizing social norms such as the imperative to assert or liberate a sexual identity or to affirm or realize a norm of sexual fulfillment. The knowledges, experts, institutions, and communities that enforce this disciplinary order of sexuality have been made into a site of politics. In this regard, queers struggle for an order of bodies, desires, pleasures, and intimacies beyond sexuality, an order that would be fluid, protean, and tolerant of expansive sexual-intimate choices between consenting adults.

The transgendered movement is sometimes taken as exemplary of queer politics. With strong roots in the lesbian/gay movement, yet critical of the latter's enforcement of normalizing gender norms that render transgendered individuals deviant, the queer impulse of this movement lies in criticizing dominant norms of gender and sex. In particular, transgendered people (e.g., transsexuals, transvestites, drag queens, and gender benders) challenge norms that enforce a rigid alignment of sex, gender, and sexual expression—that is, norms of normality and health that assume that sex (an assigned status of female or male depending primarily on genitalia) dictates correct gender identity (socially appropriate feminine and masculine traits), which, in turn, dictates a correct (i.e., normal, natural, healthy, or right) sexuality, that is, heterosexuality. Thus individuals who are said to be born male will and should (if healthy and normal) exhibit the correct masculine roles and behaviors, one of which is an exclusive heterosexual orientaton. From a transgendered standpoint, this alignment of sex, gender, and sexuality is a historically created, socially enforced order closely intertwined with a system of sexuality that produces dichotomously sexed bodies, genders, and sexualities. Hence, the aim of this movement is not to legitimate more sexual and gender identities but to change the very system that produces only male/female sexed bodies, selves gendered as either men or women, and mutually exclusive heterosexual/homosexual sexual identities (Bornstein 1994; Feinberg 1993).

ETHICAL-POLITICAL IMPLICATIONS

To recapitulate, I have argued that at one level social conflict involves challenges to aspects of a system of sexual hierarchy. There are, for example, struggles over civil rights (e.g., to enact antidiscriminatory legislation to protect sexual minorities or reproductive rights), political and cultural representation (e.g., regarding media and popular images of sexual minorities), and resources (e.g., sex education programs, HIV prevention programs, and funding for family planning and birth control practices). Many of the most publicized social conflicts in the sphere of sexuality, from gay marriage, the porn wars, and sex education programs, to efforts to legitimate diverse types of families are struggles of this sort. Although these conflicts are socially divisive, they are not a threat to a system of sexual hierarchy, as they sustain the sexualization of selves and identities, normative heterosexuality, and the tight alignment of sex, gender, and sexuality.

Conflict at the level of moral logics and sexual values, as it involves clashes between sexual communities and challenges to the very sexualization of bodies and identities, suggests challenges to hegemonic social norms and institutions that organize and regulate sexual-intimate practices. By way of a conclusion, I wish to consider some of the potential political and ethical implications of the latter cultural conflicts and developments.

I have suggested that a key site of sexual conflict pivots around the moral logics that justify social norms, rules, and therefore a system of sexual hierarchy, and I have proposed that in contemporary America there is an opposition between a morality of the sex act and a communicative sex ethic. The former appeals to some notion of a fixed or transcendent social and moral order that gives to sexual desires and practices an inherent meaning and social role. The latter asserts that sexual-intimate practices have no intrinsic social and moral meaning; their meaning is derived by agents in a social context, and the moral status of particular sexual practices hinges on the presence or absence of certain formal qualities of the social interaction, for example, consent, respect, and reciprocity. In the communicative sexual ethic, transcendent moral imperatives or norms are replaced by broad ethical guidelines that leave a lot of room for individual discretion, judgment, and ambiguity.

A communicative sexual ethic has potentially significant political-ethical implications. If sexual practices have no intrinsic meaning, if their moral sense involves understanding the contextualized meaning and social role of such practices and appealing to formal aspects of the communicative practice, then such an ethical standpoint legitimates a plurality of sexual practices and patterns of intimacy, including different kinds of families. Put differently, a communicative sexual ethic suggests that many sexual-intimate acts would lose their broader social and political significance. If, for example, S/M was not interpreted from a Christian standpoint as immoral or as abnormal from a psychiatric standpoint, if S/M was approached as an act judged solely by whether the agents found it meaningful (as pleasure, love, or for its spiritual or therapeutic effects) and whether the practice was consensual and responsible, its symbolic function as a marker of the moral state of the agents or society would diminish considerably. In effect, consensual S/M between adults would become a matter of aesthetic taste, not ethical judgment, and therefore would not be the site of dense social regulations, for example, laws, cultural pollution, public harassment and violence, and medical stigmatization. Accordingly, insofar as a communicative sexual ethic would become an integral part of American culture and institutional practices, such that everyday judgments would be focused on particular acts and are guided by contextually informed, minimalist, and consequentialist reasoning, we would anticipate a sexual-intimate culture less organized around normalizing judgments and therefore less likely to create populations of deviant identities and outsider sexual communities. This would be a culture where large stretches of social practice related to bodies and intimacies would lack moral and political weight. Indeed, this cultural logic implies a social logic anticipating the end of "sexuality"—that is, the end of a regime that enforces a uniform sexualization of bodies and selves, a tight alignment of sex, gender, and sexuality, and a normal/abnormal moral binary. For underpinning or implicit in a communicative sexual ethic is a view of the historical and sociopolitically constructed character of sexuality. The critique of naturalization and normalization makes possible a political project that challenges not only particular aspects of a system of sexual stratification but the very regime of sexuality. If the lesbian and gay movement represents a paradigm case of the former, the queer and transgendered movements imagine an order of bodies, desires, selves, intimacies, and solidarities "beyond sexuality."

The issue I conclude with addresses the credibility and coherence of such a sexual ethic and culture. In other words, is there a compelling logical basis or argument to be made in defense of what has been presented as a sociocultural fact? Would such a culture have the resources to establish moral boundaries and rules, and is such an ethical position logically defensible? In other words, if we abandon a transcendent standpoint or some notion of an order of things disclosed through the medium of secular reason or religion that provides grounds of judgment, standards of assessment, and substantive ideals and ends, what are we left with to provide guidelines, standards, and ends?

A chief feature of the morality of the sex act is that it makes assumptions about what sex is and, on that basis, proscribes sexual norms. For example, if we assume that the meaning and purpose of sex is to express and consolidate "love," only those sex acts and social interactions are legitimate that exhibit the qualities of love. Although such an ethical position provides strong normative and regulatory guidance, it also devalues and sometimes pollutes or stigmatizes a wide range of very different kinds of behaviors that deviate from such social norms. In other words, a morality of the sex act inevitably suppresses, devalues, pathologizes, and renders immoral a heterogenous cluster of practices, many of which seem freely chosen, involve only adults, are meaningful to the agents, and lack any obvious "harm" to the individual or to others. This hostility to difference, especially in a sexual culture characterized by a plurality of sexual values, patterns, identities, and communities has made it less credible. Indeed, from the vantage point of a reflexive, pluralistic culture, the presumption of a nonsituated, objectivist moral position has diminishing plausibility. Thus any sexual ethic that relies for its normative clout on the assumption that sexuality has a determinate, fixed meaning and therewith an ideal social form and role is today suspected of ethnocentrism and imperial designs. Plainly put, it is as if only a moral logic that abstracts from the clash over sexual meanings and values has compelling logical force.

This is precisely the basis of the claim to moral authority of a communicative sexual ethic. It assumes that sex acquires diverse, often conflicting social meanings and purposes. Moreover, this ethic's proponents hold that the clash of sexual values is inevitable and irresolvable, as such conflicts are implicated in a conflict of world views. Accordingly, a communicative sexual ethic intends to find a normative standpoint beyond this clash of values that can provide guidance and yet preserve the integrity of many sexual differences. Ethical judgment thus would focus on the communicative context of the sexual exchange, not on the sex act itself. Consensus is said to be more likely achieved if minimal normative conditions are sufficient to legitimate social practices. Such a formalistic and minimalist ethical standpoint has the advantage of being nonjudgmental with regard to substantive sexual values and respectful of a wide range of sexual differences yet providing guidance and establishing moral boundaries (see Seidman 1992; Weeks 1995).

Because a communicative sexual ethic holds that the sex act itself has no intrinsic moral significance, that only the social exchange or some general features of the interaction give sex practices their moral import, how do we decide which features of the social interaction are to carry moral significance and how do we justify those decisions? In order to avoid grounding a sexual ethic on substantive values, only formal, minimal aspects of communication can serve as normative standards, not the intentions, motives, or ends of the interaction. Such formal normative considerations must be able to provide general guidelines and yet permit many differences. Hence, the task is to identify some general, formal aspects of communicative practice that can function as normative standards, such as the consensual, responsible, and reciprocal dimensions of communication, which might be said to carry normative weight in abstraction from the meaning and qualities of the practices themselves.

Although I think that some form of a communicative ethic best resonates with a society increasingly organized around differences, some of which run deep and will persist in the long term, there are some difficulties. The formalism of this ethical position, an inevitable consequence of shifting the site of normative judgment from the "content" to the "form" of social practices, renders it weak as a normative guide in many instances. Thus although a communicative sexual ethic would be effective in proscribing rape, sexual coercion, sex between children or sex between adults and children, and legitimating a range of presently proscribed sexualities (e.g., same-sex intimacies, S/M, bisexuality, bondage, fetishisms, nonmonogamy), it would provide only very weak, if any, guidance with respect to, say, conflicts over pornography and abortion rights, and would have virtually nothing to say about broader value conflicts that relate to normative questions about the place of sex in a good society. For example, conflicts over whether pornography should be allowed in public places and, if so, which ones, and questions about the morality of sex industry workers, are largely outside the purview of a communicative sexual ethic; that is, some of the most important conflicts over sexuality involve a clash over sexual and social values. Of course, a communicative sexual ethic does not exclude public comment on such issues, but it does assume that they will ultimately be resolved at the level of interest and pragmatics.

Perhaps these concerns simply mean that there will be areas of conflict where strong notions of reason-based consent will give way to forging a culture of pragmatic accommodation. There is, though, an additional difficulty: a communicative sexual ethic does not avoid substantive value commitments. Does not an appeal to consent, responsibility, or reciprocity presuppose a particular sociocultural standpoint ("modernity" or a secular, reflexive culture) and a particular set of substantive values (individualism, autonomy, choice, mutuality)? A communicative sexual ethic assumes the credibility and normatively compelling character of these substantive values.

Although this argument does not in my view undermine a communicative sexual ethic, it does mean that such an ethic cannot pivot its claim to legitimacy on the basis of lacking any substantive value commitments. Its cultural currency revolves around articulating general standards that provide rough normative guidelines while respecting a wide range of sexual choices and differences. However, to the extent that these general standards (e.g., consent, responsibility, reciprocity) imply substantive values and particular sociohistorical conditions, such an ethic must provide a rationale for these values and conditions. Several options are available. Least credible today, at least in Anglo-American and many European nations, is a transcendent appeal to human nature or reason or natural law to provide a decontextualized and presumably nonethnocentric justification. Williams (1985) and others have proposed strategies of ethical justification that are antifoundational and ethnocentric, though without imperial designs. In place of foundational or transcendent justifications of normative standards, they propose community-and-tradition-based and pragmatic types of rationales. Unhappy with both transcendent and pragmatic justifications, these authors have proposed a Habermasian-inspired position that advances a discursive ethic underpinned by an evolutionary theory of history (e.g., Benhabib 1992; Honneth 1996). Whereas the latter offers a strong defense of general norms and a weak defense of difference, pragmatics has the reverse strengths and liabilities. Perhaps the details of these disagreements are less important than the sociocultural shift they indicate. Whether or not these debates mark some type of broad or global shift in the social terrain, one point seems compelling: the question of how to handle differences of sexuality, race, nationality, or ableness without assuming they occupy a social and moral position of inferiority, transience, the past, or irrationality is a central part of American culture and politics.

NOTES

1. Nineteenth-century middle America did not proscribe all sexual-intimate differences. For example, youth dating and courting that involved sexual-affectional intimacy

were legitimate (Rothman 1987; Lystra 1989), and same-sex intimacies, especially between women, acquired a degree of social acceptance (see note 2).

2. The extent to which nineteenth-century American culture was not organized around sexual identity categories is further suggested by the lack of a language of identity to describe same-sex intimacies (Fadermann 1981; D'Emilio and Freedman 1988; Smith-Rosenberg 1975).

3. There is another aspect of the politics of sexual difference that should at least be mentioned, namely, the formation of public sexual communities and the pressure they exert to have their differences publicly recognized and valued. To the extent that sexual communities such as the lesbian and gay community or the S/M community elaborate unique social perspectives (e.g., distinctive epistemological standpoints) and values (e.g., sexual-intimate values) or can be shown to exhibit distinctive modes of social oppression (e.g., the ability to "pass" suggests the need for unique strategies to address job or housing discrimination, which typically takes the form less of direct discrimination than anticipatory discrimination), a case can be made that the state and social institutions should respect and respond to these social differences. In other words, the formation of public sexual cultures, like the formation of feminist or race-based or religious-based public cultures raises forcefully the question of "group or minority recognition or rights." Political philosophers (e.g., Kymlicka 1995; Margalit and Raz 1995) have made the case that differences around, say, race, gender, or ableness in a society that discriminates along these dimensions makes them into sociocultural or collective differences. To the extent that such differences get elaborated into cultural communities, and to the extent that some of these differences run deep or extend into core values and beliefs and practices, doubts have been raised about a strictly individualistic-liberal model of a democratic polity (cf. Minow 1990; Taylor 1994; Young 1990).

REFERENCES

Adam, Barry. 1987. *The Rise of a Gay and Lesbian Movement*. Boston: Twayne.

Benhabib, Seyla. 1992. *Situating the Self*. New York: Routledge.

Bornstein, Kate. 1994. *Gender Outlaw*. New York: Routledge.

Boswell, John. 1994. *Same-Sex Unions in Premodern Europe*. New York: Villard Books.

Bray, Alan. 1995. *Homosexuality in Renaissance England*. New York: Columbia University Press.

Brown, Peter. 1988. *The Body and Society*. New York: Columbia University Press.

Califia, Pat. 1982. "A Personal View of the History of the Lesbian S/M Community and Movement in San Francisco." Pp. 50–68 in *Coming to Power*, edited by Samois. Boston: Alyson.

Chauncey, George, Jr. 1994. *Gay New York*. New York: Pantheon.

D'Emilio, John. 1983. *Sexual Politics, Sexual Communities*. Chicago: University of Chicago Press.

D'Emilio, John, and Estelle Freedman. 1988. *Intimate Matters*. New York: Harper & Row.

Duberman, Martin. 1986. *About Time*. New York: A Sea Horse Book.

Faderman, Lillian. 1981. *Surpassing the Love of Men*. New York: Morrow.

———. 1991. *Odd Girls and Twilight Lovers*. New York: Columbia University Press.

Feinberg, Leslie. 1993. *Stone Butch Blues*. Ithaca, New York: Firebrand Books.

Ferguson, Ann. 1989. *Blood at the Root*. Boston: Pandora Press.

Michel Foucault. 1978. *The History of Sexuality: An Introduction.* New York: Pantheon.

Gay, Peter. 1986. *The Bourgeois Experience.* Vol. 2, *The Tender Passion.* New York: Oxford University Press.

Goldberg, Jonathan. 1992. *Sodometries.* Stanford: Stanford University Press.

Honneth, Axel. 1995. *The Struggle for Recognition.* Cambridge, Mass.: Polity.

Katz, Jonathan Ned. 1983. *Gay/Lesbian Almanac.* New York: Harper & Row.

————. 1995. *The Invention of Heterosexuality.* New York: Penguin.

Kymlicka, Will, ed. 1995. *The Rights of Minority Cultures.* New York: Oxford University Press.

Laqueur, Thomas. 1990. *Making Sex.* Cambridge: Harvard University Press.

Lystra, Karen. 1989. *Searching the Heart.* New York: Oxford University Press.

Margalit, Avishai, and Joseph Raz. 1995. "National Self-Determination." Pp. 79–92 in *The Rights of Minority Cultures*, edited by Will Kymlicka. New York: Oxford University Press.

Martin, J. L. 1986. "AIDS Risk Reduction Recommendations and Sexual Behavior Patterns among Gay Men." *Health Education Quarterly* 13: 347–58.

Minow, Martha. 1990. *Making All the Difference.* Ithaca, N.Y.: Cornell University Press.

Rothman, Ellen. 1987. *Hands and Hearts.* Cambridge: Harvard University Press.

Rotundo, Anthony. 1989. "Romantic Friendship: Male Intimacy and Middle-Class Youth in the Northern United States, 1800–1930." *Journal of Social History* 23.

Seidman, Steven. 1991. *Romantic Longings.* New York: Routledge.

————. 1992. *Embattled Eros.* New York: Routledge.

Smith-Rosenberg, Carroll. 1975. "The Female World of Love and Ritual: Relations between Women in Nineteenth-Century America." *Signs* 1: 1–29.

Taylor, Charles. 1994. "The Politics of Recognition." Pp. 25–73 in *Multiculturalism*, edited by Amy Gutmann. Princeton, N.J.: Princeton University Press.

Turner, Charles, et al. 1989. *AIDS.* Washington, D.C.: National Academy Press.

Weeks, Jeffrey. 1977. *Coming Out!* London: Quartet.

————. 1995. *Invented Moralities.* New York: Columbia University Press.

Young, Iris. 1990. *Justice and the Politics of Difference.* Princeton: Princeton University Press.

PART THREE

Social Change and New Forms

of Social Connection

CHAPTER NINE

Multiple Markets: Multiple Cultures*

VIVIANA A. ZELIZER

THREE REPORTS from the multicultural front:

Item 1: In the 1850s the most common coins in the United States were Mexican, seconded by British, French, Dutch, and other European silver fractional coins; circulating alongside some five thousand or more state bank notes—often personalized with elaborate designs of local landmarks, individuals or events; as well as multiple privately issued tokens, paper notes, and coins. It took vigorous and sustained state intervention to create, by the early twentieth century, a single, standardized, national currency (Helleiner, forthcoming; Zelizer 1994; Doty 1995).

Item 2: *Fortune* magazine reports that teenagers around the world shop for a remarkably similar series of products: Reebok sports shoes, Procter & Gamble Cover Girl makeup, Nintendo videogames, PepsiCo's PepsI Max, Kodak cameras, Motorola beepers. When a New York City advertising agency videotaped teens' bedrooms in twenty-five countries, it was hard to tell whether the rooms were in Los Angeles, Mexico City, or Tokyo: walls were uniformly decorated with similar posters, closets full of the same baggy Levis, NBA jackets, Timberlands or Doc Martens shoes (Tully 1994).

Item 3: Inner-city kids, Carl Husemoller Nightingale documents in a study of Philadelphia youth, share in mainstream consumerism, passionate for Coca-Cola and McDonald's, yearning for the newest Reeboks, warm-up suits, BMX bikes, Nintendo videogames. A couple of parents told Nightingale that their son "learned to say 'Michael Jordan' before 'mommy'" (1993: 153). Increasing economic and social exclusion of African American youth, Nightingale tells us, has paradoxically taken place along with a "process of cultural inclusion" into "the orbit of American materialism and consumption" (189, 136).

* I am grateful for advice, information, criticism, and research assistance variously to Richard Alba, Bernard Barber, Miguel Centeno, Lizabeth Cohen, Paul DiMaggio, Eric Helleiner, Douglas Holt, Daniel Horowitz, Jenna Weissman Joselit, Michael Katz, Julie Nelson, Alejandro Portes, Neil Smelser, Shira Stone, Charles Tilly, and Julian Zelizer. For response to oral presentations of this paper I thank colleagues at the Center for Advanced Study in the Behavioral Sciences, the Institute for Advanced Study, and Harvard University. I am also grateful for fellowships from the National Endowment for the Humanities at the Institute for Advanced Study and the John Simon Guggenheim Memorial Foundation.

If we had only these three reports, we would not be too concerned about issues of multiculturalism and value diversity. Economic development, these reports suggest, nationalizes and homogenizes cultural distinctions. At least superficially, all three items argue that over the long run the economy generates increasing connectedness and uniformity within a standardized consumer culture. In fact, most observers consider the economy to be insulated from the disturbances of multicultural politics. Battles for diversity after all, are being fought in courts, campuses, schools, churches, and museum boards, not inside shopping malls.

What usually worries critics of multiculturalism lies beyond the economic sphere, in the apparently independent process of political and moral fragmentation. From this perspective, either economic logic is irrelevant to the growing tensions in the political and moral worlds, operating within its own self-contained territory, or else political and moral fragmentation conflict with economic change. With the hypotheses of independence, the economy becomes the only—but precarious—basis for solidarity; with the hypothesis of conflict, political and moral divisions eventually undermine the consensus that sustains joint economic effort. In either hypothesis, the economy remains a zone little fragmented by multicultural distinctions.

Such views rest on three common assumptions: first, we are facing a threat of multiculturalism and diversity that weakens national culture and solidarity; second, the economy is the only area of common ties, and third, the economy is an unsatisfactory connector—flattening, individualizing, and morally stultifying.

A closer look at how economic practices work leads to a very different view: that precisely parallel processes operate within the economy as operate within other zones of cultural activity, such as politics, religion, language, or education. What's more, clear analysis of how the economy works provides guidelines for thinking through multiculturalism in noneconomic zones. Scrutiny of economic change yields surprising hypotheses concerning noneconomic change.

Contrary to three widespread ideas that diversity undermines connection, that the economy is becoming the only zone of common bonds, and that economic ties lack moral fiber, evidence at hand supports a different line of argument:

1. Connectedness and diversity do not contradict each other but appear as different aspects of the same large-scale processes.

2. Like other areas of social life, economic relations contain extensive differentiation that distinguishes symbolically and morally contrasting social ties.

3. The economy therefore intersects with other aspects of social life in combining morally significant connectedness and differentiation.

4. Multiplication of cultural forms does not in itself usually threaten large-scale solidarity; the threat arises mainly, or perhaps exclusively, when it involves segmented, segregated, unequal circuits of communication and exchange.

How can all this be true of an economy so many observers and critics see as the enemy of moral solidarity? Despite appearances to the contrary, the economy contains intense cultural differentiation: in market transactions of any kind, people are continually creating, modifying, and protecting particular systems of meaning as they strive to differentiate their various social ties. Whatever else they do, economic transactions serve to distinguish social relations and their symbolic and moral meanings. As in all other areas of cultural life, furthermore, the economy operates at two levels: Seen from the top, economic transactions connect with broad national symbolic meanings and institutions. Seen from the bottom, however, economic transactions are highly differentiated, personalized, and local—meaningful to particular relations. No contradiction therefore exists between uniformity and diversity: they are simply two different aspects of the same transaction. Just as people speak English in a recognizably grammatical way at the same time that they pour individual and personal content into their conversations, economic actors simultaneously adopt universalizing modes and particularizing markers.

The cases of money and consumption will show precisely how this conjunction works. After a survey of changing forms and uses of money, this paper turns to a discussion of consumption before the 1940s and finally takes a look at consumption today.

THE CASE OF MONEY

The nationalization of legal tender stands as a powerful symbol and facilitator of unified, standardized economic life. The nineteenth-century American government intervened energetically in creating a single, homogeneous currency. The process was far from automatic: the federal government had to remove foreign currencies, tax thousands of state-issued paper currencies out of existence, outlaw an extensive production of private coinage, and suppress an extraordinary range of counterfeit monies. The outcome, however, served the expanding country in a number of crucial ways. Territorial currencies, Eric Helleiner (forthcoming) tells us, strengthened internal national economic coherence by eliminating the complications and contradictions of multiple local currencies while tangibly marking the domestic economy apart from other countries. A nationalized money promoted social as well as geographical cohesion, unifying the monetary instrument if not the economic worlds of the rich (who in the early nineteenth century used banknotes plus silver and gold coins) and the poor (who traded primarily with low-denomination copper coins and tokens, which often were not convertible into silver and gold coins). What's more, Helleiner suggests, such mass-produced territorial currencies—now decorated with elaborate national imagery—served as stronger symbolic markers of nationality than did flags, anthems, or statues.

This account of monetary standardization however, tells us only part of the story. At the same time that the government homogenized its currency, people and organizations invented new forms of monetary differentiation, turning the generalized medium into a multiplicity of distinct, personalized currencies. Looked at more closely, in fact, the history of monetary differentiation appears in two versions. In one case, people converted the same available legal tender that fully connected them with the national economy into a particularized currency. They did so by creating elaborate and extensive systems of earmarking monies, thereby sorting ostensibly homogeneous legal tender into distinct categories. Depending on how, when, and, most importantly, for what type of social exchange it was used, the same physically indistinguishable dollar became a wage, a bonus, a tip, a gift, an allowance, or charity. In many cases, the differentiation followed religious, ethnic, racial, gender, or age distinctions.

In a second variety of monetary differentiation, people and organizations—despite the federalization of currency—created segmented, local media, in the form of tokens, coupons, scrip, chits, tickets, grocery orders, money orders, trading stamps, or even cigarettes, which typically were not legal tender within the larger economy. At the extreme, artists traded with their own designed trompe l'oeil paintings of money, defying prosecution (for examples of both types of monetary differentiation, see Zelizer 1994). In general, the effect of the first mode of monetary differentiation was integration, increased involvement of participants in national circuits of exchange and consumption, whereas the effect of the second was segmentation, formation of segregated circuits that insulated their participants from the larger economy. Notice, however, that in neither case did the nationalization of currency result in the expected monetary uniformity. Instead, people simultaneously participated in the national economy and yet sustained their own particular social relations and meaning systems as they did so.

Observers might argue, however, that postmodern money may finally spell the end of monetary variety. Between the push of supranational currencies, such as Europe's projected European Currency Unit (ECU) and the global reach of electronic cash, how can national, local, or personal monetary distinctions survive? Yet, if anything, differentiation is increasing. Even the bills of the Euro notes as it happens, carefully designed to avoid "national bias"—they will feature no people or words, only images of nonexistent, anonymous bridges and monuments—will still retain a small space for each country to print its own national symbol (Andrews 1996: 35–36).

Within the United States, the hard-won but relatively brief, century-and-a-half state monopoly in issuing legal tender is rapidly dissipating. Take for instance, the small but symbolically powerful local-currency movement. About thirty American cities and towns are now printing their own, fully legal, local currency (the government regulates the physical dimension of notes—smaller than dollar bills—and requires its issue in denominations valued at a minimum of $1). An estimated $1.5 million in Ithaca Dollars—which must be spent in local transactions—have been traded so far in Ithaca, New York, the community-currency pioneer. During the 1996 mayoral race, the *New York Times*, 21 January 1996, reported, "all three candidates clamored to take the homegrown money as donations." An instructional Hometown Money Starter Kit, produced by the Ithaca Dollar inventor, Paul Glover, has sold to over 600 communities in forty-seven states. The local-currency movement not only enables commercial exchanges but also, claim its sponsors, builds community ties, forging social along with monetary bonds (see Graham 1996; Nieves 1996; Meeker-Lowry 1995).[1]

Local currencies are not the only instance of differentiation; obvious cases are frequent-flier credits, traveler's checks, transit cards, and food stamps. In addition, credit card companies as well as banks are eagerly creating an array of new digital monies, ranging from VISA's smart card, Visa Cash—which requires no password, signature, or identification—to Internet currencies such as Digicash and Cybercash, and including a Citicorp currency. Remarkably, as a *New York Times* (Gleick 1996: 54) story points out, the government is staying away from the production or even the regulation of the new digital cash: "virtually no one in or out of Washington," notes the report "thinks that the government should step in, take charge and issue an electronic currency." Thus, to the dismay of the more highly regulated banks, nonbank institutions are increasingly getting into the money business.

As critics of multiculturalism might well fear, some of the new monetary creations and differentiations have dimensions of ethnicity, race, class, gender, and sometimes sexual orientation. Consider affinity cards, which are issued by a given community or organization and whose proceeds are earmarked for that group. For example, the Rainbow Card, introduced by VISA, the Travelers Bank, and Subaru, with the endorsement of Martina Navratilova, is earmarked for gay and lesbian communities. The Unity Visa Card, issued by the Boston Bank of Commerce, aims at the African American community, while the Armenian Exchange U.S.A. MasterCard credit card (now defunct) was developed for the Armenian community. These three cards stand out from most affinity cards by distributing their benefits not to a specific organization such as the Sierra Club or the Elvis Presley Memorial Foundation but rather to a socially defined collectivity (*Wall Street Journal*, 6 November 1995; Bakalian 1993: 435). Communities also invent strategies that earmark legal tender in ways that dramatize their economic leverage. Under the NAACP's "Black Dollar Days" program, for instance, blacks were asked to register their collective purchasing power by paying with $2 bills and Susan B. Anthony silver dollars (see Austin 1994: 165). For similar reasons, some time ago, the gay community circulated dollar bills inscribed with the words "gay money" or a pink triangle (*Baltimore Sun*, 22 June 1993).

When it comes to class, the nineteenth-century division of currencies finds its contemporary equivalent in the class-segregated monetary worlds of the urban poor. Mostly closed off from electronic cash transactions, automated teller machines, and credit cards, the poor, including recent immigrants, increasingly rely on fringe banking institutions, such as pawnshops and commercial check-cashing outlets (Caskey, 1994). The enormous (and hugely profitable) business in migrant remittances to Central America and elsewhere, in which money leaves New York or Los Angeles in electronic dollars and arrives in remote villages in pesos or dinars, simply marks the latest stage in a century-old process of monetary differentiation (see Case 1996; Mahler 1995: 142–44).

Here, as in all the cases we've surveyed, the distinction recurs: the overall trend runs toward larger and larger scale standardized monetized transactions incessantly and simultaneously particularized by the participants in these transactions. Particular practices and understandings, from this perspective, do not contradict but support national practices. However, some portion of the population, notably the poor, recent immigrants, and racial minorities find themselves caught in segmented monetary circuits that separate them from the mainstream economic world. Rotating credit associations, for example, produce distinct local circuits of money but clearly integrate their users into the host economy. The problem for African Americans, as Mark Granovetter (1995: 141–42) points out, is that they lack precisely these local circuits that serve simultaneously their own purposes and integrate them into the national economy. In the perspective of multiculturalism, the problem therefore is not differentiation but exclusion.

CONSUMPTION BEFORE THE 1940s

Consumption processes parallel the incessant integration and differentiation of money. Recall *Fortune*'s report on a teenage global consumer culture. This culture reaches, as Nightingale indicates, even into the economically and socially marginalized inner cities. Such diffusion suggests that mass-produced standardized goods and services—the Michael Jordan sneakers, baggy jeans, McDonald's, Taco Bells of the 1990s—may operate as irresistible cultural homogenizers. Cultural particularisms, from this perspective, surrender to the shared pleasures of a nationalized—and increasingly internationalized—material culture. In an age of diversity, it seems, commonality can be found only at the mall. As William Leach puts it in his *Land of Desire* (1993: 5)—an account of the rise of consumer culture in the United States—"no immigrant culture—and, to a considerable degree, no religious tradition—had the power to resist it, as none can in our own time. Any group that has come to this country has had to learn to accept and to adjust to this elemental feature of American capitalist culture."

The assumption that, for better or worse, a culture of consumption inevitably dissolves ethnic, religious, racial, and other particularisms, has a long history. In the 1920s, as Lizabeth Cohen (1990: 100) documents in her account of Chicago's workers' consumer world, eager advertisers predicted that mass consumption would surely homogenize Americans, creating an extraordinarily profitable mass market. Ethnic leaders, meanwhile, although deeply concerned with this threat to ethnic solidarity, shared the advertisers' prognosis of a culturally corrosive consumerist ethos. Other observers worried as well. Leach (1993: 387) reports New York journalist Samuel Strauss's distress at the spread of what he called "Consumptionism":

> American business had already created the largest domestic market in history; but now, he [Strauss] observed, the movement was reaching into other countries. Strauss

was worried about this trend and warned that deeper market intrusions would lead to the destruction of local communities and of local cultures, or of what he called "particularism."[2]

Advocates of this view were of course right, to some degree. The national and global expansion of standardized and rationalized consumer goods and services—what George Ritzer (1996) calls the "McDonaldization" of society—has been extraordinary. But, as with money, it is only part of the story. Although the two phenomena are different, we find parallel processes in the case of money and mass consumerism. With money, the central standardizing agent was the state; with commodities, a complex web of firms, merchants, and media promoted the recognition and adoption of standardized goods.

The transformation of commodities clearly followed an ambivalent path. At the same time that the American economic machine was spewing out new standardized items, increasingly aiming at a global market, people were continually refashioning mass-produced goods to create particularized products. As we saw in the discussion of legal tender, the same goods that circulated as national markers served as differentiators on the local level. The vast recent outpouring of studies concerning consumption makes it easier to identify the multiple circuits by which this differentiation occurs.[3]

The process was clearly visible in the 1920s. By that time, mass-produced, consumer goods had flooded the American market: shoppers nationwide demanded such brand-name products as Campbell's soup, Uneeda biscuits, Crisco oil, Kodak cameras, Singer sewing machines, Ivory soap, Colgate toothpaste, Wrigley's chewing gum, Quaker Oats, Kellogg's Toasted Corn Flakes, and Coca-Cola. Marketing experts, advertisers, department stores, chain stores, and mail-order businesses combined efforts in creating the new national market for standardized goods (see Strasser 1989; Leach 1993).

Once in the hands of consumers, however, mass-produced goods turned into markers of distinctive sets of relations and meanings. In her compelling account of Chicago's industrial workers during the 1920s, Lizabeth Cohen (1990: 105–106, 135) shows us how ethnicity shaped their consumption. Take the example of the popular Victor Victrola. Italian immigrants, along with other shoppers, bought phonographs. But Italian families gathered around their new acquisition listening to recordings of Caruso or Italian folk songs, thus cementing rather than dissolving ethnic solidarities. So did other immigrant groups, including the small Mexican community, turning Chicago into a busy center for the foreign record industry. Radios, too, were adapted into particularized media, as different groups tuned into stations that broadcast ethnic news and information.

When it came to food, local city groceries, Cohen (1990: 129, 110) explains, combined "standardized products with local, particularly ethnic, culture," offering Italian housewives escarole, dandelion leaves, and many varieties of pasta, while Jewish homemakers shopped for kosher meat or challah bread. Despite the predictions of advertisers and others, Cohen (1990: 119–20) concludes that:

Chicago's ethnic workers were not transformed into more Americanized, middle-class people by the objects they consumed. Buying an electric vacuum cleaner did not turn Josef Dubrowolski into *True Story*'s hero, Jim Smith. Instead, workers consumed on their own terms, giving their own meanings to new possessions.

Accounts of immigrant consumption choices before the 1920s portray a similar dual world where goods served at the same time as national connectors and as ethnic, and sometimes class and racial, particularizers. To continue with Lizabeth Cohen's (1986) findings, take the case of furnishings in working-class immigrant homes between 1885 and 1915. To the dismay of middle-class Progressive reformers who advocated the newly fashionable plain and "dust-free" home decorations and furniture, immigrant families stubbornly adorned their homes with carpets, drapes, and elaborately designed wallpaper at the same time that they embellished their domestic spaces with bureaus, chiffoniers, and buffets. Their choices, Cohen tells us, were shaped by a distinctive material culture, which associated such consumer goods with the luxury of affluent European rural upper-class families. Ironically, while middle-class reformers bemoaned what they saw as a threat to Americanization and the cultural homogeneity of taste, immigrants defined their distinctive selections of mass-produced goods as a pathway into, not away from, the American social world (see also Joselit 1990: 33).

Or consider the case of Jewish immigrants. Andrew Heinze's (1990) study of New York's Lower East Side during the decades before World War I finds Eastern European Jews captivated by America's consumer culture yet simultaneously marking their purchases with what Heinze describes as a distinctive Jewish American cultural imprint. Whether it was a mass-marketed piano in the parlor (to play Jewish sheet music), or a new suit of clothes, a brand-name product, or a summer vacation in the Catskills, Jews imbued each item with particular meanings, most notably as symbols of their new American Jewishness. What's more, Jewish immigrants were soon incorporating mass-marketed goods into the celebration of traditional ritual events, such as the Sabbath, Chanukah, or Passover. Earmarking mass-produced goods was one strategy of personalization. A second was the request for special, separate goods, as in consumer demand for kosher meat, or Italian pasta, or special ritual goods.

Consumer differentiation, however, was not just the work of buyers. By the turn of the century at least some marketing experts and merchants had noted the ethnic, religious, and racial earmarking of consumer goods, thereby discovering the potential profits of segmented marketing (Strasser 1989: 139–42; Cohen 1990: 113–15). After the 1890s, for instance, major brand names advertised in New York Yiddish newspapers. Procter and Gamble's 1911 campaign introduced Crisco vegetable shortening—duly rabbinically certified—announcing that "The Hebrew Race has been waiting 4000 years for Crisco." After discovering the substantial profits involved in marketing kosher food, Procter & Gamble, General Foods, and Heinz 57 Varieties added kosher products to their production (see Joselit 1994: 187–88; Heinze 1990: 159). Significantly, as Jenna

Joselit's vivid account of Jewish material culture shows, mass-produced kosher food items actually served to reinforce ritual eating practices by making permissible food more readily available. Even "Jewish bacon," a kosher meat invention that tasted just like the ritually forbidden bacon, was selling in Jewish delicatessens by the mid 1930s. By the late 1920s and early thirties, American manufacturers had expanded their Jewish trade and were producing a variety of ritual objects such as menorahs, kiddush cups, or talis clips. In such ways, marketers reinforced, rather than watered down, ethnic spheres of meaning and practice (Joselit 1994: 187, 193, 154–58).[4]

Mass-produced goods often passed through three phases: profusion of competing forms produced by multiple firms; temporary predominance of one or a few well-marketed versions of the good; subsequent proliferation of differentiated but centrally produced and distributed goods aimed at different markets. Henry Ford's Model T almost crowded out the wide range of motor vehicles produced before World War I only to see a new multiplication of makes and models after 1930. Similarly, American manufacturers of breakfast cereals continue to innovate for niche markets after an era in which corn flakes and a few other varieties dominated grocery shelves. Throughout such three-stage processes, consumers continue to differentiate, adapt, and subordinate available goods to their own particular cultural practices and social relations. Eventually, manufacturers and marketers start to follow their lead.

This excursion into early-twentieth-century consumerism calls attention to two versions of product differentiation; in the first, people select and adapt mass-produced goods, while in a similar process, marketers channel mass-produced products to particular markets. In a second version, people demand special, particularized goods, while marketers tailor goods for segmented markets.

CONSUMPTION TODAY

Were the 1920s and 30s simply the ethnic moment of American history? After all, Lizabeth Cohen (1990: 325) persuasively argues that by the end of the Great Depression mainstream consumer culture finally overtook the "cultural communities" of the 1920s, as chain stores with their uniform products increasingly displaced local merchants while national network radio, with its standardized messages shut off—or at least quieted—the sounds of local ethnic programming. Ethnic solidarities did not disappear, Cohen claims, but increasingly America's cultural world became divided by class, not ethnicity or race.[5]

Cohen's picture, however, is incomplete. Class differences certainly became salient in the 1940s and 50s, but two other developments likewise deserve attention: first, the extension of consumer culture actually produced differentiated markets corresponding to different ethnic, religious, or racial traditions; second, new groups of immigrants relived some of the same process of negotiation with the American marketplace as their predecessors had experienced in the 1920s. Thus we find that the dual processes of differentiation and connection with the national market continued beyond the 1930s. In fact, in a later article on shopping malls after World War II, Cohen stresses the new segmentation. Mass consumption, she tells us, "was supposed to bring standardization in merchandise and consumption patterns. Instead, diverse social groups are no longer integrated into central consumer marketplaces but rather are consigned to differentiated retail institutions, segmented markets, and new hierarchies" (1996: 1080).

To follow up that important lead, let us look briefly at consumption today. Much of what we know comes from consumer researchers and marketing experts. Indeed, the professionalization of market research actually emerged from and facilitated the creation of differentiated marketing strategies for various segments of the American population. Since the 1980s, consumer researchers have paid increasing attention to ethnic, or multicultural, consumerism. Earlier studies adopted the standard procedures of empirical social science, survey research, measurement of consumer propensities, use of ethnicity as one variable among many, and so on. More recently, a group of investigators, attentive to the differentiated cultural content of goods, are calling for a new "ethnoconsumerism" (Venkatesh 1995) involving interpretive approaches—using ethnographies and personal interviews for delving into ethnic cultural worlds (see also Sherry 1991; Costa and Bamossy 1995; Holt 1995, 1997).[6]

As they do so, consumer researchers uncover revealing parallels between the new immigrant populations from Mexico, Latin America, and Asia, and the Italian, Irish, or Polish 1920s communities that Lizabeth Cohen writes about. Now as then, for instance, ethnic grocers and ethnic media provide tangible ethnic markers.[7] Consider the persistence and significance of small grocery stores—bodegas—in Hispanic neighborhood culture. In a Puerto Rican barrio in Philadelphia, bodegas, one study tells us (Kaufman and Hernandez 1991), supply their largely Hispanic clientele with "an environment of Latin culture in the foods, smells, and sounds," along with a number of other informal services, including employment information. With business conducted about half the time in Spanish, the "bodeguero" offers customers, along with mainstream products, an ample supply of Hispanic goods such as plantains or viandas. In interviews with and participant observation of twenty-three Mexican immigrants in a southern California town, Lisa Peñaloza (1994: 42–43) noted the significance of ethnic foods: local stores stocked salsas, chilies, and spices, along with fresh meat and produce (her respondents rejected packaged, prepared, and canned goods).[8]

In both instances, Hispanic customers marked their ethnicity with special products but at the same time participated in mainstream consumerism. Clients of the Philadelphia bodegas, for instance, also shopped in the supermarket for bulk purchases. This simultaneous consumer involvement took place with media as well: Mexican immigrants in the Peñaloza study (1994: 45–46) tuned into Spanish-language television channels and radio but also watched and listened to English programs. (My own listening to Spanish language radio confirms this mixture, with Julio Iglesias following Madonna and Spanish-language ads for McDonald's jostling promotion of specifically Hispanic products).[9]

At the same time, a growing Latino population and an expanding non-Latino demand for Latino products has opened up a niche for immigrant or Latino entrepreneurs. In Los Angeles, for instance, anthropologist Robert M. Alvarez (1990: 100) reports: "The distribution of Mexican fruit-commodities . . . is controlled by Mexican and Mexican American entrepreneurs. Mexicans buy fruit in Mexico, sell and distribute to both the wholesale market in Los Angeles as well as to retailers who sell in Mexican neighborhoods throughout the city."[10]

The demand for Mexican products, Alvarez tells us, has led to intense market competition. While formerly, small Mexican retailers dominated the trade in Mexican produce, "Today . . . large chain stores boast not only Mexican departments but entire supermarkets that are dedicated to Mexican clientele. . . . Chorizo counters, huge meat departments specializing in Mexican cuts, panaderias (bakeries of fresh baked sweet bread and tortillas), and even Mariachi bands attract Mexican clientele" (107).

Recognizing the growing purchasing power (estimated by one report at an annual $650 billion, McQuillen 1996) of new Hispanic and Asian immigrants, marketing specialists and retailers have pushed head-on into the ethnicity business. Armed with 1990s expertise and technologies—including innovations such as telemarketing or special ethnic telephone yellow pages as well as ethnic consultants and bilingual operators—undreamed of by the 1920s pioneers, marketers are prepared to take on ethnic tastes (see, e.g., Mulhern and Williams 1994; Mathews 1995).[11]

Using zip code research on consumer preferences, marketers learn, among other things, about the "flavor boundaries" of each zip code cluster of residents: "Hispanic Mix Residents" report the authors of *The Clustering of America* (Weiss 1988: 128), "don't just favor tacos, beans and rice but exhibit a more subtle cultural bias in their preference for products ranging from cigarillos to rum to bottled water." While mass-marketing may not be as "dead" as the president of a Florida Market Segment Research firm proclaims (McQuillen 1996), supermarkets, chain stores, and retail stores are aggressively targeting ethnic populations, both adapting their products to ethnic neighborhoods as well as opening specialized retail stores. Thus while firms such as Frito-Lay and Quaker adjust their standard products to Hispanic tastes (Kaufman and Hernandez 1991), a number of retail stores offer special ethnic products.

Increasingly aware of the complexities of ethnic differentiations, retailers address variations within communities, noting for instance that Hispanics are not homogeneous shoppers but that choices vary among Cubans, Mexicans, Puerto Ricans, Peruvians, and others. In Union City, New Jersey, Cuban-born Abel Hernandez recognizes Latino heterogeneity by decorating his Mi Bandera supermarket—which draws some six thousand to eight thousand customers each weekend—with flags from the different Latin American countries, along with a U.S. flag (Hammel 1995: 74).

Or take the Good Fortune supermarket stores in southern California (under the corporate name "99", 9 being a good luck number for the Chinese), where buyers can select among national brands plus countless Oriental specialties. Versions of almost identical products (such as teas and herb drinks, canned pigeon and quail eggs, sauces, grain products) carrying, however, different brand names, are stocked in various locations of the store. Chinese, Japanese, Korean, or Vietnamese customers know the difference. Ivan Chien, vice president of Good Fortune's retail operations, explains, "They all have distinct preferences based on their own cultures and customs, and they demand exactly the right items, and in the particular brands they have always known" (De Santa 1991). So do Asian Indians. In the Subzi-Mandi Indo-Pakistani Grocery in Flushing, Queens, customers shop for Indian foods and spices, including Parle Glucose Biscuits, Indian's most popular cookie, shipped from Bombay. The store manager notes with some wonder that in America you can pick from "50, 100 kinds of cookies," yet "they still want their own" (Lewnes 1993: 18).

In the world of consumerism, we see once again deep and variable forms of differentiation. On the one hand, consumers and marketers adapt mass-products to particularized circuits. On the other, consumers demand, and marketers create, special ethnic products that nevertheless remain embedded in the national circuit. Increasingly, a new circuit forms in which special products are subsequently incorporated into mainstream consumption, as in the case of ethnic shelves in supermarkets or the spread of Mexican restaurants. In fact, today non-Latin firms such as Pillsbury, Campbell Soup, PepsiCo, Nestle, and Kraft dominate the North American market for Mexican-style—or what some call "gringo"—food, adapting its flavors and intensities to American tastes (Collins 1996).[12] Some circuits of consumption, however, remain more segregated from the national circuits of distribution, as with the bodegas, where suppliers from the customers' regions of origin often stock the shelves with products that are not widely available on the American market but cater to the particular tastes of ethnic and immigrant groups.

Similar processes occur in all populations, although the mix will vary in degree or kind. Take the case of African American consumer patterns. In Chicago, Lizabeth Cohen (1990) found that, unlike white ethnic workers, blacks stepped early into mainstream mass culture, having joined by the 1920s the commercial world of chain stores, brand-name products, and popular music. Yet they never became integrated into a homogeneous white-dominated, middle-class consumer culture. Instead, Cohen claims, in a world of residential and economic segregation, consumption became a means of achieving influence, independence, laying the groundwork for a new urban black identity. "With mass culture as raw material," blacks, Cohen tells us, "fashioned their own culture during the 1920s that made them feel no less black." In fact, consumer goods she notes "would take on special cultural significance within black society that was often unintelligible to whites" (157, 154).

Recent interpretations of current black consumption patterns suggest a similar cultural creativity. Racial independence is achieved, in this view, by " 'blackening' the most mass of mass . . . produced goods so as to subvert domination and the generally received meaning of the thing," as when black men and women bleach their hair blond (Austin 1994: 160). To be sure, other observers of the same phenomenon treat it less favorably, arguing that poor African Americans acquire the consumer ambitions of white, middle-class Americans without having the means to acquire goods easily. This results in destructive and even lethal competition for popular goods, such as gold jewelry, leather jackets, or sneakers (see, e.g., Nightingale 1993).

However we read this controversy, marketers have to some degree approached African Americans as another distinctive ethnic market. Starting in the 1930s, but taking off only by the 1960s, consumer researchers and marketing specialists zeroed in on black consumers, documenting, for instance, blacks' preference for brand-name products and prestige items (see Edwards 1932; Bauer and Cunningham 1970; Nightingale 1993: 138–44).[13] As in the case of ethnic marketing, some firms tailored their promotion of mass products to a black clientele while others produced a distinct "soul market" of food, music, and clothes (Weems 1994). More recently, Nightingale (1993: 141) reports, mass marketers have targeted inner-city teenagers; jewelry manufacturers display, for instance, "hundreds of huge, low-carat gold 'bamboo' earrings, 'fat rope' or 'herringbone' gold chains with gold BMW and Mercedes logos or gold guns hanging from them, thick gold bracelets, and 'four-finger' gold rings" while Nike, Reebok, and other sportswear manufacturers glamorize their sneakers or warm-up suits.

CONCLUSIONS

Our review of changes in monetary practices and consumption unexpectedly clarifies what is at issue in multiculturalism. We have seen first how the nationalization of currency and mass production of goods did not dull cultural differentiation; instead the fingerprints of multiculturalism are all over the economy. Even currency and mass-produced goods behave like culturally differentiated media.

We've also seen how easily we confuse differentiation with segregation from central circuits of American life. In fact, major trends in the U.S. economy have combined differentiation with connection. The analysis of economic processes shows us the two are perfectly compatible in a wide range of areas: there is no contradiction between connectedness and diversity. The same currency, the same consumer product can have at the same moment universal and local meaning. Indeed, in recent years, we've seen mass markets themselves reaching out to specialized markets with ethnic focus, connecting the group with the central circuit of production. Unexpectedly, capitalized modern markets may increase ethnic options and therefore diversity. Critics have thought otherwise because they have conflated mass production with uniformity and differentiation with segregation.

The economic zone posing the greatest threat to national circuits connects groups in exclusive ways, cutting them off from the central circuit. To the extent that populations are actually excluded and discriminated against there is serious concern. But voluntary differentiation has always characterized the U.S. economy; consumers, producers, and distributors have worked to integrate specialized markets into the national economy. The moral and political problems center not on differentiation or the presence of multiple cultures but on forced inequality. Under conditions of segmented inequality, for example, cultural differences in consumption often become markers in intergroup conflict. What matters in the long run is how segmented markets are connected to the mainstream.

Why then have so many observers assumed an inescapable tension between diversity and common values? Because looking from the top, they fail to capture the duality of representations, where we find outward uniformity yet diversity in its local adaptation. Therefore the illusion persists of a struggle between connectedness and diversity, which, depending on the observer, takes two common forms. In the first view, differentiation appears as fragmentation and a threat to unity. In the second, unity or nationalized cultures loom as a menace to differentiation, seemingly obliterating all particularisms. A 1993 symposium on the subject shows how intimately the two views cohabit. In the conclusion to his essay on the "Erosion of Mass Culture," Paul Croce (1993: 16) warns:

> The clustering of mass culture has created a gridlock. . . . In a polarized cultural setting, people confront questions about health care, the environment, abortion, race relations, and a host of other knotty issues as partisans of their subculture's values, without talking to or even listening to other values.

A few pages away, an essay by David Pearson (1993: 22) on the troubles of our times says:

> This is the real post-mass culture, a mass-mediated fanfaronade in all its brilliant diversity offering us, its supplicants, in the end, a bare modicum of discretion. The more we partake of the mass media's standardized diversity, the more our lifestyles become individuated. Yet, the more we partake, the more we resemble one another on the fundamental level of consumers. This is far from a victory of the sovereign individual over the mindless homogeneity of mass culture.

Both observers act out the illusion of an irreconcilable contest between unity and diversity. In another version, political theorist Benjamin Barber (1995) goes so far as to portray a cosmic struggle between Jihad and McWorld, pitting the forces of religious and ethnic fragmentation against the inexorable economic homogenization of the world. The economic side of this illusion resonates with moral sensitivities and fears that if we all eat at McDonald's we'll end up with the same soul, or that standardized Hallmark cards will homogenize sentiments. Yet this fear couples oddly with the opposite fear: that America is disintegrating into hermetic and hostile subcultures. The dilemma, we've seen, is false. Each time there is an increase in scale, we find people particularizing, adapting to local circuits.[14]

We could pursue this theme in other areas of economic life, such as access to credit, categories of payments, or systems of work. One more unexpected example linked to consumption is the nationalization of holidays. Consider this selection from the mid-nineteenth-century's vast assortment of local civic holidays reported by Leigh Schmidt (1995: 33–4) in his account of American holidays: New York City's republican Evacuation Day, Irish Catholics' St. Patrick's Day, Scots' St. Andrew's Day, patrician Knickerbockers' St. Nicholas's Day, New Englander's Pilgrim Day, and Charlestown's Bunker Hill Day. "Ethnic particularity, eclecticism, and localism," Schmidt notes, "seemed to impede national observances at every turn" (33). Yet, by the end of the century national holiday traditions had been installed, largely propelled by the expansion of a consumerist economy and culture. Merchants, recognizing the commercial potential of holiday celebrations, displayed, promoted, and in the process nationalized both holiday observances and material symbols, such as the mass-produced greeting cards, Valentine cupids and hearts, Santa Clauses, or chocolate Easter bunnies. "The consumer culture," Schmidt concludes, "more than folk tradition, local custom, or religious community increasingly provided the common forms and materials for American celebrations" (297).

Yet, as in the case of currency and other consumer goods, people and groups, even as they shared in the increasingly nationalized, standardized, consumer-oriented celebrations, found ways to simultaneously particularize their holidays. Mary Waters (1990) has shown that contemporary Americans attach themselves to symbolic ethnicity by means of holidays, celebrations, foods, and other representations of their origins. This process was already well underway a half-century ago. By the 1920s, for instance, American Jews had revitalized the languishing holiday of Chanukah into what Jenna Joselit (1994: 229) calls a "functional equivalent" to Christmas, shopping for and exchanging gifts. Even the Christmas Club savings concept was adapted to Chanukah: "Save For Chanukah" ads by the East River Savings Institution appeared in Yiddish newspapers—although printed in Yiddish, the ads pictured a young couple standing next to a Christmas tree (Joselit 1994: 234, and personal communication). In the 1960s, African Americans fashioned their own December holiday of Kwanzaa, drawing not only from Christmas, but also from African harvest festivals, Chanukah, and New Year's Eve. Although Kwanzaa was intended to counter the commercial orientation of dominant holidays, it has now incorporated consumerism in its practice: the production of videos and books, Kwanzaa cards and wrapping paper, along with Afrocentric clothes, art work, jewelry, and music (Schmidt 1995: 300–301; Austin 1996). Recent Indian immigrants are likewise constructing dual holiday celebrations. One study reports Indian immigrant families celebrating Thanksgiving with turkey and stuffing combined with curries and other Indian foods (Mehta and Belk 1991: 407). Armenian families, meanwhile, serve their Thanksgiving turkey with rice pilaf, boreog, and stuffed vine leaves (Bakalian 1993: 366).

Recall the three common beliefs with which we began: that the United States faces a threat of fragmentation caused by the proliferation of distinct cultures and the resistance of recent immigrants to cultural assimilation; that the economy differs from other areas of social life because it dissolves such cultural distinctions, drawing people directly into standardized, large-scale circuits of exchange; that the economy thereby constitutes an unsatisfactory connector to the precise degree that differentiation occurs in other spheres, given that economic relations undermine solidarity and moral commitment that would otherwise form in those spheres. So far as the evidence from monetary transactions and consumption tells, all three beliefs are deeply inadequate. Money and consumption show us the simultaneity and compatibility of connectedness and differentiation, with the chief threat to national solidarity arising not from cultural differentiation but from the formation of segregated, unequal circuits of exchange. The economy, it turns out, differentiates and proliferates culturally in much the same way as other spheres of social life do, without losing national and even international connectedness. Although we may differ vigorously on the justice or efficiency of present-day economic institutions, we can by no means dismiss them as an amoral realm in which obligation, distinction, identity, and meaning vanish. On the contrary, a clear-eyed look at economic transactions reveals a world charged with moral meaning, a world of deeply felt and well-nuanced social relations.

NOTES

1. "Time dollars"—chits used to regulate a barter system of exchange of services such as child care, housecleaning, tutoring, or reading to the blind—provide still another strategy of currency differentiation, by creating an independent alternative to legal tender while using legal tender as the unit of account. See the *New York Times*, 29 September 1996, p. 16, on the successful use of "time dollars" in inner cities.

2. For a thorough discussion of American attitudes toward consumption between 1875 and 1940 see Horowitz (1985).

3. For some earlier classics see Veblen ([1899] 1953); Douglas and Isherwood, (1979); Bourdieu (1984). DiMaggio (1990, 1994) and Agnew (1994) provide excellent syntheses of the literature on consumption. Here I focus on ethnicity, neglecting for the most part both class and gender, for which there is an extensive literature. That literature shows among a great many other things the great predominance of women in purchasing and planning for household consumption. See, for example, the recent edited collection by De Grazia and Furlough (1996)

4. Similarly, ethnic marketing targeted Mexicans, and Spanish-language radio programming aimed at the same audience, in Los Angeles during the 1920s and 1930s (Sanchez 1993: 171–87).

5. For the purposes of this article I am not dealing with the vast literature on the politics of ethnicity. Note, however, that Gans's (1979) concept of "symbolic" ethnicity illustrates the simultaneity of connectedness and differentiation. For more recent discussions of that issue, see also Waters (1990).

6. Frenzen, Hirsch, and Zerillo (1994: 412) observe that: "Sociology has an under-explored resource in the databases comprised by . . . descriptive market studies of consumers' attitudes and behavior on a wide variety of topics and issues."

7. See for example, Dugger 1996: 25, 28; Mendosa 1996: 72; Armann 1995: 56, 58.

8. In her study of Latino immigrants in Long Island, anthropologist Sarah Mahler (1995) points out that managing small-scale ethnic food businesses offers women with children a conveniently flexible occupation. Maria Cristina Garcia (1996: 87) documents a complementary adaptation in Miami: the success of cantinas, Cuban-owned home-delivery food services targeted to busy Cuban working women, supplying their families with traditional Cuban specialties such as lechon asado, boliche, or arroz con pollo. Mahler attributes the spread of ethnic food services in Long Island, along with other immigrant-centered businesses—such as the multipurpose agencies that handle travel, insurance, remittances, and legal services—to immigrants' segregation from mainstream institutions (139–45).

9. Significantly, one of the most frequent advertisements in Spanish-language television stations are for the various schools and home-study programs that teach English (Rohter 1996).

10. Obviously this connects with the overlapping literatures on ethnic enclaves and transnational migrant networks. For an orientation to these literatures, see Portes 1995: 1–41; 1996: 151–68.

11. For similar merchandising trends in the revival of Yiddish culture among American Jews, see Halter (forthcoming).

12. More generally, the top ten firms (Procter & Gamble; AT&T; McDonald's; Anheuser-Busch; Sears, Roebuck & Co.; Philip Morris; Colgate-Palmolive; JC Penney; Ford Motor Co.; Quaker Oats Co.) advertising in Hispanic markets are non-Latin. Goya, the largest Hispanic firm, ranks only twenty-seventh. By 1995, overall advertising in Hispanic markets had surpassed $1 billion (Zate 1995: 50, 52). Even in the zone of Latin music (estimated to be 300 million and growing) mainstream American firms are moving in (Mendosa 1996b: 72). Meanwhile the number of Hispanic-owned businesses—estimated at more than 1.35 million in 1996—has also been increasing rapidly, at about 12% a year (Mendosa 1996a: 10).

13. Peiss (1996: 327) notes that as early as the 1880s and 1890s white-owned patent medicine companies aimed at a black consumer market. By the 1900s, however, African American entrepreneurs had built their own vigorous trade in hair care and cosmetics for black women. See also Rooks 1996.

14. Following Appadurai's (1990) analysis of global culture, Castells (1996) identifies similar dual processes of connection and differentiation occurring in the worldwide transformation of communications, especially as exemplified by computer networks. See also Regev (1996).

REFERENCES

Agnew, Jean-Cristophe. 1994. "Coming Up for Air: Consumer Culture in Historical Perspective." Pp. 19–39 in *Consumption and the World of Goods*, edited by John Brewer and Roy Porter. New York: Routledge.

Alvarez, Robert M. 1990. "Mexican Entrepreneurs and Markets in the City of Los Angeles: A Case of an Immigrant Enclave." *Urban Anthropology* 19: 99–124.

Andrews, Edmund L. 1996. "Europeans Report Breakthrough in Monetary Union Effort." *New York Times*, 14 December.

Appadurai, Arjun. 1990. "Disjuncture and Difference in the Global Cultural Economy." *Public Culture* 2 (spring): 1–24.

Armann, Claudia. 1995. "The Audience Is Listening." *Hispanic Business* 17 (December): 56, 58.

Austin, Regina. 1994. "'A Nation of Thieves': Securing Black People's Right to Shop and to Sell in White America." *Utah Law Review* (no. 1): 147–77.

———. 1996. "Kwanzaa and The Commercialization of Black Culture." Philadelphia: University of Pennsylvania Law School. Unpublished paper.

Bakalian, Anny. 1993. *Armenian-Americans: From Being to Feeling Armenian*. New Brunswick, N.J.: Transaction.

Barber, Benjamin R. 1995. *Jihad vs. McWorld*. New York: Time Books.

Bauer, Raymond A., and Scott M. Cunningham. 1970. *Studies in the Negro Market*. Cambridge, Mass.: Marketing Science Institute.

Bourdieu, Pierre. 1984. *Distinction*. Cambridge: Harvard University Press.

Case, Brendan M. 1996. "Cashing In on Immigration." *New York Times*, 14 September.

Caskey, John P. 1994. *Fringe Banking: Check-Cashing Outlets, Pawnshops, and the Poor*. New York: Russell Sage Foundation.

Castells, Manuel. 1996. *The Rise of the Network Society*. Cambridge, Mass.: Blackwell.

Cohen, Lizabeth. 1986. "Embellishing a Life of Labor: An Interpretation of the Material Culture of American Working-Class Homes, 1885–1915." Pp. 261–78 in *Common Places: Readings in American Vernacular Architecture*, edited by Dell Upton and John Michael Vlach. Athens: The University of Georgia Press.

———. 1990. *Making A New Deal: Industrial Workers in Chicago, 1919–1939*. New York: Cambridge University Press.

———. 1996. "From Town Center to Shopping Center: The Reconfiguration of Community Marketplaces in Postwar America." *The American Historical Review* 101 (October): 1050–81.

Collins, Glenn. 1996. "The Americanization of Salsa." *New York Times*, 9 January.

Costa, Janeen Arnold, and Gary J. Bamossy, eds. 1995. *Marketing in a Multicultural World*. Thousand Oaks, Calif.: Sage Publications.

Croce, Paul Jerome. 1993. "Erosion of Mass Culture." *Society* 30 (July/August): 11–16.

De Grazia, Victoria, with Ellen Forlough. 1996. *The Sex of Things*. Berkeley: University of California Press.

De Santa, Richard. 1991. "California's Oriental Stores: The Ultimate Niche Marketers." *Supermarket Business* 46 (November): 25–30.

Di Maggio, Paul. 1990. "Cultural Aspects of Economic Action and Organization." Pp. 113–36 in *Beyond the Marketplace*, edited by Roger Friedland and A. F. Robertson. New York: Aldine de Gruyter.

———. 1994. "Culture and Economy." Pp. 27–57 in *The Handbook Of Economic Sociology*, edited by Neil J. Smelser and Richard Swedberg. Princeton, N.J.: Princeton University Press; New York: Russell Sage Foundation.

Doty, Richard G. 1995. "Surviving Images, Forgotten Peoples: Native Americans, Women, and African Americans on United States Obsolete Banknotes." Pp. 119–25 in *The Banker's Art*, edited by Virginia Hewitt. London: British Museum Press.

Douglas, Mary, and Baron Isherwood. 1979. *The World of Goods*. New York: Norton.

Dugger, Celia. 1996. "A Tower of Babel, in Wood Pulp." *New York Times*, 19 January.

Edwards, Paul K. 1932. *The Southern Urban Negro as a Consumer*. New York: Prentice-Hall.

Frenzen, Jonathan, Paul M. Hirsch, and Philip C. Zerillo. 1994. "Consumption, Preferences, and Changing Lifestyles." Pp. 403–25 in *The Handbook of Economic Sociology*, edited by Neil J. Smelser and Richard Swedberg. Princeton, N.J.: Princeton University Press; New York: Russell Sage Foundation.

Gans, Herbert. 1979. "Symbolic Ethnicity: The Future of Ethnic Groups and Cultures in America." Pp. 193–200 in *On the Making of Americans: Essays in Honor of David Riesman*, edited by Herbert Gans. Philadelphia: University of Pennsylvania Press.

Garcia, Maria Cristina. 1996. *Havana USA*. Berkeley: University of California Press.

Gleick, James. 1996. "Dead as a Dollar." *New York Times Magazine*, June 16, pp. 26–54.

Graham, Ellen. 1996. "Community Groups Print Local (and Legal) Currencies." *Wall Street Journal*, 27 June, p. B1.

Granovetter, Mark. 1995. "The Economic Sociology of Firms and Entrepreneurs." Pp. 128–65 in *The Economic Sociology of Immigration*, edited by Alejandro Portes. New York: Russell Sage Foundation.

Halter, Marilyn. 1998. "Longings and Belongings: Yiddish Identity and Consumer Culture." In *Yiddish Culture Then and Now*. Omaha, Neb.: Creighton University Press. Forthcoming.

Hammell, Frank. 1995. "An Ear for the Exotic." *Supermarket Business* 50: 73–82.

Heinze, Andrew R. 1990. *Adapting to Abundance*. New York: Columbia University Press.

Helleiner, Eric. n.d. "Historicizing Territorial Currencies: Monetary Space and the Nation-State in North America." *Political Geography*, forthcoming.

Holt, Douglas B. 1995. "How Consumers Consume: A Typology of Consumption Practices." *Journal of Consumer Research* 22 (June): 1–16.

———. 1997. "Postructuralist Lifestyle Analysis: Conceptualizing the Social Patterning of Consumption in Postmodernity." *Journal of Consumer Research* 23 (March): 326–50.

Horowitz, Daniel. 1985. *The Morality of Spending*. Baltimore, Md.: John Hopkins University Press.

Joselit, Jenna Weissman. 1990. "'A Set Table': Jewish Domestic Culture in the New World, 1880–1950." Pp. 21–73 in *Getting Comfortable in New York: The American Jewish Home 1919–1939*, edited by Susan L. Braunstein and Jenna Weissman Joselit. New York: The Jewish Museum.

———. 1994. *The Wonders of America*. New York: Hill and Wang.

Kaufman, Carol J., and Sigfredo A. Hernandez. 1991. "The Role of the Bodega in a U.S. Puerto Rican Community." *Journal of Retailing* 67 (December 22): 375.

Leach, William. 1993. *Land of Desire*. New York: Pantheon.

Lewnes, Alexia. 1993. "The Two Worlders." *Brandweek* 34: 16–21.

Mahler, Sarah J. 1995. *American Dreaming*. Princeton, N.J.: Princeton University Press.

Mathews, Ryan. 1995. "Marketing to a New World of Taste: Ethnic Marketing at Supermarkets." *Progressive Grocer* 74 (July): 73.

McQuillen, Daniel. 1996. "Cities of Gold." *Incentive* 170 (February): 38–40.

Meeker-Lowry, Susan. 1995. "The Potential of Local Currency." *Z Magazine* July/August: 16–22.

Mehta, Raj, and Russell W. Belk. 1991. "Artifacts, Identity, and Transition: Favorite Possessions of Indians and Indian Immigrants to the United States." *Journal of Consumer Research* 17 (March): 398–411.

Mendosa, Rick. 1996a. "A Million and Counting." *Hispanic Business* 18 (July/August): 10.

———. 1996b. "Music to Their Ears." *Hispanic Business* 18 (July/August): 72.

Mulhern, Francis J., and Jerome D. Williams. 1994. "A Comparative Analysis of Shopping Behavior in Hispanic and Non-Hispanic Market Areas." *Journal of Retailing* 70 (September 22): 231.

Nieves, Evelyn. 1996. "Ithaca Hours: Pocket Money for Everyman." *New York Times*, 21 January.

Nightingale, Carl Husemoller. 1993. *On The Edge: A History of Poor Black Children and Their American Dreams*. New York: Basic Books.

Pearson, David E. 1993. "Post-Mass Culture." *Society* 30 (July/August): 17–22.

Peiss, Kathy. 1996. "Making Up, Making Over: Cosmetics, Consumer Culture, and Women's Identity." Pp. 311–36 in *The Sex of Things*, edited by Victoria De Grazia with Ellen Furlough. Berkeley: University of California Press.

Peñaloza, Lisa. 1994. "Atravesando Fronteras/Border Crossings: A Critical Ethnographic Exploration of the Consumer Acculturation of Mexican Immigrants." *Journal of Consumer Research* 21 (June): 32–54.

Portes, Alejandro. 1995. "Economic Sociology and the Sociology of Immigration: A Conceptual Overview." Pp. 1–41 in *The Economic Sociology of Immigration*, edited by Alejandro Portes. New York: Russell Sage Foundation.

———. 1996. "Transnational Communities: Their Emergence and Significance in the Contemporary World-System." Pp. 151–68 in *Latin America in the World-Economy*, edited by Roberto Patricio Korzeniewicz and William C. Smith. Westport, Conn.: Praeger.

Regev, Motti. 1996. "Rock Aesthetics and Musics of the World." Department of Sociology, Hebrew University, Jerusalem. Unpublished paper.

Ritzer, George. 1996. *The McDonaldization of Society*. Thousand Oaks, Calif.: Pine Forge.

Rohter, Larry. 1996. "In Spanish, It's Another Story." *New York Times*, 15 December.

Rooks, Noliwe M. 1996. *Hair Raising*. New Brunswick, N.J.: Rutgers University Press.

Sanchez, George J. 1993. *Becoming Mexican-American: Ethnicity, Culture, and Identity in Chicano Los Angeles 1900–1945*. New York: Oxford University Press.

Schmidt, Leigh Eric. 1995. *Consumer Rites: The Buying and Selling of American Holidays*. Princeton, N.J.: Princeton University Press.

Sherry, John F., Jr. 1991. "Postmodern Alternatives: The Interpretive Turn in Consumer Research." Pp. 548–91 in *Handbook of Consumer Behavior*, edited by Thomas S. Robertson and Harold H. Kassarjian. Englewood Cliffs, N.J.: Prentice-Hall.

Strasser, Susan. 1989. *Satisfaction Guaranteed: The Making of the American Mass Market*. New York: Pantheon.

Tully, Shawn. 1994. "Teens: The Most Global Market of All." *Fortune*, 16 May, 90–97.

Veblen, Thorstein. [1899]1953. *The Theory of the Leisure Class*. New York: Mentor.

Venkatesh, Alladi. 1995. "Ethnoconsumerism: A New Paradigm to Study Cultural and Cross-Cultural Consumer Behavior." Pp. 26–67 in *Marketing in a Multicultural World*, edited by Janeen Arnold Costa and Gary J. Bamossy. Thousand Oaks, Calif.: Sage Publications.

Waters, Mary. 1990. *Ethnic Options*. Berkeley: University of California Press.

Weems, Robert E., Jr. 1994. "The Revolution Will Be Marketed: American Corporations and Black Consumers during the 1960s." *Radical History Review* 59: 94–107.

Weiss, Michael J. 1988. *The Clustering of America*. New York: Harper & Row.

Zate, Maria. 1995. "A Billion-Dollar Year for Media Spending." *Hispanic Business* 17: 50, 52.

Zelizer, Viviana A. 1994. *The Social Meaning of Money*. New York: Basic Books.

CHAPTER TEN

Uncommon Values, Diversity, and Conflict in City Life*

CLAUDE S. FISCHER

PROLOGUE

THE FIRST DAY that I meet my undergraduate class in "American Society" at Berkeley, I challenge their notion that America is especially diverse culturally. The Berkeley campus is a hotbed of ethnic consciousness and students typically frame issues in terms of race and nationality. Many believe, at least implicitly, that ethnicity creates wide social and cultural differences. But on that first day, while scanning faces that are freckled pink topped with blonde hair, olive-colored framed by black hair, and ebony capped with kinky hair, I contest that presumption. Typically, these students have ancestors from all over the world, from Africa, Asia, Latin America, Eastern Europe, and Western Europe. But virtually every one of them agrees, for example, that people should choose their own spouses, that each person deserves equal respect from the law and equal opportunity for success, that "one person, one vote" is a political ideal, and that the perfect home is a detached single-family house in which each child has a separate bedroom. These beliefs or values are, in the context of human history and geography, exceedingly odd; few of the students' ancestors would understand, much less agree with, those views. Yet, so powerfully absorbing is American culture that long-enduring, antipodal values, such as parental rights to arrange marriages, vanish within a generation's residence in this country. The human rainbow that is my class only underlines the homogenous quality of our culture. *E pluribus unum* indeed!

City people, more than others, resist assimilation, cling most tightly to foreign ways, and even personify cultural diversity. Popular and scholarly concerns that "modernization" dissolves moral solidarity have long focused on cities. I assume that we can learn much about the dynamics of cultural diversity in this nation by looking at American cities' experiences with diversity. From that experience, I draw several tentative lessons:

* This is a revision of a paper prepared for a conference on Common Values, Social Diversity, and Cultural Conflict, at the Center for Advanced Study in the Behavioral Sciences, Stanford, California, October 17–19, 1996.

- Despite resistance, ethnic cultures have been absorbed and are still being absorbed into the "mainstream" American culture.
- Because cultural diversity along ethnic lines is in decline, the novelty of the current era lies less in the reality of ethnic diversity than in the explicit ideology of ethnic diversity.
- In the end, cultural diversity rests less on ethnic heterogeneity than on the emergence of new subcultures organized around class, religion, lifestyles, and other interests and identities. Urban places generate such subcultures and so, perhaps, do modern media of communications and transportation.
- Moral order is precarious in a diverse environment, but order can be sustained without a moral consensus.

The City and Diversity

Since the nation's founding, confrontations among its diverse cultures have been most intense in the cities. Most non-English immigrants confronted other immigrant groups and felt pressed by the dominant Anglo-Protestant culture in the cities. Organized resistance to assimilation most often happened, and cultural diversity made its strongest stands, in the cities. Most Americans have long read the city as "foreign"—and, significantly, as the "lost community," too.

The intense bond between urban life and diversity was evident to the founding fathers and the generations that followed. For Jefferson, cities, with their landless workers, immigrants, and mobs, represented a threat to yeoman democracy. New York City, whose inhabitants spoke eighteen different languages by 1650, in many ways signified a heterogeneity that threatened American virtue (see, e.g., Bender 1988). Populists often invoked the specter of urban "Rum, Romanism, and Rebellion" or its variants to mobilize rural and small-town voters. Do-gooders of the nineteenth century understood, as a matter of course, that cities were the wandering grounds of lost souls. To redeem the fallen might require removing them from the city to places where a "natural community" could sustain individuals' integration into a moral order.[1] Struggles, often violent ones, over culture—that is, over ways of life, rather than material interests, although these two are not so easily untangled—racked American cities. Roy Rosenzweig (1985), for example, describes recurrent battles in late-nineteenth-century Worcester, Massachusetts, over how the public parks would be used and the Fourth of July celebrated: with the sober reserve of the Protestant middle class or the boisterous drinking of Catholic immigrants. ("Italian Celebrates: Couldn't Speak English but Could Fire Revolver Shots," read one Worcester newspaper headline.) Similar accounts are available for cities around the nation.

The parks and parade routes were just two of the urban battlegrounds upon which immigrants struggled against native Protestants intent on at least controlling, if not assimilating, them. Other front lines were schools (fighting over, for example, compulsory education and Protestant moral instruction), workplaces (punctuality, drinking, and Sabbath work), police departments (jobs, enforcement of liquor, gambling, and drug laws), churches (ethnic succession, and styles of worship), and, certainly, neighborhoods.[2]

Lest this list imply that urban cultural diversity was solely *ethnic* diversity, we should remember that nineteenth-century American cities also generated tension and even violence along other dimensions of difference, such as religion, class, and age. For example, revivalist movements mobilized many middle-class Americans to force piety and discipline on their employees and neighbors, and an atheistic labor movement arose in Chicago (Johnson 1978; Nelson 1991). A distinct middle class, with its own organizations, neighborhoods, and consciousness, developed in the major cities of the East Coast during the antebellum years; and in roughly the same period, workingmen created solidarity, unions, and their own class consciousness (Blumin 1989; Wilentz 1984; Gorn 1987). Around the turn of the century, young, single women formed a notable part—a problematic part, for many observers—of the urban workforce, with distinctive "youth" lifestyles and neighborhoods (Meyerowitz 1988; Peiss 1986).

Guardians of Anglo-Protestant culture worked hard to keep the lid on the urban caldron of diversity by "Americanizing" newcomers through schooling, social work, and propaganda. Although immigrants often resisted such outreach—for example, scoffing at settlement-house social workers—and tried to defend their ways of life—for example, by supporting Catholic schools—there seems to have been no organized ideology against cultural assimilation. In fact, immigrant groups often sought ways to syncretize their cultures with Americanism, to argue that being true to one's own culture was, in some fashion, part of being a "real" American (e.g., Meagher 1986). And assimilation did occur, probably less because of conscious Americanization and more as the result of occupational mobility, social interaction, and participation in the wider mass culture of twentieth-century America (see, for example, Alba 1990; 1995; Waters 1990; Cohen 1989; and Morawska 1994).

Today, too, the metropolis is the cockpit of cultural clashes. (The phrase "culture wars," as used by, say, Pat Buchanan, describes a struggle between an often urban cosmopolitanism and a typically rural provincialism, but I am referring here instead to divisions within our urban areas.) American cities are where peoples of the world congregate. In 1994, 95% of enumerated noncitizens lived in America's metropolitan areas as compared with 77% of native-born citizens; 50% of the noncitizens lived in metropolitan center cities, compared with 30% of the native-born.[3] Moreover, more than half of recent immigrants resided in only five of the metropolitan areas.[4] In 1990, foreign-born residents constituted 45% of the population of Miami, 38% of the population of Los Angeles city, and 34% of San Francisco's population (U.S. Bureau of the Census 1995a). In addition, African Americans disproportionately live in metropolitan areas, particularly in the center cities. One well-known consequence of this urban diversity is conflict—ranging from simple intergroup tension to political struggles over schools to violent racial battles—conflict that tends to be greater in frequency and depth the larger the city (Fischer 1984: 151–52; see, e.g., Olzak, Shanahan, and West 1994; Olzak, Shanahan, and McEneaney 1996; Portes 1984; and Baldassare 1994). Such conflict is often read as showing the absence of common values and community in cities.

Contemporary American cities also spawn distinct but *nonethnic* cultural groups, too: art worlds, gay communities, young singles crowds, "yuppies," even welfare "underclasses" (on the last example: Rank and Hirshl 1988; Hirschl and Rank 1991). These nonethnic communities often conflict, too, over housing, school policies, domestic partner legislation, policing, and so on.

Nonethnic subcultures differ in many ways from ethnic ones. In principle, for example, the former are chosen rather than assigned by birth, they seem short-lived rather than deeply rooted, they connect people more to friends than to family, and they arise from within the national culture rather than outside it. However, even these distinctions are fuzzy. (Today, it is not obvious that being born into, say, an Italian American family is more fateful than being born to parents who are political radicals, or artists, or in a drug scene.) Nonethnic differences can be as divisive as ethnic ones. Struggles over school curricula are initiated by evangelical communities, over public space by youth groups, and over natural resources by committed environmentalists. As American subcultures, they do fight their battles within a common discourse—for example, in the language of individual rights—but that may make the battles even more bitter and lasting.

Cultural diversity and cultural tension are endemic to cities, the more so the larger the cities. Why? As I have elaborated elsewhere (Fischer 1984; 1982; 1995), population centers generate diverse subcultures by attracting migrants from widely dispersed places and by concentrating distinct sets of people in such numbers that they form social networks of shared interests. In larger cities, those networks grow to "critical masses" needed to build institutions, institutions that, in turn, foster self-conscious and active subcultures. These subcultures expand and encompass members' personal networks more completely than is likely in smaller places. The city is diverse—a "mosaic of little worlds that touch but do not interpenetrate," in the famous words of Robert Ezra Park (1967: 40)—but individuals' own networks, located inside those little "worlds"—are not diverse. In fact, they are probably less diverse than the personal networks of comparable rural people. These subcultures (some call them "communities") frequently conflict over material or cultural issues or both.

Disagreement and conflict form the negative side of the diversity coin. That same diversity provides the excitement and creativity of city life. Both the appreciated and the abhorred qualities of cities result from their multiple cultural worlds. Ethnic communities are just one kind of cultural world that flourish in cities—and not the most distinctive ones at that. The really distinctive subcultures are those that rarely have counterparts in rural areas—for example, the ballet world, sex workers, computer hackers, lesbians, and political junkies.[5] Moreover, nonethnic subcultures proliferate and grow over time, while the viability and distinctiveness of minority ethnic subcultures typically fade as the pressures from the dominant culture to assimilate win out (see next section).

HISTORICAL CHANGES

How have these patterns of urban diversity changed over American history?

The degree of *ethnic* diversity in American cities has fluctuated wildly over the last couple of centuries. Although the colonial cities were heterogenous, peoples from the British Isles and northwest Europe largely defined their motley character. The flood of Germans and Irish during the mid–nineteenth century increased both urban diversity and polarization. The next big influx, around the turn of the century, of Italians, Jews, and others from southern and eastern Europe, raised the proportion of Americans who were born outside the nation's borders to 15%. This inflow, mixed with anxieties about labor unrest, contributed to a backlash of nativism, racism, eugenics, and political moves to close the borders. Borders did close in 1924. By 1970, only 5% of Americans were born abroad. The immigration reforms of 1965 reversed the tide yet again. In 1994, 9% of U.S. residents had been born abroad, largely in Latin America and Asia (U.S. Bureau of the Census 1996a) and they differed much more from natives than had the European immigrants. (In that light, perhaps we should be surprised that the nativist reaction to "brown" and "yellow" immigrants today is notably milder than nativist reactions were to "white" immigrants in earlier eras.)

The immigrants of earlier waves have assimilated, some virtually disappearing into the American mainstream. (I use the term "assimilation" broadly, to mean both adoption of dominant cultural perspectives and incorporation of group members into the larger society's social structures, such as jobs and neighborhoods.[6]) Germans and Scandinavians, for example, barely count as ethnic anymore, except in a few colorful tourist locations.[7] The Irish, Italians, Poles, and so on, are rapidly on their way to complete melting. The Jews appear not far behind (at least as an *ethnic* group).

One indicator of assimilation is spatial distribution within urban areas. The Europeans have moved out of their turn-of-the-century enclaves and spread out, so that European ethnic neighborhoods—although a few discernible ones can still be found, especially in cities such as New York—are few and house few of the remaining group members. The process seems slowed in very large urban centers, but spatial assimilation has been largely inexorable (see Massey 1985; Lieberson 1980; Zunz 1982; Bodnar 1985; Alba, Logan, and Crowder 1996).

Probably the most fundamental indicator of assimilation is intermarriage. The data show strong declines in the rate of within-group marriage among the immigrant groups of the late nineteenth century—to the point, among Jews, of virtual collective panic. Like spatial assimilation, group intermarriage seems slowed down in the larger cities, but the historical trend is clear nonetheless.[8]

What of the "new" immigrants? Are they following the same trends toward assimilation, or have we entered a new era, one of ethnic persistence? Answering these questions is difficult because the tide of immigrants continues to replenish the ethnic neighborhoods, reinforce mother tongues, and provide marriage partners. Nevertheless, the trend lines look similar to those of the Europeans: increasing spatial dispersion away from enclaves, loss of language in later generations, and increased intermarriage with outgroup Americans.[9]

To be sure, I have grossly summarized complex patterns. Some groups have assimilated more quickly (e.g., the French); others more slowly (e.g., Italians); some have been ambivalent (e.g., Jews); and others have been fiercely resisted (e.g., African Americans). The new immigrants face greater hurdles than the Europeans did, because they are not only foreign but also, like blacks, racially distinct. Also, cultural assimilation, when it does come, ought not to be equated with "making it" in America, as the travails of Chicanos show. Still, what is striking is the pervasiveness and power of assimilation. That the Jews, people who have for millennia successfully persisted as "strangers" in foreign lands, should find their cultural identity threatened in America as it has been nowhere else where they have lived in large numbers is testimony to the absorptive power of this society.

The great exception to this pattern of assimilation is, of course, African Americans. They became *more* segregated from whites during the twentieth century as they moved into northern, urban ghettoes. Intermarriage rates between blacks and whites remain—although recently rising—below 5 %.[10] Culturally very American and historically more American than most groups, African Americans remain unincorporated.

Excepting the African American case, the contemporary patterns of assimilation do not seem qualitatively different from those of earlier eras. Even in the urban environment so supportive of ethnic cultures, America is absorbing the second and third generations into the conventional culture. Some have even suggested that the recent immigrants, many of whom are well educated and previously exposed to American popular culture, are more ready and able to assimilate than were earlier immigrants.

What may be new and substantially different is that an *ideology* of diversity, of multiculturalism, exists today that did not exist before. This ideology thrives most visibly among some elites in universities, politics, media, and even corporate management (see Hollinger 1995). Whether it affects everyday assimilation in neighborhoods, on jobs, or in dating is an open question, however. The celebration of ethnicity seems to have followed the rise of the "black pride" movement that succeeded the civil rights movement. For Latinos, Indians, and Asians, emulation seems logical. But for other Americans the celebration of difference may be partly a defensive reaction to these moves (everyone needs "roots" to participate) and partly a romantic reaction to the success of assimilation (much like the adoration of nature that emerged from the centers of the urban-industrial order).

In a nation of multiculturalism—as opposed to a nation of segregated cultures—it is also possible to merge an ethnic identity with other identities, with occupational or lifestyle identities, even with the national identity itself. A "real" American, in this sense, is a hyphenated American. (On my first visit to San Francisco, I watched Chinese girls wearing Scottish kilts march in a Columbus Day parade. What could be more American?) This expression of ethnicity is far from that found in the culturally segregated ethnic villages or ghettoes of Europe, or even in the immigrant enclaves a few generations ago.

If the clear trend for (nonblack) ethnic groups is assimilation, what about those nonethnic subcultures—occupational, leisure, lifestyle, and ideological groups—fermenting in cities? There is little hard evidence about the rate of such groups' formation, or of their divergence from the mainstream norms, except insofar as they become criminal, but one could fairly speculate that in both respects diversity may be increasing. (Some of the research on intermarriage suggests a shift from ethnic to class endogamy, for example.) To the extent that cities generate subcultural diversity because they bring people together, creating what Durkheim called "dynamic density," then the further bringing together of people in contemporary society made possible by planes, highways, and electronic communication may, in turn, be accelerating the formation of novel subcultures (Fischer 1995: 549–50). The urban experience suggests, paradoxically, that as the society becomes more diverse, the individuals' own social networks become less diverse. More than ever, perhaps, the child of an affluent professional family may live, learn, and play with only similar children; the elderly factory worker may retire and relax only among other aged members of the working class. Ironically, then, the worries about a "disuniting of America" may be misdirected by focusing on *ethnic* diversity.

A columnist for a computer magazine phrased his concerns about the dark side of telecommunications development in an essay entitled "The End of Common Experience." Given the arrival of narrow-casting television and individualized Internet exchanges, he wrote,

> the good news is that people with specific interests can find lots of similar-minded people with whom to interact. The bad news is that people whose behavior already tends toward the antisocial will likely find increased support for their tendencies, unmoderated by interaction with the rest of the world. . . . Not only is there the potential for the weird to get weirder but for the supposedly normal among us to become less tolerant, because we have less exposure to those who are different (Machrone 1996).

The history of urban diversity suggests that some of this concern may be well placed.[11]

SEEKING ORDER IN A DIVERSE COMMUNITY[12]

Studying the city's diversity provides lessons for understanding the nature and consequences of diversity in the wider society. The problem of "moral order" in the metropolis is a classic one. European fathers of social science (Durkheim, Tonniës, Simmel, and so on) wondered how moral order—regular, predictable, and harmonious social action founded on shared values and understandings— could survive in the heterogeneity of the city and, by extension, in the hetero- geneity of modern society. Underlying their discussion was the *assumption* that public order required a moral consensus. The American tradition, too, sought moral order in the city. The Puritan's idealized "city upon a hill" presumed concord among citizens; the evangelical reformers of the nineteenth century tried to recreate a harmony they remembered from their small-town childhoods; and American sociologists, too, searched for the source of a morally based order.[13] Yet, American efforts to sustain a moral consensus were repeatedly disappointed. Puritan towns declined into strife and division; immigrant groups rejected reformers' efforts at taming them. Moral order is elusive in the city; the "decline of community" seems ever-constant.

Cities generate moral *dis*order: misunderstandings, tension, and even conflict among people over ends, over means, and even over definitions of the situation. Yet, they rarely degenerate into Hobbesian wars or anarchy. By understanding the sources of disorder and the solutions that sustain order, we gain some in- sight into the larger issues of moral order in a diverse American society.

Cities produce problems of moral order at the *micro* level. Urban life, more so than life in small places, puts us in problematic *public*[14] settings, ones in which shared understandings are weak and expectations are unclear. The distin- guishing condition of public encounters in urban communities—in bus stations, ticket lines, stores, subways, on the streets—is that they are typically encoun- ters in a "world of strangers" (to quote Lyn Lofland [1973]).[15] We must deal, at least tacitly, with people whom we do not know personally, whom we do not recognize, and, most important, who are obviously different from us in many ways. In such encounters among people from different subcultures, behavioral expectations are neither shared nor certain. How near or far to sit, to make eye contact or not, to speak or not—these elementary norms vary from group to group and carry different implications for each. Then, should an untoward event occur, alternative interpretations make action ambiguous. If a man and woman start yelling at each other, is this an everyday dispute or the beginning of a physical assault? Would intervention be welcome or resented? If teenagers bois- terously shout obscenities, is this delinquency or just high spirits? In situations such as these, urbanites in public places often lack a common definition of the situation and normative guide to action. Order at the level of individual experi- ences is tentative and fragile. Anxiety about it is pervasive and consequential. For example, fear of crime is bred at least as much by the perception of public disorder, especially of loitering minority youth, as by actual incidents of crime (see, e.g., Taylor and Covington 1993; Rountree and Land 1996).

Fragility characterizes the order among social groups in the urban "mosaic of little worlds," as well. The heterogeneity of subcultures I have described means that cities, in Louis Wirth's ([1938] 1969: 160) phrase, "comprise a motley of peoples and cultures of highly differentiated modes of life between which there often is only the faintest communication, the greatest indifference, the broadest tolerance, occasionally bitter strife, but always the sharpest contrast"—hardly a *moral* order. Conflict, sometimes bitter, certainly arises in small towns, too, yet intergroup conflict in large cities is of a different magnitude, more pervasive, extensive, and serious. Cities tend to be rent by many cleavages, rather than one or two, by race, nationality, class, business, age, and lifestyles, all at once; often, cultural differences are themselves the grounds of dispute.[16] In addition, the stakes are often enormous, and interests in those stakes divide along group lines—for example, the struggles between black neighborhood activists and heavily Jewish teachers' unions over controlling the New York City school system.

Given these forces of disorder, why doesn't everything fall apart? Sometimes it does—individuals fight, cities split into civil war. More often, however, things do not fall apart; they just hang together tenuously. It is remarkable how well order is sustained in the most improbable cases. Robert Edgerton (1979) has described how 450,000 people, more than live in Kansas City, can crowd a small stretch of Southern California beach wearing virtually no clothes but with few problems. Every working day, people of diverse colors and cultures jam together, check-to-cheek and elbow-to-rib, in New York's subways with only rare disturbances. How is this possible? How is order sustained in the morally disunited city? I can speculate about how an amoral order is sustained.

At the personal level of public encounters, one solution to the threat of moral anarchy is *avoidance*. Americans (more so than Europeans) have dealt with urban anxiety by residential segregation. John Schneider, for example, has shown how in mid-nineteenth-century Detroit spatial segregation helped reduce middle-class encounters with public disorder; similarly, racial segregation today reduces whites' crossing paths with blacks whom they find threatening (Schneider 1980; Liska, Lawrence, and Sanchiriko 1982). *Wariness* is a related strategy. An on-guard attitude can help forestall upsetting encounters; that stance often distinguishes the urban veteran from the rural "hayseed." *Stereotyping* is also useful, providing guides, whether ill-founded or not, to interaction among people of different backgrounds.[17] *Coercion* is a historically common solution—blatantly present in police states that enforce the cultural understandings of the ruling group, more subtly so in democratic societies (e.g., Dray-Novey 1993). Several scholars have explored another kind of solution: a *public etiquette*—proper manners such as "selective inattention," nonverbal cues of recognition, careful physical spacing, and what might be called "elevator behavior"—that lubricates what might otherwise be frictional situations. Such etiquette seems most developed in cities.[18]

I have excluded from this list of "solutions" any recourse to a moral consensus, although one might consider public etiquette as a minimal sort of consensus. There may be more than this minimum, however. Popular outrage—at, say, horrific crimes such as child kidnappings—and popular celebrations—for, say, sports-teams' victories such as the Yankee's world championship in 1996—show that diverse people can share some values. Still, the point here is that order can be sustained in public encounters without much in the way of shared values.

Disorder also threatens at the level of groups. Here, too, cities seem to maintain order with amoral solutions. Some cities have managed to stay relatively *homogenous*, sometimes by rigid entry controls (e.g., Redfield and Singer 1954). Conflict often increases as the numbers of a subordinated group grow, and keeping them at bay can work, at least for a while.[19] Neighborhood *segregation*, maintained by physically walled quarters in medieval cities or politically walled suburbs in American metropolises, also reduces intergroup confrontations. So does strong *domination* of the city by a single and unified group. What is probably most common in American cities, after residential segregation, is order through *negotiation* among diverse groups. Sometimes it is tacit negotiation, as when police ignore illegal activities favored by particular groups, and sometimes it is explicit negotiation that may involve shifting coalitions of interests. Such negotiations are usually unequal ones. Behind the negotiation lies the latent threat of disorder—of disruptive strikes, ethnic violence, withdrawal, and the like. Moreover, negotiated solutions chronically need patching and are usually on the verge of collapse. Therefore, negotiation compounds the general sense that urban life is morally chaotic and tenuous. It is.

CONCLUSION

The urban struggle to sustain order in the midst of diversity—an endemic problem in city life—suggests lessons for understanding the national "community." Ethnic diversity, although a vivid and sometimes troubling reality, is declining. The sociology students of varying hues whom I described at the beginning of this paper think alike much more than they imagine. They differ significantly, however, from Americans of other ages, regions, and educational backgrounds; they even think differently than Berkeley students outside letters and science. American cultural diversity on nonethnic or -racial dimensions of human affiliation is probably increasing. Achieving a societywide consensus on values beyond perhaps a few fundamental ones such as democracy becomes more difficult. The urban experience suggests that order can be sustained even without a moral consensus, by various devices, some not pleasant. Perhaps the best such device is negotiation based on shared procedural understandings. This aspiration is a far more modest one than is the goal of a morally cohesive society. It forecasts continuing, even worsening, tensions and misunderstandings. But it may be the best we can hope for in a diversifying society.

NOTES

1. For example, reformers tried to round up street urchins in New York and ship them off to live with rural families. See on these matters, e.g., Boyer 1978.

2. On some of these points, see, for example, Ravitch 1974; Brown and Warner 1992; Glenn 1992; Bodnar 1985: esp. chs. 5 and 7; and Bayor 1978.

3. The figures for naturalized citizens are 94% metropolitan and 39% center-city (U.S. Bureau of the Census 1996a).

4. Roger Waldinger (1989) reports that 46% of immigrants arriving between 1965 and 1980 lived in New York, Los Angeles, Chicago, San Francisco, and Miami. Uncounted and more recent immigrants are probably even more likely than others to be in those places, especially Los Angeles.

5. Of course, some particular subcultures tend to be disproportionately rural, such as people heavily involved in hunting. But overall the generalization holds.

6. In principle, cultural adaptation and structural incorporation need not be tied together. One can imagine an English-speaking, Protestant, Anglicized Chicano who nevertheless lives in a *barrio* and holds a "Mexican" job or imagine a totally observant Hasidic Jew who nevertheless lives in suburban Salt Lake City and works as a professional athlete—but these images require quite an imagination. In practice, cultural and structural assimilation go together strongly, excepting, as we usually must, the case of African Americans whose culture is deeply American but many of whom are shut out from much of the society. Sometimes, assimilated people express their ethnic heritage consciously, but this most often involves "symbolic ethnicity" (Waters 1990). Such expressions, in fact, often simply underline a group's assimilation—for example, having a float in a patriotic parade, displaying cultural traditions in a public school classroom, or mobilizing politically. All these are *American* forms of action, totally unfamiliar in the traditional culture.

7. See, for example, on waning Norwegian identity, Schultz 1991. A 1991 report in the *New York Times*, 18 March, noted that only two Norwegian-language newspapers were left in the country from more than 100 originally.

8. Lieberson and Waters (1988: 199) report that in-group marriage rates among Polish Americans dropped from 47% for the generation born before 1915 to 20% for the generation born after 1945; the drop was from 66% to 27% for Italians. (The decline was less dramatic for the Irish, Germans, and English, because, having heavily intermarried by the early twentieth century, Americans of partial Irish, German, or English ancestry are so common that even nationality-blind marriages often involve people with some partial heritage in these groups.) On Jewish assimilation, see, e.g., Goldscheider and Zuckerman 1984 and Lipset and Raab 1995 and many other warnings about intermarriage in almost any Jewish community publication. On reduced intermarriage within cities see, e.g., Bernard 1980 and Alba 1990. On ethnic intermarriage in general, see Kalmun 1991, Stevens 1985, and Alba and Golden 1986.

9. On spatial assimilation, see, e.g., Massey and Denton 1987. On intermarriage: rates of Mexican–Mexican marriages have dropped from 83% in the pre-1915 cohort to 71% in the post-1965 cohort, despite the vastly increased numbers of Mexicans in the United States (Lieberson and Waters 1988: 199; see also Farley 1996: table 6-5). The proportion of Hispanics married to other Hispanics has stayed about the same for the last 25 years (U.S. Bureau of the Census 1996b: 55), but in the face of an approximate tripling of the Latino population, that stability implies much intermarriage in later generations. On language change among Mexican Americans, see Lopez 1978. Intermarriage among Asians follows similar patterns. Even by 1980, the out-marriage rate among third-generation Japanese Americans was 40%, and the out-marriage rate among Chinese Americans, despite continuing immigration, was 26% (Montero 1980). In 1990, only about half of young native-born Asian men and one-fifth of young native-born Asian

women married other Asians of whatever specific nationality (although those proportions were up from 1980, probably because of the immigration flow) (Farley 1996: table 6-5).

10. On segregation, see Massey and Denton 1993 and Harrison and Weinberg 1992. On intermarriage: In 1994, about 4% of married blacks were married to a white spouse (up from about 1% in 1970—U.S. Bureau of the Census 1996b: 55). A recent study points out the pace at which black–white intermarriage is growing: 12% of new marriages by blacks in 1993 were with a white, up from 3% in 1970 (study reported by Holmes [1996]).

11. Urbanites *do* have *exposure* to different others, but that impersonal exposure may just aggravate intergroup estrangement.

12. Some material in this section is drawn from an earlier paper: "Rethinking Urban Life: Order and Disorder in the Public Realm," presented to the American Sociological Association, San Francisco, August 1982.

13. A classic in this latter genre is Zorbaugh's (1928) *The Gold Coast and the Slum.* He finds the differences in values among communities of affluent WASPS, Sicilian immigrants, and young singles totally problematic.

14. Distinguishing public from private here is critical. Some analyses of urban mores describe urbanites' private lives as mirrors of the public encounters described below. That is a major error, upon which I shall not elaborate here (see Fischer 1984).

15. These encounters are the dramatic texts for other analysts, too, such as Erving Goffman, Stanley Milgram, William H. Whyte, and Robert Edgerton.

16. One sign of this tension is the finding that although residents of large cities are less prejudiced than small-town people, as that is conventionally measured, urbanites are likelier to see other cultural groups as community problems, e.g., complaining that Asians "buy up everything" in the neighborhood, or that public behavior by gays can make one "feel like a minority" (Fischer 1982: ch. 18).

17. E. M. Bruner (1973) describes the use of popular stereotypes to regulate public interaction in Indonesia. Sally Engle Merry (1981) describes a similar process in a Boston housing project.

18. David Hummon, in his study of how people think about city and town, quotes a San Franciscan:

> I'm a city person. . . . I feel comfortable in the city, I can get around. I know how to deal with people on a very informal basis. There are certain rules: how to get along in a city, what to expect from people you don't know. In a small town, I think there is much more of a personal level of what's expected. . . . I think a lot of small town people—that really throws them for a loop. They can't understand how everybody's just getting along [in the city] (Hummon 1980; see also Hummon 1990).

19. This is the story of black–white relations in American cities. The era of nostalgic harmony was typically the era during which the blacks were few and weak in power. As their numbers grew, so did conflict. See, for example, Osofsky 1971, Drake and Cayton 1945, and Karnig 1979.

REFERENCES

Alba, Richard. 1990. *Ethnic Identity: The Transformation of White America.* New Haven, Conn.: Yale University Press.

———. 1995. "Assimilation's Quiet Tide." *The Public Interest* 119 (spring): 3–18.

Alba, Richard D., and Reid M. Golden. 1986. "Patterns of Ethnic Marriage in the United States." *Social Forces* 65: 202–23.

Alba, Richard D., John R. Logan, and Kyle Crowder. 1996. "White Ethnic Neighborhoods and the Assimilation Process: The Greater New York Region, 1980–1990." Department of Sociology, State University of New York at Albany. Unpublished paper.

Baldassare, Mark, ed. 1994. *The Los Angeles Riots: Lessons for the Urban Future.* Boulder, Colo.: Westview Press.

Bayor, Ronald H. 1978. *Neighbors in Conflict: The Irish, Germans, Jews, and Italians of New York City, 1929–1941.* Baltimore: Johns Hopkins University Press.

Bender, Thomas. 1988. "New York in Theory." Pp. 53–65 in *America in Theory*, edited by Leslie Berlowitz, Denis Donoghue, and Louis Menand. New York: Oxford University Press.

Bernard, R. M. 1980. *The Melting Pot and the Altar.* Minneapolis: University of Minnesota Press.

Blumin, Stuart M. 1989. *The Emergence of the Middle Class: Social Experience in the American City, 1760–1900.* New York: Cambridge University Press.

Bodnar, John E. 1985. *The Transplanted.* Bloomington: Indiana University Press.

Boyer, Paul. 1978. *Urban Masses and Moral Order in America, 1820–1920.* Cambridge: Harvard University Press.

Brown, M. Craig, and Barbara D. Warner. 1992. "Immigrants, Urban Politics, and Policing in 1900." *American Sociological Review* 57: 293–305.

Bruner, E. M. 1973. "The Expression of Ethnicity in an Indonesian City." Pp. 251–80 in *Urban Ethnicity*, edited by Albert Cohen. London: Tavistock.

Cohen, Lizabeth. 1989. "Encountering Mass Culture at the Grass Roots: The Experience of Chicago Workers in the 1920s." *American Quarterly* 41: 6–33.

Drake, St. Clair, and Horace Cayton. 1945. *Black Metropolis: A Study of Negro Life in a Northern City.* Chicago: University of Chicago Press.

Dray-Novey, Alison. 1993. "Spatial Order and Police in Imperial Beijing." *Journal of Asian Studies* 52: 885–922.

Edgerton, Robert B. 1979. *Alone Together: Social Order on an Urban Beach.* Berkeley: University of California Press.

Farley, Reynolds. 1996. *The New American Reality: Who We Are, How We Got There, Where We Are Going.* New York: Russell Sage Foundation.

Fischer, Claude S. 1982. *To Dwell Among Friends: Personal Networks in Town and City.* Chicago: University of Chicago Press.

———. 1984. *The Urban Experience.* San Diego: Harcourt Brace.

———. 1995. "The Subcultural Theory of Urbanism: A Twentieth-Year Assessment." *American Journal of Sociology* 101: 543–77.

Glenn, Susan A. 1992. *Daughters of the Shtetl: Life and Labor in the Immigrant Generation.* Ithaca, N.Y.: Cornell University Press.

Goldscheider, Calvin, and Alan S. Zuckerman. 1984. *The Transformation of the Jews.* Chicago: University of Chicago Press.

Gorn, Elliott J. 1987. " 'Good-Bye Boys, I Die a True American': Homicide, Nativism, and Working-Class Culture in Antebellum New York City." *Journal of American History* 74: 388–410.

Harrison, Roderick J., and Daniel H. Weinberg. 1992. "Racial and Ethnic Segregation in 1990." Paper presented to the Population Association of America, May.

Hirschl, Thomas A., and Mark R. Rank. 1991. "The Effect of Population Density on Welfare Participation." *Social Forces* 70: 225–35.

Hollinger, David A. 1995. *Postethnic America.* New York: Basic Books.

Holmes, Steven. 1996. "Black–White Marriages on Rise, Study Says." *New York Times,* 4 July.

Hummon, David. 1980. "Community Ideology," Ph.D. diss., Department of Sociology, University of California, Berkeley.

————. 1990. *Commonplaces: Community Ideology and Identity in American Culture.* Albany: State University of New York Press.

Johnson, Paul. 1978. *A Shopkeeper's Millennium: Society and Revivals in Rochester, New York, 1815–1837.* New York: Hill and Wang.

Kalmun, Matthus. 1991. "Shifting Boundaries: Trends in Religious and Educational Homogamy." *American Sociological Review* 56: 786–800.

Karnig, A. A. 1979. "Black Economic, Political, and Cultural Development: Does City Size Make a Difference?" *Social Forces* 57: 1194–1211.

Lieberson, Stanley. 1980. *A Piece of the Pie: Blacks and White Immigrants since 1880.* Berkeley: University of California Press.

Lieberson, Stanley, and Mary C. Waters. 1988. *From Many Strands: Ethnic and Racial Groups in Contemporary America.* New York: Russell Sage Foundation.

Lipset, Seymour Martin, and Earl Raab. 1995. *Jews and the New American Scene.* Cambridge: Harvard University Press.

Liska, A. E., J. J. Lawrence, and A. Sanchiriko. 1982. "Fear of Crime as a Social Fact." *Social Forces* 60: 760–70.

Lofland, Lyn. 1973. *A World of Strangers.* New York: Basic Books.

Lopez, David Lopez. 1978. "Chicano Language Loyalty in an Urban Setting." *Sociology and Social Research* 42: 267–78.

Machrone, Bill. 1996. "The End of Common Experience." *PC Magazine,* 22 October, 85.

Massey, Douglas S. 1985. "Ethnic Residential Segregation: A Theoretical Synthesis and Empirical Overview." *Sociology and Social Research* 69: 315–50.

Massey, Douglas S., and Nancy A. Denton. 1987. "Trends in the Residential Segregation of Blacks, Hispanics, and Asians: 1970–1980." *American Sociological Review* 52: 802–25.

————. 1993. *American Apartheid.* Cambridge: Harvard University Press.

Meagher, Timothy J. 1986. "Irish, American, Catholic: Irish-American Identity in Worcester, Massachusetts, 1880 to 1920." In *From Paddy to Studs: Irish-American Communities in the Turn of the Century Era, 1880 to 1920.* Westport, Conn.: Greenwood Press.

Merry, Sally Engle. 1981. *Urban Danger: Life in a Neighborhood of Strangers.* Philadelphia: Temple University Press.

Meyerowitz, Joanne J. 1988. *Women Adrift: Independent Wage Earners in Chicago, 1880–1930.* Chicago: University of Chicago Press.

Montero, Daniel. 1980. *Japanese Americans: Changing Patterns of Ethnic Affiliation over Three Generations.* Boulder, Colo.: Westview Press.

Morawska, Eva. 1994. "In Defense of the Assimilation Model." *Journal of American Ethnic History* 13: 75–87.

Nelson, Bruce C. 1991. "Revival and Upheaval: Religion, Irreligion and Chicago's Working Class in 1886." *Journal of Social History* 25: 233–53.

Olzak, Susan, Suzanne Shanahan, and Elizabeth H. McEneaney. 1996. "Poverty, Segregation, and Race Riots, 1960 to 1993," *American Sociological Review* 61: 590–613.

Olzak, Susan, Suzanne Shanahan, and Elizabeth West. 1994. "School Desegregation, Interracial Exposure, and Antibusing Activity in Contemporary Urban America." *American Journal of Sociology* 100: 196–241.

Osofsky, Gilbert. 1971. *Harlem: The Making of a Ghetto*, 2d ed. New York: Harper & Row, Harper Torchbooks.

Park, Robert Ezra. 1967 [1916]. "The City: Suggestion for the Investigation of Human Behavior in the Urban Environment." Pp. 1–46 in *The City*, edited by R. E. Park and E. W. Burgess. Chicago: University of Chicago Press.

Peiss, Kathy. 1986. *Cheap Amusements: Working Women and Leisure in Turn-of-the-Century New York*. Philadelphia: Temple University Press.

Portes, Alejandro. 1984. "The Rise of Ethnicity: Determinants of Ethnic Perceptions among Cuban Exiles in Miami." *American Sociological Review* 49: 383–97.

Rank, Mark R., and Thomas A. Hirschl. 1988. "A Rural-Urban Comparison of Welfare Exits: The Importance of Population Density." *Rural Sociology* 53: 190–206.

Ravitch, Diane. 1974. *The Great School Wars: New York City, 1805–1973; A History of the Public Schools as Battlefield of Social Change*. New York: Basic Books.

Redfield, Robert, and M. Singer. 1954. "The Cultural Role of Cities." *Economic Development and Cultural Change* 3: 53–77.

Rosenzweig, Roy. 1985. *Eight Hours for What We Will: Workers and Leisure in an Industrial City, 1870–1920*. New York: Cambridge University Press.

Rountree, Pamela, and Kenneth C. Land. 1996. "Perceived Risk versus Fear of Crime: Empirical Evidence of Conceptually Distinct Reactions in Survey Data." *Social Forces* 74: 1353–76.

Schneider, John C. 1980. *Detroit and the Problem of Order, 1830–1880*, Lincoln: University of Nebraska Press.

Schultz, April. 1991. " 'The Pride of Race Had Been Touched': The 1925 Norse-American Centennial and Ethnic Identity." *Journal of American History* 77: 1265–95.

Stevens, Gillian. 1985. "Nativity, Intermarriage, and Mother-Tongue Shift." *American Sociological Review* 50: 74–83.

Taylor, Ralph B., and Jeanette Covington. 1993. "Community Structural Change and Fear of Crime." *Social Problems* 40: 375–97.

U.S. Bureau of the Census. 1995. *City and County Data Book, 1994*. Washington, D.C.: GPO.

————. 1996a. "The Foreign-Born Population: 1994." Current Population Survey Report P20-486. Washington, D.C.: GPO. Web site: http://www.census.gov:80/population/socdemo/foreign/tab-1.dat (September 4).

————. 1996b. *Statistical Abstract of the United States 1995*. Washington, D.C.: GPO.

Waldinger, Roger. 1989. "Immigration and Urban Change." *Annual Review of Sociology* 15: 211–32.

Waters, Mary C. 1990. *Ethnic Options: Choosing Identities in America*. Berkeley: University of California Press.

Wilentz, Sean. 1984. *Chants Democratic: New York City and the Rise of the American Working Class, 1788–1850*. New York: Oxford University Press.

Wirth, Louis. [1938] 1969. "Urbanism as a Way of Life." Pp. 143–64 in *Classic Essays on the Culture of Cities*, edited by R. Sennett. New York: Appleton Century Crofts.

Zorbaugh, Harvey. 1928. *The Gold Coast and the Slum*. Chicago: University of Chicago Press.

Zunz, Olivier. 1982. *The Changing Face of Inequality*. Chicago: University of Chicago Press.

CHAPTER ELEVEN

Changes in the Civic Role of Religion*

R. STEPHEN WARNER

> Modernity urgently needs to be saved from its most unconditional supporters.
>
> —*Charles Taylor*

CONTRASTING THE CIVIC ROLE OF RELIGION IN 1960 AND 1996

BY THE END of the 1950s the United States had achieved a working consensus on the place of religion in society, consisting of two aspects. First, religious *identity* was relegated to a "private" realm, to be left uncontested and largely unexamined. Another way of putting this is that religion was considered a legitimately "ascribed" category. As Will Herberg (1960) put it, to be a Protestant, a Catholic or a Jew were three equally acceptable and morally unquestionable ways of being a good American. Indeed, so legitimate was religious identification that no one disclaiming a personal religion was likely to receive a public hearing, and those affirming no religious preference in opinion polls were, in fact, largely marginal members of society.

Second, however, it was also considered entirely proper for religious institutions, especially the National Council of Churches, to make pronouncements on matters of national public policy, with the guiding assumption that, on fundamental matters of *ethics and morality*, all religion speaks with one voice. If religious identities were ascriptive, religion's teachings were universalistic. This was the ethnographer's (if not the philosopher's) wisdom behind Dwight Eisenhower's often quoted remark, "Our government makes no sense unless it is founded on a deeply felt religious faith—and I don't care what it is" (Herberg 1960: 84).

There were limits on this consensus. It did not extend to those other than Christians and Jews, it included some under its umbrella (particularly Catholics and Jews) only at the cost of their adopting Protestant manners (Cuddihy 1987),

* An earlier draft of this paper was presented at the conference on Common Values, Social Diversity, and Cultural Conflict, Stanford, California, October 17–19, 1996.

For comments and suggestions, I am indebted to Nancy Ammerman, Anne Heider, Frank Lechner, Lowell Livezey, Robert V. Robinson, Frank Senn, Michael R. Warner, Elfriede Wedam, Robert Wuthnow, Fenggang Yang, and my fellow participants in the Stanford conference. For the stimulus to write this paper, I thank Neil Smelser and Jeffrey Alexander.

it was not shared by fundamentalist Protestants (Ammerman 1987), and it depended to some extent on an external enemy, a shared anticommunism. The public space allowed for religion was also a highly gendered space, a masculinist version of "public," a matter to which I shall return in the conclusion.

But the consensus was nonetheless real. It passed tests and made differences. The electoral margin of John Kennedy in 1960 was razor-thin, but his victory dealt a heavy blow to politically acceptable anti-Catholicism. In the years surrounding the Kennedy presidency, religious leaders successfully (not without challenge and not without great courage) mobilized the legitimacy of religion in support of the civil rights movement and civil rights legislation (Wood 1981). Dr. Martin Luther King, Jr.'s career depended on a religious consensus he both invoked and helped to build.

To speak of such a religious consensus today—of the great moral authority exerted by King in his "Letter From Birmingham Jail"—is to speak about a bygone era. Today, religious proclamations, especially at the national level, are more likely to appear divisive than morally commanding. "Ecumenical" bodies like the National Council of Churches "can no longer plausibly claim to be the primary, privileged vehicles of Christian unity" (Heim 1996: 781) let alone of the national conscience, and at the opposite pole, the claims of Ralph Reed's Christian Coalition are widely understood as partisan pleading.

Forty years ago, in order to allay suspicion and claim respectability, King and his colleagues gathered under the banner of the Southern *Christian* Leadership Conference, invoking both the unifying label of Christianity and the prestige of the ministry as a profession in American society at large and African American society in particular in the 1950s. By contrasting example, the new journal *Books and Culture*,[1] appearing in a format and size virtually identical with the *New York Review of Books*, announces itself "a *Christian* Review" in self-conscious recognition of its alternative, outsider status, insinuating itself with allies as a welcome cry in the wilderness and virtually daring adversaries to take offense.

Badges of religious identity—from the "Christian" label to the crosses, yarmulkes, and hijab coverings worn by today's college students—are increasingly asserted in order to invite recognition from the like-minded, embolden comrades, confound enemies, and invite inquiries from those open to persuasion. Although symbols of this kind may be no more than assertions of the individual identities of their bearers, many onlookers experience them as unwanted efforts at proselytization; some, especially the Christian and Muslim ones, may indeed be so intended. In these and other ways, religious identities have become not only more assertive but also more contested. Instead of having one's religious identity be taken for granted, one may now be expected to defend and claim it. Likewise, if one's religious identity doesn't suit, change to a more suitable one is not out of the question.

Change may be to a deeper embrace of one's ascribed religion (as in the "return" of Jewish youth to an orthodoxy they'd never known [Davidman 1991] and the head coverings increasingly adopted by second-generation Muslim college students), conversion to a different religion, or, with hardly a ripple of social sanction in much of the middle class, the abandonment of religion altogether. Thus, in my current[2] undergraduate sociology of religion class in (ascriptively) Catholic Chicago, I have substantial proportions of students who, baptized Catholic, claim to have left that identity to become "Christian" as well as those who, baptized Catholic, now affirm no religion.

It is not that the American religious order has collapsed. Sociologists of religion are divided on the "secularization thesis," some (e.g., Roof and McKinney 1987; Hadaway et al. 1993) arguing that there has been substantial erosion from a more sacralized past, others (e.g., Greeley 1989; Finke and Stark 1992) insisting that today's patterns are continuous with the past, with religious involvement remaining high. Yet no one disputes the enormous size and significance of religious institutions in the United States, the more than three hundred thousand local congregations, the billions of contributed dollars, the countless hours of volunteer time, the one-third of Americans (more or less) who attend church or religious services every week (see, for details, Hodgkinson and Weitzman 1993; Gallup 1996). Thus there is far more volatility in *perceptions of religion's influence* than in *self-reported church attendance* (Gallup 1996: 28–29, 54–55; Warner 1988a: 179–80).

For the sake of argument, I shall overdraw the change in religious culture: whereas a generation ago religious identities were taken to be ascribed and religion's teachings to be universalistic, today religion appears to be particularistic but religious identities appear to be achieved. (For a more developed but also more circumscribed statement, see Warner 1988a, especially pp. 52–53.) It is the implications of this admittedly overdrawn scheme of change—religion is no longer taken for granted, but it is also no longer unifying—that I explore in this paper.

Changes in Religious Infrastructure since 1960: The Watershed Year of 1965

Although there are many sources of the huge changes experienced by our society since 1960, not least of them the Vietnam War, let us look at the roots of this cultural change in specifically religious institutions, focusing on one watershed year, 1965. Nineteen sixty-five not only was the year that Lyndon Johnson dramatically escalated the war in Vietnam, it was also the year that membership rolls peaked and began to decline in almost all of the mainline Protestant denominations—Presbyterian, Methodist, Northern Baptist—and also the year that Oral Roberts University opened in Tulsa, Oklahoma. By 1972, as conservative bodies like the Assemblies of God and the Southern Baptist Convention continued to grow and the more liberal mainline Presbyterians, Methodists, and Episcopalians to decline, National Council of Churches executive Dean Kelley (1977) caused a ruckus with his scathing analysis of liberal malaise, *Why Con-*

servative Churches Are Growing. A quarter century later the trend of mainline decline and conservative growth continues.

Sociologists of religion have refuted the notion that the decline of the mainline churches was the result of their outspoken stance in favor of civil rights (Hoge and Roozen 1979). It had deeper demographic causes, being characterized more by a failure to recruit newcomers than a loss of erstwhile adherents. More controversial is whether their decline was in other ways brought about by the churches' own actions (Finke and Stark 1992) or by factors beyond their control (Hoge and Roozen 1979; cf. Iannaccone 1996). Uncontested is that the decades of mainline decline have meant a dramatic loss of the confidence felt by their predecessors that they spoke for the whole society.[3]

In sheer numbers of local churches, the mainline Protestant decline has been matched by conservative Protestant growth—evangelical, fundamentalist, pentecostal, and charismatic (Warner 1994: 56). But this does not mean that the mainline "place" has been taken by the conservatives, for it is a place Protestants no longer occupy. It is a mistake to see in the vociferousness of the organized "religious right" a mere protest against and attempt to reverse the Protestant displacement of the 1960s (a period that has been called the "third disestablishment" of religion in America [Roof and McKinney 1987]), for the conservatives had suffered their own great defeat a half-century before, in the fundamentalist-modernist battles of the 1920s (Longfield 1991). For them, the mainline debacle of the 1960s was a vindication and a so-far-unrealized opportunity to grab the mantle of American moral stewardship, not to recapture a hegemony that, in fact, they had not known for generations. Yet, the conservatives were surely emboldened by the mainline decline.

Corresponding changes in the institutional structure of American Protestantism have been analyzed by Wuthnow (1988) and others. (1) The historic denominations—the Presbyterian Church (USA), the United Methodist Church, the United Church of Christ—have been greatly weakened, partly because of internal divisions, both as organizations and as centers of identification. (2) Policy preferences have been increasingly articulated by religious "special-purpose groups," from the Christian Coalition through Bread for the World and People for the American Way to Clergy and Laity Concerned. (3) Material, human, and moral resources have increasingly devolved to the level of the local church, which in turn has become the focus of much religious loyalty and identity, in a widespread pattern I call "de facto congregationalism" (Warner 1994: 73–82).

Nineteen sixty-five also saw the conclusion of Vatican II. If any religious voice has made a credible bid for the role of conscience of American society formerly occupied by the National Council of Churches, it is the National Conference of Catholic Bishops, whose pronouncements on war and the economy have won admiration, respect, and serious commentary far beyond the already wide confines of the communion for which the bishops claim to speak (Burns 1992). Yet, vocal dissension within the church—on the part not only of those on the left, who think the church insufficiently progressive on issues of gender, but also those on the right, for whom the bishops are too radical on disarmament and redistribution—undermines the bishops' claim to be speaking for all Catholics. Meanwhile, their "consistent ethic of life" stance (against abortion but also against the death penalty) sits astride the conservative–liberal divide in American politics. As such it might promise to mediate left–right conflict but instead seems to provoke suspicion and distrust among potential allies on both sides (Wedam 1997).

Two events of 1965 had major implications for the civic role of religion in the black community. First was the passage of the Voting Rights Act, the crowning legislative achievement of the civil rights movement. The 1965 act fully enfranchised African Americans for the first time, with the consequence that politics as a career became more open than ever before to African Americans. One result was to weaken the relative monopoly on leadership that had previously been enjoyed by African American clergy, even though religious institutions continue to play a more important role in African American society than in most other sectors of the United States. Later applications of the Voting Rights Act, now under assault in the courts, have meant that the interests and grievances of African Americans were more likely to be articulated directly by legislators representing majority African American constituencies; thus the black church was no longer the only institutional sphere for the direct expression of group interests.

But 1965 was also the year of the assassination of Malcolm X, soon to assume the status of hero-martyr. Many in the diverse Muslim movements among African Americans, from Louis Farrakhan to Warith Deen Mohammed, claim his legacy, and indeed his legacy is ambiguous. Yet, part of that legacy is the appeal of Islam to young African American men and a further weakening of the leadership monopoly of African American Christian clergy. Far too radical for most whites, tarnished by antisemitic spokesmen, and morally too conservative to make easy alliance with secular liberals, African American Muslims remained isolated for years. Only recently, with the decline of African American confidence in political institutions and a renewed moral conservatism in public African American discourse, has there reemerged a major civic role for two African American religious leaders: Louis Farrakhan and Jesse Jackson (Wills 1996).

We have a situation—liberal and conservative Protestants stalemate each other, one side attracted to African American clergy's claims for economic justice and the other to their critique of ghetto-oriented liquor advertising, pornography, and gangsta rap; Catholics appear unable to present a united front; and Jews remain a small minority without a stable coalition partner—in which there seems little near-term possibility for an institutionalized locus to articulate whatever latent civil religious consensus might emerge from the interchange between the common value system and the end-of-century empirical reality.

I see signs of a reconstruction emerging from another innovation of 1965, one having profound implications for the religious landscape of the United States. For 1965 was also the year that the Immigration and Nationality Law was amended by the Hart-Celler Act and signed into law by President Johnson, with eventual results that would astonish those who deliberated it. Thirty years later, nearly 1 million immigrants per year enter the United States, most of them legally, most of them from non-European countries. For example, in 1992–93, the top ten sending countries were Mexico, China, Philippines, Vietnam, the former Soviet Union, the Dominican Republic, India, Poland, El Salvador, and the United Kingdom (Ungar 1995).

Contrary to stereotype, however, the religious effect of the new immigration is not so much an increasing de-Christianization of America as the de-Europeanizing of American Christianity and the intensification of religious identification. The great majority of new immigrants are Christian (mostly Catholics, evangelicals, and pentecostals); they are, after all, disproportionately from Latin America. Those from Asia, particularly Korea and Vietnam and even from India and overwhelmingly from the Philippines, are disproportionately self-selected from already Christian segments of the sending countries' population. The many Muslim immigrants have, among other things, helped shape African American Islamic movements in orthodox directions. Immigrant Buddhist temples provide an institutional home for European-American converts (Numrich 1996). Immigrant Hindus are learning to be religious in their own American way (Williams 1988; Kurien 1998). I explore the religious implications of the new immigration in the next section.

FROM SOCIETAL CONSCIENCE TO CULTURAL REPRODUCTION

The picture I have drawn is a centrifugal one of increasing complexity and decreasing centralization. It is not, however, a picture of fragmentation or entropy. There are signs of systematization, but to appreciate them it is necessary to turn one's gaze away from the demoralized mainline Protestants and the alternatively brash and defensive conservative Protestants to smaller minorities, particularly African Americans, Jews, and new immigrants. For the sensibility that today informs efforts at religious reconstruction is not that of the bearer of the collective conscience but that of the sojourner.

My interpretation of the crosses, yarmulkes, and hijab coverings seen on college campuses today is that they represent efforts to build morale internally more than efforts to threaten or persuade others externally. The energies behind the politically oriented Christian Coalition are dwarfed by the culturally oriented energies going into the new "megachurches" (Trueheart 1996; Eiesland 1998), popular local assemblies that mobilize generous tithes and volunteer labor. In congregations new and old, in midweek campus Bible studies, and in Muslim Student Association Friday prayers, participants learn and tell each other what they have (and are supposed to have) in common, particularly religious narratives and group ritual; in group discussions they adapt inherited principles to contemporary realities (Livezey 1998); they enjoy the power of singing, moving, and eating together (Warner 1997); they bear each other up; they find places where their individual gifts can be put to good use; and just by being together they affirm the ways in which they are different—perhaps in their attire, their facial features, their skin color, their language, their ritual, or their moral code (Ammerman 1987)—from those outside the space in which they gather.

Yes, aggressive religious rhetoric is abundant. As a white European-American Christian with mainline Protestant affiliations, I hear aggressive-sounding talk issuing from conservative Protestants and some Muslims, although I am sure that differently situated observers would perceive aggression to be issuing from different sources. But even so, I argue that Promise Keepers and the Million Man March are primarily efforts at cultural reproduction—on a national scale. To be sure, the March was also intended to demonstrate to Congress the potential power of a mobilized African American constituency, but the motivation of most participants—and the memory they carried away—was to experience the exhilaration of gathering with so many like-minded and like-appearing others.

A month before our meeting at Stanford, I attended a gigantic four-hour-long Christian "crusade" rally, sponsored by one of Chicago's largest African American churches[4] but held, presumably to address the city at large, in the 10,000-seat pavilion on my public university campus. Featured were a Grammy-winning gospel troupe, the church's 400-voice choir, the enthusiastic singing and clapping of thousands of worshippers, and a forty-minute sermon by the church's distinguished, widely honored, and politically influential pastor. His manifest message was that our society needs Jesus, and the integrity of such an event requires both theologically and sociologically that there may be in the assembly one or more who do not already recognize that. Yet, the overwhelming effect was to celebrate, reinforce, and nurture the commitment of the multitudes attending, who must have been encouraged by the number turning out and the enthusiasm of their response. It isn't foolish anymore to preach to the choir.

Jews, African American Christians, and immigrants set the tone for religion in America today. As sojourners, they know that religion cannot be taken for granted but must be actively produced, renegotiated, and reproduced into the next generation (Feher 1998; Kurien 1998; León 1998; Wellmeier 1998; Yang 1999). As unmistakable minorities, they do not assume that their beliefs and mores will be supported by messages coming from the surrounding society, so they actively teach their children—and remind themselves—what they are supposed to value and how they are supposed to behave.[5] In Stephen Carter's recent essay on behalf of religious seriousness, he was most passionate about what I call the right of religious reproduction. "[N]o nation that strips away the right of parents to raise their children in their religion is worthy of allegiance" (Carter 1993: 192; Warner 1994–95).

Even churches of the old Protestant main line have taken to using the "children's message" or "children's sermon" as the pastor's means of speaking over the heads of the young ones to impart to their elders first principles of theology that it would be embarrassing for all concerned to acknowledge that they have forgotten or never learned in the first place. Jettisoning the "cultural invisibility within which the North American upper middle class hides itself from itself" (Rosaldo 1993: 203), wise clergy recognize that even mainline Protestantism is today a counterculture.

Subcultural religious reproduction does not require antagonism towards one's neighbor. In the United States, religion is the preeminent institution for the mediation of cultural difference. In the United States, religious difference is the most legitimate cultural difference (Herberg 1960; Williams 1988; Warner 1993), and in our history religion has tended to moderate difference (Hepner 1998). Therefore the softening of manners or liberalization of social mores, a characteristic of America Tocqueville noticed a century and a half ago, can advance along with religious particularism.

Religious particularism primarily takes not a political but a constitutive form, in which the differences that are emphasized are the founding myth (e.g., scriptural narrative, stories of the prophets) and the distinctive religious style (e.g., liturgy, music, dress, language). For example, Jewish services, even in Reform synagogues, now emphasize the use of Hebrew and the wearing of yarmulkes to a degree unknown a generation ago, thus accentuating their Jewishness (Wertheimer 1993: 95–113). That we are not talking about across-the-board conservatism or a mere "return to tradition" is clear when we recognize that many Reform Jewish women, as well as men, now wear yarmulkes. To cite another example, many churches that are open to gay men feature the "highest," most arcane liturgy (Reed 1989; Warner 1995: 94). Social liberalism and religious conservatism can go hand in hand.

Both to ensure their own survival as communities and to meet the needs of their individual and family constituents, today's religious institutions put at least as much of their energy into articulating their particularities as they do into addressing, whether in a civic, evangelistic, or antagonistic spirit, those outside.

IMPLICATIONS FOR SOCIETY AT LARGE

In concluding, I briefly address two issues, first, whether the new particularism I have outlined threatens civil order and, second, whether it represents a retreat from societal responsibility. I answer both questions in the negative.

In a society historically less open, less mobile, less tolerant, less deeply individualistic, and less affluent than ours, the kind of particularism I have claimed prevails in American religion today might well be worrisome. But in the United States, motion across communal boundaries is to be expected and is very often positively valued (which is precisely why groups stress their differences). Religious switching and racial-ethnic intermarriage are commonplace (the former very frequent among liberal and conservative Protestants [Roof and McKinney 1987: 164–70] and the latter among Asians and Hispanics [Farley, ch. 5]). Mass media–driven and peer youth cultures are hugely pervasive (Denby 1996;

Dyson 1996), and the children of immigrants are increasingly unable to speak the first language of their parents (Chai 1998; George 1998). Despite divisive battles over abortion, sexual orientation, and women's ordination, increasing tolerance and liberalism on racial and gender issues pervade our society (Di-Maggio et al. 1996). Those who formally reject the standards of secular society are drawn by the allure of its honors (I have in mind the respect paid to academic credentials by the most outspoken of conservative Protestants). Although incomes are highly unequal, unemployment is low.

It is doubtful that we can rely much longer on the older religious regime to shore up the civil values that legitimate such liberal social values.[6] Meanwhile, the religious cultural reproduction of the sort that I see promoted in black churches, white evangelical churches, Hispanic/Latino churches, synagogues, and immigrant congregations presupposes at least implicitly what mainline churches proclaim explicitly: that society is worth the church's while. It is worth the effort to raise children so that they can have a decent life in it and can raise their children in turn to have a decent life. The successful formula that Jews are perceived to have concocted—being simultaneously different and assimilated—is invoked as a model by immigrant Hindus and Chinese Christians, as I discovered on site visits to their communities for the New Ethnic and Immigrant Congregations Project. Religion as an identity of esteemed difference is recurrently being rediscovered by other new Americans (Feher 1998; McAlister 1998).

This, perhaps cyclical, religious emphasis on subcultural reproduction does not represent a retreat from societal responsibility; instead it is an effort to repair structural and cultural underpinnings of society beginning at home, a religious form of thinking globally but acting locally.

Although religion's public face is less visible and less unifying at the national level today than a generation ago, local religious communities, individually or through local ministerial alliances, still make themselves felt to their neighbors. They promote charitable causes, from providing meals to elderly shut-ins to housing the homeless. They provide services, including resale shops, family counseling, after-school tutoring and courses in English as a second language. They host concerts and community meetings. They lobby city hall to collect the garbage, close down crack houses, and award development contracts to socially responsive builders.[7]

Perhaps the most important way local religious communities—"congregations"—contribute to the social order is through the development of "social capital," the "network of skill and trust that makes civic life possible" (Ammerman 1997: 347). Churches are places of meeting for diffuse purposes outside the family, places where relationships of trust are built up with people who, while perhaps not strangers, are also not kin. They are arenas where skills of leadership and discussion are inculcated. Robert Putnam (1995) has argued that many middle-class-based voluntary associations are in steep decline, but an important exception to his rule is found in American congregations, *and especially the congregations of racial, ethnic, and cultural minorities.* The black church is the classic nursery of African American oratorical skills, and for many subordinate ethnic groups the pentecostal and evangelical movements' emphasis on "testimony" provides a legitimate occasion for rank-and-file public speaking. "Because people of all economic and educational levels belong nearly equally to congregations (whereas other voluntary associations are disproportionately middle and upper class), congregations are the single most widespread and egalitarian providers of civic opportunity in the United States" (Ammerman 1997: 364).

But the new religious particularism may also help repair our culture. The theory of modern culture I depend on here is broadly that of Talcott Parsons (1951), that the universalistic and individualistic, justice- and achievement-oriented (and often masculine) "gesellschaftlich" values of the modern American "public sphere" depended intimately on an infrastructure of particularistic and collective, relational and ascriptive (and often feminine) "gemeinschaftlich" values of the "private sphere." Parsons articulated this theory in his AGIL and pattern-variable schemes, where he tried to make clear that one side always needed the other,[8] that A and G (economy and polity) always needed I and L (societal community and fiduciary), or, in terms of the 1950s, that Dad always needed Mom. For Parsons, modern society involved a system of role differentiation into two spheres. Thus, the modern occupational sphere required for its balancing—indeed for its completeness—the modern family. Tocqueville had seen the same thing about the United States a century before Parsons.[9]

But Parsons's insight, and the societal balance it articulated, was lost sight of in the 1960s (Warner 1988b). What happened is that public culture took public values all too much at face value.[10] An example is the early career of renowned theologian Reinhold Niebuhr, whose peripatetic lecturing depended intimately on a pastoral household (in Detroit) that his widowed mother effectively ran (Fox 1985: 69). What seems to have happened from midcentury onward was that American middle-class culture in general and mainstream Protestantism in particular increasingly lost sight of its necessary grounding in nurturance, which was relegated to lesser status and lesser urgency. By the 1950s, public intellectuals positively dismissed community-building and nurturance ("suburban captivity") as unworthy of the churches (Winter 1962). In an odd way, this self-styled prophetic rhetoric represented just as much the triumph of a masculinist perspective as did the adolescent fixations of *Playboy* and the beats and hippies (see Barbara Ehrenreich, *The Hearts of Men*). In fleeing from the claims of family and parish to the greater good of the "public sphere," too many intellectuals lost sight of the classical wisdom, recently restated by Charles Taylor (1989: 511), that "a dilemma doesn't invalidate the rival goods. On the contrary, it presupposes them."

It must be said that public intellectuals did not alone trivialize the private sphere. Social processes did that too. The suburbs were far more removed from the "public" world than had been true of the urban neighborhood: work was farther away, the commute was longer, and the bedroom community was more isolated.[11] Meanwhile, it had always been part of the formula that those responsible for child-rearing should be educated, and these educated women had longer life expectancies and greater aspirations. Betty Friedan (1963) articulated their anger and bewilderment a generation ago, but today a broad spectrum of American subcultures want to renew attention to nurturance.

Those who were less enmeshed in urban middle-class life were less affected by postwar privatizing trends. Hence, African Americans, working-class Americans, rural Americans (the midcentury heartland of evangelicalism), and, of course, those who had not yet come to the United States were less affected by the decay of attention to the "private sphere." Their religious institutions and cultures had not yet forgotten that new generations need to be nurtured. It is the sociological wisdom of their religious institutions that is setting the tone for the cultural role of U.S. religion at the end of the twentieth century.

NOTES

1. *Books and Culture: A Christian Review*, vol. 2, no. 4 (July/August 1996), features essays by Eugene Genovese, Eric Metaxas, and Harry Stout, among others. Along with Stout, the masthead lists Nathan Hatch, George Marsden, Mark Noll, and others as editors.

2. This was written during the fall semester of 1996.

3. The essays and particularly the photographs collected by historian William Hutchison (1989) speak eloquently about that vanished confidence.

4. Specifically the Apostolic Church of God, whose guiding spirit and senior pastor is Rev. Arthur Brazier. For extensive analysis of Brazier and his ministry, see Browning 1991. The date of the rally was September 13, 1996.

5. Liberal critic David Denby (1996: 48–49) shares their outrage at the culture's effect on children but cannot bring himself to apply the authoritarian measures of religious conservatives. Speaking of his children and the media with exasperation, he cries, "There is so much to forbid—perhaps a whole culture to forbid! . . . How can you control what they breathe?"

6. "We agree surprisingly well, across great differences of theological and metaphysical belief, about the demands of justice and benevolence, and their importance. . . . So why worry that we disagree on the reasons, as long as we're united around the norms? It's not the disagreement which is the problem. Rather the issue is what sources can support our far-reaching moral commitments to benevolence and justice. . . . The question . . . is whether we are not living beyond our moral means in continuing allegiance to our standards of justice and benevolence" (Taylor 1989: 515, 517).

7. This paragraph and the one following draw for orientation and illustrative material on a number of recent and ongoing research projects on the role of religious institutions in local community life, including the "Springfield Project" (Demerath and Williams 1992) and the Program on Non-Profit Organizations (Hall 1997), but especially the Congregations in Changing Communities Project (Ammerman 1997, Becker 1999, Eiesland 1999) and the Religion in Urban America Program (Livezey 1996, 1998), to both of which I am deeply indebted.

8. See the dedication of *The Social System* to his wife, Helen, the "indispensable balance-wheel" (Parsons 1951: v).

9. "The Americans have applied to the sexes the great principle of political economy which now dominates industry. They have carefully separated the functions of man and of woman so that the great work of society may be better performed" (Tocqueville 1969: 601). With the advance of technology and the increased salience of specific skills, gender ascription becomes less functional (Marwell 1975). That the "private sphere" need no longer be "women's place" nor the "public sphere" men's is one progressive perception I attribute to such movements as Promise Keepers and the Million Man March, for whom concerns of parents are once again to be brought into the quasi-public arena of football stadiums and the Washington Mall. Yet the various functions, I and L as well as A and G, or however one wishes to classify them, continue as needs of the society.

10. Because I see the new particularism strengthening these essential I and L activities, my interpretation of religious conservatism necessarily parts company with that of Lechner (1985), for whom "fundamentalism" represents "dedifferentiation." Yet Lechner recognizes that those who "retreat to . . . traditionalist security bases" thereby add complexity to their lives and thus become even more "quintessentially modern" (167).

11. "[A] man's job, is usually related, directly or indirectly, to large organizations of industry and union which have considerable influence on the national life; by contrast, his neighborhood, life with family, at church, or in a local association has little or no connection with his job or even with the interests and problems which fill his mind during the day. . . . The sphere of residential activities . . . (family problems, nurture of the young, neighborhood interests, informal association, and general consumer activities) . . . is a very private aspect of modern life" (Winter 1962: 156–57).

REFERENCES

Ammerman, Nancy Tatom. 1987. *Bible Believers: Fundamentalists in the Modern World.* New Brunswick, N.J.: Rutgers University Press.

————. 1997. *Congregation and Community.* New Brunswick, N.J.: Rutgers University Press.

Becker, Penny Edgell. 1999. *Congregations in Conflict: Cultural Models of Local Religious Life.* New York: Cambridge University Press.

Browning, Don S. 1991. "Congregational Care in a Black Pentecostal Church." Pp. 243–277 in *A Fundamental Practical Theology: Descriptive and Strategic Proposals.* Minneapolis: Fortress.

Burns, Gene. 1992. *The Frontiers of Catholicism: The Politics of Ideology in a Liberal World.* Berkeley: University of California Press.

Carter, Stephen L. 1993. *The Culture of Disbelief.* New York: Basic Books.

Chai, Karen. 1998. "Competing for the Second Generation: English-Language Ministry at a Korean Protestant Church." Pp. 295–331 in *Gatherings in Diaspora: Religious Communities and the New Immigration,* edited by R. Stephen Warner and Judith G. Wittner. Philadelphia: Temple University Press.

Cuddihy, John Murray. 1987. *The Ordeal of Civility,* 2d ed. Boston: Beacon.

Davidman, Lynn. 1991. *Tradition in a Rootless World: Women Turn to Orthodox Judaism.* Berkeley and Los Angeles: University of California Press.

Demerath, N. J., III, and Rhys H. Williams. 1992. *A Bridging of Faiths: Religion and Politics in a New England City.* Princeton, N.J.: Princeton University Press.

Denby, David. 1996. "Buried Alive: Our Children and the Avalanche of Crud." *The New Yorker* 72 (July 15): 48–58.

CHANGES IN THE CIVIC ROLE OF RELIGION

DiMaggio, Paul, John Evans, and Bethany Bryson. 1996. "Have Americans' Social Attitudes Become More Polarized?" *American Journal of Sociology* 102 (November): 690–755.

Dyson, Michael Eric. 1996. *Between God and Gangsta Rap: Bearing Witness to Black Culture*. New York: Oxford University Press.

Eiesland, Nancy L. 1999. *A Particular Place: Exurbanization and Religious Response in a Southern Town*. New Brunswick, N.J.: Rutgers University Press. Forthcoming.

Feher, Shoshanah. 1998. "From the Rivers of Babylon to the Valleys of Los Angeles: The Exodus and Adaptation of Iranian Jews." Pp. 71–94 in *Gatherings in Diaspora: Religious Communities and the New Immigration*, edited by R. Stephen Warner and Judith G. Wittner. Philadelphia: Temple University Press.

Finke, Roger, and Rodney Stark. 1992. *The Churching of America, 1776–1990: Winners and Losers in Our Religious Economy*. New Brunswick, N.J.: Rutgers University Press.

Fox, Richard Wightman. 1985. *Reinhold Niebuhr: A Biography*. New York: Pantheon.

Friedan, Betty. 1963. *The Feminine Mystique*. New York: W. W. Norton.

Gallup, George H., Jr. 1996. *Religion in America, 1996*. Princeton, N.J.: Princeton Religion Research Center.

George, Sheba. 1998. "Caroling with the Keralites: The Negotiation of Gendered Space in an Indian Immigrant Church." Pp. 265–94 in *Gatherings in Diaspora: Religious Communities and the New Immigration*, edited by R. Stephen Warner and Judith G. Wittner. Philadelphia: Temple University Press.

Greeley, Andrew M. 1989. *Religious Change in America*. Cambridge: Harvard University Press.

Hadaway, C. Kirk, Penny Long Marler, and Mark Chaves. 1993. "What the Polls Don't Show: A Closer Look at U.S. Church Attendance." *American Sociological Review* 58 (December): 741–52.

Hall, Peter Dobkin. 1997. "Founded on the Rock, Built upon Shifting Sands: Churches, Voluntary Associations, and Non-Profit Organizations in Public Life, 1850–1990." Working paper of the Program on Non-Profit Organizations, Yale University.

Heim, S. Mark. 1996. "The Next Ecumenical Movement." *Christian Century* 113 (August 14–21): 780–83.

Hepner, Randal L. 1998. "The House that Rasta Built: Church-Building and Fundamentalism among New York Rastafarians." Pp. 197–234 in *Gatherings in Diaspora: Religious Communities and the New Immigration*, edited by R. Stephen Warner and Judith G. Wittner. Philadelphia: Temple University Press.

Herberg, Will. 1960. *Protestant, Catholic, Jew: An Essay in American Religious Sociology*, 2d ed. Garden City, N.Y.: Doubleday.

Hodgkinson, Virginia A., and Murray S. Weitzman. 1993. *From Belief to Commitment: The Community Service Activities and Finances of Religious Congregations in the United States*. Washington, D.C.: Independent Sector.

Hoge, Dean R., and David A. Roozen, eds. 1979. *Understanding Church Growth and Decline, 1950–1978*. New York: Pilgrim.

Hutchison, William R., ed. 1989. *Between the Times: The Travail of the Protestant Establishment in America, 1900–1960*. Cambridge: Cambridge University Press.

Iannaccone, Laurence R. 1996. "Reassessing Church Growth: Statistical Pitfalls and Their Consequences." *Journal for the Scientific Study of Religion* 35 (September): 197–217.

Kelley, Dean M. 1977. *Why Conservative Churches Are Growing*. 2d ed. San Francisco: Harper and Row.

Kurien, Prema. 1998. "Becoming American by Becoming Hindu: Indian Americans Take their Place at the Multicultural Table." Pp. 37–70 in *Gatherings in Diaspora: Religious Communities and the New Immigration*, edited by R. Stephen Warner and Judith G. Wittner. Philadelphia: Temple University Press.

Lechner, Frank J. 1985. "Modernity and Its Discontents." In *Neofunctionalism*, edited by Jeffrey C. Alexander, 157–76. Beverly Hills, Calif.: Sage Publications.

León, Luís. 1998. "Born Again in East LA: The Congregation as Border Space." Pp. 163–196 in *Gatherings in Diaspora: Religious Communities and the New Immigration*, edited by R. Stephen Warner and Judith G. Wittner. Philadelphia: Temple University Press.

Livezey, Lowell W. 1996. "Congregations and their Publics." Address presented to a conference on "Leading Congregations that Matter" at the Louisville Institute, October 10–11.

———. 1998. "Family Ministries at Carter Temple CME Church." In *Tending the Flock: Models of Congregational Family Ministries*, edited by K. Brynford Lyon and Archie Smith, Jr. Louisville, Ky.: Westminster/John Knox.

Longfield, Bradley. 1991. *The Presbyterian Controversy*. New York: Oxford University Press.

Marwell, Gerald. 1975. "Why Ascription? Parts of a More or Less Formal Theory of the Functions and Dysfunctions of Sex Roles." *American Sociological Review* 40 (August): 445–55.

McAlister, Elizabeth. 1998. "The Madonna of 115th Street Revisited: Vodou and Haitian Catholicism in the Age of Transnationalism." Pp. 123–160 in *Gatherings in Diaspora: Religious Communities and the New Immigration*, edited by R. Stephen Warner and Judith G. Wittner. Philadelphia: Temple University Press.

Numrich, Paul David. 1996. *Old Wisdom in the New World: Americanization in Two Immigrant Theravada Buddhist Temples*. Knoxville: University of Tennessee Press.

Parsons, Talcott. 1951. *The Social System*. Glencoe, Ill.: Free Press.

Putnam, Robert. 1995. "Bowling Alone: America's Declining Social Capital." *Journal of Democracy* 6 (1): 65–78.

Reed, John Shelton. 1989. "'Giddy Young Men:' A Counter-Cultural Aspect of Victorian Anglo-Catholicism." *Comparative Social Research* 11: 209–36.

Roof, Wade Clark, and William McKinney. 1987. *American Mainline Religion: Its Changing Shape and Future*. New Brunswick, N.J.: Rutgers University Press.

Rosaldo, Renato. 1993. *Culture and Truth: The Remaking of Social Analysis*. Boston: Beacon.

Taylor, Charles. 1989. *Sources of the Self: The Making of Modern Identity*. Cambridge: Harvard University Press.

Tocqueville, Alexis de. 1969. *Democracy in America*. Edited by J. P Mayer and translated by George Lawrence; Garden City, N.Y.: Anchor.

Trueheart, Charles. 1996. "Welcome to the Next Church." *The Atlantic Monthly* 278:2 (August): 37–58.

Ungar, Sanford J. 1995. *Fresh Blood: The New American Immigrants*. New York: Simon and Schuster.

Warner, R. Stephen. 1988a. *New Wine in Old Wineskins: Evangelicals and Liberals in a Small-Town Church*. Berkeley and Los Angeles: University of California Press.

———. 1988b. "Sociological Theory as Public Philosophy." (Review essay on Jeffrey C. Alexander, *The Modern Reconstruction of Classical Thought: Talcott Parsons*. Vol. 4 of *Theoretical Logic in Sociology*.) *American Journal of Sociology* 94 (November): 644–55.

————. 1993. "Work In Progress toward a New Paradigm for the Sociological Study of Religion in the United States," *American Journal of Sociology* 98 (March): 1044–93.

————. 1994. "The Place of the Congregation in the American Religious Configuration." Pp. 54–99 in *New Perspectives in the Study of Congregations*, edited by James P. Wind and James W. Lewis. Vol. 2 of *American Congregations*. Chicago: University of Chicago Press.

————. 1994–95. "Oh Ye of Little Faith." (Review essay on Stephen Carter's *The Culture of Unbelief.*) *The Responsive Community* (winter): 68–72.

————. 1995. "The Metropolitan Community Churches and the Gay Agenda: The Power of Pentecostalism and Essentialism." Pp. 81–108 in *Sex, Lies, and Sanctity: Religion and Deviance in Contemporary North America*, edited by Mary Jo Neitz and Marion S. Goldman. Greenwich, Conn.: JAI Press.

————. 1997. "Religion, Boundaries, and Bridges: The 1996 Paul Hanly Furfey Lecture." *Sociology of Religion* 58 (fall): 217–238.

Warner, R. Stephen, and Judith G. Wittner, eds. 1998. *Gatherings in Diaspora: Religious Communities and the New Immigration*. Philadelphia: Temple University Press.

Wedam, Elfriede. 1997. "Splitting Interests or Common Causes: Styles of Moral Reasoning in Opposing Abortion." Pp. 147–68 in *Contemporary American Religion: An Ethnographic Reader*, edited by Penny Edgell Becker and Nancy L. Eiesland. Walnut Creek, Calif.: Altamira Press.

Wellmeier, Nancy J. 1998. "Santa Eulalia's People in Exile: Maya Religion, Culture, and Identity in Los Angeles." Pp. 97–122 in *Gatherings in Diaspora: Religious Communities and the New Immigration*, edited by R. Stephen Warner and Judith G. Wittner. Philadelphia: Temple University Press.

Wertheimer, Jack. 1993. *A People Divided: Judaism in Contemporary America*. New York: Basic Books.

Williams, Raymond Brady. 1988. *Religions of Immigrants from India and Pakistan: New Threads in the American Tapestry*. Cambridge: Cambridge University Press.

Wills, Garry. 1996. "A Tale of Three Leaders," *New York Review of Books* 43, no. 14 (September 19): 61–74.

Winter, Gibson. 1962. *The Suburban Captivity of the Churches: An Analysis of Protestant Responsibility in the Expanding Metropolis*. New York: Macmillan.

Wood, James R. 1981. *Leadership in Voluntary Organizations: The Controversy over Social Action in Protestant Churches*. New Brunswick, N.J.: Rutgers University Press.

Wuthnow, Robert. 1988. *The Restructuring of American Religion: Society and Faith Since World War II*. Princeton, N.J.: Princeton University Press.

Yang, Fenggang. 1999. *Chinese Christians in America: Conversion, Assimilation, and Adhesive Identities*. University Park, Pa.: Penn State University Press. Forthcoming.

PART FOUR

Rethinking Diversity and Social Solidarity

CHAPTER TWELVE

National Culture and Communities of Descent*

DAVID A. HOLLINGER

DESCENT AND NATIONALITY have never had an easy time with one another in the era of the modern nation-state. Descent and nationality generate their own solidarities, overlapping but almost never coterminus, each making claims of contingent intensity and range upon each other and upon individuals. The tension between descent and nationality has been an especially prominent feature of the United States, where descent communities are many in number and historically unequal in status, and where the national community is officially committed to treating individuals equally regardless of descent.

The oldest of the world's major constitutional regimes, founded under the aegis of Enlightenment universalism, has only gradually and incompletely ceased to be "a white man's country" with a predominantly Anglo-Protestant national culture. The principle of separation of church and state long served to address the relation of the national, civic community to what was taken to be the most potent of the nation's subnational and transnational cultures. But this principle, which proved difficult enough to apply fairly to the religiously defined cultures for which it was designed, gave little guidance when these ostensibly consenting cultures were substantially supplemented, if not replaced, in the cultural politics of the nation by cultures associated with communities of descent. The Old Republic has faced, in the early decades of its third century, demands for public support of ethnoracially defined, diasporic cultures, some of which are identified by color distinctions the diminution of which has been a goal of many liberal and radical movements in the history of the United States.

These contingent relations of civic nationality and communities of descent in the United States are now enacted on a world stage structured by two features. First, whatever capacity nation-states may have to serve as guarantors of rights, providers of welfare, and agents of democratic-egalitarian values is under severe pressure from a capitalist economy that achieves greater and greater integration and concentration on a global basis. Second, the cultural life of nation-states is increasingly subject to particularization by descent communities, even while multinational corporations disseminate elements of a commercially functional "universal" culture flowing largely from the high-tech societies of the

* This essay is reprinted from *Reviews in American History* (March 1998), with the permission of the Johns Hopkins University Press. For helpful suggestions based on an earlier version of this essay, I thank Kwame Anthony Appiah, Thomas Laqueur, Louis Masur, Yuri Slezkine, and Robert Wiebe.

North Atlantic West. In this world-historical context, those who defend the nation-state are divided on the question of the "national culture" in the United States. We should try to avoid anything answering to this name, argue many critics of nationalism who view national culture as necessarily monolithic, coercive, and exclusive to a particular community of descent.

Yet national culture has been identified by David M. Potter (1962: esp. 934, 937) and a number of other theorists as the most significant factor in the making and sustaining of national solidarity.[1] And the United States possesses some political and demographic features that may neutralize the most troubling aspects of national culture in ways that theorists of nationalism have not confronted as directly as they might.[2] These features of the United States can compel the attention of anyone who recognizes the centrality of nation-states to the contemporary world, who appreciates the contribution of culture to national solidarity, and who finds narrow the cultural programs associated with the most widely discussed of nationalist movements in the past and present. Three contrasts between the United States and a number of other nations and protonations are most salient.

First, this nation of immigrants—and of descendants of immigrants and of slaves and of conquered peoples—is more conspicuously diverse, ethnoracially, than are the communities on behalf of which nationalist movements of varying intensity and success have recently been launched or renewed by Basques, Croats, Flemings, Kurds, Macedonians, Quebecois, Scots, Serbs, Sikhs, Slovakians, Tamils, and Ukrainians. Second, the United States, as a nation whose population derives from a number of different European countries, as well as from Africa, Asia, and Latin America, displays a greater range of descent communities than do most of the established, major nation-states of Europe, Asia, and Latin America to which the United States is accustomed to comparing itself, including Argentina, China, France, Germany, Italy, Japan, Mexico, Spain, Sweden, and the United Kingdom. Third, the United States differs in one striking respect from France, with which it has long shared a civic principle of nationality antithetical to the common-descent principle of nationality exemplified most notably by Germany and Israel. Unlike France, the contemporary United States espouses a pluralist ideology that encourages voluntary associations on a variety of subnational and transnational bases. France ignores and often resists the display of non-French affiliations on the part of its citizens, even as it welcomes Senegalese, Moroccan, Hungarian, and other immigrants into its national community on officially equal terms with descendants of Descartes and DeGaulle. When France urges its immigrants to "become French," France is more totalizing in its cultural demands than is the contemporary United States in its response to immigrants.

To call attention to these contrasts is not to adopt an "American exceptionalist" perspective but merely to establish a rudimentary comparative framework for exploring the question of the national culture. Empirical generalizations concerning how one nation differs from certain other specified nations need not imply that this nation is immune to the working of whatever laws influence the character and behavior of other nations, nor need such generalizations imply the operation of the providential hand invoked once again, astonishingly, in Seymour Martin Lipset's (1996: 14) recent book defending "American exceptionalism."[3] The discourse of American exceptionalism from John Winthrop onward has no doubt helped to generate and sustain imperialist impulses, but it has also instilled in critics a fear that even the most modest of favorable contrasts of the United States to one or more other specific nations will be misconstrued as a failure to condemn American sins and hypocrisies with sufficient conviction.[4] Of attacks on these sins and hypocrisies there can never be enough, but the perspective yielded by comparison is too valuable to be eschewed out of fright that it will inevitably mystify the United States.

History has placed the contemporary United States in a position to develop a national culture less dependent on any one particular community of descent than are most other comparable national or protonational solidarities. But the claims of descent communities on the cultural identities of individuals within the United States are strong and have been appropriately strengthened by the recognition that empowered Anglo-Protestants long ignored, or actively suppressed the particular cultures carried by many of the descent communities that have gone into the formation of the nation. Any discussion of the question of the national culture in our own time must begin with the cultural significance now assigned by public authority and private convention to communities of descent, especially those commonly, if unscientifically, called "races." Hence the question of the national culture is best approached not through Tocqueville—rich as the insights of this standard point of entry to the question remain even after more than a century and a half—but through a pivotal, yet underanalyzed, moment in recent history: *Regents of University of California v. Bakke* (483 U.S. 265: 311–13).

Culture was tightly linked to color-coded descent communities when Justice Lewis Powell, struggling in 1978 for a way to justify preferences in academic admissions for historically disadvantaged ethnoracial minorities, declared such preferences potentially permissible if their aim was to diversify the "ideas and mores" of campuses. Powell was part of the five-justice majority that invalidated the affirmative action program of the medical school at the University of California at Davis on the grounds that this program's setting aside of places for nonwhites violated Title VI of the Civil Rights Act of 1964. The latter prohibited the use of "race," Powell and his colleagues concluded in *Bakke*, as a basis for deciding who could or could not participate in a federally funded program. But Powell, in a paragraph that became the constitutional foundation for affirmative action programs in higher education, went on to distinguish group preferences as such from group preferences in their capacity as instruments of cultural diversification. The ethnoracial status of an individual could be taken into account amid other considerations, Powell said, in the interests of achieving a diverse campus environment. Powell explained that the nation's future depended on leaders exposed to "ideas and mores . . . as diverse as this Nation of many peoples."[5]

Powell's device for saving group preferences from the nation's egalitarian principles would not have worked as well as it has for two decades had it not embodied a large measure of easily recognized truth about the relation of color to culture.[6] The overwhelming majority of people within each of the four non-white categories named in the Davis program—"Blacks," "Chicanos," "Asians," and "American Indians"—had been subject, directly or indirectly, to racist conditions that endowed them with life experiences different from the average white person's. The cultural life of all Americans—including empowered whites—obviously derived in part from the operation of a color hierarchy of long standing, the ordinance of which over particular groups had increased or decreased in specific locales at different times. The customs, tastes, and values that came to be stereotypically associated with each ethnoracial group had been affected, moreover, not only by the unequal distribution of power and prestige among ethnoracial groups but also by distinctive historical matrices made up of a variety of languages, religious orientations, and points of geographic origin. The mantra that "race" is constituted by culture as well as by color may be misleading, but it is not altogether false. Powell's formulations gained additional credibility from a popular and enduring presumption in the North Atlantic West that what Powell called "ideas and mores" were largely ethnoracial phenomena in any case. If this presumption had been somewhat discredited by its extreme development in Nazi cultural doctrine and practice, the presumption, in more benign forms, lived on.

Yet this presumption was increasingly on the defensive in the United States between World War II and the 1970s, rendering Powell's reassertion of it in a progressive cause ironic. The Immigration and Nationality Act of 1965 eliminated the restrictions on immigration that had been enacted in 1924 on the basis of the blatantly racist belief that the distinctive "ideas and mores" of Asians and of southern and eastern Europeans made it impossible for such people to become part of a democratic, humane society. The children of pre-1924 immigrants had, in fact, achieved a remarkable degree of structural assimilation in a society increasingly willing to call itself "a nation of immigrants," even though this term left out of account the segments of the population incorporated through enslavement and conquest. The massive intellectual attack on racism carried out by anthropologists, biologists, historians, sociologists, and other scholars from Gunnar Myrdal onward cut to ribbons the old doctrinal fabric in which communities of biological descent were woven together with necessary cultural consequences. These antiracist scholars disseminated the knowledge that the genes producing skin color and morphological traits did not generate the habits, attitudes, and dispositions stereotypically associated with the standardized ethnoracial groups. The civil rights movement of the 1950s and 1960s was directed, in part, against the notion that Negroes were burdened with race-specific social traits that prevented successful integration. The bulk of the government's antidiscrimination remedies, including the affirmative action programs developed during the administrations of Lyndon Johnson, Richard Nixon, and Gerald Ford, were designed to help not culture-bearing communities but individuals whose physical appearance put them at risk of mistreatment or who inherited a legacy of mistreatment suffered by their ancestors. *It was thus possible to be "color-conscious" rather than "color-blind" in public affairs without assuming that persons of a given color were possessed of a particular culture.*

To be sure, a highly publicized upsurge of interest in ethnic cultures took place during the decade prior to *Bakke*. Yet the ethnic enthusiasms of the early and mid-1970s were not as color-coded as those of the 1980s and 1990s. The new ethnic consciousness of the 1970s was most energetically displayed by segments of the white population celebrating Polish, Italian, Irish, Jewish, and other ethnicities. They did so in antiphonal relation to the celebration of black culture that had become conspicuous by the end of the 1960s. Hence, the exaltations of cultural diversity and the attacks on melting-pot-style assimilation most prominent in the years immediately preceding *Bakke* did not automatically follow the logic of affirmative action. According to that logic, the cultural distinctions within the white population were beside the point. Before *Bakke*, the appreciation for cultural diversity, and the development of affirmative action programs, were obviously grounded in some of the same political impulses, but the two proceeded in greater independence from each other than they did after *Bakke*.

It was during the 1980s, in the wake of Powell's reasoning in *Bakke*, that culture and color were more closely associated. Organizers of the movement to appreciate cultural diversity relied increasingly on the categories used in affirmative action programs sustained by courts following Powell's lead. These affirmative action programs rightly focused on nonwhite groups identified largely by physical characteristics that had historically triggered prejudicial treatment at the hands of whites. Multiculturalism was never about "diversity" as such. If it were, campuses would make a concerted effort to increase the number of Promise Keepers in their midst. Multiculturalism was about certain kinds of diversity and not others. The salient distinctions were those of the five classic color categories, which, while owing little of their prominence to culture and geography, were with increasing frequency assigned cultural and geographic labels: *black* (African American), *brown* (Hispanic, or Latino, and in the Southwest often Chicano), *red* (Indian, or Native American, and later Indigenous Peoples), *white* (European American), and *yellow* (Asian American).[7]

The cultural differences among various groups of white people diminished in significance when "culture" became a surrogate for "race." Diminished in significance also were cultures that transcended color lines. These included cultures defined regionally, religiously, and nationally. Pentecostal Christianity is a vital part of the lives of many millions of Americans, but its culture has been almost entirely ignored by the multiculturalist movement. Whatever claims might be made for a national culture were also given short shrift in a multiculturalist milieu, as it was under the name of "American" culture that so many cultural contributions by nonwhites had been ignored or undervalued. The very idea of a national culture was often condemned by celebrants of cultural diversity. Multiculturalist initiatives in schools often functioned, then, as affirmative action programs for cultures associated with the nonwhite ethnoracial groups who had been the victims of white prejudice.

There were excellent reasons for this. The cultural creativity of nonwhites had indeed been given insufficient attention in American education and public discussion. Multicultural efforts to correct these omissions were magnificently successful as measured by textbooks, anthologies, curricula, and the picture of American life displayed in the popular media. Especially did multiculturalism succeed in reinforcing, and winning more widespread respect for, an African American culture developed over many generations under conditions imposed by traditional, racist understandings of the color line. Multiculturalism's alliance with affirmative action also served symbolically to welcome nonwhites in new places; multiculturalism tried to provide schools, colleges, and universities with an environment that nonwhites, whatever their individual values and tastes, could see was intended as a warm response to their presence.

Yet the alliance of multiculturalism with affirmative action had five other, closely related, problematic effects that make the overall legacy of the alliance difficult to assess. First, the alliance interrupted the demanding struggle—already underway in the United States between World War II and the 1970s—to decouple culture from descent communities in the interests of maximizing the opportunities of every individual to affiliate culturally as he or she might choose. Second, the alliance narrowed into distinctly color-coded categories the revision, already underway in the 1960s and 1970s, of the nation's cultural self-conception from a predominantly Anglo-Protestant, masculinist one into a self-conception more responsive to many different kinds of diversity. Third, the alliance placed an enormous political burden on cultural programs to diminish inequalities that were deeply embedded in the social and economic life of the nation, and were thus hard to reach from within the sphere of "cultural identity." Fourth, the alliance, by making "culture" something of a euphemism for "race," encouraged the implicit translation of the ideal of "racial equality" into one of "cultural equality." The old presumption that culture was a field for freewheeling critique, including arguments to the effect that some cultures were decidedly more appealing than others, was put on the defensive as a version of the rightly unutterable claim that some "races" were superior to others. Thus there was an incentive to speak in a voice of appreciation about cultures associated with nonwhites, and to speak more critically about any culture ascribed to the white people collectively responsible for the mistreatment of nonwhites. Fifth, the alliance, by treating much of culture as an ethnoracial phenomenon, rendered more credible a practice that invites more detailed scrutiny here: the construction of genealogies for culture in the apparent interest of perpetuating the power of, or in the interest of newly empowering, a given descent community.

The most widely discussed contemporary example of this practice is associated with Martin Bernal's (1987) *Black Athena*. This work speaks to the desire of some readers to treat the great artistic monuments of the ancient Mediterranean, including Athens, as the contributions of a descent community continuous with black people in the United States today. Bernal himself does not assert, to be sure, that Homer, Socrates, and Euclid had black skin, but these claims are sometimes made by Afrocentrists who draw part of their inspiration from his work. Critics complain that the idea of "blackness" relevant to ancient Egypt as well as to ancient Greece is anachronistic in the United States at the end of the twentieth century. Yet it was surely the possibility of claiming Athenian and Egyptian artifacts for a disadvantaged descent community in our own society that helped to make *Black Athena* a famous book. I invoke the controversy over *Black Athena* not to rehearse again the arguments over the validity of its claims. Other scholars, closer to the relevant sources and historiographies, have debated the merits of the work.[8] I mention this controversy simply because it is so convenient a point of entry to the political commodification of historical artifacts in the interests of communities of descent.

Such commodification is anything but new. Power-intensive genealogies for culture long predate the alliance between multiculturalism and affirmative action by which these genealogies have been reinvigorated. Yet this reinvigoration renders the dynamics of these genealogies all the more in need of analysis at a time when the relationship among culture, descent, and consent is a matter of widespread engagement.

I hope it is not pretentious to invent the term "the will to descend" to refer to the deep-seated drive to claim politically potent historical artifacts for a contemporary descent community. This "will" can be construed as a variation on Nietzsche's "will to power."[9] The will to descend is a sharpened and politicized form of more generic phenomena, the desire for noble ancestors, and the pride most people take in the cultural contributions of their kin and of their larger descent community, however widely or narrowly they may define its boundaries. But the will to descend is much more specific than either of these, often benign, genealogical preoccupations. *The will to descend consists in the claiming, on behalf of a particular descent community, of contributions to civilization the value of which is already recognized in a social arena well beyond the particular descent community on behalf of which genetic ownership of those contributions is being asserted.* The capacity of certain artifacts, achievements, and ideas to function as cultural capital in a contemporary struggle is what renders the claiming of them a potentially empowering step. Such artifacts, achievements, and ideas include Christianity, Stonehenge, democracy, Greek philosophy, and the Great Zimbabwe Ruins. The people who made such things as these are the sort of people from whom it can be good politics to descend.

Isn't it wonderful that Copernicus was Polish? And that Columbus was Italian? And how truly wonderful, as Madison Grant proclaimed in 1916, that Jesus Christ was "Nordic." The New York intellectual Grant revealed this finding to the public in his influential book *The Passing of the Great Race*. Grant's discovery was reassuring to many people in his own ethnoracial group, the northwestern Europeans who felt their position to be declining as a result of racial mixing and of the rise of "inferior races." That the founder of one's own magnificent Christianity might be Jewish could be a disquieting thought to sensitive Anglo-Protestants absorbing the social milieu of the Lower East Side of New York. But, happily, this anomaly in the Progressive Era's Nordic suprema- cist paradigm had been eliminated by Grant's research. The man of Galilee had been one of their own, after all (Grant 1916).

Grant's category of "Nordic" has long since been discredited, along with his fanciful claims about the descent community of Jesus and about the disastrous consequences of intermarriage. But Grant's project is one of many historic ex- amples of the will to descend that may help us understand its character and to diminish the frequency with which we are misled by its powerful appeal.

The idea that democracy came out of the medieval German forests—popular among American and British historians and political philosophers in the late- nineteenth century—was a product, at least in part, of the will to descend. Sturdy Saxon stock was said to have been responsible for developing a sound political culture first in Germany, then in England, and finally in America. The German-forest theory of democracy's origins suited well the interests of the people of northwestern European ancestry who were triumphant in the politics of their own time.

Many examples of the will to descend respond to a threat, or to an oppor- tunity, in relation to a descent community's relative position in the world as understood by persons claiming to speak for that community. A new group seeking empowerment through genealogy may be reacting to a revolution in rising expectations and/or to a suspicion that the cultural contributions of this group's past members have been stolen or destroyed by members of other groups. Or a historically privileged ethnoracial group, like that of Madison Grant, may feel on the defensive and may believe that its traditional position is being threatened by rival groups or by a failure of nerve within the leadership of the established group.

These threats or opportunities sometimes appear quite suddenly but in other instances constitute enduring features of a given society's sense of its relation to the rest of the world. Russian cultural patriots, for example, have long felt that westerners have stolen credit for innovations actually contributed by ethnic Russians. Russian scholars of the technologically sensitive 1920s found that once the historical record was examined objectively—free of bourgeois ob- fuscation—it became clear that the foundation of modern natural science had been laid by M. V. Lomonosov, the steam engine had been invented by I. I. Polzunov, radio had been invented by A. S. Popov, the first airplane had been built by A. F. Mozhaiskii, and the first electric light bulb had been created by P. N. Iablochkov and A. N. Lodygin.[10]

Not all examples of the will to descend seem as fanciful to our ears today as does that of Russian ethnocentrists with Soviet authority at their disposal. Euro- pean scholars of the late eighteenth and nineteenth centuries "fabricated," as Bernal has phrased it, an ancient Greece flattering to the racist self-image of Europeans, erasing an understanding that the magnificent culture of Periclean Athens had drawn upon African and Asian foundations. The least-contested aspect of *Black Athena* tells the story of the reassigning of classical Greece from a partly Afro-Asiatic ancestry long acknowledged to a new, predominantly European ancestry. It was indeed this retroactive ethnoracial "cleansing" of ancient Athens that gave Grant the opportunity to claim Jesus. The Savior had probably been Greek, Grant asserted, and hence "Nordic."

Yet another example, this one from our own time, involves indigenous peoples. A few years ago some public school officials in the state of New York became attracted to the idea that the Iroquois Confederation had influenced the Constitution of the United States. Some historians were quick to insist that this link was weak, if not speculative, but this particular cultural genealogy was magnificently functional.[11] Here was an opportunity to make American history more inclusive, to integrate indigenous peoples into the very foundations of the Great Republic. The reassigning of the Constitution to an ancestry that included the Iroquois would have a more beneficial effect on our troubled, ethnoracially divided society, it would seem, than would retaining the old, exclusively European ancestry. And the claim about Iroquois influence might not have been that much more speculative, after all, than some of the other ideas about American history that have been taught to eighth graders. Myth-making had gone forward with remarkably little resistance when it was about the Pilgrims, defenders of the Iroquois influence theory had some cause to complain.

It is interesting to contemplate the wholesome work that multiculturalism might be able to accomplish on the basis of the will to descend if a central authority was in a position to authorize the redistribution of cultural resources and was unrestrained by historical evidence. This authority might survey the various ethnoracial groups to build up an inventory of items whose value was widely appreciated across ethnoracial lines. Upon the discovery that this cultural capital was not equitably distributed among the various groups, the authority might then go about redistributing this capital in the interests of ethnoracial equality. If the Germans and the Italians had too many of the items appreciated in the polity as a whole, then the authority might reassign some of their goods—Bach and Beethoven? Dante and Michelangelo?—to other groups. Items of the greatest importance to the functioning of the national community as whole, such as enthusiasm for diversity, would have to be distributed especially widely in order that virtually every group could feel that it had helped to endow the United States with this precious cultural commodity. In this case, it would be vitally important that Japanese Americans, and others whose community of descent had been popularly understood to be unresponsive to diversity, be credited with having helped to provide the world with the virtues of tolerance and open-mindedness, and with a great capacity for empathic identification with alterity.

Something like this has already happened, but the process of cultural theft has been carried out by empowered white Americans and has been masked by the prevailing epistemic regime. The cultural creativity of black people within the United States has been often appropriated and the creators themselves largely erased from cultural history. Michael Rogin (1996) and a number of other scholars in several disciplines throughout American studies are energetically engaged in correcting this appropriation and effacement, but the upshot of these corrective projects need not be the reassertion of an ethnoracially essentialist cultural genealogy.[12] Whether Italy or India has been the historic site of a given idea's most energetic development need not create a compelling incentive or disincentive for any person of any descent to accept it; to note this ought to be a platitudinous restatement of the classic critique of the genetic fallacy. The origin of "cosmopolitanism" in Europe and in the Enlightenment, for example, does not "in any way" discredit it, Kwame Anthony Appiah (1997) recently observed, "either for non-Europeans or, for that matter, for Europeans." The truth about the origin and sustaining conditions of a particular idea, artifact, or orientation ought to be sufficient. Such truths need not be a threat to the self-esteem of any American of any community of descent unless his or her identification with a given descent community is so narrow and monolithic as to preclude other, simultaneous identities and solidarities.

Appreciation for the value of multiple identities and solidarities, especially those transcending color, has increased in the 1990s and has helped to stimulate a new engagement with civic nationality in the United States. This appreciation has been prompted, in part, by the dead end of "identity politics," lamented by a chorus of ideologically dispersed voices.[13] This appreciation also responds to the resurgence of nationalism in the post–Cold War world. "Being national is the condition of our times," Geoff Eley and Ronald Grigor Suny (1996: 32) declared. These simultaneous recognitions—the ubiquity of nationalism abroad and the limitations of identity politics at home—have created the immediate conditions for a more sympathetic view of a civic nation-state like the United States that is relatively responsive to ethnoracial diversity and thus differs massively from the national solidarities in the Balkans and elsewhere producing headlines about "ethnic cleansing." In an utterance characteristic of the new openness to liberal varieties of nationalism, Eley and Suny declare that nationalism need not, "like racism," lead to "a politics of blood," but "could potentially lead" to the "acceptance, even celebration, of difference."[14]

Yet the notion of a national culture as applied to the demographically diverse United States has been resisted even by many who defend the national community and are explicitly "patriotic" about it. This is true, for example, of two of Appiah's (1996, 1997) recent essays, "Against National Culture," and "Cosmopolitan Patriots," which together present one of the most rigorous and sophisticated arguments yet offered against the viability of the concept of national culture for the United States.

What Appiah most likes about the United States—and what inspires "patriotic" emotions in him—is the relative ease with which its citizens can cultivate a variety of important identities without diminishing their loyalty to the national community and to the state. Many people, the Ghanaian-rooted Appiah observes of citizens of his adopted country, have "loved America . . . exactly because it has enabled them to choose who they are and to decide, too, how central America is in their chosen identity." In order to sustain this condition what is essential is "only," Appiah insists, "that all of us share respect for the political culture of liberalism and the constitutional order it entails." Appiah distinguishes sharply between this "political" culture and a "national" culture, which he represents as a much more comprehensive coordination of thought and feeling on a multitude of human issues including, for example, abortion. Appiah is so adamantly opposed to the notion of "shared core values" that he explicitly denies that this term can be fairly used to refer to a "mutual commitment" to the democratic institutions of the nation, about which he is firmly "patriotic." What is crucial for Appiah is that democratic institutions can entail "a great diversity of meanings" for those who adhere to those institutions. Yet that diversity is not so great as it first appears. Essential to the "political culture" Appiah is willing to advance on behalf of the national community are certain values: the classically liberal values of respect for "human dignity and personal autonomy" (1997: 629–31, 633, 635).

Appiah puts an extremely fine point on the distinction between the "political" culture he endorses and the "national" culture he says should never be built around it. Appiah warns against "centering every American on shared values, shared literary references, and shared narratives of the American nation," but by phrasing this practice as a form of coercion—the *centering* of *every* American life—Appiah reduces the effectiveness of his argument to a case against a compulsory national curriculum. He thus fails to deal with what he elsewhere acknowledges is a pluralistic environment for cultural conversation in the United States, within which political meanings are worked out not only in schools that are locally controlled but in "family and church, reading and television, and in . . . professional and recreational associations" (1997: 630).

It is in exactly that extended, polycentric environment that the "political" culture Appiah admires can become "national" without violating Appiah's own soundest insights and instincts. And it is there that a variety of literary connections to this political culture are worked out: Mark Twain, an emblem for many contradictions within what Appiah would call the "political culture" of the United States, and for the "black" elements within "white" culture, has sustained a claim to being a national poet for the United States comparable to Pushkin for Russia, Dante for Italy, Goethe for Germany, Cervantes for Spain, and Shakespeare for England. That national poets—those most credited with bringing a national language to its fullest powers—also belong to all humankind should be beyond dispute, but this need not mean they cannot be presented as part of the "culture" of a particular nation.

Appiah displays little understanding of the historically rooted character of the democratic institutions and practices he celebrates. The constitutional order of the United States is not simply the embodiment of a list of abstract liberal values; rather, it is a finite historical entity with a record of specific tragedies, successes, failures, contradictions, and provincial conceits too easily lost from view in Appiah's reduction of it to an instrument of cosmopolitanism. It can and should be such an instrument, enabling a host of consenting affiliations, but there is no reason why the United States cannot become, for some of its citizens, a solidarity to which one is attached with the same sense of belonging that

Appiah assigns to religious, professional, local, and gender solidarities. This feeling of deep attachment to the United States was manifest in the abiding engagement of many Americans with Ken Burns's television series on the Civil War first broadcast in the fall of 1990.

The shared memories and practices that are often said to be essential to any personally sustaining solidarity can develop around a civic community over time, just as they do around a community of descent. Indeed, the distinction between an ethnic and a civic community can be exaggerated. Some affiliations now considered ethnic in many parts of the world have been created over centuries by civil authority out of what were once distinctive descent communities. As mixture of descent increases in the United States, the integrity of the old, standardized communities of descent is weakened. The greater the number of Americans who claim more than one community of descent, the less ordinance does any one of these communities have over the others, and the more room is made within the economy of identity for the national community as a "descent community" of a kind: the kind produced by ethnoracial mixing.

One theorist who grasps more fully than Appiah does the capacity of the United States to inspire feelings of belonging is Bernard Yack (1996) who, in a commentary on Ernest Renan's theory of nationalism, insists that at least "two things" make a viable nation: "present-day consent and a rich cultural inheritance of shared memories and practices." Without consent, Yack continues,

> our cultural legacy would be our destiny, rather than a set of background constraints on our activities. But without such a legacy there would be no consent at all, since there would be no reason for people to seek agreement with any one group of individuals rather than another. Focusing exclusively on one or the other component of national identity inspires the contrasting myths of enthonationalism and [of] civic theories of political community . . . that exaggerate, on the one side, our inability to change, build on, and improve the communal ties we have inherited and, on the other, our capacity to recreate ourselves in the image of our liberal theories.[15]

Yack's formulation is consistent with an appreciation for the capacity of narrative to help constitute a national culture, especially one thin enough in its prescriptive content to allow for the simultaneous flourishing of multiple identities and loyalties. A national narrative true to the history of democratic institutions in the United States is ideally suited to convey the "diversity of meanings" of those institutions Appiah wishes to preserve. Part of "the story" to be told is how the boundaries of the national solidarity came into being, how and when they were challenged and sometimes changed, and by whom. How has the United States drawn and redrawn its social borders to accommodate, repel, or subjugate this or that group? How has racism and the struggle against it proceeded in a sequence of distinctive settings? Answers to these vital questions are among the proudest products of recent scholarship. These answers can help constitute the story the nation tells about itself and can thus partake of the "national culture" without precluding the telling of other empirically warranted stories about subnational and transnational solidarities, including communities of descent.

The United States now finds itself in a position to develop and act upon a cultural self-image as *a national solidarity committed—but often failing—to incorporate individuals from a great variety of communities of descent, on equal but not homogeneous terms, into a society with democratic aspirations inherited largely from England.* There is much more to the history of the United States than this, but it is a defensible focus for a national narrative. Historians can be expected to disagree among themselves on exactly how the narrative of the nation should be constructed, but this understanding of what the story should be primarily about may enable more scholars to tell more truths to more people about more of the nation's character than can other, comparable charters for the telling of the national story. This conception of the national story affords ample room to display two truths now vouchsafed to historians, but often resisted by much of the public: the great extent to which the flourishing of the United States has depended on the exploitation of nonwhites, and the relative weakness, during most of the national history, of egalitarian ideals.

This conception of the national story has the additional advantage of incorporating some insights from the strongest of recent scholarship on the dynamics of nationality. Against those who depict nations as either primordial extensions of kinship or as instruments of modernizing elites in a distinctly industrial world,[16] historian Prasenjit Duara (1996: esp. 161) argues that ancient and contemporary nations are best understood like other political solidarities: they are contingent, historical entities that achieve their shape by hardening certain boundaries and softening others on a field of fluid relationships among groups that may be defined by a variety of different principles, including language, religion, and kinship. Among the means by which a community's boundaries are achieved, maintained, and altered are narratives, which, Duara rightly observes, "are necessarily selective," repressing some "historical and contemporary materials as they seek to define a community." The materials thus left out "are fair game," Duara adds, "for the spokesmen of those on the outs or on the margins of this definition who will seek to organize them into a counternarrative of mobilization."[17]

Recent controversies over the Smithsonian's *Enola Gay* exhibit and over the National History Standards can remind us how some of the "materials" de-emphasized by historians trying to shape the national narrative are brought back into discursive play by the Air Force, the Congress, and others who offer themselves as the champions of the "outs." Who is "in" and who is "out" depends, obviously, on the context, but these quarrels over the American story illustrate the soundness of Duara's understanding of national narratives. The task of formulating critical scholarship in terms that can work within a national narrative accessible to the public is challenging, and the contending interests that seek to control that narrative are formidable. The national culture of the United States will always include a semiofficial national narrative, no matter what historians do or do not do in relation to it. If professional historians do not try to influence that narrative, and hence the national culture of which it is so vital a part, others will control that narrative and that culture even more fully than they now do. Historians should have no client but the truth, but one truth about the world in which they practice is that it confronts them with choices about how and where to disseminate the knowledge they attain.

NOTES

1. This essay remains, after nearly four decades, one of the wisest discussions of its topic.

2. Much of the recent theoretical and comparative literature on nationalism has surprisingly little to say about the case of the United States. This is true, for example, of three of the most important collections of the 1990s: *Nation and Narration* (Bhabha 1990), *Nationalism* (Hutchinson and Smith 1994), and *Becoming National: A Reader* (Eley and Suny 1996). Even Benedict Anderson (1991), who understands that the United States is one of the largest and most enduring nationalist projects in modern history, provides only episodic treatment of it while discussing "creole nationalism" in his influential book *Imagined Communities: Reflections on the Origins and Spread of Nationalism*.

3. Although Lipset makes several sound points about how the United States differs historically from certain other industrialized nations, his claims are hard to sort out from "red herrings" that follow from his uncritical reliance on the concept of "exceptionalism." Is "exceptional" used simply as a synonym for "unique," and if so, in relation to what? Or does this usage imply an "exception" to a general pattern explicable by a uniform set of rules? Or is the United States exceptional in the more radical sense that its history cannot be explained by the same set of rules that explains the condition and character of other national societies?

4. For recent explorations of the imperialist element in the cultural life of the United States, see the studies collected in Kaplan and Pease 1993.

5. For a powerful analysis of Powell's opinion, see Post (1996).

6. It is possible that Powell's reasoning will continue to provide constitutional sanction for some affirmative action programs. I write in the past tense in 1998, when the legal future of group preferences is uncertain.

7. For an account of the institutionalization of the ethnoracial pentagon in American life following a 1977 directive of the federal Office of Budget and Management to the Bureau of the Census, see Hollinger 1995: 19–50. This account emphasizes the fact that culture abounds in every segment of the pentagon, expresses the hope that ethnoracially defined cultures can be perpetuated more on the basis of voluntary commitment than by social authority, and identifies traditional racism as the chief obstacle to a more voluntary foundation for ethnoracial cultural affiliation in the United States.

8. An important collection of critical essays is *Black Athena Revisited* (Lefkowitz and Rogers 1996). For Bernal's response to this book, see Bernal 1996.

9. The following several paragraphs develop a concept I sketched briefly in an essay published only in Italian (Hollinger 1996: 55–68).

10. For this example, I am indebted to Yuri Slezkine (1996).

11. For scholarly opinion on the question of Iroquois influence on the Constitution, see "Forum" 1996.

12. See also Clover 1995.

13. For two very different critiques of the politics of identity by "progressives," one centering on the perspective of local communities and the second on that of the national community, see Anner 1996 and Lind 1995.

14. For a brief consideration of the appeal of "liberal nationalism" in relation to the demands of social justice in the contemporary United States, see Hollinger 1997.

15. See also Margalit 1997.

16. These two approaches to nationalism are associated above all with the writings of Anthony Smith and Ernest Gellner, respectively.

17. See also Prasenjit Duara 1995. Although Duara presents himself as a poststructuralist, he is one of the few contemporary students of nationalism who continue to draw inspiration from Potter's "Historian's Use of Nationalism and Vice Versa." See Duara 1996: 172.

REFERENCES

Anderson, Benedict. 1991. *Imagined Communities: Reflections on the Origins and Spread of Nationalism*, rev. and ext. ed., 2d ed. New York: Verso.

Anner, John, ed. 1996. *Beyond Identity Politics: Emerging Social Justice Movements in Communities of Color*. Boston: South End.

Appiah, Kwame Anthony. 1996. "Against National Culture." Pp. 175–90 in *Text and Nation: Cross-Disciplinary Essays on Cultural and National Identities*, edited by Laura Garcia-Moreno and Peter C. Pfeiffer. Columbia, S.C.: Camden House.

———. 1997. "Cosmopolitan Patriots." *Critical Inquiry* 23 (spring): 617–39.

Bernal, Martin. 1987. *Black Athena: The Afro-Asiatic Roots of Classical Civilization*. New Brunswick, N.J.: Rutgers University Press.

———. 1996. "Whose Greece?" *London Review of Books*, 12 December, 17–18.

Bhaba, Homi, ed. 1990. *Nation and Narration*. New York: Routledge.

Clover, Carol J. 1995. "Dancin' in the Rain." *Critical Inquiry* 21 (summer): 722–47.

Duara, Prasenjit. 1995. *Rescuing History from the Nation: Questioning Narratives of Modern China*. Chicago: University of Chicago Press.

———. 1996. "Historicizing National Identity, or Who Imagines What and When." Pp. 151–77 in *Becoming National: A Reader*, edited by Geoff Eley and Ronald Grigor Suny. New York: Oxford University Press.

Eley, Geoff, and Ronald Grigor Suny, eds. 1996. *Becoming National: A Reader*. New York: Oxford University Press.

"Forum: The 'Iroquois Influence' Thesis—Con and Pro." *William and Mary Quarterly* 3, ser. 53 (July): 587–620.

Grant, Madison. 1916. *The Passing of the Great Race*. New York: Scribner.

Hollinger, David A. 1995. *Postethnic America: Beyond Multiculturalism*. New York: Basic Books.

———. 1996. "La 'narrazione di inclusione' e la 'ricerca degli antenati': la storiogria americana nell fase multiculturale." Pp. 55–68 in *La storia americana e le scienze sociali in europa e negli stati uniti*, edited by Daniele Fiorentino. Rome: Encyclopedia Italiana.

Hollinger, David A. 1997. "National Solidarity at the End of the Twentieth Century: Reflections on the United States and Liberal Nationalism." *Journal of American History* 84 (September): 559–69.

Hutchinson, John, and Anthony D. Smith. 1994. *Nationalism*. New York: Oxford University Press.

Kaplan, Amy, and Donald E. Pease, eds. 1993. *Cultures of United States Imperialism*. Durham, N.C.: Duke University Press.

Lefkowitz, Mary, and Guy MacLean Rogers, eds. 1996. *Black Athena Revisited*. Chapel Hill: University of North Carolina Press.

Lind, Michael. 1995. *The Next American Nation: The New Nationalism and the Fourth American Revolution*. New York: Free Press.

Lipset, Seymour Martin. 1996. *American Exceptionalism: A Double-Edged Sword*. New York: W. W. Norton.

Margalit, Avishai. 1997. "The Moral Psychology of Nationalism." Pp. 74–87 in *The Morality of Nationalism*, edited by Robert McKim and Jeff McMahan. New York: Oxford University Press.

Post, Robert. 1996. "After Bakke." *Representations* no. 55 (summer): 1–12.

Potter, David M. 1962. "The Historian's Use of Nationalism and Vice Versa." *American Historical Review* 67: 924–50.

Rogin, Michael. 1996. *Blackface, White Noise: Jewish Immigrants in The Hollywood Melting Pot*. Berkeley: University of California Press.

Slezkine, Yuri. 1996. *Arctic Mirrors*. Ithaca, N.Y.: Cornell University Press.

Yack, Bernard. 1996. "The Myth of the Civic Nation." *Centennial Review* 10: 208–209.

CHAPTER THIRTEEN

Does Voluntary Association Make Democracy Work?

JEAN L. COHEN

ABOUT 25 YEARS AGO, post-Marxist critics of socialist authoritarianism revived the concept of civil society (Cohen and Arato 1992: 1–26). The remarkable historical success of the concept was due to its convergence with a dualist strategy for democratization first in the East and then in Latin America. This strategy was based on the idea of the self-organization of society: the rebuilding of social ties, politically relevant collective action, and independent publics outside state-controlled communication, but it also aimed at creating political publics and institutions that would be responsive and accountable to the electorate.

In Western Europe the concept also caught on in the post-Marxist milieux of the "new" social movements, which challenged forms of domination within liberal democracies that differed from class oppression yet persisted and had systematic bases despite formal equality. There the focus was on the further democratization of already existing civil societies and political publics: on the expansion and strenghtening of basic rights, on the reduction of social hierarchies, on voice and justice for stigmatized and discriminated-against groups, on the revitalization of civil associations and publics, and on the increase of access and influence of these on political society. Theorists like Bobbio, Habermas, Lefort, Offe, Melucci, Rosanvallon, and Touraine anticipated such a possibility very early. It is hoped that Andrew Arato and I were able to contribute to it in our writings during the previous decade (Cohen and Arato 1992: 492–563; Cohen 1982).

Today the political context and projects associated with the discourse of civil society have changed. In the United States, interest in the concept has exploded—a somewhat belated development vis-à-vis the European debate but in certain respects continuous with an earlier indigeneous American discussion.

The current American debate has strong affinities with the approach of the pluralist school of the 1950s. Both draw on the sociocultural tradition of political analysis introduced in the nineteenth century by Alexis de Tocqueville's study of American democracy (Tocqueville 1969). The pluralists developed the Tocquevillian concept of a civic culture and focused on the relation of cultural and social factors (including participation in the autonomous associational life of civil society) to responsive and effective democratic government. In contrast, the postwar pluralist discourse of civil society was aimed primarily at explaining the "difference" between societies prone to totalitarianism and *stable* democracies.

The intermediary bodies and overlapping forms of plurality and identity characteristic of associations in civil (as distinct from "mass") society were deemed a sign of successful "modernization." When brought together with a universalistic and egalitarian political culture, these allegedly secured cross-cutting solidarities, fostered tolerance, and limited the nature of demands and ideological agendas on the part of elites and social actors (Almond and Verba 1963). Accordingly, a civic culture was believed to protect society against destabilizing mass mobilization and social atomization characteristic of totalitarian movements and states.[1]

The ideological context in the United States is quite different today, as are the stakes of what has become a hotly contested concept open to competing interpretations and political projects. Now it is the crisis of the welfare state—not the threat of a totalitarian state—that is at issue. Now it is dissatisfaction with the cultural and social effects of "successful" and "normal" rather than "failed" modernization that motivates the renewal of the discourse of civil society. And now there is the fear that models of social integration, civic engagement, and associational life that were once taken for granted are being strained by new forms of social diversity, institutional transformation, and economic and technological change.

Apparently, neither the centralized state nor the magic of the marketplace can offer effective, liberal, and democratic solutions to the problems of "postindustrial" civil societies in a context of globalization. Statist correctives threaten freedom, but social injustice is exacerbated when the state completely abandons the field to market forces: both "reforms" can be socially disintegrative, oppressive, and unjust. Given the political impossibility of continuing the welfare state model in the old way and the undesirability of returning to market magic, it is understandable that the discourse of civil society has become so widespread and so contentious. Indeed, welfare state legality has shifted emphasis toward the administration and the courts and triggered calls for revitalizing and protecting both democracy and community.

To be sure, much of this was already true in the 1980s (Cohen and Arato 1992), but what strikes us today is the ubiquity with which the term "civil society" is invoked in response. No longer an arcane concept deployed by a select group of political and social theorists, the term has entered the speech of politicians, journalists, and public intellectuals on all sides of the political spectrum from Pat Buchanan and Newt Gingrich to Bill Clinton and Bill Bradley (Bradley 1995; Skocpol 1996). "Civil society" has become a slogan for the 1990s in part because it appears to offer an alternative center for political and economical initiatives, but the idealized, one-dimensional version of the concept that is being revived is hardly up to the task, in my view.

This paper addresses the contemporary American discourses of civil society with an eye to the politics of theory and the political effects of rhetoric. I focus on two of the most prominent recent interventions in the civil society debate: the neorepublican stance of Robert Putnam and his school, and the communitarian version of the political theorists who gather around the journal *The Responsive Community*.[2] Civil society in these approaches has become so reduced that the normative thrust of the concept, along with its relevance to democracy and contemporary problems, is being obscured. Nearly everyone in the current discussion has come to equate civil society with traditional forms of voluntary association (including "the" family), and nearly everyone assumes that the "intermediary bodies" created by voluntary association are in decline in contemporary America—the debate is over the causes of the decline and what to do about it.

This conceptualization of civil society is theoretically impoverished and politically suspect. When combined with the discourse of civic and moral decline, it undermines democracy instead of making it work, threatens personal liberty instead of enhancing it, and blocks social justice and social solidarity instead of furthering them. Unless this model is corrected, the current revival of the discourse of civil society in the United States will play into the hands of social conservatives who aim to retraditionalize civil life and to substitute local "volunteerism" for the public services and redistributive efforts of the welfare state, as if these are the only options we have. The conservatives pretend that we can have a vital, well-integrated, and just civil society without states' guaranteeing that universalistic egalitarian principles inform social policy regardless of which social institution or level of government carries it out. If civil society discourse is left in this form, we will not be able to articulate, much less resolve, the critical problems facing democratic polities in the coming century. My claim is that it matters very much, both politically and theoretically, which concept of civil society we use and seek to foster.

THE CONCEPT OF CIVIL SOCIETY

Whether we take Hegel or Tocqueville as our starting point, the concept of civil society made available to us by nineteenth-century theorists was rich and multi-leveled. "Civil society" was understood as a sphere of social interaction distinct from the economy and state, characterized by voluntary association, civil publics and the media of communication (at that time, print), and sets of subjective legal rights. The rule of law and the autonomous administration of justice were central to civil society because although the latter creates itself spontaneously, it cannot on its own institutionalize or generalize its norms and orientations ("habits of the heart"). A legal system and a legal culture committing practitioners to the norms of impartiality were crucial to the process by which the particularistic goals and projects of associated individuals within civil society could be informed by, made compatible with, or generalized into the universalistic principles of modern constitutional democracies (Knox 1967: 83–116; Habermas 1996).[3] These dimensions of civil society reciprocally influenced or mediated the institutionalized political publics (parliaments as well as parties and political organizations) and legal publics (courts, juries) of the political system proper.

The twentieth-century European discussion of civil society has added two crucial components to this understanding. The first is an emphasis on the importance of informal social networks and self-organizing social movements, as distinct from more formal voluntary associations and institutions, to the vitality and reproduction of an autonomous civil society (e.g., Touraine 1981; Melucci 1980, 1985; Offe 1985). Recognition of this dimension allows one to shift between two perspectives: civil society as a dynamic, innovative source for articulating new concerns, developing projects, forming new identities, and generating and contesting new norms, and civil society as institutionalized civic autonomy. It also allows one to see how in its dynamic capacity (collective action) the institutional shape of civil as well as political institutions, social as well as other forms of power, can be targeted in struggles over democratization.

The second contribution of twentieth-century analysis is the communicative model of the public sphere developed primarily by Jurgen Habermas and his followers (Habermas 1989; Cohen and Arato 1992). The category of the public sphere was already present in eighteenth- and nineteenth-century understandings of civil society, but its normative weight and its role in mediating between the particular and the general were not clarified until relatively recently.

In the public sphere people can discuss matters of mutual concern as peers and learn about facts, events, and the opinions, interests, and perspectives of others. Discourse on values, norms, laws, and policies generates politically relevant public opinion. Moreover, through its generalized media of communication, the public sphere can mediate among the myriad minipublics that emerge from associations, movements, religious organizations, clubs, local organizations of concerned citizens, and simple socializing. The public sphere is a decentered anonymous matrix of communication about common concerns, comprising the full gamut of networks and modes of communication that allow for the contestatory, agonistic, and rhetorical as well as deliberative expression and formation of public opinion(s). The latter is meant, in turn, to influence the debates within political and legal publics proper (legislatures, courts) and to bring under informal control the actions and decisions of rulers and lawmakers (the principle of responsiveness). The concept of the public sphere thus brings together the normative and the empirical, the universal and the particular.[4] It is, in my view, the normative core of the idea of civil society and the heart of any conception of democracy.

As already indicated, voluntary association is an important aspect of a vital civil society, but focusing exclusively on this dimension is impoverishing, to say the least. So is the degeneration of "civil society talk" into rhetoric about the decline of morals and civic virtue. It is also backward-looking and politically dangerous.

VOLUNTARY ASSOCIATION, SOCIAL CAPITAL, AND WORKABLE DEMOCRACY

Robert Putnam's (1993: 173–75) claim in his extraordinarily influential book *Making Democracy Work* that democratic government is more responsive and effective when it faces a vigorous civil society is, of course, one that I embrace.

He argues convincingly that horizontally organized voluntary associations that cut across social cleavages are more likely to nourish wider social cooperation, to reinforce norms of reciprocity, and thus to "make democracy work" than hierarchical segmental organizations or clientelistic structures.[5] A civic culture of "generalized trust" and social solidarity, peopled by citizens willing and able to cooperate in joint ventures, *is* an important societal prerequisite of a vital democracy.

Nevertheless, Putnam's approach is unsatisfactory, in part for methodological reasons. He reduces civil society to the dimension of voluntary association and construes the latter as the *sole* source of what he calls social capital. The feature of the social context that matters most to the performance of democratic institutions, in Putnam's analysis, is the presence or absence of a civic culture. The indicators of civicness that he cites are similar to those mentioned in the civic culture studies of the 1950s: the number of voluntary associations, the incidence of newspaper readership (a sign of interest in and being informed about community affairs), electoral turnout, and a range of civic attitudes including law abidingness, interpersonal trust, and general cooperativeness—so far so good.

Indeed, Putnam's historical chapters provide a rich description of the emergence of civicness and what it needed to take root, at least in the north of Italy. Here, in addition to the dense network of associational life and the oaths of mutual assistance sworn by members of associations in the early Communes, Putnam mentions the importance of institutions and institutionalized norms, such as the professionalization of public administration and credible state impartiality in the enforcement of laws, for the maintenance of social trust. Strong and autonomous courts, reliable administrative state structures, and *confidence* that the administration of justice, enforcement of contracts, and legislation would be impartial seemed to be a sine qua non for the networks of civic associations to succeed in generating solidarity outside the bonds of kinship (Putnam 1993: 128, 147).[6] Thus on the descriptive level, at least, the charge of reductionism seems inappropriate.

The important concluding theoretical chapter of the book, Social Capital and Institutional Success, however, *is* open to such a charge. For there, history, tradition, culture, normative orientations, and their transmission over time are analyzed in terms of the concept of inherited "social capital"—defined as the social stock of trust, norms, and networks that facilitate coordinated actions— whereas the *source* of social capital and of its generalization is narrowed down to involvement in secondary associations. We are left with a weak theoretical framework and an unconvincing analysis. Unfortunately, this framework is greatly influencing the American civil society debate.

The crucial chapter on social capital asks how "virtuous circles" generate, generalize, and transmit traditions of civic engagement through centuries of radical social, economic, and political change. Putnam dismisses the classic Hobbesian solution, "third party enforcement." If cooperation for the common good requires trust in everyone's willingness to contribute equally, a "third party enforcer" like the state should enable subjects to do what they cannot do on their own, namely, trust one another. But apparently the use of force is expensive, and impartial enforcement is itself a public good subject to the same dilemma it aims to solve: what power could ensure that the sovereign does not defect? Nor, as the new institutionalists suggest, will the best institutional design ensure impartiality even if it entails the participation of the affected parties in defining the rules, the subjection of violators to sanctions, and low-cost mechanisms for resolving conflicts. For the same dilemma apparently obtains vis-à-vis the institutionalist understanding of the state as impartial lawgiver that confronted the state as Hobbesian sovereign, namely, the problem of infinite regress: trust and generalized reciprocity are presupposed for the establishment of the institutions in the first place.

Putnam accordingly turns away from state structures to "soft" sociocultural solutions. Dense networks of civic involvement are both a sign and a source of social capital. Participating in horizontal voluntary associations lubricates cooperation and generates social trust, thus allowing dilemmas of collective action to be resolved (1993: 165–66; 1995a: 67). Apparently, such participation produces "moral resources" that can be transmitted over generations (inherited) and whose supply increases through use—stocks of social capital tend to be self-reinforcing and cumulative. Inheritance of a stock of social capital renders voluntary cooperation in a community easier and thus makes democracy work (1993: 167, 176–77, 182).

Although Putnam does say that trust has two sources—norms of reciprocity and networks of civic engagement—the first is primarily a function of the second (Levi 1996: 47).[7] Dense networks of associations entail repeated exchanges of what he calls "short-term altruism" and "long-term self-interest"—I help you out now in the expectation that you will help me out in the future. These rational exchanges, and the direct experience of reliability, repeated over a period of time, encourage the development of a norm of generalized reciprocity.

That voluntary association is *evidence* of social cooperation and trust is both undeniable and almost tautological, but why is it construed as the only significant source of social capital? Why are democratic political institutions, the public sphere, and law absent from the theoretical analysis of how social trust is developed? The answer is obvious: once the state is defined and dismissed as a third-party enforcer, once law is turned into sanctions that provide for a certain level of social order but no more, once institutions are dismissed as irrelevant to social trust because their genesis already presupposes social trust, and once a vital civil society is reduced to the presence or absence of intermediate voluntary assocations, no other source of social trust is conceivable.

As others have already pointed out, the theory has many flaws.[8] One of the most serious flaws is the failure to say just what generalizes the social trust produced within voluntary associations. How does intergroup trust become trust of strangers outside the group? Why does the willingness to act together for mutual benefit in a small group like a choral society translate into willingness to act for the common good or to become politically engaged at all? Indeed, *is the interpersonal trust generated in face-to-face interactions even the same thing as "generalized trust"?* I don't think so.

Let me be clear here. I don't doubt that trust lubricates cooperation or, more important, that general abstract *norms* of reciprocity allow the reconciliation of self-interest and solidarity. I am not convinced, however, that the trust that emerges within particular associations is sufficient for producing generalized trust or, in the language I prefer, belief in the legitimacy of institutionalized norms, acceptance of the universalistic principles of reciprocity and societywide social solidarity, and confidence that these will orient the action both of powerful elites and average citizens. What is very odd is that Putnam offers no mechanism for explaining how these emerge.

I believe that the use made of the concept of social capital is at fault. Obscuring more than it illuminates, this concept allows one to avoid the difficult task of showing that the particular trust built up between specific individuals in one context can be transferred without further ado to other contexts, to strangers, or to society at large. In short, prior to addressing the issue of what generalizes social capital, we need to ask whether "inherited social capital" is the right concept to use for *six* rather different things: interpersonal trust, social solidarity, general norms of reciprocity, belief in the legitimacy of institutionalized norms, confidence that these will motivate the action of institutional actors and ordinary citizens (social solidarity), and the transmission of cultural traditions, patterns, and values.

The metaphor of social "capital" allows the theorist to finesse the generalization issue and to blur these distinctions by suggesting a false analogy between direct interpersonal social relations and economic exchanges on the market. Capital accumulated in one context can of course be invested in another place: it can easily be saved, inherited, and exchanged regardless of its particular form because there is a universal equivalent for it—money—and an institutional framework for the exchange—the market economy. As the medium of exchange and the universal equivalent for all forms of wealth, money solves the generalization issue. Impersonal contractual market relations are possible because money in a market system substitutes for direct communications in the coordination and integration of actions (see Habermas 1984: 113–99 on this point). Of course, even the market presupposes *confidence* that the value of money is backed up by the banking system and that contractual obligations are recognized and enforced by states.

Interpersonal trust, on the other hand, is by definition specific and contextual—one trusts *particular* people because of repeated interactions with them in specific contexts in which reciprocity is directly experienced. Interpersonal trust generated in face-to-face relationships is not an instance of a more general impersonal phenomenon, nor can it simply be transferred to others or to other contexts. Indeed, it is entirely possible that without other mechanisms for the generalization of trust, participation in associations and membership in social networks could foster particularism, localism, intolerance, exclusion, and generalized mistrust of outsiders, of the law, and of government. Without other mediations, there is no reason to expect that the forms of reciprocity or trust generated within small groups would extend beyond the group, or, for that matter, that group demands would be anything other than particularistic.

The argument that repeated interaction games within small-scale face-to-face groups of strategic calculators can generate universal norms of law abidingness or reciprocity is unconvincing. Repeated interaction within a group may help generate local norms of reciprocity among members, because each learns gradually to expect that the other will cooperate (Coleman 1990: 251, 273).[9] Interpersonal trust involves not only the experience of reliability of the other but also the moral obligation of the trusted person to honor the trust bestowed upon him or her and the mutual expectation that each understands this principle and will be motivated internally to act accordingly.

For interpersonal trust to turn into generalized reciprocity, or to foster general law-abidingness, however, the universalistic normative expectation itself would have to be presupposed *as a norm* in a wide variety of contexts. The *obligatoriness* of reciprocity and law-abidingness, and the motivation to act accordingly, over and above the experience and hence expectation of regularity of behavior of particular others, and in distinction from simply contingent prudent behavior, requires something more than the repetition of sets of strategic interactions. In short, for impersonal, general trust of strangers to be conceivable and warranted, other factors would have to mediate (on the concept of warranted trust, see Warren 1996). The principle of reciprocity would have to be institutionalized on the one side, and the aspiration/motivation to be trustworthy would have to become part of one's identity, as it were, on the other. Thus the analysis does not escape the problem of infinite regress.

In order to see what role institutions play here, one would have to understand law and the state not just as a third-party enforcer. At the very least the two-sidedness of law—law as sanction *and* law as institutionalized cultural values, norms, rules, and rights would have to be theorized. Only then would it be possible to reflect on the role of law and rights in substituting *universalistic* norms as functional equivalents for personalized trust and substituting confidence in abstract institutions (backed up by sanctions) and belief in their legitimacy and purpose for direct interpersonal ties. For example, legal norms of procedural fairness, impartiality, and justice that give structure to state and some civil institutions, limit favoritism and arbitrariness, and protect merit are the sine qua non for societywide "general trust," at least in a modern social structure. So is the expectation that institutional actors will live up to and enforce the norms of the institutional setting in which they interact. Rights, on the other hand, ensure that trust is warranted insofar as they provide individuals the opportunity to demand that violations of legitimate reciprocal expectations be sanctioned.

It makes little sense to use the category of generalized trust to describe one's attitude toward law or government. One can trust only people because only people can fulfill obligations. But institutions (legal and other) can provide functional equivalents for interpersonal trust in impersonal settings involving interactions with strangers, because they, as it were, institutionalize action-orienting norms and the expectation that these will be honored.

What Durkheim (1958) once called "professional ethics" does indeed have affect "civic morals." If one knows one can expect impartiality from a judge, care and concern from a doctor, protection from police, concern for the common good from legislators, and so on, then one can develop confidence (instead of cynicism) that shared norms and cultural values will orient the action of powerful others. But confidence of this sort also presupposes public spaces in which the validity of such norms and the fairness of procedures can be challenged, revised, redeemed, or reinforced through critique.[10]

The point here is that Putnam's narrow theoretical framework prevents him from articulating these complex interrelations. Nevertheless, even with its flaws, *Making Democracy Work* is open to a more sophisticated interpretation. After all, the book traces the effects of institutional reform in Italy: the devolution of important powers from a centralized state to newly created regional political public spaces, closer to the populace and open to their influence. Moreover, many of the vital elements of a richer society-centered analysis were at least mentioned in the text. Even though Putnam misinterprets his own data, his research suggests that well-designed political institutions are crucial to fostering civic spirit because they provide enabling conditions—a political opportunity structure—that could become an incentive to civil actors to emerge and a target of influence for them once they do (see Urbinati 1993: 573). The path not taken in the theoretical chapter of this book was nonetheless made available.

The recent work on civil society in the United States is all the more disappointing in this regard. Far from broadening the analytical framework, the new research is guided exclusively by the methods and categories of that final chapter. "Civil society" is cast in very narrow terms. As I already indicated, it is the link of the reductionist conception of civil society to the discourse of civic decline that makes this approach ambiguous, and so prone to ideological misuse.

SOCIAL DECAPITALIZATION IN AMERICA?

In a series of recent articles, Putnam and his associates argued that low electoral turnout and declining membership in political parties in the United States are part of a much wider phenomenon: the gradual disappearance of American "social capital" (Putnam 1995a, 1995b, 1996). Given the alleged centrality of social capital to civic engagement and effective, democratic government, its erosion is presented as a serious cause for alarm.

The startling discovery of "social decapitalization" emerged out of the application of the method and concepts of Putnam's work on Italian civic culture to the American context. Accordingly, the presence of secondary associations, deemed the most reliable empirical indicator of social capital, is *the* independent variable used to test the vitality of American civil society. The research does indeed show a drastic decline of membership in such associations, beginning in the second half of the twentieth century.[11]

These findings would not be so alarming if functional equivalents for the old group were emerging. But according to the research, they are not. "Counter-trends" such as the emergence of new mass-membership organizations like NOW, and the explosion of interest groups represented in Washington such as the American Association of Retired Persons (AARP), are only apparent, for these groups are really tertiary, "mailing-list" organizations rather than second-ary associations. The latter are characterized by face-to-face interactions and direct horizontal interpersonal ties of people who actually meet one another, whereas the former involve abstract impersonal ties of people to common sym-bols, texts, leaders, and ideals and not to one another (Putnam 1995a: 71; 1996: 35). According to the theory of social capital, associational membership should increase social trust, but apparently membership in tertiary groups does not yield the kind of social connectedness that generates social capital.

Compared with the civic generation born between 1910 and 1940, the post-war baby boom generation that matured in the sixties and all those that fol-lowed are disturbingly "postcivic." Indeed, the phenomenon of decline is gener-ational, all other factors having been controlled for (Putnam 1996: 35–43). What caused this decline, if we assume that it is real?

Putnam says that the decline was caused by the arrival of television, a new medium of communication that became prevalent while the sixties generation was maturing. Television viewing is the only leisure activity that inhibits partic-ipation outside the home, coming at the expense of nearly every social activity. Analyzing General Social Survey data from 1974 through 1994, and controlling for factors such as education, age, and income, Putnam found that TV viewing is negatively correlated with social trust, group membership, and voting turnout (Putnam 1996: 46–48). People who watch too much TV are no longer neigh-borly; they don't socialize, join clubs, or form the sorts of secondary associa-tions that would foster civic orientations. Apparently the culture industry is finally having the effect so feared by its critics: the transformation of American civil society into a mass society.[12]

I do not find this account persuasive. First, other analysts show that not all the data on civicness point to decline. In a recent major study, Sidney Verba and his colleagues (Brady, Schlozman, and Verba 1995: 68–91) do not find that the falloff in voter turnout is part of a general erosion in voluntary activity or political participation. They have reported increases in certain forms of civic activism such as membership in community problem-solving organizations. Some older types of associational membership and activities have even been expanding both numerically and qualitatively. Moreover, different loci and sorts of social activity may serve purposes similar to those of traditional forms of secondary association (Schudson 1996: 17–18). Putnam's research screens out such innovations in social connectedness.

Equally important is the phenomenon of "shifting involvements" noted many years ago by Albert O. Hirschman (1982). The political engagement of contem-porary citizens is episodic and increasingly issue-oriented. Membership in polit-ical parties, labor unions, and traditional voluntary associations may have de-clined, but the willingness of Americans to mobilize periodically on local and national levels around concerns that affect them cannot be deduced from this fact. The new action repertoires invented by civic and political actors cannot be assessed adequately by criteria derived from older forms.[13]

Indeed, to discount the new types of association, mobilization, and public engagement of the sixties and seventies simply because they differ from traditional secondary associations makes little sense. These allegedly uncivic generations, and their successors, created the first consumers' movement since the 1930s, the first environmental movement since the turn of the century, public health movements, grassroots activism and community organizing, the most important feminist movement since the pre–World War I period, the civil rights movement, and innumerable transnational NGOs and civic movements, all of which have led to unprecedented advances in rights and social justice (Schudson 1996: 20).

This highly civic activism is not the product of disassociated individuals mobilized by direct mailings or glib leaders. It draws instead on myriad small-scale groups different in kind from Putnam's preferred intermediary organizations but most certainly involving face-to-face interpersonal interaction and oppositional public spheres, as well as more generalized forms of communication. In other words, the forms of association out of which mass mobilizations emerge nowadays might not involve organized groups with official membership lists, but they can and often do involve discussion groups, consciousness-raising groups, self-help groups, and the like that are continuously cropping up and disappearing but surely are signs of the ability to connect and act in concert. Moreover, top-down and bottom-up forms of political mobilization are not incompatible.[14]

Why is all this dismissed or ignored? If one starts from the assumption that only a certain form of secondary association is the source of social capital, then obviously if it wanes, the conclusion of overall decline is unavoidable—it is an artifact of the method. But one cannot measure the vitality of civil society by comparing only one indicator (statistics on membership in secondary associations). The normative structure and identity of society have different manifestations in different contexts and epochs. The real question is why certain forms of civic activity appear when they do. Surely the "political opportunity structure" afforded by the state and "political society," legal developments, and the level and type of organization of economic life along with the nature of other dimensions of civil society would have to be analyzed, including, to be sure, the form and impact of the mass media, in order to arrive at an answer (Skocpol 1996: 23).

If one does not screen out "functional equivalents" for traditional forms of voluntary association at the outset, then the relationship of new media of communication to new forms of collective action and engagement could be analyzed along with their (alleged) potential to undermine old ones.

Indeed, if the analyst had the normative concept of the public sphere at his or her disposal, the "two-sidedness" of all mass media would be apparent. Generalized forms of communication, from the printed word to radio, television, and now cyberspace do not necessarily displace or degrade interpersonal communication, nor do they perforce "privatize" or block civic engagement.[15] They could even foster it by enabling the extension of communications and networks beyond local contexts.[16] The public media of communication are, along with law, an important mechanism by which the particular and the universal, the local, the national and international (meanings, norms, and issues) are interrelated. Even media that have little claim to be interactive, such as TV, might foster discussion about the content of what is broadcast despite the fact that reception may initially be private. Interactive media can of course do more. In short, there is no zero-sum relation between deliberation and mass media, between direct face-to-face discussion and indirect communication.

Moreover, generalized media of communication are themselves institutions subject to the norms of the public sphere and hence are open to critique if access to them or their functioning violates these norms. Indeed, one might note that today the autonomy and integrity of civil publics and personal communication are explicitly asserted and institutionalized as public norms, and they are better protected by law and courts than ever before. Certainly, compared with the 1950s, First Amendment protections for public, political, and personal expression are incomparably stronger, as are legal protections of personal autonomy rights. To focus only on aspects of the media that privatize and trivialize, and to conclude that the amount of time spent with such media is both a sign and a cause of the erosion of social capital, is thus highly misleading.

I do not doubt that the old sorts of associations that fostered civicness for certain segments of the population are disappearing. Nor do I want to claim that functional equivalents are flourishing and that there is nothing to think about. Assuredly some social, economic, and structural changes have undermined the traditional shape of civil society and rendered some of the old avenues of participation and influence obsolete. We may well be in a political context now in which *institutional redesign* of various aspects of the political system is necessary to strengthen new sorts of civil sociality. It is not necessary to choose between an institutionalist and an associationalist path to the creation of social trust; these can be mutually interdependent and reinforcing. But where to look and what is to be done will only be obscured by backward-looking analyses focused on reviving old forms of association that may no longer be appropriate. Even more serious, such an approach plays into the hands of those who are far more concerned with pushing back the achievements of welfare states and reviving traditional and authoritarian forms of civil society than with its further democratization.

Strange Bedfellows: The Rhetoric of Decline and Suspect Agendas

The two groups that deploy the discourse of civil society most effectively are the Republican right, and the neocommunitarian movement associated with the journal *The Responsive Community*.[17] Both define civil society in terms of traditional forms of voluntary association, and both lament their decline. Unlike Putnam and his associates however, the former explicitly target the welfare state, and the latter blame the rise of an amoral culture of expressive (and secular) individualism and a legalistic focus on individual rights for the alleged disintegration of social capital. I shall briefly comment on the first, as it is not particularly new, and then turn to the more nuanced analysis of the second.

The civil society discourse of the Republican right is straightforward: it argues, in Newt Gingrich's words, for "replacing the welfare state with an opportunity society" (see Skocpol 1996: 20–21). Market incentives, volunteerism, and localism are presented as the alternative to big government and the best way to revitalize initiative and independence in America. Centralized national "interventionist" government is blamed for both economic stagnation and social disintegration: it displaces voluntary association and creates dependence, undermining both individual initiative and the sense of personal and civic responsibility.

This discourse conflates the market and business with civil society, placing local self-help and charity in a zero-sum opposition to national public policy. It is hardly a project for a "reflexive continuation of the welfare state."[18] Proponents of this agenda do not seek to honor universalistic principles of social justice by means less obtrusive than top-down legal ordering, which might avoid the administrative penetration and fragmentation of social life, a real concern in my view. Instead the discourse functions as a thinly veiled cover for dismantling public services and redistributing wealth to the top—already a highly successful project in the United States. In the current context of corporate internationalization, globalization of labor markets, downsizing, outsourcing, capital flight, growing economic disparity, and the corresponding decline of secure or career-oriented jobs, not to mention the veritable disappearance of work in certain communities, this discourse is both disingenuous and destructive (Wilson 1996a, 1996b). It obscures the fact that when unregulated, the capitalist economy itself has corrosive effects on community, solidarity, and family that can scarcely be mitigated by volunteerism or moral exhortation.

The latest communitarian version of the discourse of civil society seems to be aware of this problem. As Michael Sandel (1996) puts it in his recent book, *Democracy's Discontent*, not only big government but also "big economy" undermine responsibility, virtue, and character. On closer inspection, however, it turns out that it is above all the misguided focus of public policy since the seventies on growth, redistribution, and rights without regard for moral concerns that has undermined civil society. This policy orientation is both effect and cause of a deeper disintegrative development: the triumph of a culture of expressive individualism, a corresponding fragmentation of social life, and moral impoverishment of our public discourse. The "procedural republic" with its neutrality toward substantive values and its rights orientation not only has missed the moral boat but actively contributes to moral decay.

The communitarians thus choose a *values* discourse predicated on the premise that only good people make good citizens. Their central thesis is that we are facing a potentially disastrous decline of good values in the United States. Accordingly, the emphasis is on reviving substantive ethical (and religious) discussion in the public sphere so as to arrive at a new consensus on core values (Sandel 1996: 21, 318–51). "Formative" public policies guided by an explicitly articulated, shared substantive conception of the good, oriented toward inculcating the proper values and shaping preferences in the right direction, are needed to reintroduce an ethic of responsibility, social solidarity, and virtue into the worldview of citizens. Communitarians assume that in order to be well integrated, society requires a "thick," extensive, nationally articulated substantive value consensus on a wide range of public *and* private issues. Strengthening civil society's institutions is the first priority of such "soulcraft," for these are the primary agents of character formation. The state and law are important, but instead of granting rights and entitlements they should encourage talk about virtue and ethics, institutionalize the right values, and foster strong civil institutions that will help integrate people into what will be, in effect, a refurbished American civil religion.

This assessment of the problem (and the proposed solution) is deeply misleading. It is based on four misconceptions. The first is the assumption that a thick, substantive, societywide value consensus is necessary for social integration in modern societies. The second is the equation of open, public pluralization of forms of life with social fragmentation and disintegration. Communitarians, third, also tend to construe the concern for self-realization and social responsibility as mutually exclusive. Fourth, and finally, they assume that the rights orientation of contemporary Americans undermines our sense of community, our moral impulses, and the democratic legitimacy of our political system.[19]

It is not difficult to articulate theoretically what's wrong with each of these notions. Ever since Durkheim (1933; see also Habermas 1984, 1987), social theorists have known that social integration in a modern differentiated society does not depend on a nationwide value consensus. Although a general acceptance of the abstract moral principles undergirding America's (and every) constitutional democracy *is* important, these are compatible with a variety of cultural systems of evaluation. They are, moreover, open to different institutionalizations, which vary with the prevailing conception of the cultural and ethical identity of the society.[20]

Contestation over past institutionalizations and struggles over cultural hegemony—over the power to name, signify, and interpret norms and national identity—are not necessarily signs of social disintegration or moral decay. Instead, open, public, even conflictual pluralization and individuation of forms of life can be a response to change that has the potential to realize these principles in less exclusionary, less hierarchical ways. A relatively thin conception of national identity together with political principles that accommodate diversity and acknowledge the equal claim of everyone to participate and to live openly according to their evaluations could foster rather than undermine social inclusion and social solidarity.[21] Democratic affirmation of the right to do so could strengthen local and national community, as well as the principles of democratic citizenship.

The communitarian thesis of value decline and social fragmentation is neither self-evidently true nor politically innocent. Social contestation over institutionalized public values and cultural models *is* evidence that a once-hegemonic conception of the American way of life is being challenged and decentered. But to call this a sign of corruption is a rhetorical ploy that positions one particular set of values and identities as "the moral" and all others as deviant. In short, it conflates one conception of the good with the morally right.

The four misconceptions are thus, in my view, a political project aimed at retraditionalizing civil society, at homogenizing our social and cultural life, and at reimposing a particular conception of American national identity on our political and civil institutions, to which citizens would have to assimilate or risk stigma and exclusion. Under the guise of reviving republican civic virtue, neo-communitarian rhetoric effaces the elective affinity between the universalistic principles undergirding modern civil society and plurality (see Alexander, ch. 1 in this vol.). Let me turn to a concrete example, their analysis of "the" family, to make my point.

Although communitarians vary on whether the intermediary associations of civil society include primarily churches, neighborhood groups, and the usual list of locally based voluntary associations, or additionally unions and social movements, all agree that the family is *the* institutional core of a modern and civil society. Indeed, the family is now the most important "voluntary" association because it is the place where the capacity for collaborating in other secondary intermediary associations emerges. It is here that competence and character are first formed, solidarity and trust first experienced, values first learned. Only in well-functioning families do children develop the healthy self-confidence and independence of mind crucial to citizenship along with the civic virtues of cooperation, self-restraint, and concern for the common good (Glendon 1991: 115; Sandel 1996: 104–18; Galston 1991: 222; Galston 1995: 139–49; Whitehead 1992: 1–2; Elshtain and Buell 1991: 262–66; Struening 1996: 135–54). Of course, the other mediating institutions of civil society matter. But it is from the family that we first inherit social capital! Social connectedness and the ability to participate constructively in the other associations of civil society presuppose the health of this core institution. "Family values" and the values produced in the family are thus at the center of the communitarians' civil society discourse.

Needless to say, they also argue that the sort of family that imparts the virtues necessary to a vital civil society and a democratic polity has been in decline for the past thirty years. Why else would we need a family-values discourse? The well-known statistics on rising divorce rates, out-of-wedlock births, single-parent families, teen pregnancy, female-headed households, the postponement of marriage, the rising incidence of premarital sex, and so on are cited in all their works as evidence of an alarming moral decline and a dangerous unraveling of community (Glendon 1991: 133–34; Sandel, 1996: 112–15; Galston 1995: 140–41n. 1; Elshtain 1995: 3–8). Among the alleged consequences of these trends is the failure of children to learn the virtues that make for responsible, self-reliant, self-controlled, independent, productive, cooperative, and civically virtuous citizens. Apparently, only one family form can generate the proper values and social capital necessary to a vital civil society: the intact two-parent heterosexual nuclear family with children, based on a companionate marriage construed as a lifetime commitment of love, solidarity, fidelity, and responsibility. In short, the communitarians' family-values discourse places the blame for poverty, drug use, and civil privatism on cultural developments and on family composition rather than on structural factors in economics and politics. They have successfully shifted public policy debate away from asking how to ensure that all households can attain an adequate standard of living, health care, and housing toward how to fortify the two-parent family. This argument revives the American tradition of blaming poverty on the moral failings of the poor, especially women.[22]

But why has this family form along with the other institutions of civil society so drastically declined? Instead of pointing to the impact of new technologies, like Putnam, the communitarian movement blames a huge shift in cultural values. In short, we are reaping the bitter harvest of the permissive culture of the 1960s, Putnam's first "postcivic" generation. The rise of a new self-indulgent and irresponsible "expressive" individualism and the triumph of the "voluntarist" conception of the self are the chief culprits here.

Echoing the story told by Robert Bellah (1985) in *Habits of the Heart*, neo-communitarians insist that the focus on self-realization initiated by sixties radicals leads people to view intimate relationships and all other associations solely as contexts for self-fulfillment and hence as temporary or endlessly renegotiable (Galston 1992: 7; cf. Giddens 1992). An older American culture of individualism based on self-control and a willingness to assume responsibility for oneself, one's family, and one's community used to reinforce the citizen's sense of civicness. But this ascetic individualism has been replaced by an ideal that emphasizes personal happiness over all other concerns. This ideology undermines the capacity of individuals to exhibit civic virtue or social solidarity, both of which require commitment and self-restraint. Strong, inner-directed people striving for independence, yet sharing the same family values and work ethic, have given way to narcissists whose only value is their own self-fulfillment.

The new voluntarist conception of moral obligation fostered by contemporary liberal theory has also played its destructive part. Taking their cues from Michael Sandel's jeremiad against the liberal ideal of the "unencumbered self" and the "procedural republic," communitarians insist that a widespread contractualist conception of morality has weakened Americans' sense of obligation to family and local and national community. We are obligated to fulfill only those ends that we have chosen (Sandel 1996: 11–14). The image of the sovereign authentic self, recognizing obligations only if they are voluntarily assumed by the moral agent, misconstrues and erodes the moral fabric of that all-important community—the family—with important consequences for the rest of social and civic life. The thin consensus on procedural principles touted by liberal contractualists, which goes with the voluntarist conception of the self, is deemed insufficient for civic virtue, especially given our increasing diversity in ethnic, religious, and moral makeup. In short, it cannot provide the shared understandings necessary for a well-integrated polity.

It is to the development of liberal jurisprudence, however, that we must look for an explanation of how the cultural orientation of a relatively small minority became spread to the population at large. According to the communitarian analysis, the "rights revolution" begun in the 1950s and consolidated in the sixties and seventies is the culprit. The "legalization" of American society, the saturation of political discourse with "rights talk" began with the civil rights movement and accelerated when the Warren Court decided to vigorously exercise the power of judicial review as a means of protecting individual rights from state injustice (Glendon 1991: 1–30).

The tendency (instigated by lawyers) of collective actors to articulate social and political issues as rights-based claims fostered, and was in turn reinforced by, the vast expansion of the role of courts and judges in the political system. Legalistic rights talk, with its emphasis on personal liberty and entitlement, has had a "colonizing effect" on our moral intuitions and discourses.[23] By turning almost every political issue and passing desire into a claim for rights, the ever-expanding process of legalization *generalized* egoism and undermined alternative moral discourses along with the institutions in which these are generated (Glendon 1991: 4–5, 77). It also allegedly undermined common values and exacerbated tendencies toward fragmentation by encouraging entitlement claims and identity politics on behalf of particularistic groups who aggressively assert their interests with no thought to the common good.[24] Post-1950s liberal jurisprudence, in short, brought the expressivist conception of the self along with a contractualist legalistic model of obligation and association to the population at large.

Small wonder that the rights revolution is considered most destructive in the domain of "intimate association." The constitutionalization of key aspects of family law that began in the 1960s, in particular the discovery of "fundamental" *individual* privacy rights in this domain, has allegedly had deleterious effects on the associational life of civil society because it has privileged individualistic over community values.[25] It transposes contractualist assumptions from the market to spheres of life with which they are incompatible. The rights revolution in family law thus introduced a destructive atomization and an adversarial relationship into otherwise solid family communities, pitting one member's rights against another's and undermining the bases of social trust and cohesion. This disruption has undermined social capital by destroying the ability to conceive oneself as responsible for the effect of one's actions on others or as concerned with the well-being of community members.

Given this diagnosis of American civil society's decline, the solution is obvious: replacement of the rights-oriented with a responsibility-based family and social policy, and replacement of entitlement talk with a discourse of duty in the political and legal public spheres. Alongside a good deal of moral exhortation, communitarian journals are filled with authoritarian policy proposals geared toward reinforcing the two-parent family; discouraging divorce, out-of-wedlock sex, and (unmarried!) teen pregnancy; and undoing various allegedly destructive, individualizing rights in the domain of intimate association. The discourse of reinvigorating the most important of civil associations, the family, is thus linked to a clear, socially authoritarian project of retraditionalization and uniformity.

It is not hard to see who the targets of this discourse are nor to challenge some of the empirical claims and their meaning. For example, although it is true that Americans have a high divorce rate, 79% of households include a married couple according to the 1990 census, down undramatically from 82.5% a decade earlier (Morone 1996: 37).[26] Marriage has hardly become a minority lifestyle.[27]

The figures on marriage, divorce, single-parenthood, and sexual standards do indicate ethical change, but this change cannot be understood as the demise of the family. Only one particular family form is losing ground: the 1950s model of the patriarchal nuclear family composed of a heterosexual couple married for life—a male breadwinner, a female homemaker, and children—and this for complex economic as well as cultural and political reasons.[28] Indeed, what has disintegrated is not the family but the consensus on what a proper family is, on what form a good intimate relationship must take, and, more precisely, about the nature of women's (and men's) roles and gender/sexual identity.[29]

Pluralization of forms of intimacy, however, is not the same as the disintegration of family values. There *is* conflict and uncertainty over how best to realize the general values appropriate to the domain of intimacy: love, care, loyalty, mutuality, trust, reciprocity. Decoupling of these from one ethical model of intimate relations means that they may be realized in a variety of ways. Communitarian rhetoric steers us away from reflection on these important issues by miscasting the dissolution of the cultural hegemony of one form of intimate life as a phenomena of moral decline, positioning one particular ethical model as the moral norm against which every other form appears as morally suspect.

This rhetoric must be understood for what it is: a political intervention in the battle between those who insist that there is only one right way (to be backed up by law) to conduct intimate relations and those who argue that a plurality of types of intimate association can realize the relevant values as long as they do not violate the moral principles that regulate interaction generally.

The more general theoretical claim that the expansion of individual rights in the domain of intimate association undermines community and mutual responsibility is also profoundly misleading, politically motivated, and based on flawed premises. The relevant personal rights protect individuals if and when the solidarity of the love community breaks down, against the unjust use of power and force by the stronger party—they are not the cause of the breakdown. Such rights do not pretend to substitute for the ethical forms of love and commitment that are "beyond justice." They do, however, protect a relationship of respect that the law will enforce when all else fails. Moreover, equal rights for women and men in the domain of intimacy foster relations of reciprocity by mitigating differences in power and opportunity. Protecting against the terrible effects of unwarranted trust, they facilitate warranted trust.

The criminalization of spousal violence and marital rape, decisional autonomy regarding sexual and reproductive decisions for women, equal voice over familial affairs, equal access to marital property, legal regulation of family support, egalitarian exit options when the ethical substance of the family dissolves, and the like do not turn marriage into a contractual economic exchange relationship. But legalization of this sort does bring moral principles of justice to bear on intimate relations, by acknowledging the individuality, legal standing, personal autonomy, and claims to self-realization of all adult family members. It thereby provides the minimal basis for a companionate marriage to live up to its own egalitarian ideal.

Indeed the companionate ideal of the family construed as a voluntary association based on love, mutuality, reciprocity, esteem, and care among members presupposes, under contemporary conditions, the norm of equality and the value of happiness in intimate relations. It *is* easier to ensure the *stability* of marriage when one member of the couple is subordinate and dependent without any meaningful exit option. But modern companionate marriage is not supposed to rest on such things.

The communitarian wants it both ways: the family is somehow to be *in* but not *of* civil society. When cast as the most important voluntary association mediating between the individual and the state, the family must be located within and not, as Hegel had it, outside of civil society in the realm of nature. This means that the principles of justice must also apply to it. But, like Hegel (Knox 1967: 112), the communitarian discourse also constructs the family as based on a "contract to transcend contract"—as a natural association and an affective community innocent of the conflicts of self-interest, power dynamics, and egoism characteristic of contractual voluntary relations generally. Contractual relations and rights allegedly destroy this community. The family is thus "beyond justice," not subject to the principles or risks of civil society.

The trick is to pretend that full legal standing and protections for intimate associates, and the ability consensually to order the terms of one's intimate association, turns families into contractual business relationships with no ethical content beyond the rights of its members. By implication we must return to the old status understanding of the family with its internal hierarchies.

The choice, however, is not between status and contract, for as any serious student of civil society knows, most forms of civil association elude this dichotomy.[30] Moreover, the very idea of voluntary association entails the free creation, entry, and maintenance of the group because of the solidarity, support, recognition, or happiness it affords its members. Of course, responsibilities and duties arise in all such association. It is ludicrous to allege that rights (especially those according equal status to both genders) undermine responsibilities because every right and every relationship carries with it reciprocal duties.[31] There is no reason why the ethical content that is "beyond justice" cannot inform such associations along with the principles of justice. Nor is there any reason to revive the Kantian dichotomy between duty and happiness, as if the only choice we have regarding failed intimate relationships is "moral" renunciation (self-denial of a life of love and happiness) or "immoral" narcissism. To trot out "the best interests of the child" as an argument for restricting rights in the domain of intimacy is utterly polemical and counterproductive.

I do not want to be misunderstood. There has been real and radical change in the domain of intimacy over the past three decades, and families *are* under enormous stress today. The application of the ideal of self-realization to this domain *is* new, but it does not indicate immoral egoism or the decline of values. Instead, it heightens expectations for intimate relations (especially for marriage and family) and an equalization of these between the genders. Self-actualization, trust, and being there for others are not opposites, as the simplistic dichotomous thinking revived in communitarian rhetoric implies—they belong together.

The problems and insecurities plaguing intimate among other forms of associational life today are not due to cultural (or ethnic) diversity, value dissensus, vice, or the pluralization of family forms. Institutional change, economic uncertainty, and dislocation on the one side, and greater gender equality, expanded mobility, and opportunities on the other, render all associational forms looser and more fragile. These raise many complex theoretical and legal issues. How to regulate intimate associations once the old "consensus" on "the" patriarchal nuclear family has broken down, and on what legal paradigm, is one of them.

I cannot address these questions here, but I can say that moralizing, backward-looking rhetoric or policy proposals do not help. One should beware of reviving a bad old American tradition of sowing moral panic and scapegoating relatively powerless groups in times of economic stress and social change. The very rights that constitute civil society and protect plurality and civic and personal autonomy, and that allow voluntary associations including intimate ones to emerge, may be sacrificed to an authoritarian cultural populism in the name of virtue and social solidarity. The discourse of declining family values and disintegration of civil society diverts us from the real issues by constructing our policy problems as moral meltdowns, making them more difficult to address.[32]

CONCLUSION

What connection does this sort of jeremiad, or the discourse of the Republican right, have to do with Robert Putnam's approach to civil society? One cannot accuse him of advocating the demise of the welfare state or blaming the expansion of civil rights and declining personal morals for social decapitalization.

Indeed, in *Making Democracy Work* the family was dismissed as a primitive substitute for social capital, not a source of it. Strong kinship ties were actually found to hinder strong civic traditions and to block the generalization of social trust. But there is a revealing shift in Putnam's views on the family in the texts where the discourse of decline dominates. In "Bowling Alone," we are suddenly told that "the most fundamental form of social capital is the family"

(1995a: 50). We are also told that the "massive evidence" of loosened family bonds "may help to explain" the theme of social decapitalization (1995b: 73). By the time he wrote "Strange Disappearance," Putnam was citing the increase in divorce rates, single-parent families, teen pregnancies, and the like as "unequivocal" evidence of family decline (1996: 41). His new claim is that successful marriage is statistically associated with greater social trust and civic engagement! Although not *the* main cause of social decapitalization, the "disintegration of the family" is now deemed to be an important accessory to the crime.[33]

This remains so far a minor strain in Putnam's work, but it derives from an analytic approach that offers no conceptual counterweight to the main theoretical claim of conservative communitarians, who, as we have seen, have already appropriated his core concept, social capital. Because law, rights, and the public sphere play no theoretical role in his analysis, Putnam has no conceptual means to counter the thesis that legalization itself—in particular, the expansion of personal individual rights and entitlement claims, actually causes the disintegration of civil society and civic capacities.[34] The step from here to the moralizing values discourse of social conservatives is not a large one, but it takes us further and further away from the real issues that a civil society discourse can and should raise.

I have argued in this paper that a narrow conception of civil society obscures and miscasts important problems, not that these problems do not exist. There is no question that the welfare-state paradigm, corresponding forms of legalization, and established modes of civic engagement, political participation, and social integration are all in crisis today. However, the dichotomous thinking that counterposes civil society to the state, duties to rights, custom to code, informal to formal sociation (as the source of trust), and status to contract lead to an overhasty conclusion of social decapitalization and a set of false policy choices.

If we had a richer concept of civil society and a more abstract understanding of its cultural presuppositions, the discovery of the erosion of one type of civic institution would not have to lead to a claim of general civic decline. Given different methods, functional equivalents for older forms of associationalism could become visible, along with new types of civic action targeting an altered environment of civil, economic, and political institutions. The question of whether the political public spheres including the party and electoral systems are sufficiently receptive to new forms of civic engagement of citizens aimed at influencing them could then be addressed. This in turn could point to consideration of the role of government in encouraging or discouraging civic participation.[35] It could also direct attention to the institutional structure of the state and its impact on and receptivity to organizational initiatives in civil society. Last, but hardly least, there would be room to consider the role of law and rights not only in establishing and protecting civil society but also in facilitating civil initiatives and generalizing social solidarity and confidence.

Such considerations do not replace a societalist analysis with a state-oriented one. Rather, if we had a rich conception of civil society that included the civil public sphere, we could fruitfully consider the reciprocal lines of influence among it, the state, and the economy. This perspective could point us to an important range of questions begging for serious research. For example, what is an optimal relation (or division of labor) among the state, civil society, and the market under contemporary conditions? What institutional reforms or redesigns are necessary to accomplish the material goals of the welfare-state-destroying incentives for individual and group initiative? How would the principle of subsidiarity apply when issues of efficiency, democratic values, social justice, and social autonomy are raised? What type of federalism can encourage democratic participation and citizen initiative without feeding into parochialism and local intolerance?

If the neocommunitarian claim that expansion of individual personal rights and entitlements destroys the ethical content of civil associations is unconvincing, excessive reliance on courts and judicial review to discover fundamental personal rights nevertheless does strain democratic legitimacy. What legal paradigm could guarantee the basic rights of civil society without sacrificing public to private autonomy? What conception of constitutionalism could protect the plurality of forms of life within civil society from intolerant majorities without privatizing or reifying "difference" (see Alexander and Smelser, ch. 1 in this vol.)? Are there ways to institutionalize civil and political publics so as to lessen tension between democracy and rights, between public and personal freedom? Indeed, how can the media of communication, which are crucial to the generalization of norms of reciprocity, be more receptive to civil input without allowing the power of money to control the agenda of debate and to silence others? And last, what effect do structural factors such as the flight of real capital have on the vitality of civil institutions? (see Tarrow 1996: 396). To address these questions we must drop the rhetoric of moral and civic decline.

NOTES

1. It also protected against "segmental pluralism"—the bad kind of groupness that precludes cooperation across "primordial" or ideological identities. But these pluralists were all partisans of the welfare state and of rights despite their critique of mass society. The hostility of the model to movements was aimed at "totalitarian" forms of collective action. This was thus quite different from the later neoconservative discourse of "ungovernability" that emerged in the 1970s. On the other hand, the pluralist model was wed to what one can call the assimilitationist mode of incorportation of groups into civil society and the polity: tolerance of difference was based on the expectation that people confined their group identities (religion, ethnos, sexuality, racial cultures, etc.) to the private sphere—these were to be abstracted away from in public life. Assimilation of formerly excluded and newly arrived groups involved Americanization in public and the privatization of difference. This model has been under attack since the 1970s. The discourse of diversity, multiculturalism, and the current contestation over the meaning of civil society must be understood on this terrain.

2. The main figures of the neocommunitarian movement are Amitai Etzioni, a professor of sociology at George Washington University; William Galston, a political philosopher and former professor at the University of Maryland, now domestic policy advisor to President Clinton; Maryann Glendon, a Harvard law professor; and Michael Sandel, a Harvard professor of political science. Their journal, edited by Etzioni, *The Responsive Community: Rights and Responsibilities*, sees itself as the voice of a new movement for communitarian values.

3. Law has a foot in both civil society and the state. It institutionalizes generalized norms of the public sphere that constrain state (as well as individual) action. It is also the carrier of state (or class) imperatives. The basic rights established in constitutional liberal democracies construct the terrain of civil society on which social actors clash over cultural evaluations and interpretations of norms, identities, modes of inclusion/exclusion, and the like, but states also construct privileged or stigmatized group identities through legalization and classification according to their own imperatives or the imperatives of powerful private actors. Thus legalization can be highly ambiguous. On the liberal paradigm of civil society, law must be formal, general, abstract, and neutral. Legal formalism allegedly protects against privilege and bias. The defenders of the liberal paradigm of law and the liberal conception of civil society are thus blind to the role of private power in undermining the worth of liberty of those formally entitled to have rights.

4. There are, of course, differentiated and institutionalized civil and political publics, weak and strong. But this way of conceptualizing the public sphere precludes granting legitimacy to any group or institution claiming to embody or represent the public, endowed with the authority to define what is a matter of public concern. Moreover, the line between public and private, along with the question of who is to be included in the public, cannot be decided once and for all.

5. Putnam knows that all networks and associations mix the horizontal and the vertical but insists nonetheless that the basic contrast between horizontal and vertical linkages, between weblike and maypolelike networks, is reasonably clear. But isn't it possible for people to belong to both sorts of organizations? Does Putnam insist on full congruence between civil and political institutions? For a critique of this idea see Rosenblum 1994: 67–97.

6. I use the word *confidence* advisedly. What is at stake is analytically distinct from interpersonal trust, that is, the trust of concrete individuals. Confidence that the administration of justice will be impartial, or that the legislative process is fair, responsive, and representative rests on the shared understanding that the principles of impartiality, fairness, equal concern and respect, and so forth, have been institutionalized as norms and that these are internalized by the institutional actors as well as by those subject to these institutions. It is thus possible to lose trust in a particular lawmaker or judge without losing confidence in the legal system or the legislative process as a whole. Their legitimacy rests on the belief that generally they function in a manner appropriate to their institutionalized norms.

7. See also Putnam 1993: 171–74.

8. Portes and Landolt (1996) have stressed the circularity of the argument, while Tarrow (1996) points to the confusion of the indicators with the causes of civicness. Levi (1996) has noted the sloppiness of the definitions, which make it almost impossible to differentiate among social capital, interpersonal trust, and generalized reciprocity, as well as the absence of a definition of trust in Putnam's work. Skocpol (1996) notes the one-sidedness of the society-centered analysis to the neglect of other important actors, most notably government, and factors such as the structure and nature of the state. Although I

agree with these criticisms, we must beware of overcorrecting here. The society-centered analysis is itself a corrective to one-sided, state-centered approaches. What we need is a model broad enough to capture both dimensions.

9. Coleman (1990) shows that under the assumption of rational action, norms can arise, but he gives no argument about the emergence of norms in general. Nor does he address the deeper issue of how values (standards used to evaluate evaluative standards) emerge. I don't believe this can be answered within a rational-choice framework. Putnam's work suffers from the same deficiency.

10. As Claus Offe (1996: 23) recently put it in a brilliant analytical paper on trust, democratic citizens build "generalized" trust on the basis of what they know about institutions and their ability to orient action, not on the basis of what they know about political elites (whom they in fact do not know).

11. Putnam (1996: 35–36) indicates an erosion of roughly 25–50% of membership over the last three decades. See also Putnam 1995a: 67–70.

12. It is bizarre to present the adult generation in the 1950s as the paragon of civicness or the 1950s and early 1960s as an era of the generalized social trust that makes democracy work. This period was the heyday of McCarthyism (hardly noteworthy for generalized trust), institutionalized racial segregation, exclusion of women from a wide range of economic and political institutions and associations (hardly a model of cross-cutting plurality), a pervasive ideological (and economic) movement to push women out of the labor force and into the housewife role (something that did not exactly foster egalitarian gender norms or undermine familism).

Civil privatism and authoritarian cultural and social conservativism would seem a more apt characterization of that period than civic virtue. Indeed, if voluntary association was alive and well in the fifties, this is proof that it does not suffice to render a political culture civic or to generate generalized trust or active egalitarian participation in public life. Moreover, I suspect that economic expansion and the impact of the New Deal had a good deal more to do with the effectiveness of government than the vitality of the Elks Club.

13. Tarrow (1994) and others have argued that social movements can produce lasting effects on political culture by legitimating new forms of collective action and by establishing a permanent place for issues on the public agenda that remain alive even in a general context of demobilization. See also Cohen 1985. For an interesting albeit controversial recent discussion of the relation between movements and state forms see Dryzek 1996.

14. Nor are direct and more mediated forms of communication. Ties to common leaders, texts, symbols, and ideals can inform and foster horizontal styles of association and interpersonal interaction by providing points of reference for discussion and for mobilization when the time comes. Skocpol (1996: 25) points to the Christian Coalition as a successful example of a secondary association that melds top-down and bottom-up styles of political mobilization.

15. Pippa Norris (1996) convincingly shows that the data do not permit one to claim that civic and political disengagement vary unambiguously and positively with the sheer amount of TV that one watches. What matters more is the content of what one watches. Given the diversity of channels, programs and choices, from *Nightline*, *60 Minutes*, *CNN World News*, *NPR*, *Meet the Press*, and C-Span to the information available now on the Internet, it might even be the case that Americans as a whole are better informed about national and international issues then ever before.

16. See Norris 1996: 475–76. The problem of disentangling the direction of causality that plagues all cross-sectional survey analysis is not resolved regardless of how one comes down on this issue. It is not clear whether those that are already actively involved in public life turn to the news networks for more information or whether tuning into TV news or reading about public affairs encourages people to become more active in public affairs and civic life. Either way, the charge that television is the root cause of the lack of trust in American democracy is unproven and implausible.

17. My remarks here regarding neocommunitarians reference primarily the works of communitarians associated with A. Etzioni's journal, *The Responsive Community*. For a representative sampling of their work see Etzioni 1995. I do not address the far more complex theoretical and political positions of theorists like M. Walzer and Charles Taylor, who are not part of this movement although they are labeled communitarians.

18. See Cohen and Arato 1992: 11–15, 468–91 for a critique of neoconservative critiques of the welfare state and for a discussion of its reflexive continuation.

19. For two critiques see Cohen 1992: 66–98 and McClain 1994.

20. On the general abstract principles informing every constitutional democracy see Habermas 1996: 82–132.

21. Just how thick or thin a national consensus or identity is necessary is a matter of heated debate. Among those who claim a thin consensus suffices are Rawls (1993) and Habermas (1995: 255–82). See Hollinger 1995 and Lind 1995 for arguments for a thick national identity in the United States.

22. This discourse has not gone unchallenged. Many analysts have questioned the claim that it is the wrong family composition or divorce that causes poverty and dysfunctionality. See Stacey 1994: 119–22; Skolnick and Rosencrantz 1994: 59–65; and Young 1995: 536–42. Others (Morone 1996) have noted that the halcyon days of stable marriage featured dependent women without significant career options and thus argue that the low divorce rates of the past do not necessarily reflect an earlier generation's greater committment to family, and virtue, but rather women's lack of the means and rights to mobililty and independence.

23. According to Mary Ann Glendon (1991: 4), this introduced an entirely new focus to constitutional law. Prior to that time, the principal emphasis of constitution jurisprudence was not on personal liberty as such but on the division of authority between the states and the federal government and the allocation of powers among the branches of the central government. "Today the bulk of the Court's constitutional work involves claims that individual rights have been violated."

24. What the communitarians have in mind is affirmative action demanded not only by African Americans but by a variety of ethnoracial and "special interest" groups all in the name of redressing past discrimination and/or protecting the value of diversity. These claims raise thorny issues that I cannot address here. One thing is clear, however: incantations about civic virtue and common values will redress neither the wrongs and injustices caused by discrimination nor the harms caused by misrecognition.

25. The Supreme Court privacy decisions from *Griswold v. Connecticut*, to *Eisenstadt v. Baird*, to *Roe v. Wade*, down to *Casey v. Pennsylvania* are at issue here. See Sandel 1996: 94–119 for a recent restatement of this position. See also Cohen 1992a for a discussion and critique of these arguments.

26. People divorce and then remarry, creating "blended families" with children from more than one marriage, ex-spouses, stepparents, half-siblings, and several sets of grandparents (Cherlin 1992).

27. Divorce rates have not risen since the late 1970s. Moreover, the claim of a general decline of moral values with the weakening of religiosity is also unconvincing. According to recent surveys, 95% of Americans profess a faith in God, 87% say adultery is "always wrong," and 75% belong to a church. Church attendance has risen as much as 30% in the past two decades. Not only are these the highest figures in the Western world, they indicate no decline in the United States over time (Morone 1996: 31–32). But even if divorce rates are high and even if marriage were to decline, one should avoid identifying marriage with family.

28. One of the most important of these is the entry of women, and especially young mothers into the labor force.

29. The demographic data refer to the decentering of marriage vis-à-vis intimacy. Functions and events that were once fused on the old hegemonic model of the nuclear family—marriage, domesticity, parenthood, child rearing, love, sex—have become disaggregated and recombined in a variety of types of intimate and kin relationships (see F. F. Furstenberg, Jr. 1995: 245–57 and ch. 7 in this vol.). Furstenberg sums up the situation by stating that marriage is no longer the master event that orchestrates the onset of sexual relations, parenthood, departure from the home, or even the establishment of a household.

30. Legal marriage and legally acknowledged family forms involve a range of legally acknowledged statuses with attendant rights and duties: husband, wife, father, mother, kin, grandparent, and so forth.

31. See McClain 1994 for an excellent critique.

32. I am paraphrasing Morone 1996: 36–37. The quality of intimate relationships and not their particular structure is what matters. Instead of a moralizing discourse that stigmatizes a variety of forms of intimacy outside "traditional" marriage, including divorce, one should be thinking about the ethical quality of relationships (are they reciprocal, egalitarian, fair, solid, caring, fulfilling, just) and how to help ease the demands and strains on working parents, married or single. On this, see Seidman in this volume.

33. If we combine these claims with the strong relationship noted between the decline in traditional (gender segregated) associational memberships like the PTA that relied heavily on the volunteer work of housewives and the increase in working mothers since the 1960s, a very conservative message does seem to be implied in the recent texts. It is hard to avoid the impression that despite disclaimers, the changing role of women plays a large role in the apparent decline of civicness. See Levi 1996: 52.

34. Given his too narrow conception of the sources of social trust (face-to-face relationships), he has no other place to turn for an explanation of the apparent "decline" of social capital. The TV explanation on its own is simply too weak—hence the tendency to place more and more weight on the family.

35. For an argument that governmental structures greatly affect civil society's capacities, see Dryzek 1996.

References

Almond, Gabriel, and Sidney Verba. 1963. *The Civic Culture: Political Attitudes and Democracy in Five Nations*. Princeton, N.J.: Princeton University Press.

Bellah, Robert N., Richard Madsen, William M. Sullivan, Ann Swidler, and Steven M. Tipton. 1985. *Habits of the Heart: Individualism and Commitment in American Life*. Berkeley: University of California Press.

Banfield, Edward. 1958. *The Moral Basis of a Backward Society.* Chicago: The Free Press.

Bradley, Bill. 1995. "America's Challenge: Revitalizing Our National Community." *National Civil Review* 84 (2): 94.

Brady, Henry E., Kay L. Schlozman, and Sidney Verba. 1995. *Voice and Equality.* Cambridge: Harvard University Press.

Calhoun, Craig. 1992. *Habermas and the Public Sphere.* Cambridge: MIT Press.

Cherlin, Andrew J. 1992. *Marriage, Divorce, Remarriage.* Cambridge: Harvard University Press.

Cohen, Jean L. 1982. *Class and Civil Society: The Limits of Marxian Critical Theory.* Amherst: University of Massachusetts Press.

———. 1985. "Strategy or Identity: New Theoretical Paradigms and Contemporary Social Movements." *Social Research* 52 (4): 663–716.

———. 1992. "Redescribing Privacy: Identity, Difference, and the Abortion Controversy." *Columbia Journal of Gender and Law* 3 (1): 43–118.

Cohen, Jean L., and Andrew Arato. 1992. *Civil Society and Political Theory.* Cambridge: MIT Press.

Coleman, James. 1990. *Foundations of Social Theory.* Cambridge: Harvard University Press.

Durkheim, Emile. 1933. *The Division of Labor in Society.* New York: Macmillan.

———. 1958. *Professional Ethics and Civic Morals.* Glencoe, Ill.: The Free Press.

Dryzek, John. 1996. "Political Inclusion and the Dynamics of Democratization." *American Political Science Review* 90 (Sept.): 475–88.

Elshtain, Jean. 1995. *Democracy on Trial.* New York: Basic Books.

Elshtain, Jean-Bethke, and John Buell. 1991. "Families in Trouble." *Dissent* 38 (2): 262–66.

Etzioni, Amitai, ed. 1995. *Rights and the Common Good: The Communitarian Perspective.* New York: St. Martin's Press.

Furstenberg, F. F., Jr. 1995. "Family Change and the Welfare of Children: What Do We Know and What Can We Do About It?" Pp. 245–57 in *Gender and Family Change in Industrialized Countries,* edited by A. M. Jensen and K. O. Mason. Oxford: Clarendon Press.

Galston, William. 1991. *Liberal Purposes.* New York: Cambridge University Press.

———. 1992. "New Familism, New Politics." *Family Affairs* 5: 1–2.

———. 1995. "A Liberal-Democratic Case for the Two-Parent Family." Pp. 139–49 in *Rights and the Common Good,* edited by Amitai Etzioni. New York: St. Martin's Press.

Giddens, Anthony. 1992. *The Transformation of Intimacy.* California: Stanford University Press.

Glendon, Mary Ann. 1991. *Rights Talk.* New York: Free Press.

Habermas, Jurgen. 1984, 1987. *The Theory of Communicative Action. Vols. 1 and 2.* Boston: Beacon.

———. 1989. *The Structural Transformation of the Public Sphere.* Cambridge: MIT Press.

———. 1995. "Citizenship and National Identity." *Theorizing Citizenship.* New York: SUNY Press.

———. 1996. *Between Facts and Norms.* Cambridge: MIT Press.

Hirschman, Albert. 1982. *Shifting Involvements.* Princeton, N.J.: Princeton University Press.

Hollinger, David. 1995. *Postethnic America.* New York: Basic Books.

Knox, T. M., trans. 1967. *Hegel's Philosophy of Right.* New York: Oxford University Press.

Levi, Margaret. 1996. "Social and Unsocial Capital: A Review Essay of Robert Putnam's *Making Democracy Work.*" *Politics and Society* 24 (1): 45–55.

Lind, Michael. 1995. *The Next American Nation.* New York: Free Press.

McClain, Linda C. 1994. "Rights and Irresponsibilities." *Duke Law Journal* 43: 989–1037.

Melucci, Alberto. 1980. "The New Social Movements: A Theoretical Approach." *Social Science Information* 19.

————. 1985. "The Symbolic Challenge of Contemporary Movements." *Social Research* 52 (4): 789–816.

Morone, James A. 1996. "The Corrosive Politics of Virtue." *American Prospect* 26 (May/June): 30–39.

Norris, Pippa. 1996. "Does Television Erode Social Capital? A Reply to Putnam." *Political Science and Politics* 29 (3): 476–79.

Offe, Claus. 1985. "New Social Movements Challenging the Boundaries of Institutional Politics." *Social Research* 52 (4): 817–69.

————. 1996. "Trust and Knowledge, Rules and Decisions: Exploring a Difficult Conceptual Terrain." Paper delivered at "Democracy and Trust" conference at George Washington University, Washington, D.C. Nov. 7–9.

Portes, Alejandro, and Patricia Landolt. 1996. "The Downside of Social Capital." *American Prospect* 26 (May/June): 18–21.

Putnam, Robert. 1993. *Making Democracy Work.* Princeton, N.J.: Princeton University Press.

————. 1995a. "Bowling Alone: America's Declining Social Capital." *Journal of Democracy* 6 (1): 65–78.

————. 1995b. "Bowling Alone Revisited." *The Responsive Community* 5 (2).

————. 1996. "The Strange Disappearance of Civic America." *American Prospect* 24 (winter): 34–48.

Rawls, John. 1993. *Political Liberalism.* New York: Columbia University Press.

Rosenblum, Nancy. 1994. "Democratic Character and Community: The Logic of Congruence?" *Journal of Political Philosophy* 2: 1.

Sandel, Michael. 1996. *Democracy's Discontent.* Cambridge: Harvard University Press.

Schudson, M. 1996. "What If Civil Life Didn't Die?" *American Prospect* 25:17–20.

Skocpol, Theda. 1996. "Unravelling from Above." *American Prospect* 25 (March/April): 20–25.

Skolnick, Arlene, and Stanley Rosencrantz. 1994. "The New Crusade for the Old Family." *American Prospect* 18: 59–65.

Stacey, Judith. 1994. "The New Family Values Crusaders." *Nation* 259 (4): 119–22.

Struening, Karen. 1996. "Feminist Challenges to the New Familism: Lifestyle Experimentation and the Freedom of Intimate Association." *Hypatia* 11: 1.

Tarrow, Sidney. 1994. *Power in Movement: Social Movements, Collective Action, and Politics.* New York: Cambridge University Press.

————. 1996. "Making Social Science Work across Space and Time: A Critical Reflection on Robert Putnam's *Making Democracy Work.*" *American Political Science Review* 90 (2): 389–97.

Tocqueville, Alexis de. 1969. *Democracy in America.* Edited by J. P. Mayer, translated by George Lawrence. Garden City, N.Y.: Anchor Books.

Touraine, Alain. 1981. *The Voice and the Eye.* New York: Cambridge University Press.

Urbinati, Nadia. 1993. "The Art of Tolerance." *Dissent* (fall): 572–73.

Warren, Mark. 1996. "What Should We Expect from More Democracy? Radically Democratic Responses to Politics." *Political Theory* 24 (2): 241–70.

Wilson, William Julius. 1996a. *When Work Disappears: The World of the New Urban Poor.* New York: Knopf.

————. 1996b. "When Work Disappears." *New York Times Magazine*, 18 August, 28–52.

Whitehead, Barbara Dafor. 1992. "A New Familism?" *Family Affairs* 5: 1–2.

Young, Iris. 1995. "Mothers, Citizenship, and Independence: A Critique of Pure Family Values." *Ethics* 105 (3): 536–42.

CHAPTER FOURTEEN

Civil Society and the Politics of Identity and Difference in a Global Context*

SEYLA BENHABIB

THE STRANGE MULTIPLICITIES OF OUR TIMES

THE TERM *civil society*, before it got picked up by contemporary American social commentary, was used by dissidents in Eastern Europe who reflected on non-state-centered forms of social protest and mobilization. A second, and equally significant, set of voices included those new social movements that saw civil society as their chosen terrain of mobilization (Cohen and Arato 1993). The contemporary American discourse of civil society is, by contrast, defensive about social transformation, nostalgic in its vision of the social order, and hostile toward the redistributionist state.

In this contribution I want to move the discourse of civil society beyond the jeremiads of American decline that have recently crowded the field, back to its origins in European social theory and comparative politics. I shall analyze the dilemmas of contemporary identity/difference politics and, in particular, explore how the methodological dualism of the "essentialism"/"constructivism" pair plays itself out in these various movements. My conclusion is humble: I plead for sociological skepticism vis-à-vis group-differentiated rights claims. The normative haste with which political philosophers have responded to identity/difference politics has prevented us from analyzing the social dynamics of such politics of recognition. The result has been, more often than not, a premature reification of group identities rather than a critical interrogation of their limits as well as illusions.

The various political struggles militating for the recognition of identities, or the reassertion of differences, can be distinguished into three types.

First, the term *politics of identity* initially emerged from new social movements in the late 1970s and early 1980s in western capitalist democracies.

* This article was prepared during my stay as a senior research fellow at the Institut fuer die Wissenschaften vom Menschen in Vienna, Austria, from July 1 to December 31, 1996. I would like to acknowledge the generous support of the Institute for this period. Many thanks also to Sayres S. Rudy and Christoph Sachse for discussions and comments on earlier versions of this paper during my stay in Vienna. Comments and criticisms by Jean L. Cohen, Jeffrey Alexander, David Hollinger, Neil Smelser, and Stephen Warner, made during the Stanford conference, pushed my own thinking on these issues further. Some portions of this contribution have appeared in the *Proceedings of the 1996 Macalaster International Roundtable* (Spring 1997, Macalaster College, Minnesota).

These movements (for women's rights, ecology, ethnic and linguistic autonomy, or gay and lesbian rights) were seen as expressions of postmaterialist values (Inglehart 1990), and were interpreted as signaling a shift from issues of distribution to a concern with the "grammar" of forms of life (Habermas 1981, 1984). The nature of political concerns was transformed. The struggles over wealth, political position, and access that had dominated bourgeois and working-class politics throughout the nineteenth and the first half of the twentieth centuries were replaced by struggles over abortion and gay rights, ecology and the consequence of new medical technologies, and the politics of racial, linguistic, and ethnic pride (colloquially referred to in the United States as the Rainbow Coalition).

These new issues were represented by novel groups of political actors: loosely coalesced groups of activist women, people of color, gay men and women, and concerned citizens militated for gender and ecological rights, against big science and technology, and for the recognition of language rights. There was a shift from party to movement politics. The phrase "strategy or identity" aptly captured this transformation in the politics of western capitalist democracies (Cohen 1985).

Second, although social movement politics rarely question the constitutional framework and identity boundaries of the body politic in western capitalist democracies, cultural, linguistic, ethnic, and religious separatist movements challenge precisely these markers. As examples of separatist movements one can give the Québecois aspirations in Canada as well as the search by the aboriginal peoples of Canada for more self-determination. A successfully negotiated cultural separation and constitutional compromise currently exists between the Spanish central government and the province of Catalonia. The Basque separatist movement, ETA, on the other hand presents a glaring example of an unfinished ethnic, linguistic, and regional conflict. The struggle over Kurdish linguistic, cultural, and regional rights, taking different forms in Turkey, Iran, and Iraq, is a particularly poignant example of separatism. Whereas in some cases, like the Québecois movement, the Catalan and aboriginal cultural rights movements, and movements for the linguistic and cultural demands of the Hungarian minority in Romania, such struggles aim at constitutional accommodation and compromise *within the boundaries of an existing sovereign nation-state*, other movements like those of the Basques, the IRA, and the PKK (the Kurdish Communist Party), envision the destruction or transformation of existing forms of sovereignty. I shall call forms of identity/difference politics that demand more extensive constitutional transformations than do new social movements but less than do full-blown nationalist ones, movements for "pluricultural or pluri-ethnic polities."

Third, as the Irish, Kurdish, Basquist, and Québecois movements reveal, the line separating struggles for pluricultural polities from ethnonationalism is not always hard and fast. Nationalism "requires that ethnic boundaries should not cut across political ones, and in particular, that ethnic boundaries within a given state . . . should not separate the power-holders from the rest" (Gellner 1983:

1). Nationalism is an ideology that requires that the sovereign people in a given polity be an ethnically, religiously, and linguistically homogeneous majority. It views the state as expressing the will of this people as a distinct nation; furthermore, it maintains that every people that constitutes a nation should have its own sovereign state. Nationalism is an extremely powerful ideology that in one form or another is coeval with the emergence of the modern state form. Nationalist movements are like the shadow cast by the modern European state formations since their inception.[1]

National sovereignty movements have been particularly salient in the erstwhile communist states. Not only in former Yugoslavia but in the Baltic countries and the former Soviet republics as well, the principle of "one people, one nation, one state" has come to dominate. As the continuing conflicts in the former Yugoslavia and Chechnya and the simmering hostilities in Armenia, Azerbaijan, and Kosovo indicate, the struggles for new state forms have not ended in these regions.

The coexistence in space and time of these different kinds of movements, each of which appears to struggle for the recognition of certain identity claims over others, creates the contemporary sense of "strange multiplicity" (Tully 1995). Many of the categories of modern political theory from constitutionalism to citizenship, from secularization to individualism, from the ideal of equality before the law to the concept of the nation-state are deeply unsettled by these developments. In his remarkable book *Strange Multiplicity: Constitutionalism in an Age of Diversity*, James Tully (1995: 1) seeks to rethink the European constitutional tradition in the light of these recent developments and asks: "Can a modern constitution recognize and accommodate cultural diversity?" This is "one of the most difficult and pressing questions of the political era we are entering at the dawn of the twenty-first century."

I agree with Tully about the urgency of this question, but I do not think that he addresses the central paradox afflicting all politics of identity/difference and which, in my view, is a first step in developing a theoretical understanding of demands to accommodate "cultural diversity": movements militating for identity/difference claims simultaneously posit the contingency of proposed identity definitions while arguing for their essential character. Whereas identity claims are said to be fundamental, essential, nonnegotiable, and clearly distinguishable from the claims of competitors, in the process of social and political mobilization and cultural articulation, identity claims are "created" that are negotiable, contestable, and open to political redefinition and redescription.

Tully (1995: 46) considers this issue in the following: "Of course, it is increasingly difficult to attach human identity and meaning to a coherent culture or language on common ground, given the forces of globalization and mobility. . . . However, dissolving this difficulty, and the demands it has engendered, into a homogeneous 'post-cultural' situation is to finesse rather than face the problem post-modernism sets out to address." One need not accept the postmodernist emphasis on the fragmentary, dispersed self to conclude that identity politics rest on presuppositions that are illusory from a metatheoretical point of view. How can discrete groups be identified and sustained over time? Are there such discrete identities? Should differentiated claims to rights and responsibilities be allowed in a polity on the basis of distinct group identities?

These identity-driven movements are occurring at a time when there is a great deal of second-order social analysis in all fields leading, when not to outright skepticism, at least to careful distancing from any essentialist or primordialist defense of identity claims. Ironically, sociological skepticism about identity politics and political militance on behalf of identity are features of our current discourse (Calhoun 1996).

Essentialism versus Constructivism Debates in Contemporary Theory

The terms *essentialism* and *constructivism* designate a wide range of theoretical positions in contemporary identity/difference debates. I shall treat these categories as provisional road markers, whose meaning will be delineated more sharply as we consider their usage in different contexts. Let me suggest the following working definitions: Whereas essentialists suggest that collective identities like those of gender, race, or nation have clearly delineated contours that persist, constructivists argue that the boundaries of all identities are fluid, contested and contestable, unstable over time. Some essentialists may ground identities in biology, others in anthropological universals: seeing gender characteristics as emerging from the sexual division of labor within our species is an example of such an anthropological perspective. Constructivists distrust deep, structural explanations and look at social, economic, political, and cultural struggles in history to analyze and interpret the formation of identities.

Debates among feminist theorists over the last two decades offer a particularly salient example of these alternative conceptions of identities. The transition from "standpoint feminism" to poststructuralist feminisms can be taken as paradigmatic.[2] No concept reveals the nature of this paradigm shift more explicitly than the one that is central to feminist theory, namely, gender. As an example of early standpoint feminism, the historian Joan Kelly Gadol (1984: 6) observes: "In short, women have to be defined as women. We are the social opposite, not of a class, a caste, or of a majority, since we are a majority, but of a sex: men. We are a sex, and categorization by gender no longer implies a mothering role and subordination to men, except as a social role and relation recognized as such, as socially constructed and socially imposed." Gadol makes a clear distinction between gender and sex; whereas sex is given—we as women are the opposite sex of an equally nonproblematic one, namely, men—gender is socially constructed and contested.

Poststructuralist feminism challenges precisely this dichotomy between sex and gender and the logic of binary oppositions it creates. Butler (1990: 7) writes: "Gender is not to culture as sex is to nature; gender is also the discursive/cultural means by which 'sexed nature' or a 'natural sex' is produced and established as 'prediscursive,' prior to culture, a politically neutral surface *on which* culture acts." For Butler the myth of the already sexed body is the epistemological equivalent of the myth of the given: just as the given can be identified only in a discursive framework that first allows us to name it, so too the culturally available codes of gender sexualize a body and determine the direction of that body's sexual desire. Butler's sharp critique of the distinction between sex and gender allows her to focus on how oppressive and debilitating the compulsory binarity of heterosexual logic has been for some women and men. Seeing that not only gender but also sexuality is socially *constructed* allows one to enter the terrain of political contestation around issues like sexuality and sexual identity, terrains that were hitherto thought to lie outside politics.

The shift from essentialism to constructivism within feminist debates heralds a complex transformation of theoretical as well as political sensitivities. The single most important consequence of this shift is that all identity markers, including the sexuality of the body one is born within, are now "denaturalized," rendered historical, and become complex sites of struggle among conflicting social, cultural, and psychological forces. Simone de Beauvoir's famous phrase, "One is not born, but rather becomes, a woman" (Beauvoir [1949]/1989: 267), can now be rendered as: "One is not born but is constructed as a woman through the psychosexual matrices of diverse societies and cultures at different points in history."

The principal consequence of viewing gender as well as sexuality as socially constructed is the fluidity this introduces in conceptualizations of identity. Identities, personal as well as collective, are viewed as narrative constructions resulting from social, cultural, and political struggles for hegemony among social groups who vie with one another for the dominance of certain identity definitions over others (cf., e.g., Prakash 1992; Mohanty 1992; Ashcroft, Griffiths, and Tiffin 1995).

For example, what does "we the people" mean? Originally it meant the propertied, white male heads of household of the colonies. What about the African American slave population who were considered three-fifth persons? What about the Native Americans whose presence on the territory of the colonies was not even acknowledged? What about women whose civic identity was subsumed under that of the male head of household through a practice known as *couverture?* Our identity as a "we" contains the results of collective struggles for power among cultural groups, genders, and social classes. The identity of every "we" is formed by the sedimentation of such past struggles for hegemony (Benhabib 1994a). If this is so, the history of every "we" presupposes differentiation from a "they." There is no identity without difference; to be one of a certain kind presupposes that one is different from another. Identity formation is a process of self and other differentiation.

THE POLITICS OF THE CONSTRUCTION OF CORPORATE IDENTITIES

The essentialism/constructivism divide can be applied to the formation of corporate group identities in modern welfare states. I shall use the term *corporate identities* to refer to forms of group identity that are officially recognized, sanctified, legitimized, and accepted by the state and its institutions. This usage departs from legal parlance, for in the eyes of the law, not only groups but artificial entities like cities, towns, and financial or industrial corporations have a "corporate" identity. For my purposes, what is important is the relationship between forms of group identity based on language, ethnicity, religion, and culture, as these are experienced by individual members, and forms of group identity that are recognized by the state and its institutions as legal or quasi-legal collective entities, which then confer on members of such groups certain rights and privileges. It is important to make this distinction because groups clamoring for the recognition of their corporate identities will claim that the differences of language, culture, ethnicity, and religion as they live and experience them are essential and that states and their institutions should give these essential differences public recognition by deeming them officially established corporate identity forms.

The introduction to an influential collection of essays by social philosophers and legal theorists expresses the quandaries of the creation and the undoing of identity categories in contemporary states very well. These scholars provide evidence for the volatility and contestability of the essentialist/constructivist divide: "In one sense, this work, which we term post-identity scholarship, would be unimaginable without the diversity of discourses enabled by identity politics—voices of women, gay men and lesbians, blacks and others. At the same time, the scholarship represented in these essays critiques the tendency of these discourses to obscure the differences among women, among gays, among blacks, and others, and to ignore the significance of multiple allegiances, communities, and experiences to the construction of these identities. Broadly stated, the authors assert that *in order to generate more effective legal strategies, legal consciousness should take account of the role of law in the constitution of identities and of the simultaneity of multiple identities and perspectives*" (Danielsen and Engle 1995: xii; emphasis added).

There is a new consciousness afoot among jurists and social scientists, policy makers as well as social activists, of the role of law and, more broadly, of governmental and nongovernmental policies in the constitution as well as contestation of identities. The collection called *After Identity* is a retrospective analysis of identity politics by a generation of North American legal scholars and activists, mainly from the Critical Legal Studies Movement, whose own previous work contributed to the very creation of the kinds of politics the later volume is challenging and questioning.

Sociologists like Daniel Bell (1978) had already noted in the late 1970s that the welfare state, which sought to redress social and economic inequalities among groups by rectifying their differential forms of disadvantage in society, would give rise to such corporate identities by encouraging a revolution of entitlements. An ever-growing number of social groups would be able to show that they were placed in unequal and unfair positions vis-à-vis the job market, education, housing, health care, or employment in professional and scientific institutions. By extending the net of social equality beyond mere income distribution to encompass equality of opportunity in the major sectors of a society like health, education, and housing, the welfare state created a form of public-political culture that encouraged corporate identities.

Contemporary debates about affirmative action, as well as increasing public disenchantment with affirmative action, are in part a consequence of a growing sociological sophistication on the part of the citizenry. People realize that "what the welfare state hath wrought it can also undo." Differences of race and gender, some argue, are not essential differences, as claimed by their advocates. They seem essential only because advocates and lobbyists have been strong and tenacious enough to convince lawmakers that they should protect certain group rights while discriminating against others.

Additional examples of the politics of the constitution of corporate identities are offered in the growing literature on migrant workers, postcolonials, and foreign nationals in contemporary Europe. In her book *Limits of Citizenship: Migrants and Postnational Membership in Europe*, sociologist Yasemin Soysal (1994) introduces the concept of "incorporation regimes" to describe how host countries in which foreign nationals, guest workers, and postcolonials reside come to define, delineate, and establish corporate identities. Instead of seeing the identities of these groups to be consequences of some essential features they supposedly bring with them from their home cultures, a growing social science literature is emphasizing how incorporation regimes create new corporate group identities.[3]

In recent years the most spectacular example of the construction of a corporate, collective identity resulting in a constitutional crisis has been the Québecois separatist movement. Reconstructing the development of Québecois identity, Charles Taylor (1993) emphasizes its evolution from a largely clerical, Catholic identity expressed primarily through educational policies to an increasingly autonomous regional government, encouraged by the differential tax systems and policies granted to it by the Canadian central government and referred to as "asymmetrical federalism." Will Kymlicka (1995), by contrast, sees the sources of the current Québecois claims to a separate collective identity to be rooted in the history of Canada. Whether this corporate identity should take the form of a sovereign state is still an open question, and hotly contested among the participants. There is a range of views on this issue, extending from the separatist Partie Québecois to the moderate New Democrats. Arguing that Canada is a multination as well as a polyethnic state, Kymlicka maintains that the granting of special group rights of the Anglophone, Francophone, and aboriginal communities in Canada goes back to the historical contract that founded the Canadian nation.

These diverse instances of the creation and recognition of corporate identities show the crisscrossing effects of historical circumstance and social and political policies. Indeed, the constructivist view has a great deal more analytical leverage in explaining these phenomena than does the essentializing viewpoint.

ETHNONATIONALISMS: ESSENTIAL OR CONSTRUCTED?

Ernst Gellner (1983: 55) expresses the tensions between the essentializing and constructivist visions of nationalism as follows:

> The great, but valid, paradox is this: nations can be defined only in terms of the age of nationalism, rather than, as you might expect, the other way round. It is not the case that the "age of nationalism" is a mere summation of the awakening and political self-assertion of this, that, or the other nation. Rather, when general social conditions make for standardized, homogeneous, centrally sustained high cultures, pervading entire populations and not just elite minorities, a situation arises in which well-defined educationally sanctioned and unified cultures constitute very nearly the only kind of unit with which men willingly and often ardently identify. The cultures now seem to be the natural repositories of political legitimacy.

For Gellner it is "nationalism which engenders nations, and not the other way around" (55). Human beings have always lived in some form of collectively defined constellations. From tribes to neighborhoods, from the manor of the feudal lords to old multinational empires, diverse forms of collective, political, legal, and cultural units have shaped human history. What is distinctive about nationalism is its emphasis that the commonalities of language, religion, ethnic origin, and history that are shared by a human group constitute them as a unity that clearly distinguishes them from others. Nationalism is the claim that the will to unity should take the form of a sovereign state. Ernst Renan (1882: 27), one of the main theorists of nationalism in the previous century, states: "A nation's existence is, if you will pardon the metaphor, a daily plebiscite, just as an individual's existence is a perpetual affirmation of life. . . . The wish of nations is, all in all, the sole legitimate criteria, the one to which we must always return."

The "wish of nations" to be recognized as such emerges in human history at certain points and as a consequence of certain economic, technological, and sociocultural transformations. For Gellner these are the conditions for the production of standardized, homogeneous, and centrally sustained high cultures. These conditions would include certainly, but not only, the development of a free market in commodities as well as labor, in news as well as goods. Furthermore, civil society and the state would have to be sufficiently differentiated from each other so that a sphere of autonomous culture, in the printed media and vernacular literature in particular, could develop. In addition to the institutions of the market and the cultural media, other homogenizing and disciplinary institutions like the army, the educational system, a civil bureaucracy, and, in some cases, democratic political insitutions would be a precondition of such processes.[4]

I indicated earlier that I would treat the essentialist/constructivist dichotomy as a road marker. This dichotomy is too simple to help us capture some of the deeper perplexities of identity politics in all their shapes and forms. At one level, the duality of perspectives created by the essentialist versus constructivist perspectives corresponds to the standpoints of the participant versus the observer in social and political life.

Members and theorists of movements clamoring for the recognition of identity forms, be they adherents of the women's, cultural, ethnic, or nationalist movements, must assume that their differences are so fundamental and essential to their lives as individuals and as members of collectivities that they are willing to go to the streets or barricades for them. Without a fundamental belief in the crucial significance of these identity-based differences, social movements would not motivate individuals and sustain their participation and sacrifices. So the "constructedness" of identities and the beliefs of the members of identity-based movements that their identities are essential are not compatible.[5]

For the social and political theorist, it is almost axiomatic that identity-based movements express historically contingent claims, at certain times, on account of certain other transformations in culture, politics, economics, and society. For the observer these movements do not express *given* identity-related differences but *create* them; identites are not *expressed* but *articulated*. Between the perspective of the observer and that of the participant a gap opens. It is not easy for members of identity/difference movements to accept the sociological contingency of their own claims. Between sociological enlightenment and social militancy there is a hiatus.

However, the observer's perspective must explain not only the historical and sociological contingency of these movements but also how and why they are plausible and desirable for their members. There has to be a motivational explanation of action. At this point we begin to reach the limits of an exaggerated constructivism. In human affairs not everything is possible, and not "anything goes." Analyzing the crises and contradictions of the welfare state may enable us to see why certain forms of corporatist identity are likely to emerge within these political formations. Such analyses do not account for the relationship between state actions and policies on the one hand and individual needs, desires, biographies, and motivational structures on the other. The latter lead individuals to find in a group-based identity more than simply a convenient formula for getting privileges and benefits from the welfare state. Or do they? Perhaps we have to examine more closely the interactions between the formulation of policies and the creation of identities.

Take the example of nationalisms. According to Gellner (1983: 56), "nationalism is not what it seems, and above all it is not what it seems to itself. The cultures it claims to defend and revive, are often its own inventions, or are modified out of all recognition. . . . The cultural shreds and patches used by nationalism are often arbitrary historical inventions. Any old shred and patch would have served as well. But in no way does it follow that the principle of nationalism itself, as opposed to the avatars it happens to pick up for its incarnations, is itself in the least contingent and accidental." Is it obvious that "the cultural shreds and patches used by nationalism are arbitrary historical inventions"? Isn't there an "elective affinity" between the narratives, works of art, music, and painting through which "the nation is narrated," to use homi bhabha's language (bhabha 1994: 146, ff.), and the past history as well as anticipated and projected future of this group of people? It is precisely this "elective affinity" that the student of human affairs is trying to explain.

Let me give an example unfamiliar to most European and North American students of nationalism. The creation of modern Turkey through the reforms of Atatürk can be viewed as a paradigm of civic nationalism. In order to forge a new civic identity out of the old Ottoman Empire, which prided itself in being composed of 72 "millets" (peoples, nations in the prenationalist sense of the term), Kemal Ataturk had to position the new nation of Turkey in opposition to the Persian and Arabic legacies that dominated the cultural life of the Empire. In a radical gesture, Atatürk abolished the old script, which was written in Arabic letters and was a mélange of Persian, Turkish, and Arabic, and created a new official language out of the vernacular Turkish, which was spoken quite differently in the city than in the countryside.

The new alphabet, this primary instrument of the pedagogy of the nation, reinforced a certain kind of identity in that it seemed to resolve the identity conflict that had plagued the Ottoman Empire since the eighteenth century. Positioned as a bridge between Europe and the Orient, West and East, Moslem and Oriental, yet controlling significant parts of Europe, the Ottomans had straddled an unbridgeable gap for centuries. Atatürk simply chose the West and expressed his choice most dramatically by abolishing the cultural and literary medium in which the elite of the Empire had expressed itself. So "the cultural shreds and patches of nationalism" are not arbitrary historical inventions. They have to fit together; they have to tell a story and perform a narrative that makes sense, that is plausible and coherent, and that motivates people to the point that they are willing to sacrifice their lives for it. Collective narratives can also cease to make sense, cohere, motivate, or hold people together. This appears to be the case in contemporary Turkey, where the once dominant ideology of Kemalism has fallen from grace, and new and competing collective narratives are clamoring to fill its place.

The limits of constructivism are reached around the following issues: (1) Constructivism cannot explain adequately what motivates people to consider identity-based differences as essential for them. (2) Constructivism cannot account for the "fit" between the cultural shreds and patches that movements and militants pick up from the culture around them and the identity dilemmas and options that these shreds and patches appear to resolve. (3) Constructivism, in short, can account for *contingency* but not for *coherence;* constructivism can account for *sociological distance* but not for the *motivating closeness* of ideologies.[6]

Identity Politics: A Plea for Sociological Caution

In the preceding sections I have explored the varieties of identity/difference movements coexisting on a global scale at present. I have also examined how the essentialist/constructivist dichotomy operates within the discourse of these movements—among their participants as well as among their observers. The first conclusion to be drawn is sociological caution. Such caution may help us avoid some of the pitfalls of current theorizing in these areas: neither the contemporary discourse of civil society nor that of group-differentiated citizenship rights is the right approach to take in the face of the dilemmas posed by the coexistence of these movements.

The contemporary discourse of civil society, and by this term I am referring primarily to the concept as it has been used in the work of Robert Putnam (1995) and other writers (Elshtain 1995; Fukuyama 1995; Etzioni 1993), locates "democracy's discontent" (see Sandel 1996) in the decline of voluntary associations, neighborhood networks, PTA organizations, and the like (Putnam 1995; cf. Wuthnow, ch. 2 in this volume). Little attention is paid in this literature to the interaction among patterns of voluntary participation on the one hand and transformations in work and family on the other. This deficit became sorely clear around Robert Putnam's original comments about women's declining participation in religious and civic organizations, schools, and neighborhoods.[7] It was as if the myth of the 1950s' American family with the wage-earning father and the homemaking mother could be used to explain the realities of the fragile household arrangements of the global economy of the 1990s (see Hochschild 1997).

More significantly, the discourse of civil society sets its threshold of explanation either below or above the phenomena of identity/difference politics. These social and political movements, whether on the right or the left, fall out of the purview of these theories. The model of groups privileged in these new civil society theories is the "voluntary association." This model is sorely inadequate to explain the social realities of groupings based on partially ascriptive characteristics like gender, race, ethnicity, language, and nationality. Although at its inception the discourse of civil society was developed in tandem with the experience of new social movements, it is now curiously removed from their reality. Furthermore, the contemporary discourse of civil society presupposes that the identity boundaries of the "civil body" are uncontested, but this is precisely not the case in the contemporary world. It is not only civic and political participation rates and the formation of social capital that should concern us—they surely are important enough—but the politics of inclusion and exclusion, which takes place at the boundaries of associational life as well. Declining rates of participation in traditional voluntary associations in the United States are not insignificantly correlated with the experiences of new social actors like women, peoples of color, gay men, and lesbians who felt that such organizations were oblivious to their concerns and interests.

Theories of "group-differentiated citizenship rights," by which I mean primarily the work of Will Kymlicka (1995; 1996) and Iris Young (1990),[8] are concerned precisely with the rise of the new politics of identity/difference and their consequences for contemporary liberal democracies. Arguing from within the framework of political liberalism, in recent years Kymlicka has made one of the most impressive contributions to debates about "cultural politics." His thesis is that cultural identity and its preservation are fundamental human goods, which a liberal political philosophy, based upon respect for autonomous individuals, can respect and encourage. Particularly with an eye to the historical specificities of the Canadian case, Kymlicka argues for the necessity of "group-differentiated" citizenship rights (1996: 153–71). In his view, and especially as far as the Native Americans of Canada are concerned, differential language, land, and participation rights are both justifiable and necessary.

Much of Kymlicka's position derives its plausibility from the "thick narrative" about the tripartite national contract of Canada that he tells: the Anglophone, Francophone, and Native American communities were there at the beginning of the foundation of Canada as more or less discrete entities, and respecting their autonomy in the contemporary world is thus consistent not only with philosophical argument but also with historical precedent. Whether or not Kymlicka's narrative about the peculiarities of the Canadian experience is true, it is clear that the focus on Canada allows him to avoid, up to a certain point, the thorny question of group identities and the social construction of groups in other parts of the world. Nonetheless questions emerge. Kymlicka wants to retain a certain normative naïveté about the constructivist argument concerning the potential contestability of group identities, but he cannot really do so.

Kymlicka (1995) distinguishes among "multination" states and "polyethnic" states. Multination states, like Canada and Belgium, are based on a multi-linguistic and multicultural contract. Polyethnic nations, like the United States, are formed by the coming together of various ethnic, religious, and linguistic groups largely through migrations. Whereas Kymlicka takes a pluralist position vis-à-vis the differential rights of nations, he has a curiously monistic view of the rights of ethnic groups, asking them to accept that migration means incorporation into a dominant culture and loss of the home culture.

What exactly is the basis for this distinction: is it historical precedent, which may be construed in different ways, and which in any event forms no basis for normative justification? If it is not historical precedent but rather the normative claim that culture is a good because autonomous individuals choose to identify with it and pursue it as a good, then how can we distinguish between the value of "national" culture versus the value of "ethnic" culture of a person? Take the case of a female Francophone migrant from Ivory Coast to Québec. Who can say that her identification with French language and culture should trump her identification with West African ethnic traditions? This was precisely what the Parti Québecois attempted to argue but also where it lost the immigrant vote in the elections of 1996. Were Kymlicka to apply more sociological skepticism to his scheme of group identities, his normative theory could not distinguish so clearly among multination groups and polyethnic groups and use an un-problematized concept of culture as a basis for the ascription of group rights (see Forst 1997; Benhabib forthcoming).

We need at present to bring together the discourses of critical sociological theory and that of normative political philosophy into a fruitful synthesis. Neither alone will enable us to deal with the pitfalls of identity/difference politics on a global scale. The classics of critical sociological thought, like Marx, Durkheim, and Weber, presupposed that the integrative powers and agencies of the nation-state would create docile citizens in civil society. Although the nationalities question haunts these classics and is present at the peripheries of their work, the "strange multiplicity" of the present, generated by the unraveling of the social integration apparatuses of the modern nation-state, like schools, the family, armies, and religious institutions, were out of their purview. Civil society was, in one way or another, always a "national" civil society—a German, French, Italian, or American one (Alexander and Smelser, ch. 1 in this volume).

The violence and bitterness that is accompanying the new politics of identity/difference at the global level is, among other things, a consequence of the fact that the nation-state system that was restabilized after World War II is in crisis. The globalization of financial, capital, and labor markets; the rise of global armament, communication and information technologies; and the uncontrollable worldwide consequences of ecological and immunological problems are every-where challenging the nation-state system (see, e.g., Beck 1992, 1995). Nation-states are not only facing the continual undermining of their claims to sover-eignty (that is, of their abilities to determine the material, social, and cultural conditions of their existence), they are becoming increasingly helpless to find new answers to new global problems. The worldwide movement of capital, information, and labor across borders is weakening traditional concepts of sov-ereignty as well as creating a new and unpredictable global environment in which nation-states are more often than not victims rather than agents, recip-ients rather than initiators. At stake then are problems of *system-integration* on a global scale, that is, the development of mechanisms of successful social coordination and cooperation that can solve problems of the material reproduc-tion of their society.

These problems of system integration at the global level are accompanied by the decline of mechanisms of *social integration* at the domestic level. As the power of nation-states declines internationally, their capacity to act as socially integrative agents domestically is also hampered (see Featherstone et al., eds. 1995, Featherstone 1995; Friedman 1994). The modern nation-state was not only a political unity: it also represented a new form of social integration in history. According to this model, the institutions of the modern state like those of education, the army, religion, the family, and the representative bodies in the political sphere, socialized individuals such as to turn them into "docile bodies" (Michel Foucault: 1977) and "nationals" of a particular state. This is the classi-cal ideal of nineteenth-century social theory, epitomized by G. W. F. Hegel ([1821] 1973), even if idealistically, in his *Philosophy of Right*. The state, according to Hegel, does not refer exclusively to specific political institutions and mechanisms. In its broader sense, the "state" refers to the nation that is understood as a community of individuals united around a core of "ethical values" and principles, and organized as a sovereign body politic.

The same forces that undermine the capacity of the nation-state to control the international environment also undermine the power of its institutions of socialization to be effective domestically. Schools and families are struggling against global media and entertainment industries over the hearts and minds of their children. The army in many democratic countries has ceased to be the socialization and indoctrination institution of the male soldier-citizen. Wars are frequently fought by paid professional soldiers and organizations. The United States, the greatest democracy on the globe, was among the first to transfer the right of the democratic citizen to carry arms to a group of paid professionals. After the experience of the Vietnam War it became clear that democratic legitimacy and universal military service required a "parting of arms." It is this dialectic of increasing global systemic integration, along with social and cultural fragmentation and parcelization,[9] that is posing great challenges to the social and political thought of the present.

For reasons we do not yet understand, we have entered an epoch in the development of global civil society in which the national paradigm is at an end, while paradoxically, continuing to exercise its hold on the imagination of large parts of the world's population—and in particular in the postcommunist world (see Barber 1995; Huntington 1996). To appreciate the peculiarities of the current moment, think of Slovenia. Crouched between Italy, Hungary, Austria, and Croatia, a country like Slovenia would have been considered completely unworkable in the political geography of the nineteenth and early twentieth centuries. Any nineteenth-century theory of the viable state would have included among its necessary preconditions some degree of economic autarchy and access to waterways—a kind of geopolitical viability scale. But the realities of the global economy as well as of global armament, communications, and transportation industries have rendered the political necessities of these earlier times irrelevant.[10]

Although sociological theory, for the most part, has shied away from looking at the big picture of the reconfiguration of states, nations, and civil societies, contemporary normative political theory, my own field, has found itself in the midst of a profound challenge. Questions like nationalism and group rights, which as early as the 1970s, had been on the periphery of political theory, have come to occupy center stage in the nineties. Called by history and world events to think through these new realities, political theorists have responded with a premature normativism. Schemes abound for what constitutes legitimate group rights, for secession, for acceptable and unacceptable nationalisms, and the like. We have lacked some understanding of the social forces of the present global context that have made in Charles Taylor's (1992) perspicacious phrase, "the politics of recognition" the paradigmatic form of political conflict at the end of the current epoch. We need to work out a critical social theory of a global civil society in which conflicts of redistribution appear to have given way to conflicts of recognition. I join Nancy Fraser (1997: 2) in her assessment of this context:

> The "postsocialist" condition concerns a shift in the grammar of political claims-making. Claims for the recognition of group difference have become increasingly salient in the recent period, at times eclipsing claims for social equality. This phenomenon can be observed at two levels. Empirically, of course, we have seen the rise of "identity politics," the decentering of class, and, until very recently, the corresponding decline of social democracy. More deeply, however, we are witnessing an apparent shift in the political imaginary, especially in the way in which justice is imagined. . . . The result is a decoupling of cultural politics from social politics, and the relative eclipse of the former by the latter.

As Fraser herself goes on to show in *Justice Interruptus: Critical Reflections on the "Postsocialist" Condition*, a single "from/to" scheme would be wrong. We are not simply experiencing a transition from the "politics of redistribution" to a "politics of recognition." Redistribution and recognition claims are interlaced and imbricated with one another. This is also a conclusion that my analysis of the essentialism/constructivism divide supports: all identity/difference movements struggle for the distribution of resources as well—be these land, power, representation, cultural space, or linguistic access—although the political grammar in which these struggles are currently articulated is dominated by the vocabulary of recognition rather than redistribution.

If we add to this picture, which essentially holds for the "postsocialist" struggles of advanced, capitalist civil societies of North America and Western Europe, the admixture of redistribution and recognition claims within nationalist movements in the rest of the world, then, and only then, shall we begin to fathom some of the "strange multiplicities" of the present. The contemporary discourse of civil society is still far removed from becoming a critical social theory of the new global civil society.

NOTES

1. To be sure, these brief remarks cannot do justice to the intense and complicated debates about the origins and varieties of nationalisms that have occupied historians and social scientists since the last century (cf. Eric Hobsbawm 1990 and Liah Greenfeld 1992). Not only are there different paths to the formation of the nation in the European framework—compare British, French, German, Italian, and Russian nationalisms—but the emergence of nationalist movements in the Third World as a result of anticolonial struggles present complicated sociohistorical cases, each of which requires scrutiny in its own right. Nonetheless, one generalization would safely hold across all these diverse historical instances, namely, that a nationalist movement emerges and a people is mobilized as a nation insofar as out of the multiple and myriad commonalities of everyday life a sense of special unity and belonging together can be forged. A nation must be one, and in some significant and nontrivial sense, it must be distinguishable from other nations and peoples.

2. I have dealt with these issues at greater length in my article "From Identity Politics to Social Feminism: A Plea for the Nineties" (Benhabib 1996b). The term, as far as I can tell, was introduced into feminist theory by Nancy Hartsock (1983), who analyzed the possibility of building a feminist theory along the lines suggested by Georg Lukács in *History and Class Consciousness for Marxist Theory*. A number of seminal works, mostly from the late 1970s, had the characteristic titles *Becoming Visible: Women in European History* (Bridenthal et al. 1987), *In A Different Voice* (Gilligan 1981), *Public Man, Private Women* (Elshtain 1981).

3. Whereas in countries like Germany, for example, foreign workers were absorbed into the larger society and were entitled to the protection of their civil rights as well as certain social welfare benefits, like unemployment compensation, as individuals and workers and not insofar as they belonged to ethnic groups like Turks, Greeks, and Yugoslavs, the policies of countries like Holland have followed a different route. The National Advisory Council of Ethnic Minorities created by the Dutch government in 1981 has recognized Turks, Moroccans, Tunisians, Surinamese, Dutch Antilleans, Moluccans, South Europeans (meaning Greeks, Spaniards, and Portugese), refugees, and Gypsies as official minorities (see Soysal 1994: 48). The granting of official minority status to a group entitles them to certain housing, education, employment, and welfare benefits as well as encourages the preservation of certain collective forms of cultural identity. The arbitrariness of this politics of the "construction" of corporate identities becomes clear when one considers that the Chinese and the Pakistanis in Dutch society, whom one would have thought to resemble members of other official minority groups sufficiently from a cultural point of view, were not recognized as ethnic minorities by the Dutch government because they were not deemed to be in a low enough position in society.

4. The terms *civic* and *ethnic nationalism* are used to distinguish early nation-constituting democratic movements from subsequent movements for ethnic purity and homogeneity (see Brubaker 1994; Ignatieff 1994). Whereas the French and the American Revolutions defined the nation as the democratic people and granted equal civil rights to religious minorities like the Catholics, Protestant sects of various kinds, and Jews, in the nineteenth century and after the Dreyfus affair, for example, a different kind of nationalism emerged in France. This nationalism sought to replace the category of the French national as primarily one who is the citizen of the French republic—citoyen Français—with one who is an ethnic French national—a descendant of the Franks and the Gauls. Similar nativist and nationalist movements emerged in the United States at the end of the nineteenth century against immigrants from Ireland, Italy, eastern European countries, and the Chinese. These movements sought to transform the concept of the American people, as specifed in the Constitution—*e pluribus unum*—into an *unum*, an ethnically, religiously and linguistically homogeneous entity, namely white male Protestants of northern or west European origin (see Hollinger 1995).

5. For an incisive exploration of the methodological permutations in the social sciences of the primordialism or essentialism versus constructivism divide, and an analysis of the varieties of "constructivist" social methodologies, see Sayres S. Rudy, "Global Books and Local Stories: Theory and Anti-Theory in Social Research" (1999, forthcoming).

6. Constructivism does not pay sufficient attention to the dimension of memory and to the way in which narratives of collective memory constrain identity options, by making some more plausible, may be even more necessary than others, in the self-understanding of the participants. For an exploration of these themes in the context of German national identity and its limits, see Diner 1995.

7. For an in-depth discussion of the role of the family and "family values" rhetoric in the discourse of new civil society, see Jean Cohen, "Does Voluntary Association Make Democracy Work?", ch. 13 in this volume.

8. Young and I have engaged in exchanges around the values of impartiality, the public sphere, and the moral possibility of reversing perspectives in social and political dialogue on a number of occasions (see Young 1994 and Benhabib 1994b). See also Iris Young's (1996) further critique of my project of "discourse ethics," and our exchange around deliberative democracy.

9. Even terms like *fragmentation* and *parcelization* may reflect social and political assumptions formed in the classical age of western modernity, in that they appear to privilege the emergence of seemingly unitary, national cultures. "Fragmentation" as opposed to which whole that was not fragmented? "Parcelization" as opposed to which territory that was intact? We have to begin questioning these binarisms. Viviana Zelizer's contribution, "Multiple Markets: Multiple Cultures," (ch. 9 in this volume) challenges the view of the economy as an integrator, and that of culture, politics, religion, and education as disintegrative forces. "The economy," in her view, "hosts intense cultural differentiation." What is unclear to me is whether in Zelizer's view the economy, no matter what its stage of historical development, has always and everywhere hosted "intense cultural differentiation" or whether we have reached a stage in the development of global consumer capitalism in which the creation and sustenance of "intense cultural differentiation," is necessitated by this level of economic development itself. In this paper I tend to the latter view.

10. Evidence suggests that the emergence of the European Community, as an economic, legal, administrative, and eventually cultural unity, is undermining sovereign European nation-states and carving up new regional alliances that are connecting with one another via Brussels while circumventing their own capitals (see Newhouse 1997).

REFERENCES

Ashcroft, Bill, Gareth Griffiths, and Helen Tiffin, eds. 1995. *The Post-Colonial Studies Reader*. London and New York: Routledge.

Barber, Benjamin. 1995. *Jihad vs. McWorld*. New York: Ballantine Books.

Beauvoir, Simone de. [1949] 1989. *The Second Sex*, translated by H. M. Parshley. New York: Random House.

Beck, Ulrich. 1992. *Risk Society: Towards a New Modernity*. Translated by Mark Ritter. London and New York: Polity.

———. 1995. *Ecological Politics in an Age of Risk*. Translated by Amos Weisz. London and New York: Polity.

Bell, Daniel. 1978. *The Cultural Contradictions of Capitalism*. New York: Basic Books.

Benhabib, Seyla. 1994a. "Democracy and Difference. The Metapolitics of Lyotard and Derrida." *Journal of Political Philosophy* 2 (no. 1): 1–23.

———. 1994b. "In Defense of Universalism—Yet Again." *New German Critique* 62 (spring/summer): 173–89.

———, ed. 1996a. *Democracy and Difference: Contesting the Boundaries of the Political*. Princeton, N.J.: Princeton University Press.

———. 1996b. "From Identity Politics to Social Feminism. A Plea for the Nineties." Pp. 28–41 in *Radical Democracy: Identity, Citizenship and the State*, edited by David Trend. New York: Routledge.

Benhabib, Seyla. n.d. "'Nous' et les 'Autres'. Complex Cultural Dialogues in a Global Civilization." In *Multiculturalism, Minorities, and Citizenship. Proceedings of the European University Institute Conference*, edited by Christian Joppke and Steven Lukes. Forthcoming.

bhabha, homi k. 1994. *The Location of Culture*. London and New York: Routledge.

Bridenthal, Renate, Claudia Koonz, and Susan Stuard. 1987. *Becoming Visible: Women in European History*. Boston: Houghton, Mifflin.

Brubaker, Rogers. 1994. *Citizenship and Nationhood in France and Germany*. Cambridge: Harvard University Press.

Butler, Judith. 1990. *Gender Trouble*. New York: Routledge.

Calhoun, Craig, ed. 1996. *Social Theory and the Politics of Identity*. New York: Blackwell.

Cohen, Jean. 1985. "Strategy or Identity: New Theoretical Paradigms and Contemporary Social Movements." *Social Research* (Vol. 52, no. 4): 663–716.

Cohen, Jean, and Andrew Arato. 1993. *Civil Society and Political Theory*. Cambridge: MIT Press.

Connolly, William. 1991. *Identity/Difference: Democratic Negotiations of Political Paradox*. Princeton, N.J.: Princeton University Press.

Danielsen, Dan, and Karen Engle, eds. 1995. *After Identity: A Reader in Law and Culture*. New York: Routledge.

Diner, Dan. 1995. "Gedaechtnis und Institution. Ueber ethnischen und politischen Ethnos." Pp. 37–47 in *Anderssein, ein Menschenrecht*, edited by Hilmar Hoffmann and Dieter Kramer. Weinheim: Beltz/Athenaeum.

Elshtain, Jean Bethke. 1981. *Public Man, Private Women*. Princeton, N.J.: Princeton University Press.

———. 1995. *Democracy on Trial*. New York: Basic Books.

Etzioni, Amitai. 1993. *The Spirit of Community: Rights, Responsibilities, and the Communitarian Agenda*. New York: Crown.

Featherstone, Mike. 1995. *Undoing Culture. Globalization, Postmodernism, and Identity*. Thousand Oaks, Calif.: Sage.

Featherstone, Mike, Scott Lash, and Roland Robertson, eds. 1995. *Global Modernities*. Thousand Oaks, Calif.: Sage.

Forst, Rainer. 1997. "Foundations of a Theory of Multicultural Justice." *Constellations: An International Journal of Critical and Democratic Theory* 4 (1): 63–72.

Foucault, Michel. 1977. *Disciplice and Punish. The Birth of the Prison*. Translated into English by Alan Sheridan. New York: Pantheon.

Fraser, Nancy. 1997. *Justice Interruptus: Critical Reflections on the "Postsocialist" Condition*. New York and London: Routledge.

Friedman, Jonathan. 1994. *Cultural Identity and Global Process*. Thousand Oaks, Calif.: Sage.

Frug, Gerald E. 1980. "The City as a Legal Concept." *Harvard Law Review* 93 (6): 1059–1154.

Fukuyama, Francis. 1995. *Trust: The Social Virtues and the Creation of Prosperity*. New York: Free Press.

Gellner, Ernst. 1983. *Nations and Nationalism*. London and Ithaca, N.Y.: Cornell University Press.

Gilligan, Carol. 1981. *In a Different Voice*. Cambridge: Harvard University Press.

Greenfeld, Liah. 1992. *Nationalism: Five Roads to Modernity*. Cambridge and London: Harvard University Press.

Habermas, Juergen. 1981. "Dialectics of Rationalization: An Interview," *Telos* 49: 5–33.
———. 1984. *Theory of Communicative Action*. Translated by T. A. MCarthy. Vol. 1, *Reason and the Rationalization of Society*. Boston: Beacon Press.
———. 1994. "Struggles for Recognition in the Democratic Constitutional State." Pp. 107–49 in *Multiculturalism: Examining the Politics of Recognition*, edited by Amy Gutmann. Princeton, N.J.: Princeton University Press.
Hartsock, Nancy. 1983. *Money, Sex, and Power: Toward a Feminist Historical Materialism*. New York: Longman.
Hegel, G. W. F. [1821] 1973. *Hegel's Philosophy of Right*. Translated by T. M. Knox. London: Oxford.
Hobsbawm, Eric. 1990. *Nations and Nationalism since 1780: Programme, Myth, and Reality*. New York: Cambridge University Press.
Hochschild, Arlie Russell. 1997. *When Work Becomes Home and Home Becomes Work*. New York: Metropolitan Books.
Hollinger, David A. 1995. *Postethnic America: Beyond Multiculturalism*. New York: Basic Books.
Huntington, Samuel P. 1996. *The Clash of Civilizations and the Remaking of World Order*. New York: Simon and Schuster.
Inglehart, Ronald. 1990. *Cultural Shift in Advanced Industrial Society*. Princeton, N.J.: Princeton University Press.
Ignatieff, Michael. 1994. *Blood and Belonging: Journeys into the New Nationalism*. New York: Farrar, Straus and Giroux.
Kelly, Joan. 1984. "The Social Relations of the Sexes: Methodological Implications of Women's History." In *Women, History, and Theory: The Essays of Joan Kelly*. Chicago: University of Chicago Press.
Kymlicka, Will. 1995. *Multicultural Citizenship*. Oxford: Clarendon Press.
———. 1996. "Three Forms of Group-Differentiated Citizenship in Canada. Pp. 153–71 in *Democracy and Difference: Contesting the Boundaries of the Political*, edited by Seyla Benhabib. Princeton, N.J.: Princeton University Press.
Mohanty, Chandra Talpade. 1992. "Feminist Encounters: Locating the Politics of Experience." Pp. 74–92 in *Destabilizing Theory*, edited by Michelle Barret and Anne Phillips. Cambridge, UK: Polity Press.
Newhouse, John. 1997. "Europe's Rising Regionalism." *Foreign Affairs* 76 (no. 1): 67–84.
Prakash, Gyan. 1992. "Postcolonial Criticism and Indian Historiography." *Social Text* 10 (nos. 2 and 3): 8–18.
Putnam, Robert. 1993. *Making Democracy Work*. Princeton, N.J.: Princeton University Press.
———. 1995. "Bowling Alone: America's Declining Social Capital." *The Journal of Democracy* 6: 65–78.
Renan, Ernst, ed. 1882. "Qu'est-ce qu'une nation?" Paris: Calmann Levy.
Rudy, Sayres S. n.d. "Global Books and Local Stories." In *Identities, Proceedings of the Junior Fellow Conference*, IWM, edited by Charles Lowney. Vienna, forthcoming.
Sandel, Michael. 1996. *Democracy's Discontent*. Cambridge: Harvard University Press.
Soysal, Yasemin Nuhoglu. 1994. *Limits of Citizenship: Migrants and Postnational Membership in Europe*. Chicago: University of Chicago Press.
Taylor, Charles. 1992. "The Politics of Recognition." Pp. 25–75 in *Multiculturalism and "The Politics of Recognition,"* edited by Amy Gutmann. Princeton, N.J.: Princeton University Press.

Taylor, Charles. 1993. *Reconciling the Solitudes: Essays on Canadian Federalism and Nationalism*, edited by Guy Laforest. Montreal and Kingston: McGill-Queen's University Press.

Tully, James. 1995. *Strange Multiplicity: Constitutionalism in an Age of Diversity*. Cambridge: Cambridge University Press.

Young, Iris. 1990. *Justice and the Politics of Difference*. Princeton, N.J.: Princeton University Press.

———. 1994. "Comments on Seyla Benhabib: Situating the Self." *New German Critique* 62 (spring/summer): 165–73.

———. 1996. "Communication and the Other: Beyond Deliberative Democracy." Pp. 120–37 in *Democracy and Difference: Contesting the Boundaries of the Political*, edited by Seyla Benhabib. Princeton, N.J.: Princeton University Press.

———. 1997. "Asymmetrical Reciprocity: On Moral Respect, Wonder, and Enlarged Thought." *Constellations* 3 (3): 340–64.